THE COMPLETE GUIDE TO THE
NEXTSTEP™
USER ENVIRONMENT

Michael B. Shebanek

THE COMPLETE GUIDE TO THE
NEXTSTEP™
USER ENVIRONMENT

Springer-Verlag

Michael B. Shebanek
Computing and Communications Department
University of California, Riverside
Riverside, CA 92521 USA

Published by TELOS, The Electronic Library of Science, Santa Clara, CA.
Publisher: Allan M. Wylde
Publishing Associate: Cindy Peterson
TELOS Production Manager: Sue Purdy Pelosi
Production Editor: Henry Krell
Electronic Production Advisor: Howard Ratner
Cover Designer: Circa 86
Manufacturing Supervisor: Vincent Scelta

Library of Congress Cataloging-in-Publication Data
Shebanek, Michael B.
  The complete guide to the NEXTSTEP user environment / Michael B. Shebanek.
      p.   cm.
  Includes bibliographical references and index.
  Additional material to this book can be downloaded from http://extras.springer.com.
  ISBN 0-387-97956-5 (alk. paper)
  1. NeXT (Computer)--Programming. 2. NEXTSTEP. I. Title
QA76.8.N49S48 1993
005.4'469--dc20   93-9064

Printed on acid-free paper.

© 1993 Springer-Verlag New York, Inc.
Published by TELOS, The Electronic Library of Science, Santa Clara, California.

This work consists of a printed book and a diskette packaged with the book. The book may not be translated or copied in whole or in part without the written permission of the publisher (Springer-Verlag New York, Inc., 175 Fifth Avenue, New York, NY 10010, USA) except for brief excerpts in connection with reviews or scholarly analysis. Use in connection with any form of information storage and retrieval, electronic adaptation, computer software or by similar or dissimilar methodology now known or hereafter developed is forbidden. The material on the diskette is in the public domain.
The use of general descriptive names, trademarks, etc., in this publication, even if the former are not especially identified, is not to be taken as a sign that such names, as understood by the Trade Marks and Merchandise Marks Act, may accordingly be used freely by anyone. Where those designations appear in this book and Springer-Verlag was aware of a trademark claim, the designations have been printed following the capitalization style used by the manufacturer.

Negatives prepared from the author's FrameMaker files.
Printed and bound by R.R. Donnelley & Sons, Harrisonburg, VA.

9 8 7 6 5 4 3 2 1

ISBN 0-387-97956-5 Springer-Verlag New York Berlin Heidelberg
ISBN 3-540-97956-5 Springer-Verlag Berlin Heidelberg New York

TELOS, The Electronic Library of Science, is an imprint of Springer-Verlag New York, with publishing facilities in Santa Clara, California. Its publishing domain encompasses the natural and physical sciences, computer science, mathematics, and engineering. All TELOS publications have a computational orientation to them, as TELOS' primary publishing strategy is to wed the traditional print medium with the emerging new electronic media in order to provide the reader with a truly interactive multimedia information environment. To achieve this, every TELOS publication delivered on paper has an associated electronic component. This can take the form of book/diskette combinations, book/CD-ROM packages, books delivered via networks, electronic journals, newsletters, plus a multitude of other exciting possibilities. Since TELOS is not committed to any one technology, any delivery medium can be considered.

The range of TELOS publications extends from research level reference works through textbook materials for the higher education audience, practical handbooks for working professionals, as well as more broadly accessible science, computer science, and high technology trade publications. Many TELOS publications are interdisciplinary in nature, and most are targeted for the individual buyer, which dictates that TELOS publications be priced accordingly.

Of the numerous definitions of the Greek word "telos," the one most representative of our publishing philosophy is "to turn," or "turning point." We perceive the establishment of the TELOS publishing program to be a significant step towards attaining a new plateau of high quality information packaging and dissemination in the interactive learning environment of the future. TELOS welcomes you to join us in the exploration and development of this frontier as a reader and user, an author, editor, consultant, strategic partner, or in whatever other capacity might be appropriate.

TELOS, The Electronic Library of Science
Springer-Verlag Publishers
3600 Pruneridge Avenue, Suite 200
Santa Clara, CA 95051

Trademarks

NEXT, the NeXTlogo, NEXTSTEP, NeXTcube, NeXTstation, NeXTmail, NeXTWORLD, Digital Librarian, Digital Webster, Interface Builder, Project Builder, Workspace Manager, Music Kit, and NetInfo are trademarks, and NeXTedge is a service mark, of NeXT Computer, Inc. Intel is a registered trademark of Intel Corporation. Adobe, PostScript, Display PostScript, and Adobe Illustrator are registered trademarks of Adobe Systems, Incorporated. UNIX is a registered trademark of UNIX Systems Laboratories. Times is a registered trademark of Linotype AG and/or its subsidiaries. Webster's Ninth New Collegiate Dictionary, Webster's Collegiate Thesaurus is used herein pursuant to license. *Mathematica* is a registered trademark of Wolfram Research Inc. Sun is a trademark and NFS is a registered trademark of Sun Microsystems, Inc. $T_{E}X$ is a trademark of the American Mathematical Society. FrameMaker is a registered trademark of Frame Technology Corporation. Apple and Macintosh is a trademark of Apple Computer, Inc. Microsoft Windows is a trademark of Microsoft Corporation. VT100 is a trademark of Digital Equipment Corporation. PANTONE and PANTONE MATCHING SYSTEM are registered trademarks of Pantone, Inc. Oxford is a registered trademark of Oxford University Press and is used herein pursuant to license. RenderMan is a registered trademark of Pixar. Lotus and 1-2-3 are registered trademarks and Improv is a trademark of Lotus Development Corporation. WordPerfect is a registered trademark of WordPerfect Corp. Create, TextArt and DataPhile are trademarks of Stone Design Corp. Diagram! is a trademark of Lighthouse Design, Ltd. WriteNow is a registered trademark of T/Maker Company.

Preface

This book is about the advanced, object-oriented NEXTSTEP™ user environment for NeXT and Intel-based computers. It is intended for those who already own a computer running NEXTSTEP and want to quickly learn what it can do and how to get the most out of it with the least effort. It's also for those who are considering the purchase of NEXTSTEP but want to learn more about how it works before making an investment.

Why a book on NEXTSTEP? When I set out to learn how to use NEXTSTEP several years ago, I found it extremely difficult to find information from the usual sources, such as books, magazines, user groups, and authorized dealers. NEXTSTEP users were scarce and finding a computer store that sold NeXT-related products was even more rare. There were also only a handful of NeXT user groups in existence and those that did exist met so far away that joining one of them was impractical. The manuals I received from NeXT were helpful, but I had the feeling there must be something more to it than what was written in the *User's Reference*. It didn't describe many of the shortcuts that experienced users had found or the public domain and shareware utilities that were popular and how I could use them to make my work even easier and more fun. Like may other computer users, I had used DOS and Windows-based PCs and Macintosh® computers extensively in the past and felt very comfortable with a graphical user interface (GUI). What I really needed was not a bare bones "getting started" manual but a book about how NEXTSTEP works, how its

Preface

designers intended for it to be used, and the tips and tricks that made it sing, not hum. Having discussed this issue with other NEXTSTEP users, I find that such a first experience was not unusual.

Included with this book is a floppy disk containing applications, fonts, sounds, documents, and other information useful to the new NEXTSTEP user.

The Complete Guide to the NEXTSTEP User Environment is my response to this need for more and better printed information about how to make NEXTSTEP work for you. I have found NEXTSTEP to be the most enjoyable, empowering, and exciting computing environment to date and I'm excited to share it with you. This book was written to make you feel as if you are sitting next to a veteran NEXTSTEP user who can show you the easiest way to get something done and steer you away from common pitfalls. If you have a copy of NEXTSTEP, you can experiment and try out the new commands and features as you read about them. To help you practice, several popular software utilities and many electronic files have been included on a floppy disk with book. Even if you don't have access to a computer that's running NEXTSTEP, you'll be able to follow along easily and through the many illustrations and accurately visualize how the computer will respond to your commands.

This book is intended, in part, to bridge the gap between what is available on-line and what is available in print. Where feasible, I have included portions of existing on-line documents, not because they contain new or unusual information, but because the information they contain is largely unavailable to those who do not have access to the worldwide Internet network, where most of this information is stored. When the information could not be reprinted—such as with applications, utilities, sample sounds and images— files have been provided in compressed form on the enclosed floppy disk. It is my hope that the combination of written and electronic information contained in this book will speed you quickly on your way to understanding and making great use of what I believe to be the most elegant system software available today.

Welcome to the exciting world of NEXTSTEP!

Mike Shebanek
Computing and Communications
University of California, Riverside
Internet mail: comment@velo.ucr.edu

Acknowledgments

I would like to thank the many people who were influential in bringing this book to fruition: Simson Garfinkel and Michael Mahoney for getting the project off the ground; Allan Wylde, Cindy Peterson, Henry Krell, and Howard Ratner of Springer-Verlag who treated this manuscript as if it were their own; Carol Westberg for molding jotted notes and vague ideas into a cohesive, readable work; Rick Jackson, Margaret Chan, Chet Kapoor, Jim Diamond, David Spitzler, Diane Phillips, Susan Mobley, Dave Springer, Roy West, and others at NeXT, Inc., who offered technical assistance and insightful suggestions, Mark Yoder, Mary Flynn, Paige Wuest, Wolfgang Christian, and Margie Wild for suffering through early manuscripts; Larry Sautter and Paul Lowe, who introduced me to the world of NEXTSTEP; Susan Gordon for her support and flexibility, which allowed me time to write; Kerry Boyer, Michelle Perlman, and Gene Dippel for extending themselves and providing me opportunities beyond those I deserved; and to my wife Carole for her love, understanding, encouragement, and self-sacrifice, and for reminding me each and every night, "Don't worry, it will all work out."

It did.

Contents

Preface	vii
Acknowledgments	ix
Contents of Floppy Disk	xvii
Introduction	xxi

Up and Running

1. Basic Training   **1**
    User Accounts   1
    Starting NEXTSTEP   4
    Shutting Down   7

An Inside Look

2. The NEXTSTEP Workspace	**11**
The Mouse	12
The File Viewer	15
NEXTSTEP Windows	20
NEXTSTEP Menus	24
The Application Dock	29
3. Files and Folders	**31**
Navigating with the File Viewer	31
Using Multiple File Viewers	43
Managing Windows	45
Managing Folders	47
Finding a File or Folder	55
Selecting Files and Folders	58
Compressing Files and Folders	63
Moving, Copying, and Duplicating	65
Monitoring Background Tasks	69
Using Links	70
Deleting Files and Folders	73
4. Removable Disks	**77**
Understanding Disk Formats	77
Mounting a Disk	78
Unmounting a Disk	79
Initializing a Disk	80
Copying Files to a Disk	81
5. Inspectors	**85**
Inspector Controls	86
Attributes Inspector	88
Contents Inspector	91
Tools Inspector	95
Access Control Inspector	95
The Address Inspector	98

Applications

6. Application Management — 107
- Starting Applications — 108
- Monitoring Applications — 112
- Hiding and Unhiding Applications — 114
- Auto-Starting an Application — 115
- Learning Tricks — 116

7. Application Features — 117
- Attention Panels — 118
- The Help Panel — 119
- The Save Panel — 122
- The Open Panel — 124
- Basic Text Editing — 126
- The Find Panel — 132
- The Font Panel — 134
- The Spelling Panel — 138
- The Colors Panel — 139
- Services — 150
- NeXTlinks — 152

8. Printers and Fax Modems — 159
- Getting Ready to Print — 160
- Printing — 162
- Faxing — 165
- Configuring a Printer — 172
- Configuring a Fax Modem — 176

9. Bundled Applications — 185
- Edit — 186
- NeXTmail — 187
- Preview — 195
- FaxReader — 197
- Preferences — 203
- Terminal — 205
- PrintManager — 207

Digital Librarian	209
Digital Webster	217
Digital Quotations	219
Grab	220
Demonstration Applications	222
Summary of Bundled Applications	259

10. Application Installation — **267**

Where to Install Applications	269
The Installer	270

So You Want to Know More

11. Customization — **275**

Customizing the Workspace	275
Customizing the User Environment	282
Installing New Fonts	300

12. Networking — **307**

Network File System (NFS)	308
File Transfer Protocol (FTP)	309
Internet Etiquette	319
Public Domain and Shareware	319
Novell NetWare	320
Removable Disks	327
File Conversion	328
Emulators	329

13. UNIX Commands You Should Know — **335**

UNIX Command Structure	337
Often-Used UNIX Commands	338
Pathname Shortcuts	342
Jargon	343
Special UNIX Commands	346

14. NEXTSTEP First Aid — 353
Frozen Applications — 354
System Crash Recovery — 355

15. The World of NEXTSTEP — 361
Contacts at NeXT — 361
Information in Print — 363
Information in Electronic Format — 367
User Groups — 379
Conferences and User Training — 380

Reference

Appendix A: Supported Printers — A-1

Appendix B: Internet Archive Sites — B-1

Appendix C: Buried Treasures — C-1

Appendix D: Hardware Compatibility — D-1

Glossary — G-1

Index — I-1

Contents of Floppy Disk

To help you practice, and to expand your knowledge of NEXTSTEP, several electronic files and applications are included with this book on a 1.4 MB high-density (HD) floppy disk. Before you can use these files, you will need to copy them to your home folder, or to a folder within your home folder, and decompress them using the **Decompress** command in the Workspace Manager's File menu as described in "Compressing Files and Folders" on page 63. After decompressing the files, you can drag them to an appropriate folder, such as **~/Apps**, **~/Library/Fonts**, or **~/Library/Sounds** to use them. Some of the folders on the disk contain a text file named **README** to provide further instructions and credits pertaining to the items in the folder. You can use any text processor to read the files, including the Edit application provided in the NEXTSTEP user environment.

Contents of Floppy Disk

Applications Folder (532 KB compressed)		Size
BlastApp.app	An action game in which you fly a helicopter through a cavern while avoiding surface-to-air missiles.	502 KB
Digit.app	A handy scientific calculator that works with binary, decimal, hexadecimal, and octal numbers.	186 KB
GatorFTP_486.app	A NEXTSTEP application to perform file transfers between two computers on a network using FTP.	234 KB
Documents Folder (315 KB compressed)		
README.rtf	Notes about documents.	1 KB
Incomplete Guide to the Internet.ps	Describes some of the resources available on the Internet and how to take advantage of them.	845 KB
SLIP_PPP_Paper.ps	Describes the SLIP and PPP remote access protocols	35 KB
Fonts Folder (89 KB compressed)		
README.rtf	Notes about fonts.	1 KB
Architecture-Medium.font	Sans-serif font	38 KB
AuBauer TextInitials.font	Decorative font	43 KB
Flintstone.font	Decorative	76 KB

Contents of Floppy Disk

Icons Folder (28 KB compressed)		Size
README.rtf	Notes about Icons.	2 KB
NeXT logo.tiff	NeXT company logo	14 KB
People (folder)	Photos of Avie Tevanian, Mike Shebanek., and Steve Jobs	13 KB
SP_Icons (folder)	A collection of decorative icons for customizing NEXTSTEP folders.	45 KB
Images Folder (32 KB compressed)		
color roses.eps	illustration of roses	51 KB
jiminy.tiff	Jiminy Cricket	65 KB
recycle logo.ps	International recycle logo	7 KB
Sounds Folder (131 KB compressed)		
README.rtf	Notes about sounds.	2 KB
CuicaHi.snd	System beep sound	9 KB
Drum Sounds (folder)	assorted system beep sounds	54 KB
HiHat0.snd	System beep sound	42 KB
Oops.snd	"oops" sound	23 KB
Synth Twang.snd	System beep sound	20 KB

"NEXTSTEP is probably the most respected piece of software on the planet"

Byte Magazine, October 1992

Introduction

NEXTSTEP has been heralded by many in the computing industry as one of the finest examples of system software for desktop computers—bar none. "Brilliant...almost the perfect interface...a seamless computer experience-that shames other advanced systems" says *SunWorld,* a magazine devoted to reviewing the technology of one of NeXT's greatest competitors. NEXTSTEP is not just an application, operating system, programming language, or interface. It is a highly integrated collection of programs and utilities that incorporate all of these functions into a single seamless environment in which you have full control of your computer. NEXTSTEP contains many diverse yet advanced features such as true multitasking (the ability to perform several tasks concurrently), Display PostScript®, graphical user interface, UNIX command-line environment, PANTONE® color matching, support for RenderMan® 3D rendering, the ability to fax from any application, integrated object-oriented design, and numerous bundled applications for drawing, text editing, sending electronic mail, checking spelling, document search and retrieval based on document content, and games. It is by far the most easy to use, powerful, and comprehensive collection of software available for PC users.

If NEXTSTEP has received such accolades from those in the computing industry, why do so few know much about it? Until recently, NEXTSTEP could only be run on machines manufactured by NeXT, Inc. Unless you were willing to purchase a new computer, you couldn't take advantage of

NEXTSTEP. Thus, NEXTSTEP has been known to relatively few and suffered from a lack of exposure. Recently however, NeXT made a significant change to remedy this situation. In early 1993, NeXT stopped selling computer hardware and began shipping a new version of NEXTSTEP that can run on systems that use Intel 80486 and Pentium processors, commonly known as PCs. This allows personal computer users to take advantage of all of the benefits of the NEXTSTEP user environment and applications, yet protect their investment in DOS and Windows applications.

How It Got This Way

NEXTSTEP is currently in its third incarnation. But what are its origins? Why was it built the way it was and how does it benefit you and me? An understanding of these questions and their answers will be invaluable to understanding what makes NEXTSTEP unique and how it can make the computing experience more enjoyable and productive.

In 1986, Steve Jobs, co-founder and former CEO of Apple Computer, Inc., was building a new company and was in search of an operating system for his new NeXT Computer. It had to be more robust than the Macintosh he pioneered in 1984, yet would need to be just as easy to use as the Macintosh. The operating system also needed to incorporate advanced capabilities such as multitasking, networking, and many other features that would be required to make the system successful in the marketplace of the '90s. Writing an operating system takes years, and he had to bring his product to market quickly or he faced the loss of support from his investors. He also took into consideration the sharp criticisms he had received about his Macintosh computer's incompatibility with the other computer systems.

His solution was to use the Mach operating system developed at Carnegie-Mellon University, which could be obtained inexpensively and included support for powerful multitasking and communications features. As a front end to Mach he would use the UNIX system as it was well known to may computer users, could run on many types of hardware, and could be easily made to run on top of Mach. It also provided support for multitasking, could handle multiple users on the same machine, and most of all, it could enable the NeXT Computer to communicate with the many UNIX-based computers that already existed. UNIX was also readily available and could be implemented quickly. There were several other reasons for using UNIX too. After leaving Apple Computer, Jobs no longer had access to Macintosh technology. NeXT's task would be to create a GUI that would be easy to use like the Macintosh, but with the power of UNIX. The result of that effort is NEXTSTEP, a graphical environment that is easy to use, based on the UNIX operating system, and object oriented for easy maintenance.

Object Oriented Design

If NEXTSTEP is the locomotive, object-oriented design is the coal and steam that powers it. In simple terms, being object-oriented means the software that manages the computer and its applications is composed of building blocks called objects. Objects are self-contained collections of code and data that are assembled in a myriad of ways to perform larger, more complex tasks. These software objects are most often created using a programming language named Objective C. Objective C is based on the C programming language but includes extensions that allow a programmer to implement software objects. As we shall see, object orientation has many significant implications. Because of its inherent advantages, object orientation will be the standard model for systems and application software in the decade of the 1990s.

To see how object orientation can affect you directly, let's examine a common object in many NEXTSTEP applications, the Colors panel. The Colors panel was improved significantly from Release 2.2 to Release 3 and now includes support for the PANTONE® Matching System(PMS). When users ran an application designed for NEXTSTEP Release 2.2 under NEXTSTEP Release 3, they saw something amazing. Applications that used the Colors panel displayed the new and improved version containing PANTONE options and other improvements automatically. Users didn't need to do *anything*. Developers didn't need to do *anything*. Because of the object-oriented nature of NEXTSTEP applications and the NEXTSTEP environment, applications running under the new release inherited the new features automatically. The unique ability to add functionality to an application so easily is the primary reason NeXT chose to build it using object-oriented code.

Introduction

NEXTSTEP Objects

Applications that used the NEXTSTEP 2.1 Colors panel object (left) automatically displayed the new NEXTSTEP Colors panel object (right) in every application when they upgraded to NEXTSTEP release 3.

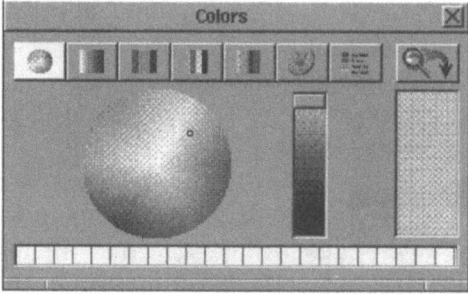
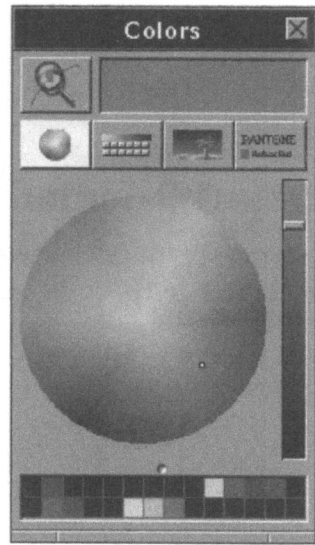

Object-oriented programming also provides numerous benefits to software developers, including NeXT. Without the use of objects, a change in code at the beginning of a *program* requires a propagation of changes throughout the rest of the code. Changes made to an object do not require changes to be made to other objects. As we saw in the previous example, a new Colors panel could be easily implemented by simply replacing the older color object with a newer one. Every application that used the color object instantly had access to PANTONE colors in the new object. Applications did not have to be recompiled or reconfigured. By enhancing the NEXTSTEP color object, NeXT enhanced every application that made use of it.

Because programming is easier for developers, more and better applications are made available sooner and at lower cost than those designed for other systems. Object orientation allows programmers to reuse and modify code much more easily than using traditional programming practice. They can add new functionality, such as the ability to access remote databases, display three-dimensional images, and open new document formats, by simply adding a standard NeXT object to their code. If you are so inclined, you too can use NeXT's standard objects to create a program to suit your needs. Several companies even sell custom objects that you can easily incorporate into your own applications. These objects are listed in the *Object Software Catalog*, available from NeXT.

Finally, since almost every NEXTSTEP application is built using standard objects provided by NeXT, each application's use of them is extraordinarily consistent. For example, the Open, Save, Color, and Font panels perform in the same manner in every application. Thus, the time you spend learning how to use one application directly transfers to the next application so you have to learn only the commands specific to the new application. Because the basics remain the same, you can get started with your second or third application much more quickly than with other systems. Through inheritance, some applications may add features to objects, but their core function will remain the same. This advantage is significant and key to NeXT's ability to provide so many powerful features. In contrast, applications built using old techniques often require you to begin from scratch with each new program.

The Display PostScript System

Another basic element of NEXTSTEP, Display PostScript, was developed jointly by NeXT Computer and Adobe Systems specifically for use in NEXTSTEP. Until Display PostScript was developed, the PostScript page description language was used exclusively in printers. PostScript is a programming language much like Fortran, Pascal, or C, that was created to describe complex graphical images and text in various typestyles. Text and images described using the PostScript language can be resized, rotated, or skewed yet be printed without distortion. Text and images described by PostScript are also device independent. This means the same image can be printed or displayed on any device, even though the devices may have differing resolutions. The higher the resolution of the printer, the better the resulting image. In combination, these two characteristics provide a method for printing or displaying scalable type and graphics at the highest resolution a device can produce, with very smooth edges or little distortion of fonts and graphic images. Having PostScript Level II built into NEXTSTEP adds the ability to manipulate calibrated color images as well as those in black and white, while increasing the imaging speed of the original Display PostScript.

Because the PostScript language is used to describe an image on the monitor as well as on the printer, you get great-looking images on the screen and very fast printing because no conversion is necessary to create printed output from an image on the screen. In computer jargon this is called

WYSIWYG (pronounced "wiz ee wig") or what you see is what you get. In simple terms, by using PostScript, NEXTSTEP delivers no surprises when you print a page.

How NEXTSTEP Is Packaged

NEXTSTEP can be purchased pre-loaded on various computer systems or it can be purchased separately. NEXTSTEP software is distributed in two parts: the user environment and the developer environment. The user environment is available in two versions, one each for computers featuring Intel processors, called **NeXTSTEP for Intel Processors**, and another for NeXT hardware, called **NeXTSTEP for NeXT Computers**. In each package you'll receive a CD-ROM containing the software, a floppy disk (or two) with which to boot the computer and load the software from the CD-ROM, and instructions. Of course you'll need a CD-ROM drive and SCSI adapter card to load the software. If your computer is on a network with other NeXT computers, you can also load the software using the network. The other machine must be running the version of NEXTSTEP you want to load, and you must have purchased the right to copy the software. This option provides a means by which you load the software without having to install and configure a CD-ROM drive on every machine.

To run the user environment, you'll need at least 120 MB of hard disk storage and at least 8 MB of random access memory (RAM). After using NEXTSTEP with this configuration for a short while, most users find 16 MB RAM (24 or more if using a color display) and 300 MB of disk storage to be more suitable. The larger disk drive is particularly important if your computer is stand-alone, not networked to a file server, in which case you'll need to store both applications and documents on your own computer.

If you are interested in developing custom applications, you'll need to purchase both the user environment and the developer environment. The two are additive. Unlike the user environment, there is only one version of the NEXTSTEP Developer disc which can be used on both Intel-based PCs and NeXT hardware. To load and run the developer environment, you'll need at least a 400 MB disk drive and 8 MB of RAM. However, a typical developer system usually contains a 660 MB hard disk and 24 MB or more of RAM. For a complete list of the applications and tools included with the NEXTSTEP user and developer releases, refer to the "Summary of Bundled Applications" on page 259.

Introduction

You may recall that NEXTSTEP was originally designed for NeXT computers that used a Motorola 68000 series central processor. Now NEXTSTEP is available for computers with Intel processors, and soon it will be available on for other processors as well. Fortunately, NEXTSTEP appears the same and works the same no matter which computer it is installed on. In this book, we will concentrate on the NEXTSTEP user environment for Intel processors and make a note where NEXTSTEP for NeXT hardware differs. If you have access to NEXTSTEP, stop from time to time to practice the concepts and instructions discussed in each chapter or section. There are many sample files and applications to provided on the enclosed floppy disk for just this purpose. If you don't have access to a computer running NEXTSTEP, don't worry. The illustrations will help you follow along, and it won't take long for you to want to try NEXTSTEP for yourself.

Up and Running

NEXTSTEP

Name
Password

1
Basic Training

This chapter presents a short but necessary description of fundamentals of NEXTSTEP that you'll need to know to get started. If you've used previous versions of NEXTSTEP and want to learn about some of the new features of release 3, you may want to skip to Chapter 3. However, if you're new to NEXTSTEP, you won't want to miss these important items.

1.0 User Accounts

One of the primary differences between NEXTSTEP and the ubiquitous DOS and Macintosh systems is that NEXTSTEP is designed to allow more than one person to use a computer at the same time. A system designed this way is called a multi-user system. As we shall soon see, this feature has many implications. Prior to accessing the computer's files and applications for the first time, you must have an account. An account consists of a *user name*, password, and location in which to store personal files. NEXTSTEP requires that you enter your user name and password before you can use the computer. This process, called *logging in*, helps keep track of each user's files and prevents one user from accessing another's files. After logging in, you will see a list of the files you have stored on the hard disk drive in your

Basic Training

private storage location, called a *home folder*. This location is also referred to as your user account. Every user has a unique home folder in which to store files, applications, and other electronic documents. Users control access to their own home folder and can prevent other users from seeing, opening, saving, or deleting items in their home folder.

1.0.0 The Me Account

Your home folder is represented by the single home icon (top). Home folders for other users are represented by the neighborhood icon (bottom).

When you start NEXTSTEP for the first time you will be immediately logged in to the special account named me. The me account does not require a password. By including this account on every system, NeXT allows a single user to get up and running very quickly. However, if you don't create a password for this account, anyone who happens to turn on the computer will have access to all of your files. Therefore, it is important to create a password for the me account as soon as you log in. Creating and changing a password is described in "Password Preferences" on page 293. After creating a password for the me account, each time you turn on the computer you will see the login panel and will have to enter your user name and password to access your files. You are not required to create a password for this account, but it is highly recommended to prevent other people who have access the computer either directly or remotely through a network, from accessing your files.

1.0.1 The Root User

NEXTSTEP, like other multi-user systems, also provides an account that has unlimited access to the files stored in the computer. This account is known as root, and the person who logs in as **root** is referred to as the *system administrator* or *superuser*. The system administrator is responsible for configuring computers and often for managing computer networks. These responsibilities include: creating user accounts and passwords, recreating a password when a user forgets it, configuring the computer to work with other computers on a network, making backup copies of the information on the computer's hard disk drive, adding additional hard disk drives and other peripherals, managing electronic mail, and performing other administrative tasks.

If you are the sole user of your computer, you may not have a system administrator to take care of these duties. In this case, you will also have to perform system administration from time to time. The tasks of the root user are so numerous a complete discussion of them would require a book of its own. However, if you find yourself in the position of system administrator for your computer system, you will want to begin by reading the on-line network and system administration files located in the **/NextLibrary/ Documentation/NextAdmin** folder. Using the Digital Librarian™ applications included with NEXTSTEP, you can index and search the contents of this folder so you can locate particular topics of interest quickly and easily. When you have exhausted this source, your next step would be to purchase a book on UNIX system administration, such as the *UNIX System Administration Handbook* by Evi Nemeth, Garth Snyder, and Scott Seebass. These sources will provide you with the necessary details of configuring and maintaining a UNIX-based system such as NEXTSTEP.

The root account is not initially protected with a password, so you'll need to create one for it. Log in as the root user and follow the procedure for creating a password described in "Password Preferences" on page 293. It is *very* important that you create a password for the root account, particularly if the computer is connected to a network, where numerous users have potential access to your computer.

Because of the unlimited power of the root user to change the computer's configuration, you should not use this account except to perform one of the root user's special duties. Instead, use the me account or your normal user account for daily work. Should you make a mistake while logged in as the root user—such as change your password, change or delete a critical configuration file, or change the access privileges to a file or folder—you could disable the computer from restarting after it is powered off.

The user who logs in as **root** is called the superuser for a very good reason. The root user has unlimited access to every file, program, and utility stored on your computer. Leaving the root account unprotected is very much like leaving your home unlocked while you leave on vacation. You are taking a great risk by allowing easy access to anyone who bothers to check the door to see if it is locked. Likewise, anyone who bothers to attempt to log in as **root** could gain access to every file in the computer and can even lock you out so that you cannot use your own computer when you return. Don't forget that root is the name used for the system administrator on almost every UNIX-based system, so it won't take long for even a novice to attempt to log in to the root account out of curiosity. Who can resist trying to become superuser? Of course, you should be very careful to avoid losing the root password as it will be exceedingly difficult to regain it.

1.1 Starting NEXTSTEP

To start running NEXTSTEP, simply turn on the power to your computer system. If you're using a PC with one or more partitions, as described in the NEXTSTEP installation guide, you'll have the choice of starting the computer using DOS, NEXTSTEP, or other system software (see Figure 1-1). Note in Figure 1-1 that no choice was entered. In such an instance, the computer will wait for several seconds and then automatically start up from the active partition, which contains the NEXTSTEP system software.

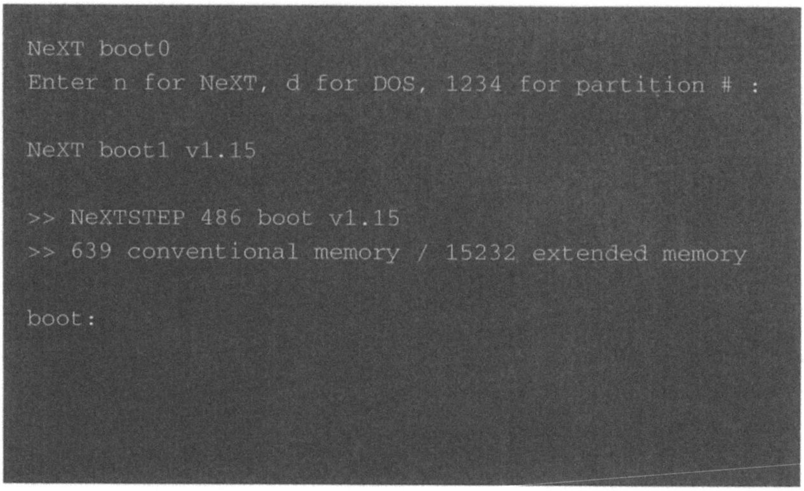

**Figure 1-1
Starting
NEXTSTEP**

If your hard disk drive has more than one partition, you can choose to boot the system software on any one of them at startup time.

```
NeXT boot0
Enter n for NeXT, d for DOS, 1234 for partition # :

NeXT boot1 v1.15

>> NeXTSTEP 486 boot v1.15
>> 639 conventional memory / 15232 extended memory

boot:
```

When you start NEXTSTEP, you'll see a long list of activities the computer must undertake to prepare NEXTSTEP for action. These activities include but are not limited to the following:

❖ Performs self-diagnostics to determine the computer's condition

❖ Loads information from the disk into its RAM

❖ Verifies the file system to make sure files are where they should be and contain the proper information

❖ Establishes itself on TCP/IP and NetWare® networks (if these are enabled and the computer is attached to such networks)

Starting NEXTSTEP

❖ Starts UNIX processes, called daemons (pronounced "dee-munz"), to provide UNIX services

❖ Presents the NEXTSTEP login panel (if the me account has been given a password).

While the computer performs each of these tasks, it displays messages on the screen so that you can monitor their progress. Should something go wrong, you can sometimes determine the problem by reviewing this list. The startup process is somewhat lengthy, depending on your computer. If you'll be using the computer again the same day, you can avoid having to load NEXTSTEP each time you want to use the computer by leaving it running and logging out rather than powering off. Then you'll only need to log in to get started the next time.

1.1.0 Logging In

If this is the first time NEXTSTEP has been used or if the me account has not been given a password, you will see the NEXTSTEP workspace immediately. However, if you have given the me account a password, you will see the login panel after you turn on the computer (see Figure 1-2). In this case, you must type a valid user name and password to gain access to your files and applications. If you don't know what your user name and password are, contact your system administrator to get them. Remember, by default, NEXTSTEP will not require a password for the me account so you may not see the login panel. However, if you do, type your user name into the Name field, press the Tab or Return key, type your password in the Password field and press Return. So that onlookers can't steal your password and access your files later, your password will not be displayed as you type it. NEXTSTEP distinguishes between upper-case and lower-case characters, so type your user name and password exactly as they were given to you, or the computer will not accept them. NEXTSTEP will verify that the name and password you entered are correct.

If either your user name or password don't match the user name and password created by the root user, the login panel will shake and the names you entered disappear. Enter your user name and password again using the procedure described above. After you have entered them successfully, the login panel will disappear and in a few moments you will see the *workspace* environment in which you do your work.

NEXTSTEP displays a bouncing NeXT logo, which acts as a screen saver, when the login panel is left alone on the screen for long periods of time. Press a key, click a mouse button, or roll the mouse to see the login panel again.

Basic Training

**Figure 1-2
Logging In**

After you NEXTSTEP's start-up procedure is finished, the login panel will appear so that you can gain access to your files and applications.

Type your user name here

Type your password here

1.1.1 Logging Out

When you are finished with a session, you should *log out*. Logging out lets NEXTSTEP know that you are leaving so that it can close the files you still have open and quit applications that are still running. Don't worry if you accidentally attempt to log out while you still have work in progress. NEXTSTEP will alert you and allow you to cancel the logout procedure or save your work before logging out. When the logout is complete, the NEXTSTEP login panel will appear again so that another user can log in and begin a session.

To log out and end a session, choose Log Out from the Workspace menu. An attention panel will appear to verify that you really want to log out (see Figure 1-3). Click Log Out to continue logging out, or click Cancel to return to the workspace to continue working with NEXTSTEP.

**Figure 1-3
Logging Out**

The Logout panel is used to end a NEXTSTEP session and power off the computer.

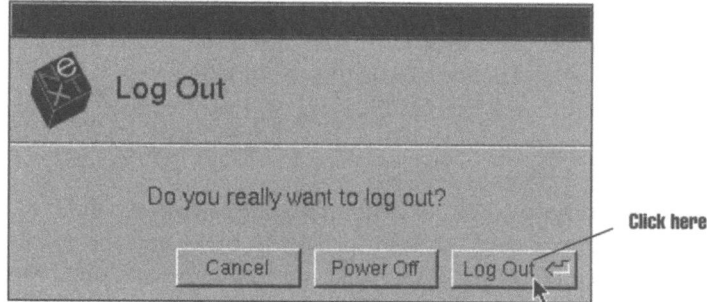

Click here

1.2 Shutting Down

You know from watching the boot process that NEXTSTEP manages not only processes you see, but processes you don't see as well. You should remain conscious of this fact when you are ready to turn off the computer.

> Unlike with DOS, you cannot merely turn off the power switch when you want to shut down the computer. This would not allow the daemons to quit gracefully, and could prevent information in volatile RAM from being saved to disk, leaving the system in an unstable state the next time you power it on. Instead, NEXTSTEP should be told to prepare for shut down before the power is actually switched off.

1.2.0 Powering Off

To initiate the power off procedure, choose Log Out from the workspace's main menu and click Power Off (see Figure 1-3). If you are using a NeXT computer, you can also press the Power key on the keyboard and click Turn it Off when the Power panel appears. Clicking Cancel in the Log Out or Power panel stops the shutdown request, keeps you logged in, and allows you to continue working in NEXTSTEP. Be sure you have saved the documents you have been working on and quit each application before choosing to power off. Should you forget to close open documents and begin the shutdown procedure, NEXTSTEP will stop and ask if you wish to save the documents before completing the shutdown. When the shutdown is complete, a panel will appear indicating that it is safe to turn off the power switch (see Figure 1-4). Do not turn off the power until you see the "CPU halted; OK to power off" message. If you have a NeXT computer, the power will be turned off automatically when it is safe.

Basic Training

**Figure 1-4
Shutting down
the Computer**

As NEXTSTEP shuts down, it displays this panel. When the OK to power off message appears, it's safe to turn off the power switch.

```
               NeXT Mach Operating System
Mar 6 12:06:45 localhost syslogd: going down on signal 15
Mar 6 12:06:48 npd[143]: caught signal, exiting
Killing all processes
continuing
unmounting swapfile.front ... done
cpu halted; OK to power off.
```

The restart button (top) and the power off button (bottom) appear only when the login panel is displayed.

1.2.1 Powering Off from the Login Panel

The power-off procedure is easy to perform when you are logged in, but what about when you're not logged in? When you log out but keep the computer running, the only thing you'll see on the screen is the login panel. Since there is no Workspace menu from which to choose Log Out, you cannot shut down or restart the computer unless you first log back in. This not only seems backward, but can be very time consuming as you must wait for the workspace to appear, removable disks to be mounted, and perhaps for auto-starting applications to start up. NeXT hardware provides a power key on the keyboard to initiate powering off, but this feature is not available on Intel-based systems.

To solve this problem, NEXTSTEP provides two buttons in the lower right corner of the login panel (see Figure 1-5). Clicking the left button presents the Restart panel. Using this panel, you can restart the computer using either NEXTSTEP or DOS, or you can cancel to keep the computer running. Clicking the right button, initiates powering off by presenting the Power panel.

Shutting Down

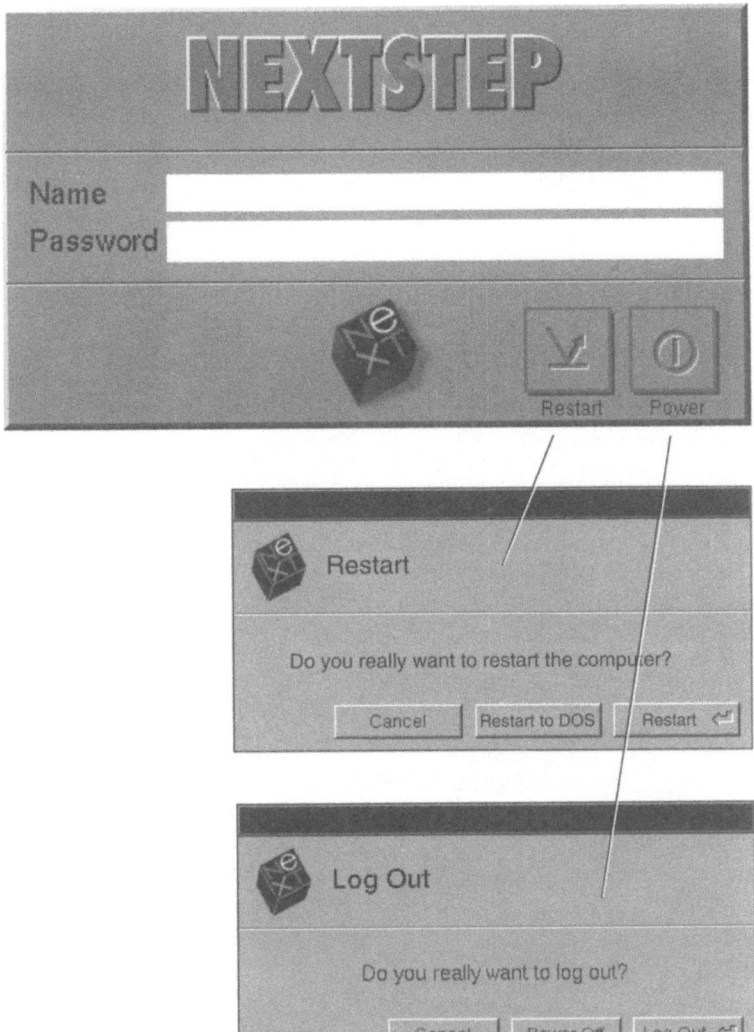

**Figure 1-5
The NEXTSTEP
login screen**

Two buttons appear in the Login screen to assist you in restarting or powering off the computer. Click the restart button to display the Restart panel (middle) or the Power Off button display the Power panel (bottom).

1.2.2 Logging Out vs. Powering Off

You may wonder if it's better to leave the computer running and log out or simply power off when not it's in use. If you are the only user, and the computer is not connected to a network, it makes sense to turn the computer off each time you finish a session. NeXT recommends that you turn off the computer if you're not going to be using it for a day or two. However, if others use the computer, or it is connected to a network, you may want to leave the computer running and simply log out to protect your files. This saves subsequent users the time and trouble of turning on each of the computer components, and waiting for the system to complete its startup procedure and present the login panel.

> If you intend to log out and power off the computer, you can skip logging out and simply begin the shutdown procedure. Powering off the computer will log you out automatically.

There are several other reasons for leaving the computer running that may not be so obvious. In NEXTSTEP, there are many daemons, which run, often unnoticed, in the background. These daemons are busy interacting with other systems on a network, or perhaps providing services to remote users. One of the more important daemons waits for electronic mail to arrive. Should your computer be turned off when a user on another system sends you mail, the daemon will not be running in order to receive it and the mail will be returned. It is also possible that other systems may be allowed to use files or applications from your system using NFS (described in "Network File System (NFS)" on page 308). In this case, others may be using your computer even when you aren't. Turning off the computer in this case would prohibit them from accessing the files or applications they might need. Computer systems are designed to run for long periods of time, so aside from the use of electricity, no damage will result. NEXTSTEP also automatically dims the display after a brief period of inactivity to prevent screen burn-in. If you are concerned about screen burn-in, you can turn off the display, but leave the CPU running.

In the next chapter, we'll examine the components of the workspace, the starting point of every NEXTSTEP session. From the workspace, you'll be able to view all of the documents and applications stored on your computer, how menus rather than typed commands can be used to manipulate these files and applications, and the "power tools" unique to the NEXTSTEP workspace. Let's go!

An Inside Look

2

The NEXTSTEP Workspace

Each time you log in, NEXTSTEP runs an application called the Workspace Manager™. The Workspace Manager is responsible for displaying the NEXTSTEP graphical user interface called the workspace (see Figure 2-1). It is in the workspace that all of your work with NEXTSTEP begins and ends. In this chapter, we will examine the parts of the workspace and take a broad look at its many features. In subsequent chapters, we'll examine each item in more detail.

The primary purpose of the Workspace Manager is to allow you to control the activities of the computer. For example, in the workspace, you can create, duplicate, organize, find, rename, and delete files and folders; start up and manage applications; access storage devices such as hard disks, CD-ROMs, and optical disks; and perform a host of other activities. The workspace may look complex at first glance, but it consists of only a few basic parts: a *File Viewer* for browsing and manipulating files, a menu containing commands, an *application dock* for easy access to applications, and a *recycler* for deleting files.

The NEXTSTEP Workspace

Up to now, you haven't needed to use the mouse, but since it is the primary means by which you control items in the workspace, it's important that you have a good understanding of how it is used. If you're handy with a mouse, you may want to skip to section 2.1 on page 15.

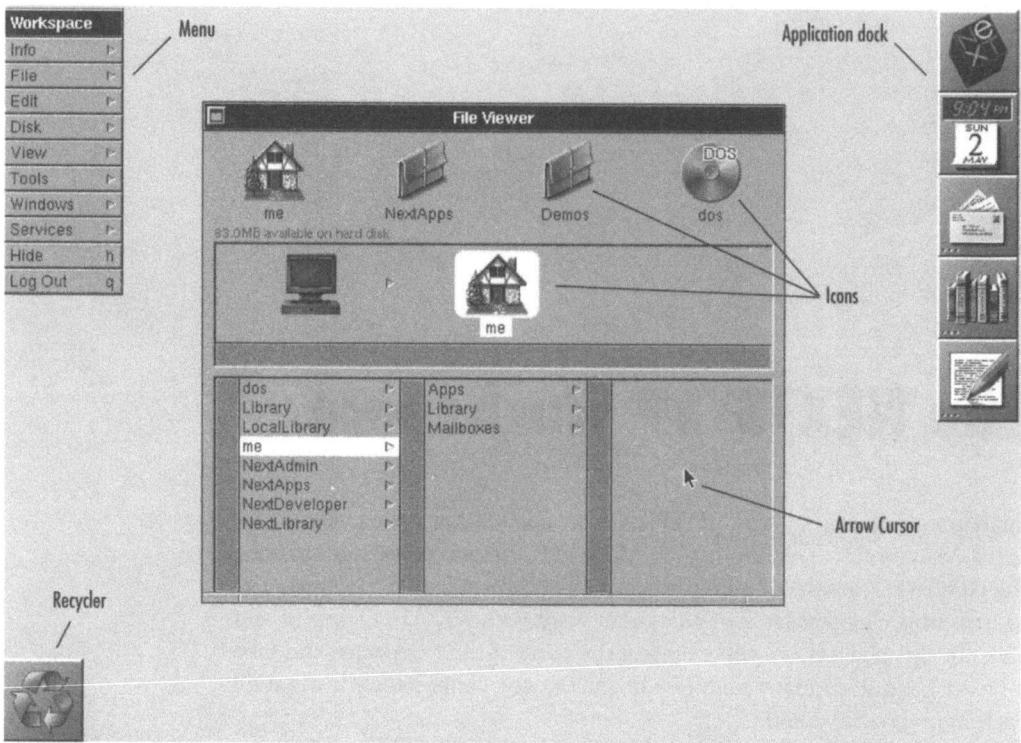

Figure 2-1
The NEXTSTEP
Workspace

2.0 The Mouse

You use the mouse to control a small pointer on the screen called a *cursor*, and to select commands from on-screen menus. It is the primary means by which you control the computer. In general, only when you enter text do you need to use the keyboard. However, you can also use the keyboard with or instead of the mouse when it is convenient.

The Mouse

Your mouse may have one, two, or three *buttons*, any of which can be used when selecting or dragging objects on the screen (see Figure 2-2). The cursor can change shape (see margin) but is always controlled by the mouse. To move the cursor around the screen, drag the mouse along a hard flat surface. As you drag the mouse, a small rubber ball located in the bottom of the mouse will move so that the mouse can detect its motion. If your computer uses an optical mouse, you may have to drag the mouse on a special reflective mouse pad in order for it to work properly. If the ball doesn't roll or you roll off the mouse pad (optical mouse only), the mouse will not detect any motion and the cursor will not move on the screen. There are three actions you can perform with the mouse:

arrow cursor
copy cursor
help cursor
I-beam cursor

- ❖ *Click*—Press and release a mouse button without moving the mouse. This action usually selects an item on the screen or activates a menu choice.

- ❖ *Double-click*—Click a mouse button two times very quickly. This action is often used to open a file or folder or start an application. The two clicks must be performed rapidly, or NEXTSTEP may interpret them as two single clicks.

- ❖ *Drag*—Press and hold down a mouse button while sliding the mouse to reposition the cursor. This action is most often used to reposition an object on the screen, or to select characters or lines of text.

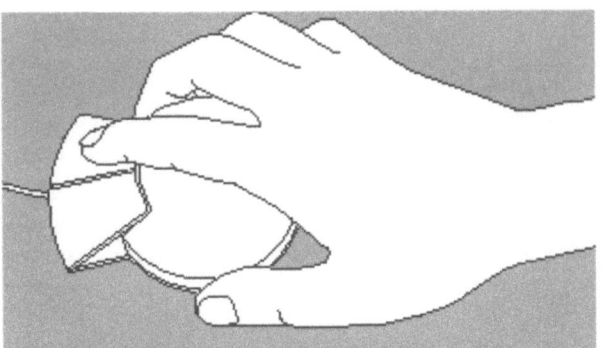

Figure 2-2
The Mouse

The mouse (NeXT ADB mouse shown here) controls the positioning of the cursor.

If you've never used a mouse, learning how may be a bit frustrating at first. But with just a little practice, you can use the mouse effectively in no time. These tips may help:

The NEXTSTEP Workspace

❖ Keep the mouse cable facing the same direction at all times to make the cursor follow a predictable pattern.

❖ Rotating the mouse in place instead of dragging it across a table will make the cursor's movement difficult to predict.

❖ If while dragging the mouse you run out of table space or bump into another object, pick the mouse up off of the table and move it so that it is in a more comfortable position. Notice that while the mouse is in the air the cursor does not move. This is because the rubber ball in the mouse is not moving while the mouse is in the air. When the mouse is in a more comfortable position, set it down on the table and continue rolling it to position the cursor. This procedure will also work even when you have a mouse button held down. Just keep the mouse button held down while the mouse is in the air.

❖ If you prefer, you can configure either button to display the current application's main menu under the cursor, no matter where the cursor is located on the screen. This shortcuts the need to continually drag the arrow cursor across the distance of the screen to make a menu selection. This feature can be turned on or off, or exchanged between the left and right mouse buttons using the Preferences application as described in "Mouse Preferences" on page 282. Because the mouse functions are interchangeable, the phrase "click a mouse button" is used to describe the button you use to point, click, and drag.

To determine how the keys on your keyboard map to the NeXT keyboard, use the Keyboard panel in the Localization preferences as described on page page 286.

From time to time you may want to take advantage of several mouse shortcuts. To extend the function of the mouse, you can press a key or combination of keys on the keyboard while you click, double-click, or drag. Table 2-1, "Mouse Action Modifier Keys" describes some of the more useful mouse shortcuts. Don't worry about learning these shortcuts right way. You can refer back to this table later when you feel more comfortable with the mouse's normal functions.

Table 2-1 **Mouse Action Modifier Keys**

Action	Description
Alternate-click	Extends a text selection to include text between the last click and the current click position.
Alternate-click a scroller	Scrolls more than one line.
Alternate-drag	Brings a window to the front but does not make the window's application active.
Command-drag	Forces NEXTSTEP to copy an item rather than move it.
Shift-click	Adds the item you click to the current selection. Shift-clicking a selected item removes it from the current selection.

2.1 The File Viewer

The window that appears in the workspace, called a File Viewer, allows you to view and manipulate the files, folders, and documents stored on your computer system. This collection of files is called the *file system*. To copy files, create new folders, name files, erase them, and perform other similar tasks, drag and drop icons in the File Viewer. Unlike with many other windowing systems, you can perform all of these tasks and more within a single window. This keeps the screen from being cluttered by unnecessary windows and allows you to focus your attention on the objects you want to manipulate rather than on the window they are in. If you've used another GUI, you may have experienced the difficulty of positioning windows on the screen in order to be able to see the item you want to drag, and the folder or window you want to drag it to. The NEXTSTEP File Viewer, avoids this frustration.

The File Viewer has three main components: the shelf, icon path, and viewing area as shown in Figure 2-3. The *shelf* is used to store items you use often and makes them easy to access. The *icon path* visually displays the current location in the file system of the selected file or folder, and always begins with the root folder. The viewing area displays the items contained in the currently selected folder. In Figure 2-3, the File Viewer displays items as icons, but we'll see later that there are also other ways to display items in the file system.

Figure 2-3
The File Viewer

The File Viewer, shown here in icon view, is used to browse the contents of the file system.

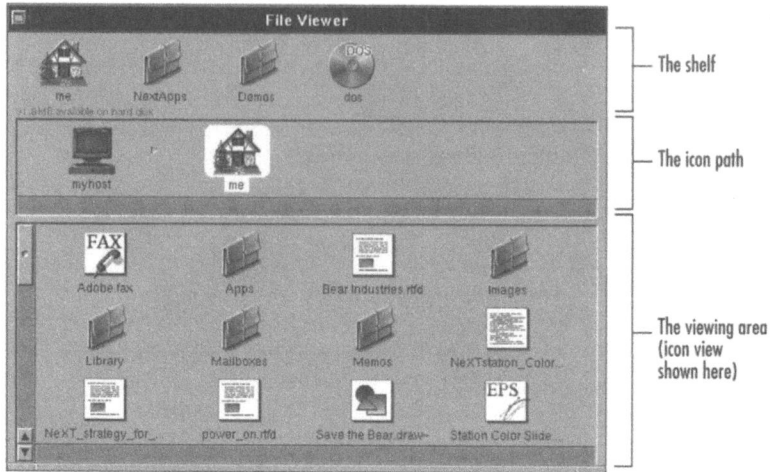

2.1.0 NEXTSTEP Icons

Folder icon

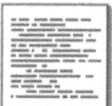

File icon

NEXTSTEP represents each item in the file system as a small picture called an *icon*. Icons visually distinguish items so you can easily identify them. For example, every folder looks the same so you can distinguish folders from documents, and documents look similar so you can tell them from folders and applications (see Figure 2-3). To uniquely identify documents that share the same icon, each document also has a name. To locate a particular document in the File Viewer, you would look for its icon and then its name. (NEXTSTEP also provides a Finder panel so you can find an item even when you don't know it's name or icon. The Finder is described further in "Finding a File or Folder" on page 55.)

Where do icons come from? NEXTSTEP has many icons built into it. Additional icons are provided by programmers who include icons with their applications to represent the applications and the documents their application creates. When you copy or install an application onto a floppy disk or hard disk, its icons are copied automatically. NEXTSTEP applies the appropriate icon according to the last few letters of a file's name, called an *extension*. Extensions always appear at the end of a file's name and start with a period. For example, documents created by the Appsoft Draw application have the extension **.drw** at the end of their names to identify them as Appsoft Draw documents. Applications append the appropriate extension to a document automatically when it is saved so you don't have to do it yourself. Since NEXTSTEP uses the extension to determine an item's icon, changing a file's extension will change its icon. Table 2-2 describes some of the file name extensions you're likely to see in NEXTSTEP.

Table 2-2 Common File Name Extensions

Extension	Document Format
.app	Application
.bshlf	Digital Librarian
.draw	NeXT Draw
.drw	Appsoft Draw
.eps	Encapsulated PostScript
.font	NeXT font
.frame	FrameMaker
.imp	Lotus Improv Spreadsheet
.ma	Mathematica notebook
.mbox	NeXTmail mailbox
.objlink	Published NeXTlink file (contains a linked graphic)
.pcd	PhotoCD ImagePac file
.ps	PostScript
.rtf	Rich Text Format©
.snd	NeXT sound
.tiff	Tagged Image File Format
.wn	WriteNow
.wp	WordPerfect

Naming Files

Applications with unknown extensions appear like this.

You can name and rename a file as many times as you want, but you should try to keep names less than 14 characters to make them easier to read. When naming a file or folder, avoid using ' " & * - / | > ^ < characters, as they have special meaning in UNIX and can cause undesirable results when using the command-line features of NEXTSTEP. Also, no two items within the same folder can share the same name.

If you change a file's name so that it no longer has a recognizable extension, NEXTSTEP will represent it with a generic document icon. Applications whose extensions are unrecognized appear in the File Viewer with a generic application icon. NEXTSTEP differentiates files from applications according to their execute *permission*. When a file's execute permission is turned on, NEXTSTEP assumes the file to be an executable application. Permissions are described in more detail in "Permissions" on page 89.

2.1.1 NEXTSTEP Folders

NEXTSTEP organizes its hierarchical file system into levels of folders within folders within folders. Folders are used to organize the many items found in the file system including documents, sounds, applications, and even other folders. The folder that contains all other folders is called the *root folder*. It has a special icon in the File Viewer that looks like a NeXTstation computer. The root gets its name from its location in the hierarchy, which when viewed graphically, looks like a tree's roots (see Figure 2-4).

There are many items in the file system, but many of them are reserved by NEXTSTEP. Only the root user can modify these items. The items you can modify are contained within your own home folder (named **me** in Figure 2-4) and its subfolders. Your home folder displays the home icon and appears in the upper left corner of the File Viewer at all times. In this folder, you can create delete, name, and rename items at any time and in any way you wish. Folders help you organize the documents you save on the computer's hard disk and floppy disks just as with paper storage systems. Using folders, you can keep documents from being mixed together and make it easier to find them later. For example, you can store all of your personal documents in a folder named **Documents** and store your business documents in a different folder called **Memos**. To further organize your work, you might create another folder named **Ad Copy** in which to keep other business files. Another advantage of the hierarchical file system is

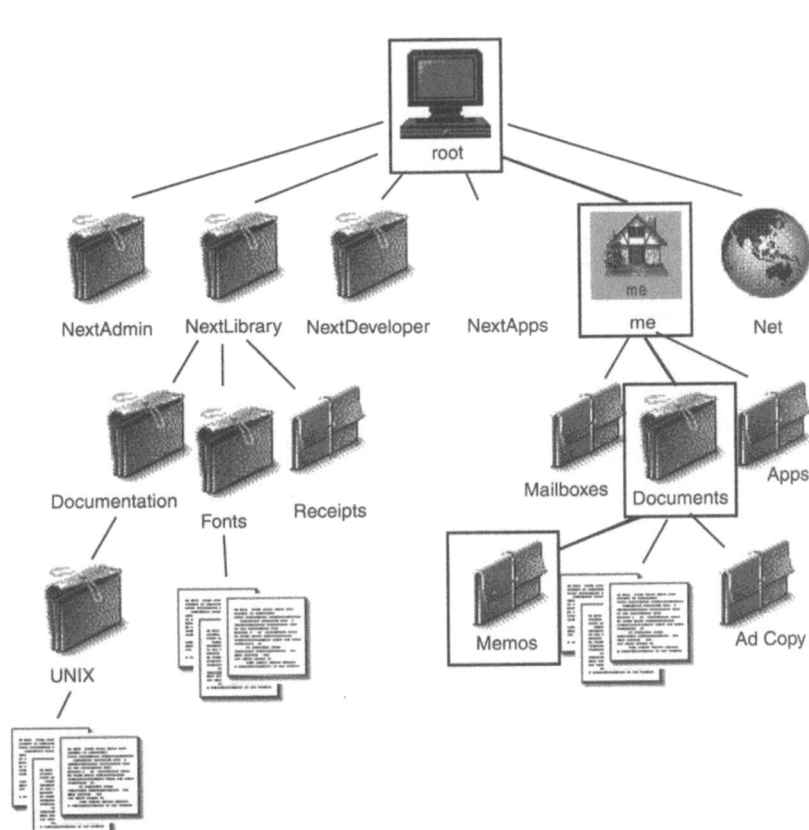

**Figure 2-4
The File System Hierarchy**

You can visualize the entire file system as the roots of a tree. Each item in the file system has a unique path through the hierarchy, called a pathname, which identifies it.

that you can manipulate many documents very easily. For example, moving the folder **Documents** would also move the files and folders it contains: **Memos** and **Ad Copy**. If you were to duplicate the **Documents** folder, every item in the folder, no matter how many, would also be duplicated. In Chapter 3, "Files and Folders," we'll examine some of the other benefits of NEXTSTEP's file system.

Pathnames

Each item in the NEXTSTEP file system is uniquely identified by the names of the folders you must pass through to find it. This sequence of folder names is called a *pathname*. All pathnames begin with the root folder, which is represented in writing by the slash (/) character. A slash character is also used to separate the names of each folder in a pathname. For example, the pathname of the UNIX folder in Figure 2-4 is **/NextLibrary/Documentation/UNIX**. This means you must look in the root for the **NextLibrary** folder, then inside the **Documentation** folder, where you will find the **UNIX** folder. When you read this pathname, say "next library documentation UNIX." You don't need to say "slash." One reason items in the same folder cannot share the same name is that the pathname to each item would be identical, and you would have no way to distinguish one from another.

Home Folder Pathname

Since most of the files you work with will reside in your home folder, the pathnames of your documents will all have the same beginning characters. For example, if your home folder is in **/users/laurel**, then every item in your home folder would have a pathname beginning with **/users/laurel**. It would convenient if we could abbreviate this portion of the pathname to make the pathname smaller and easier to write. NeXTSTEP allows you just such a shortcut; use the tilde character (**~**) to abbreviate the pathname to your home folder. (The tilde character is created by typing **Shift-`** on most keyboards). In the example above, Laurel could abbreviate the pathname to her home folder as **~/**. This abbreviation is most useful when you are using an account other then me, as /me is a relatively short pathname not much in need of an abbreviation.

Use the tilde character (~) to abbreviate the pathname to your home folder when typing out a pathname.

> The tilde shortcut represents the pathname to your own home folder, which is different for every user. For example, if your user name is **randal** the tilde would not represent **/users/laurel**, but rather **/users/randal**. Likewise, if you log in as the root user, the tilde shortcut will represent the path to the root directory, instead of your usual home folder.

2.2 NEXTSTEP Windows

NEXTSTEP displays information in movable, resizable rectangles called *windows*. NEXTSTEP windows are very similar to those found on the Macintosh and in Microsoft Windows. Because NEXTSTEP includes a window object for programmers to use, window features and controls are the same in every application. When you learn how a window works in one application, you'll know how they work in every application. The features and controls found in a typical NEXTSTEP window are described in Figure 2-5.

Not every window requires every feature or control shown in the illustration. If a feature appears in a window, use can use it. If not, the feature isn't available.

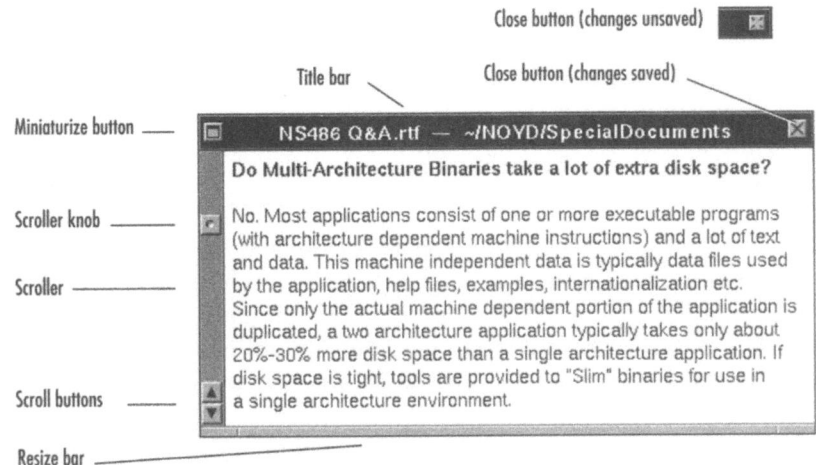

**Figure 2-5
Parts of a Window**

Every NEXTSTEP window features all or some of these controls.

The Title Bar

At the top of every NEXTSTEP window is a *title bar* (see Figure 2-6). The title bar uniquely identifies the window by displaying the name of the document it contains and, if the document has been saved to disk, the document's location in the file system. You can use the title bar to reposition a window by positioning the cursor on the title bar, pressing a mouse button, and dragging the window to a new location on the display.

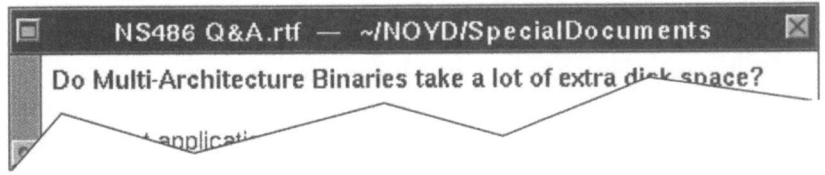

**Figure 2-6
The Title Bar**

The title bar displays the name and pathname of the document it contains.

The Miniaturize Button

It's not unusual to have many windows open while working in a single application. However, with many windows open at once, you can easily get confused and make changes to the wrong document. To solve this problem, you can miniaturize a window. Miniaturizing a window makes it very

Miniaturize button

small but does not close it. This allows you to focus your attention on a particular document while the miniaturized icon on the screen reminds you that other work is still in progress.

A miniwindow icon reflects the type of document it represents. In this example, the miniwindow represents an RTF document.

To miniaturize a window, click the *miniaturize button* in the upper left corner of its title bar (see Figure 2-6). When a window is miniaturized, it is represented as a *miniwindow* in the lower left corner of the workspace. You can reposition miniwindows anywhere in the workspace by dragging them with the mouse. To restore a miniwindow to full size, double-click the miniwindow icon.

Miniaturizing a window is not the same as closing it. A miniaturized window is still considered open although it takes up much less space, and still belongs to the application that opened it. If you quit the application to which miniwindow belongs, the application's miniwindows will be closed and disappear from the display. If you did not save the document before you miniaturized it, NEXTSTEP will display an attention panel so that you have an opportunity to save your work. If you want to close a miniwindow but not quit the application it belongs to, you must return it to a full-size window first.

Some applications display special windows that cannot be miniaturized. These windows usually display tools or information that pertain to more than one document and do not contain documents themselves. Such windows do not display the miniaturize icon in their title bar.

The Close Button

Saved

Unsaved

In the upper right corner of the title bar is a *close button*. Clicking the close button makes the window disappear. If the window contained an unsaved document, NEXTSTEP prompts you to save its contents before the document is closed. The close button indicates the state of the document displayed in the window. When the contents of the window have been saved, the close button appears with a solid X. When the X appears open instead, the contents of the window have been modified but the changes have not yet been saved to disk (see margin).

The Scroller

When an image or document cannot be fully displayed within a window, the window will display *scrollers*. To see the portion of the document that is out of view, position the cursor on the scroll knob and drag the knob up or down the scroller. A vertical and horizontal scroller will appear when portions of a document are not visible in a window. The document or image will move within the window at the same time you drag the scroller, which is not true of many other systems. For example, Macintosh computers require you to drag its scrolling object, then release the mouse button and wait for the window to be redrawn to see which part of the image is visible. You never know which portion of the image you'll be looking at until after you let go of the mouse button. Typically, you have to drag and let go several times just to get the see the portion of the text or image the way you want it. NeXT avoids this time-consuming process by moving the document or image in synchronization with the scroller.

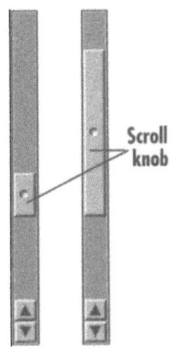

Scroll knob

In NEXTSTEP, the size of a scroll knob is just as informative as its position in the scroller. A very large scroll knob means there is little of the text that is not already visible in the window. A very small knob means much of the document is not visible in the window. You can also tell which part of the document you are viewing by noting the position of the knob in the scroller. When the knob appears at the top of the scroller, you will see the beginning of the document in the window. When the knob is at the bottom of the scroller, you will see the end of a document displayed in the window. Similarly, when the knob is positioned two-thirds of the way down the scroller, you will see the text or image that is two-thirds of the way through the document. Horizontal scrollers, when they appear, work exactly the same as vertical scrollers except that they control horizontal movement and viewing.

The length of a scroll knob indicates the proportion of text visible in the window. Very long documents have very small knobs and vice versa.

While the scroll knob can be used to traverse a long document or large image quickly, NEXTSTEP also provides *scroll buttons* for more precise scrolling. The two buttons, one for controlling each direction, are located together in the lower left corner of a window. The positioning of these arrows is much more convenient than on Windows and Macintosh systems, where these buttons are located at either end of their scrolling objects. In NEXTSTEP, you can scroll a document in either direction without having to move the cursor across the length of the scroller. Considering the large displays and windows used in graphical systems, this distance can be substantial, so making the arrow buttons close together makes them easier to reach and allows you to view a document much more quickly.

Scroll buttons provide very precise control over scrolling and appear whenever a portion of a document exists outside the boundaries of a window.

To use a scroll button, position the cursor on top of the button and click a mouse button. Clicking a scroll button repositions a document one line at a time. Holding a mouse button down while pointing to a scroll button scrolls a document continuously until you release the mouse button. In some applications, when you press the Alternate key on the keyboard while clicking a scroll button, you can quickly display the next window or page of a document.

The Resize Bar

Instead of scrolling through the contents of a NEXTSTEP window, you can resize it using the *resize bar* (see Figure 2-7). You may also want to make a window smaller in order to see other windows better or place several windows side by side. Only windows that display a resize bar can be resized. Resizable windows display a resize bar along their lower edge. To resize the length of a window, drag the middle region of the resize bar up or down. To make a window wider or narrower, drag either end of the resize bar horizontally. To resize both the width and the length of a window at the same time, drag an end region of the resize bar diagonally.

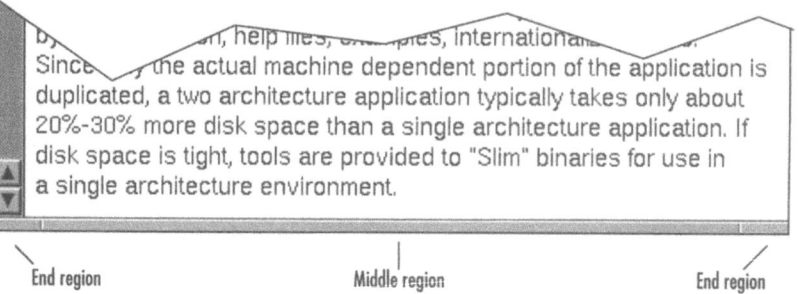

Figure 2-7
The Resize Bar

Dragging one of the corners of the resize bar allows you to change a window's width. Dragging the middle of the resize bare only changes a window's length.

2.3 NEXTSTEP Menus

Every NEXTSTEP application, including the Workspace Manager, displays a *menu* from which you can choose commands. Command menus, one of the foundations of the NEXTSTEP graphical user interface, save you the trouble of remembering and typing text commands to accomplish a task. Instead of typing, point to a command in a menu and click a mouse button. Just as with Windows and Windows NT, you need only click a menu item once to choose it. If you are a Macintosh user, you may be used to holding down the mouse button while dragging to a menu item. This is not required in NEXTSTEP, although doing so will also work.

Sometimes commands in a menu will appear gray instead of black. A gray item is disabled and cannot be chosen. Menu items are enabled and disabled as you select items in the Workspace or in an application. This prevents you from choosing an inappropriate command. When you highlight another item, change a selection, or otherwise alter the state of things, the menus will change automatically to disable commands that cannot be applied at the moment.

If a menu item displays a triangle symbol, clicking the item will display a *submenu* to its right containing more choices (see Figure 2-8). Each time you click a command that displays a submenu, it remains highlighted so you can see a trail of the commands you have selected. Only three levels of submenus should ever appear on the display at any one time This keeps the number of menu choices you must select to reach a command reasonable and prevents the display from becoming obscured by submenus. When you click a command that does not have a triangle symbol, it will be executed and the menu will remain visible. This makes it easy for you to choose another command, or the same command from the same menu, without having to open each submenu again.

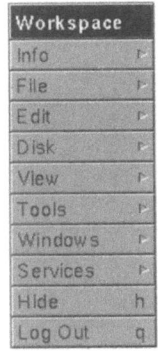

NEXTSTEP menus contain lists of commands and names of submenus. Some menu items have keyboard shortcuts (notice the Log Out item in this menu).

**Figure 2-8
Submenus**

To display Digital Librarian's Edit submenu, click Edit in the main menu. The menu will remain visible until you click an item in another menu.

For example, in the Digital Librarian application, clicking Edit displays the Edit menu (see Figure 2-8). Clicking Find in the Edit menu displays the Find menu, in which you can click any one of the several Find commands. Notice how each menu item that was selected remains highlighted to indicate how the last submenu was displayed.

When you click a highlighted menu item, it will no longer be highlighted, and any and all submenus to its right will disappear. If more than one submenu is visible, you can cause all of them to disappear by clicking the menu item in the main menu. (The main menu is always the one farthest to the left.) For example, in Figure 2-8, you could hide the Find submenu by clicking Find in the Edit submenu. To hide both the Edit and Find submenus with one click you could click Edit in the main menu. You will soon notice after using NEXTSTEP menus that you don't have to hide a submenu before choosing a command from another menu. All you have to do is click on the desired menu item; the visible submenu will disappear automatically as you make your new choice.

2.3.1 Tear-off Menus

NEXTSTEP always places the main menu in the upper left corner of the display so you can find it easily. If you prefer, you can move the main menu of any application by dragging it by its title bar. Even when you restart the application later, NEXTSTEP will remember the position of the main menu so you can find it easily. If you want the main menus of every application to appear in a particular location use the Preferences application, as described in "Menu Preferences" on page 294.

Likewise, to make access to submenus easier, NEXTSTEP allows you to *detach* and position them in a convenient location anywhere on the screen. To detach a submenu, click the appropriate menu items to make the submenu visible, then position the cursor on the submenu's title bar, and drag the menu to the right. As you drag the submenu, a close button will become visible in its title bar (see Figure 2-9). Continue dragging the menu to the desired position on the screen and then release the mouse button to drop it in place. The menu will remain there until you click the its close button. If you quit the application but don't close the torn-off menu, it will reappear in the same place the next time you start the application. This allows you to customize the positioning of each menu in an application and lets you get to work faster the next time. NEXTSTEP's ability to remember menu positions is referred to as smart menus.

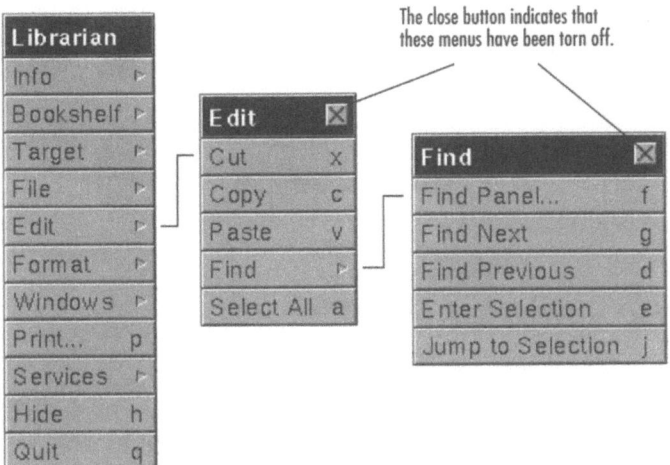

**Figure 2-9
Tear-off Menus**

When you detach a menu from its position in the main menu, it will display a close button. You can reposition the submenu by dragging its title bar. To put the submenu away, click its close button.

When a submenu is torn off, you can choose one of its menu items from the torn-off menu or from its original location in the main menu, whichever is more convenient. However, if decide to choose the menu item from the main menu, you will have to keep a mouse button pressed, instead of just clicking it, in order to make the submenu visible from the main menu.

2.3.2 Menu Command Shortcuts

In many cases, NEXTSTEP allows you to choose menu items using the keyboard instead of the mouse. You may find this much faster for choosing *commands* you use often. Menu items that can be chosen using the keyboard are said to have *keyboard alternatives* or keyboard shortcuts. Menu items with keyboard shortcuts have a letter or number after their name in the menu. To select a menu item using its keyboard shortcut, hold down the Command key (or equivalent on your particular keyboard) and type the letter or number that appears after its name in the menu.

NEXTSTEP differentiates between upper case and lower case letters so be careful when you use a keyboard shortcut. For example, typing **Command-s** executes Save and **Command-S** executes Save As. The Save As command requires you to press three keys simultaneously: Command, Shift, and s (see Figure 2-10). Many of the common Command key shortcuts are described in Table 2-3.

**Figure 2-10
Keyboard
Shortcuts**

To use a keyboard shortcut, hold down the Command key and type the letter that appears next to a menu item.

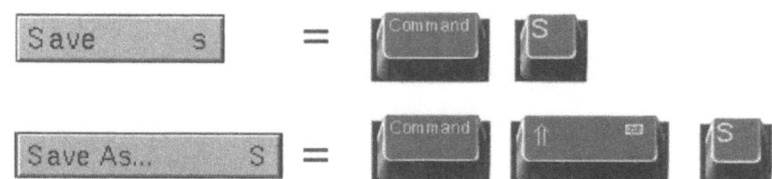

Table 2-3 Standard Menu Command Shortcuts

Command Key	Description
Command-?	Displays the ? cursor used to access the Help panel.
Command-a	Selects all.
Command-c	Copies the selected text or graphic to the pasteboard.
Command-h	Hides the current application.
Command-n	Creates a new document (or new folder in the workspace).
Command-o	Opens a document in the current application.
Command-p	Prints the current document or window.
Command-q	Quits the current application. Quitting the Workspace Manager implies logging out.
Command-s	Saves the current document.
Command-v	Pastes the item on the pasteboard into the current document or text area.
Command-w	Closes the key (current) window.
Command-x	Cuts the selected text or graphic.
Command-z	Undoes the last action.

2.4 The Application Dock

We'll examine applications in more detail in Chapter 6. But for now, let's see how the Workspace Manager allows us to access applications quickly and easily. Along the right side of the workspace is the *application dock*, which contains the icons of often-used applications for quick and easy access. The *dock* serves as a menu of applications and can be easily customized to suit your needs. When you log in for the first time, you will notice several icons are in the dock already: The Workspace Manager, Preferences, NeXTmail, Digital Librarian, and Edit (see Figure 2-11). On some systems, the recycler is located at the bottom of the dock. To add an application to the dock, drag its icon from a File Viewer and place it in an open position in the dock. To remove an icon from the dock, drag it from the dock and drop it on the workspace background. As you drag the icon from the dock, a ghost image of the icon will appear in its place. As you continue to drag, the ghost icon will disappear. After this occurs, releasing the mouse button will cause the application to be removed from the dock and the icon you are dragging to disappear.

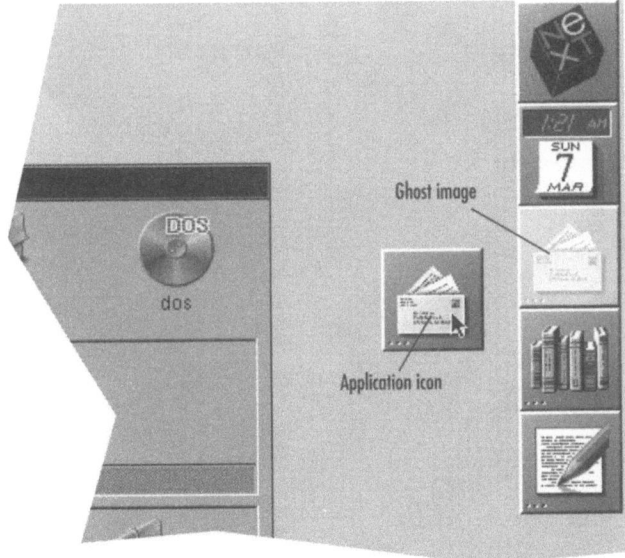

**Figure 2-11
Remove an Icon from the Dock**

To remove an icon from the dock, drag it to the left until its ghost image disappears. Releasing the mouse button then removes the application from the dock but does not erase it from the disk.

Removing an application from the dock does not destroy the application. The application still remains in its original location in the file system; only the icon in the application dock icon is destroyed. You can also rearrange icons in the dock by dragging them from one unoccupied location to another. For this reason, you may want to leave one dock position open.

The Recycler

The recycler

Depending on your computer system, the *recycler* icon may appear in the lower left corner of the workspace or at the bottom of the application dock. The recycler is used to delete files, folder, and applications. To delete a file or folder, drag its icon onto the recycler. As the cursor touches the recycler, the recycler will appear to spin. While the recycler is spinning, release the mouse button to place the icon inside the recycler. Items remain in the recycler until you retrieve them or empty the recycler. To delete the items in the recycler, choose Empty Recycler from the File menu. To retrieve items from the recycler, double-click the recycler icon to display its contents in a window, then drag the icon you want from the recycler window into an appropriate folder in the File Viewer. You'll learn a few more tricks about the recycler in the next chapter.

3

Files and Folders

Now that you know what the Workspace Manager can do, it's time to put it to work. This chapter describes the heart of NEXTSTEP, the ability to organize, find, and manipulate files quickly and easily. In it you'll learn how to find, move, copy, name, delete, and organize files and much more. This chapter shows you how to perform many of the common tasks necessary to maintain the performance and utility of your computer and provides suggestions for organizing your documents so you can find them easily when you need them.

3.0 Navigating with the File Viewer

One of the most often heard remarks about NEXTSTEP is that it consumes a great deal of disk space. Even in its smallest form, the user environment, NEXTSTEP consists of several thousand files, not including the files you create. Add to this the many files you can access through attached disk drives, CD-ROM drives, or a network, and the thought of finding a particular file can be overwhelming. While it's wonderful to have access to such vast amounts of information, the obvious problem is how to locate the files you are looking for quickly so you can make use of them. The NEXTSTEP File Viewer was designed with exactly that goal in mind. Finding or selecting an item requires you to move about using the File Viewer. To navigate, you can use the keyboard, mouse, Finder panel (discussed in section 3.4), or any combination of the three in any of three File Viewer views: browser view, icon view, or listing view.

3.0.0 The Browser View

When you log into NEXTSTEP for the first time, you'll notice the File Viewer displays the *browser* view. Traditionally, the browser has been the most recognizable part of NEXTSTEP, as only NEXTSTEP has it. The browser view is very powerful yet easy to use. One of its unique features is the ability to display several levels of the file system hierarchy at the same time, using a single window (see Figure 3-1). When you click a folder name in the browser, the contents of the folder are displayed in the next column to the right. In the browser viewer, folders are identified by a triangle symbol. If you click a folder name in the new column, the folder's contents are displayed in yet another column. When there are no more empty columns in the browser, a new one is added automatically and the contents of the previous columns scroll to the left. To see the items in a browser column that do not fit in the File Viewer, drag the scroll knob or click a scroll button to the left of the column you want to move (see Figure 3-1). If you have room on the display, you can see more columns and more items in each column by resizing the File Viewer.

The greatest advantage to using the browser is that you can see files and folders from several levels of the file system hierarchy at the same time. Unlike the icon and listing views, the browser is best used when you are searching for files in a very large file system where you will need to view the contents of folders that contain many items and when you need to navigate through many levels of the file system hierarchy quickly. Its greatest weakness is that it shows only the names of items in a folder, not icons, so it may be more difficult to identify files.

Navigating with the File Viewer

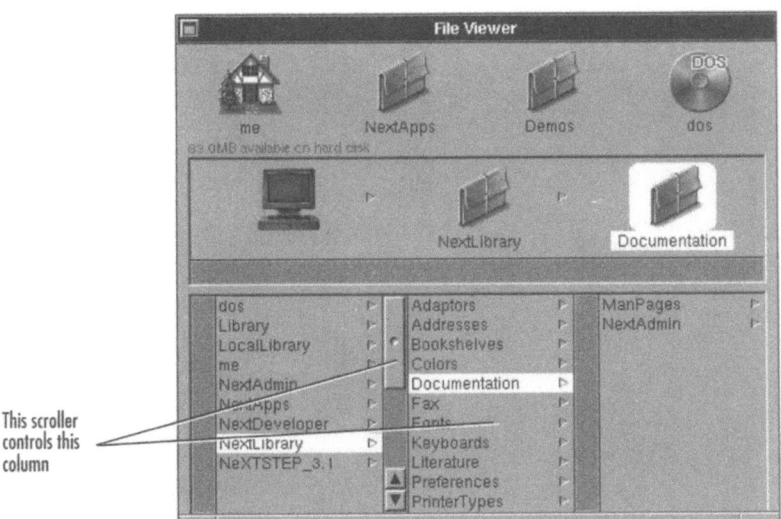

**Figure 3-1
The Browser View**

The browser view displays files and folders of several levels of the file system hierarchy at the same time. The contents of the selected folder appear in the column to the right of the folder's name.

3.0.1 The Icon View

Each time you log in, you will see the File Viewer window, and in it, the contents of your home folder. When you log in the first time, the File Viewer will display the contents of your home folder using the browser view. If you are familiar with the Macintosh or with Microsoft Windows, you may prefer seeing files and folders represented as icons. You can easily change the File Viewer to display icons as well, using the View command. Changing the way in which the File Viewer displays items in the file system does not affect any of the files and folders stored on your computer, only the way they are displayed. While in icon view, you can examine the contents of a folder, double-click its icon. When you double-click a folder icon, the File Viewer will change to display the contents of the folder. You can double-clicking any folder to view its contents.

One of the most common mistakes made by Macintosh users learning NEXTSTEP is to try to place an icon outside the File Viewer. If you want to position an icon so that it is easy to find, drag it onto the File Viewer's shelf instead.

As with the Macintosh and Microsoft Windows systems, you can drag icons in the icon view to reposition them within the File Viewer viewing area (see Figure 3-2). The File Viewer contains an invisible grid that is used to align each icon in tidy rows and columns. When you drag an icon into a new location, the icon automatically aligns itself with this grid. There is no way to turn this grid off to allow you to randomly space the icons. You can, however, change the horizontal spacing between columns, using the Preferences command as described in "Icon View Options" on

Files and Folders

Figure 3-2
The Icon View

In icon view, the File Viewer displays every file and folder as an icon rather than as a list of names as in the other views.

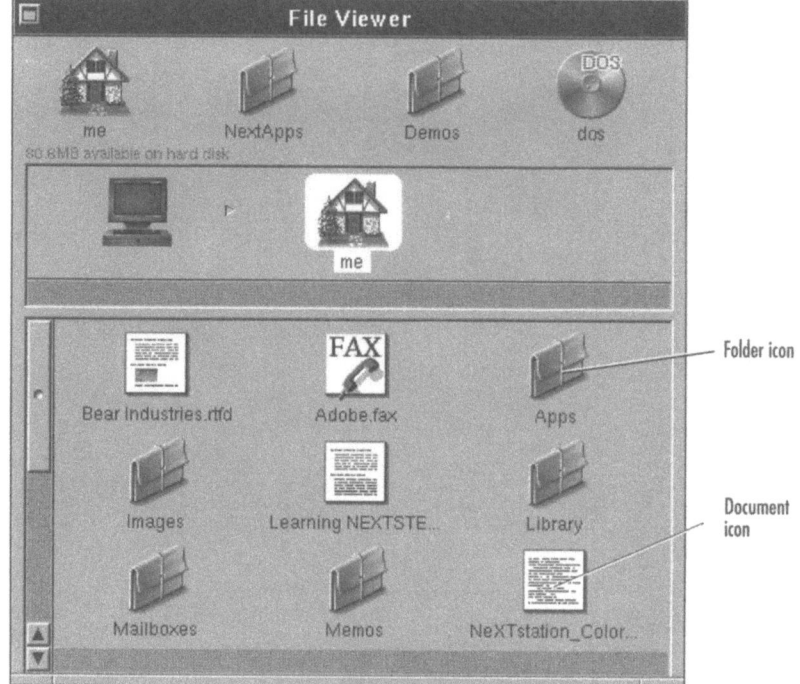

page 279. To keep file names from overlapping, the File Viewer abbreviates long file names with an ellipsis (...) so that they do not obscure icons in an adjacent columns. The file's name is not actually changed, it only appears in the File Viewer in an abbreviated form. To see the icon's full name, click the icon once to select it. It will be displayed in the icon path, and you will be able to read its complete name.

As you remove and rearrange icons in the File Viewer, gaps of space will be created, requiring you to scroll much more often to find a file you are looking for. Rather than move each icon in the File Viewer to eliminate these gaps, you can choose Clean Up Icons from the View menu to have NEXTSTEP do it for you. If there is an entire row of space, the icons below the gap will move up. Icons to the right of a gap will move left to fill in the holes. After you use this command, all of the icons will be in the upper left corner of the File Viewer viewing area (see Figure 3-3).

Navigating with the File Viewer

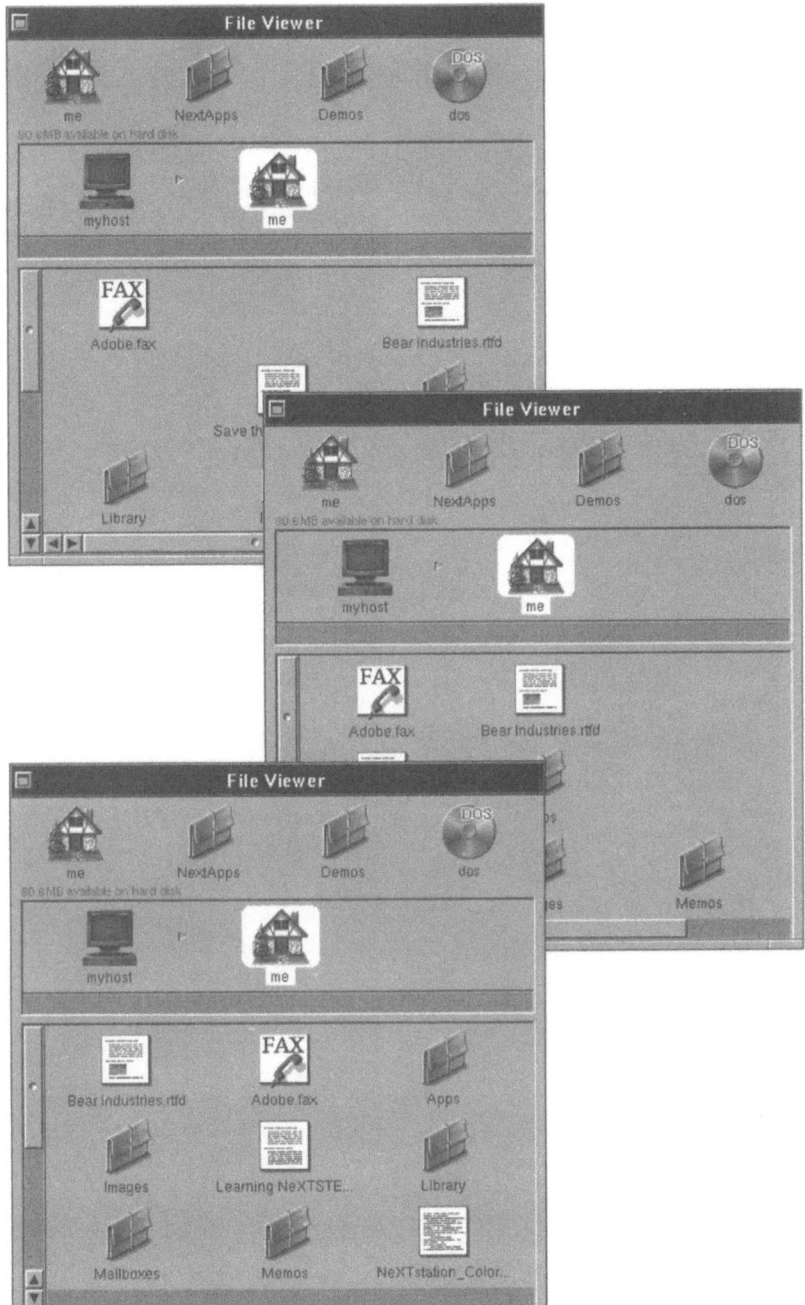

**Figure 3-3
Cleaning Up and
Sorting Icons**

When you rearrange or delete files, gaps appear in the File Viewer icon view (top left). To remove the gaps, choose Clean Up Icons (middle). This moves the icons up and to the left in the viewing area. You can also sort the icons (bottom) in various sort orders, which also fills in open gaps.

Files and Folders

You can also sort the icons to rearrange their order according to a sort method called a sort key (see Figure 3-4). This also has the effect of removing the gaps. When you first log in, NEXTSTEP sets the sort key of every folder to Name, displaying items within a folder alphabetically by their names.

**Figure 3-4
Sorting Items
in a Folder**

Using the Contents Inspector, you can choose the sorting method used to display a folder's contents.

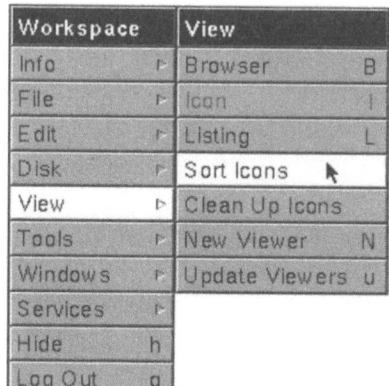
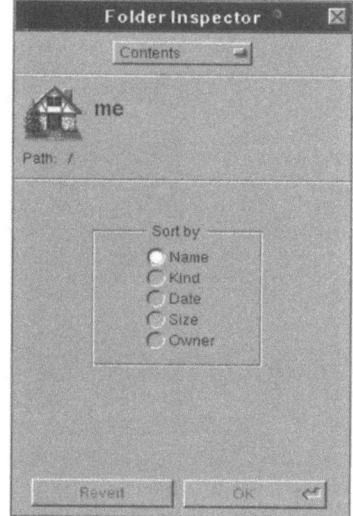

To sort the icons using the current sort key, you need only choose Sort Icons in the View menu. This will remove the gaps and rearrange the icons in order. To choose a different sort key, select the folder whose contents you would like to sort and then open the Contents Inspector by choosing Inspector in the Tools menu. In the Contents Inspector, you will see several sorting options. Click the sort order you would like to use, then click OK. NEXTSTEP will sort the contents of the selected folder immediately so you can verify the results. After you set a sort key, NEXTSTEP will remember it so you don't need to set it again.

3.0.2 The Listing View

If you are familiar with the UNIX **ls –l** command, you may find the File Viewer's listing view to be more to your liking than the icon or browser views. Choosing Listing in the View menu causes the File Viewer to display the contents of the selected folder as you might see it on a VT100-style terminal. Each item is on a separate line by name, followed by its size, date of last modification, permissions, owner, and group (see Figure 3-5). It is important to remember that the files in the folder are not changed when you select a different view, only the way in which they are displayed.

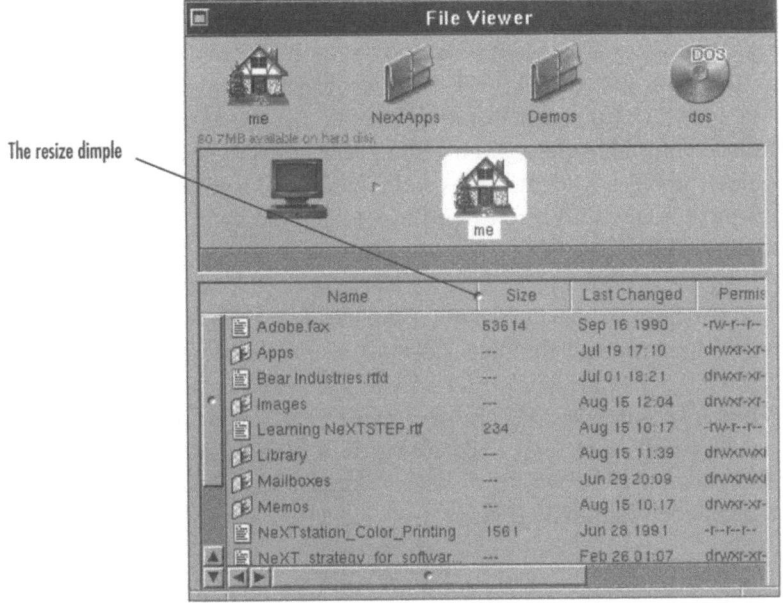

**Figure 3-5
The Listing View**

The listing view simulates the standard UNIX command ls-l and provides detailed information about each item in the selected folder.

A benefit of the listing view is that you can see detailed information about many files and folders simultaneously. A disadvantage of the listing view is that it uses generic file, folder, and application icons that serve only to distinguish files, folders, and applications. The icons do not provide any hints as to which file, folder, or application they represent.

 File

 Folder

 Application

One unique feature of the listing view is that you can resize the width of the Name column to see complete file names rather than abbreviations. To widen the Name column, drag the dimple that appears between the Name and Size column titles left or right (see Figure 3-5).

In the listing view, you can also double-click a folder icon to see its contents. However, if you double-click or drag the name of a file or folder instead of its small icon, NEXTSTEP will assume you want to change its name or select several items at once, not open it. If you select several folders or a folder name by mistake, click once on any unselected item in the listing view and select the desired files again. Also note that you cannot rearrange items in the listing view by dragging them. You must use the Sort command to arrange them in a different order.

3.0.3 The Appropriate View

In general, knowing when to use each view will come with experience, but to help you get started, here are a few suggestions. If you're used to the Macintosh or Microsoft Windows systems, use the icon view. It will be the most comfortable view as you get to know NEXTSTEP and will help you to quickly and easily identify files and folders. The icon view is also best used when there are only a few items in a folder, or when the icons in a folder are varied.

Use the browser view when all of the files in a folder share the same icon. You'll have to read the names of each icon to tell them apart anyway, so icons offer you no extra information and only take up space in the File Viewer. In this case, you can see more items in the browser view. This view displays only what you need to know, a files name, and allows you to quickly view the contents of many folders, including folders that contain tens or even hundreds of files.

If you're comfortable with UNIX and new to the graphical user interface, or if you're comparing files, perhaps their permissions or modification dates, use the listing view. This view provides more information about each file than the other views and allows you to compare this information very easily. At any time, you can switch to another view to make it easier to locate items in the file system. It's not uncommon to use the browser to locate a folder, and then use the icon view to find an item within the folder. Use the view that serves you best.

3.0.4 The Icon Path

No matter which view you happen to be using, the File Viewer always provides an icon path. The icon path is a graphical representation of the folders you opened to find the currently selected item in the File Viewer (see Figure 3-6). The icon path begins, like all pathnames, with the root (represented by a NeXTstation icon). Each time you open a folder and inspect its contents in the File Viewer, the folder's location in the file system is displayed in the icon path. Each time you select a new folder, NEXTSTEP updates the icon path so that it always represents the full path from the root to the currently selected folder.

The root icon

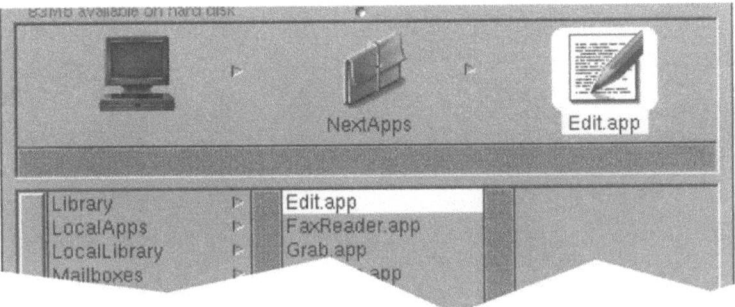

Figure 3-6
The Icon Path

The icon path graphically illustrates the pathname of the selected item in the File Viewer.

The icon path not only displays the pathname to the currently selected folder but also allows you to revisit a folder in the icon path quickly and easily. Clicking an icon in the icon path selects it and causes its contents to be displayed in the File Viewer. This feature is especially useful if you mistakenly opened the wrong folder and want to search down a new path in the file system without backtracking all the way back to the root or your home folder. When the number of icons in the path exceeds the width of the File Viewer window, the icon path will display a scroller so you can review icons in the path that are out of sight. Clicking the root folder icon allows you to begin a search into every folder in the file system.

3.0.5 The Shelf

The shelf, located at the top of the File Viewer, holds icons that you drag there so that you can access them quickly (see Figure 3-7). The home folder icon always appears on the shelf, which makes it easy to find after browsing the file system. To place an icon on the shelf, drag it from the icon path to an empty space on the shelf. In the icon view, you can drag an icon from the viewing area onto the shelf. Icons remain on the shelf until you drag them off, even if you log out or turn off the computer.

When you click a folder icon on the shelf, it becomes the selected icon, its path is displayed in the icon path, and its contents appear in the display area of the File Viewer (see Figure 3-7). By placing icons on the shelf, you can effectively take a shortcut through the file system by not having to navigate its path to select it. If you click a file or application icon on the shelf, it will also be selected, its path displayed in the icon path, and the contents of the folder in which it is located will appear in the display area of the File Viewer. Double-clicking an icon on the shelf is the same as double-clicking it in the File Viewer and causes it to be opened. Double-clicking an application icon on the shelf causes it to start.

Figure 3-7
The Shelf

The shelf is used to create file system bookmarks. Clicking an icon on the shelf highlights it, displays it or its contents in the icon path and the viewing area.

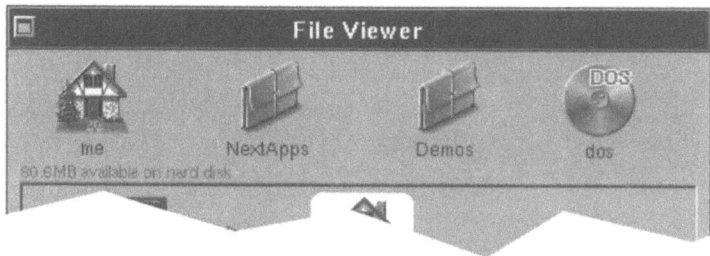

Icons on the shelf are actually pointers to the original item in the file system. If you drag an icon off of the shelf, the icon disappears, but the original file or folder remains in the file system. To remove an icon from the shelf, drag it out of the shelf area and release the mouse button. Be careful not to drop the icon onto an open document window or the file it represents may be imported into the document!

The home folder

One icon you cannot remove from the shelf is the icon that represents your home folder. It appears in the upper left corner of the shelf at all times and allows you to select and display your home folder no matter which folder is selected in the File Viewer. When you first log in, you'll notice that the **/NextApps** and **/NextDeveloper/Demos** folders have already been placed on the shelf so that you can have quick access to NEXTSTEP's bundled applications. If you want to make more space on the shelf for other icons, you can drag them off of the shelf to remove them.

Navigating with the File Viewer

You can put any icon on the shelf but only application icons in the dock, so don't fill up the shelf with application icons. Put them in the dock first.

When the shelf fills up with icons, you can resize it to hold more icons. To resize the shelf, drag its dimple up or down. (The dimple will not appear unless you have enabled the resizable shelf feature in the Workspace Manager's Preferences panel. See "Shelf Options" on page 277 to learn more about the shelf dimple.) The shelf can grow to hold more than one row of icons depending upon how far you drag the dimple (see Figure 3-8). When you resize the File Viewer window horizontally, the shelf will automatically grow too, allowing it hold more icons. The only way to increase the width of the shelf is to widen the File Viewer window; the dimple only controls the length. Changing the size of the File Viewer or the length of the shelf will cause the icons on the shelf to be rearranged or disappear, depending on the new size of the shelf. When you enlarge the shelf again, the hidden icons will reappear and return to their former positions on the shelf.

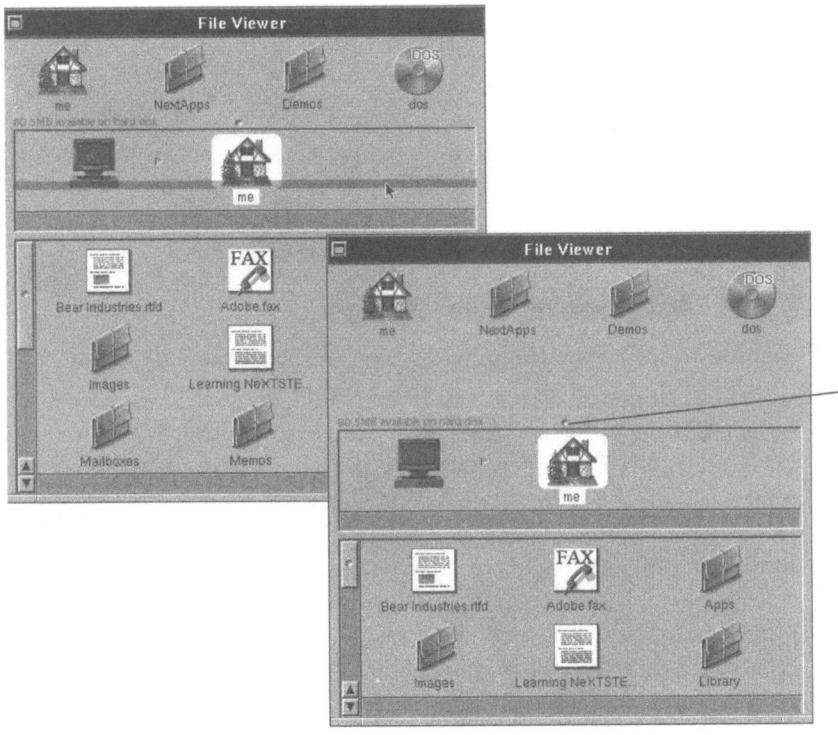

**Figure 3-8
The Resizable Shelf**

To resize the File Viewer shelf, drag the dimple up or down (top). When you release the dimple, the shelf will be resized, allowing you to add more icons (bottom).

Shelf dimple

Files and Folders

The shelf does more than just hold icons; it also displays the available disk space on the currently selected disk and the status of background processes, such as copying files and formatting disks (see Figure 3-9). By displaying this information on the shelf, NEXTSTEP doesn't need to bother you with annoying attention panels to display status messages or require you to open another window to see how much disk space is available, yet can still provide you with all of this important information about the status of the computer.

**Figure 3-9
Shelf Status
Messages**

The shelf contains two message areas, one to indicate the amount of available space remaining on the selected disk or disk partition and another to inform you of the status of background processes.

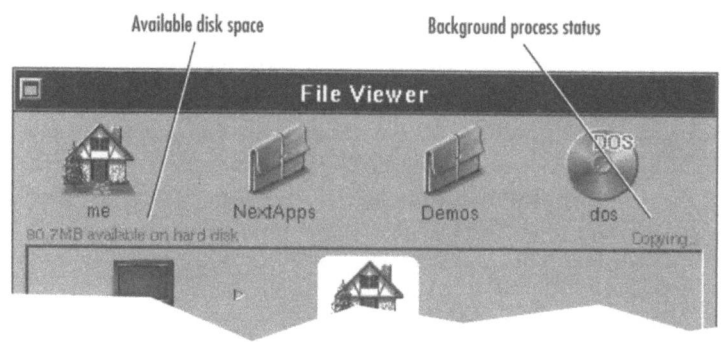

When you select a locked or read-only disk or disk partition in the File Viewer, the message describing the amount of disk space available on that will disappear. This indicates that disk is locked or read-only.

3.0.6 Keyboard Navigation

Using the mouse to select files in the File Viewer is very easy, but you can use the keyboard, too. This is called keyboard navigation. To select a file or folder using the keyboard, type a character key. For example, to select a folder named **Mailboxes**, type **m**. If two or more items begin with the letter m, you can select one by typing several characters quickly. For example, if the currently selected folder contains items named **Memos** and **Mailboxes**, then typing **m** would select **Mailboxes** because it comes before **Memos** when sorted alphabetically. If you wanted to select the item named **Memos** using the keyboard, you could type **me** quickly. Since there are no other items that begin with me, Memos would be selected. Be sure to type the letters quickly, or NEXTSTEP may think you are trying to select an item beginning with m, and then changing your mind and trying to select an item beginning with e. If the letters you type do not match any items in the folder, you will hear the system beep sound. Keyboard navigation works in all three File Viewer views: browser, icon, and listing.

When you are using the listing and browser views, you can also use the keyboard's four *arrow keys* to navigate the file system. In these views, pressing up arrow key selects the item above the currently selected item. Pressing the down arrow key selects the item below the currently selected item. Pressing the left arrow key selects the previous folder and pressing the right arrow key opens the currently selected folder. If you press the right arrow key and the currently selected item is not a folder, nothing will happen. In the icon view, only the left and right arrow keys are functional, and they select the previous and next folders respectively.

You can use the keyboard arrow keys as well as the mouse to navigate the file system.

After selecting a file or folder you can press Return to open it instead of double-clicking. Pressing Return opens a selected folder, starts a selected application, or opens the currently selected document in its default application. (Setting a document's default application is discussed in "Using the Tools Inspector" on page 110.)

3.1 Using Multiple File Viewers

NEXTSTEP is designed so that you can view and manipulate any file in the file system using a single File Viewer. However, there are many times when using two or more File Viewers is more convenient. If you feel constrained by having only one File Viewer window, a common feeling for Macintosh and Windows users new to NEXTSTEP, you can easily open another by choosing New Viewer in the View menu. The new File Viewer window is identical to the original one except for one small difference. Every File Viewer but the original one contains a close button in the title bar so you can make it disappear when it's no longer needed (see Figure 3-10). You can open as many File Viewers as necessary to complete a task, but there will always one File Viewer you cannot close.

Files and Folders

**Figure 3-10
File Viewer
Close Buttons**

Every File Viewer but the original displays a close button so you can make it disappear when it's no longer needed.

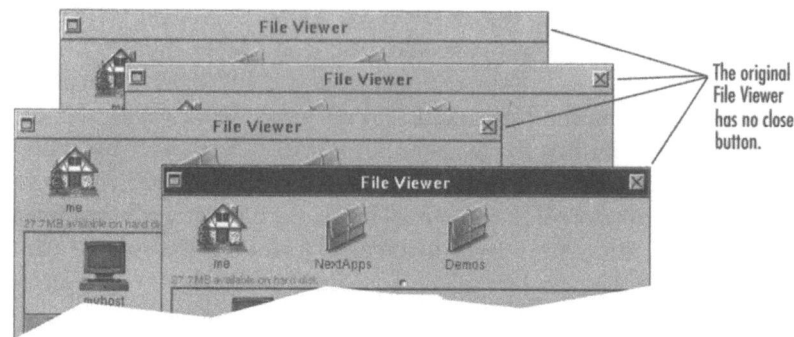

The original File Viewer has no close button.

Accessing NFS and NetWare file servers is discussed in more detail in Chapter 12.

Using two or more File Viewers, you can view the contents of two or more folders at the same time, easily copy files from one folder to another, display available NFS (Network File Service) or NetWare servers, and easily locate and manipulate files located far apart in the file system. Each File Viewer can also display a different view: browser, icon, or listing.

A new File Viewer uses the currently selected folder as its root. This allows you to use the new File Viewer as a kind of bookmark, tagging a location in the file system so that you can return to it quickly and easily without having to change the selected folder in the original File Viewer. Using more than one File Viewer makes it extremely easy to locate particular files in the file system, compare the contents of two folders, and import files into a document. Many NEXTSTEP applications allow you to drag icons from the File Viewer into an open document window to import them. So if you store the sounds, text files, and graphic images for a project in a single folder, you can open a new File Viewer using that folder as its root, and position the File Viewer so that you can see the document and the File Viewer side by side. Then, you can easily import the files by dragging them from the File Viewer to the document yet maintain access to your home folder using the original File Viewer.

To make a folder the root folder in a new File Viewer, select it in a File Viewer, and then choose Open as Folder from the File menu. As a shortcut, you can hold the Alternate key and double-click the folder's icon to open it in a new window. A new File Viewer will appear using the selected folder as its root. You can resize, change the view, reposition or miniaturize the new File Viewer just like the original File Viewer. When it's no longer needed, click the close button in its title bar to make it disappear.

3.2 Managing Windows

In every windowing system, including NEXTSTEP, it is very common to have many windows open and overlapping each other. However, this presents an interesting problem. When you choose a menu command, type a keyboard shortcut, or use keyboard navigation, which window will be affected? In NEXTSTEP, the window that is the one on top of all the others, called the *key window*, is the one affected. You can easily identify the key window because it's the only one whose title bar is black. No matter how many windows are open, there is only one key window. All others are considered to be in the background and display a gray title bar. The changing of the title bar may not seem important at first glance, but makes more sense when you consider the case in which two windows are side by side with no overlap (Figure 3-11). Which one is the key window in this case? The one with the black title bar.

Figure 3-11
The Key Window

Even when windows are not overlapping, you can easily identify the key window by its black title bar.

It's very easy to make a background window the key window. Just place the cursor so that it rests on top of any visible portion of the window and click a mouse button. If the window was opened by an application different from that of the previous key window, making it the key window also causes the application that opened it to become the *active application*, the one whose menus are visible, so that you can begin modifying the document immediately.

With most GUI systems, manipulating a background window is a two-step procedure. First you must click the background window to make it come to the foreground; then you must click again to scroll, resize, miniaturize, or move it. NEXTSTEP improves on such systems by allowing you to make a background window the key window and manipulate its controls with a single click. For example, to scroll a window and make it the key window with one click, click a background window's scroll button.

This feature can be quite unsettling if you're not expecting it so take time to practice it. If you aren't used to using a mouse, take special care not to unintentionally click a hot spot (see Figure 3-12) when you click a background window or you may close or miniaturize it accidentally.

Eliminating extra clicks of the mouse button reduces chances for error. You may not realize the value of this feature now, but as you begin to use it, you will find it extremely easy to use and very efficient. To make a background window the key window without activating a hot spot, click (don't drag) its title bar or in the contents of the window.

Figure 3-12
Window Hot Spots

Clicking or dragging a background window's hot spot will make the window the key window and perform the described action.

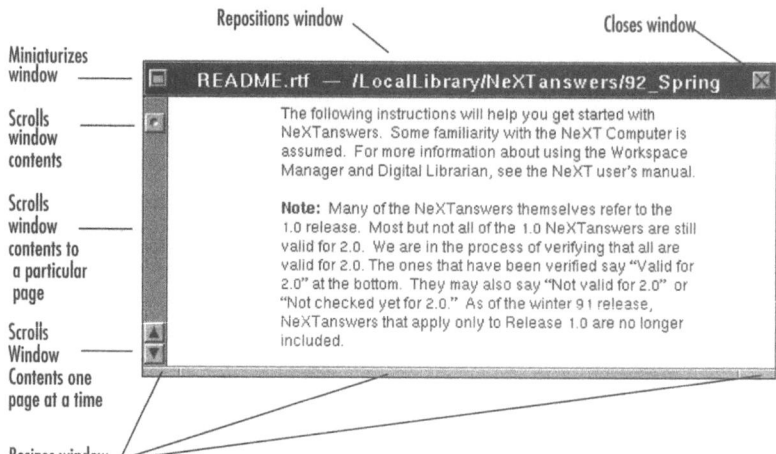

3.2.0 The Windows Menu

You can use the Windows menu to manipulate windows instead of, or in conjunction with the mouse. The Windows menu is found in every NEXT-STEP application, including the Workspace Manager. It lists every open window that belongs to the current application. For example, if you have four File Viewers open, the Windows menu will list each of them by name. To make a particular window the key window, select its name in the Windows menu. Using the Windows menu in any NEXTSTEP application, you can make a window come to the foreground even when it is completely hidden by other windows. You don't have to move the overlapping windows to bring it to the front.

If you want to arrange every window that belongs to an application so you can see at least part of them, choose Arrange in Front from the Windows menu. This is useful if one or more windows are completely hidden by another window. There are also two commands in the Windows menu that mimic window buttons: Miniaturize Window and Close Window. Choosing either of these commands has the same effect as clicking the respective window button and affects only the key window.

Next to a window's name in the Windows menu is the close button symbol. Like the close button on the title bar of a window, when this symbol displays an X, the contents of the window have been saved. When the X is only partially drawn, the contents of the window have not been saved (see Figure 3-13). You can review the list of window names in the Windows menu, to quickly see which windows have been saved and which have not.

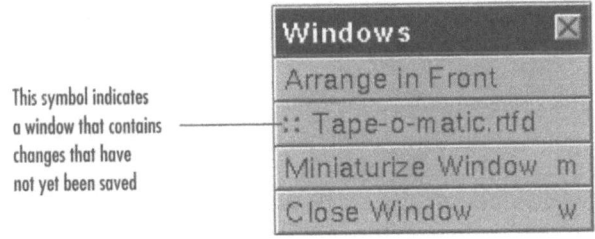

This symbol indicates a window that contains changes that have not yet been saved

**Figure 3-13
The Windows Menu**

The windows menu allows you to quickly display one of several open windows and provides an alternate means of miniaturizing and closing a window.

3.3 Managing Folders

Folders exist to organize files so that you can easily find them. Organizing your work by creating and naming folders in an organized fashion will save you countless hours searching for them later. Throughout this book, the terms folder and directory refer to the same thing. The term directory is an historic reference to the method used to organize files in UNIX and DOS systems and continues to be used today. Typically, the term folder is used in the context of the workspace, and directory is used in the context of UNIX commands in the Terminal application.

3.3.0 Creating and Naming Folders

You may create any number of folders within your home folder to organize your work. It may be possible to create folders outside your home folder but permission to do so is determined by the system administrator or the owner of the folder. Saving items outside your home folder is not always wise because it may make them more difficult to find and much easier to forget when you make backup copies of your work.

To create a new folder, choose New Folder from the File menu. A new folder named **NewFolder** will appear in the folder currently selected in the File Viewer (see Figure 3-14). The new folder will be selected automatically after it is created so you can rename it by simply typing a new name and pressing Return. If you happen to click a mouse button before you rename the folder, you will unselect it and have to select its name again before you can rename it. To do this, drag across its name to select it, then type the new name and press Return. If the folder's name is only one word long, you can double-click the folder's name to select it. If you double-click the folder's icon, it will open the folder in the File Viewer instead of select its name. If this happens, return to the previous folder by clicking its icon in the icon path of the File Viewer and try again.

You can name a folder at any time and rename it as often as you like. Like file names, folder names can be as long as you want but should be kept to about 14 characters to make them easy to read. You can use any characters you want in a folder name except for the slash character /. If you plan to use UNIX commands, you should also avoid using ' " & * - / | > ^ < as these have special meaning in UNIX commands. You cannot rename a folder on the shelf or in the browser. You can only change the name of an icon in the icon path or listing and icon viewing areas.

3.3.1 Custom Folder Icons

Folders normally display two icons: a closed folder icon and an open folder icon. You can easily colorize, replace, or create new icons and install them to give your computer a new look or make it easier to identify often used folders. To create or replace a closed folder icon, create a new 48 x 48-pixel icon using the IconBuilder application in **/NextDeveloper/Apps**, save it as in TIFF format, name the file **.dir.tiff**, and place it in the folder you want to customize. To modify the open folder icon that appears when you drop an

Managing Folders

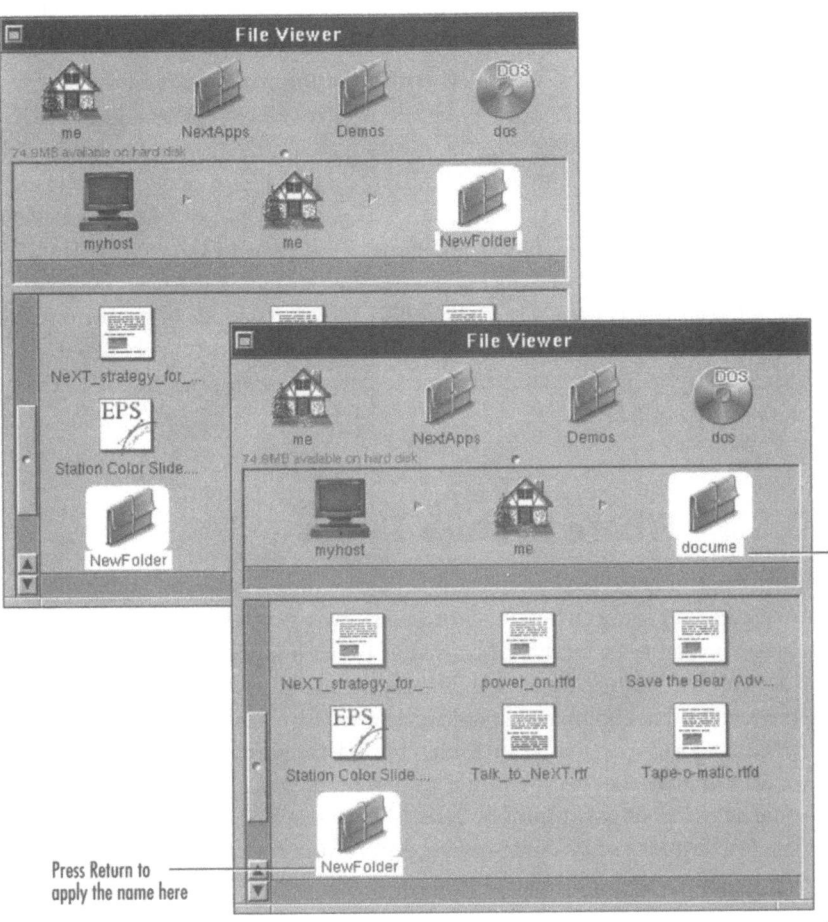

**Figure 3-14
To Create a
New Folder**

When you create a new folder, it will appear in the File Viewer in the currently selected folder (top). Rename it by typing a new name and pressing Return (bottom).

— Type a new name here

Press Return to
apply the name here

item onto a folder in the File Viewer, create a new icon and save it in a TIFF file with the name **.open.dir.tiff** and place it in the folder to be customized. The new icons will take effect immediately.

When you begin a file name with a period, the file becomes invisible in the File Viewer. This trick is often used to prevent an important file from being accidentally moved or deleted. To see these "dot" files, turn on the UNIX Expert option in the Preferences application. (See "Expert Preferences" on page 297.)

Files and Folders

3.3.2 Reserved Folders

NEXTSTEP has many reserved folders, contained in the root folder, which hold the files and applications required by NEXTSTEP to operate. These folders, which use up a significant portion of the computer's hard disk storage, cannot and should not be altered or changed except by a knowledgeable UNIX system administrator. Rather than tempt you by displaying folders that you can't change, NEXTSTEP hides them. If you are curious and want to see them, turn on the UNIX Expert option using the Preferences application (see "Expert Preferences" on page 297). You may wonder why you are not allowed access to so many folders, but these restrictions are for your protection. They allow NEXTSTEP to do all of the wonderful things it does and allow you to use the computer without becoming an expert. Not being allowed into these folders is a small price to pay to enjoy the benefits of NEXTSTEP.

3.3.3 Where to Store Things

Should you lose a file, you can find it easily using the Finder panel as described in section 3.4.

With such a large file system and so many folders reserved and invisible, how can you know where to store your own personal files? Store everything you create or modify only in your home folder or folders within your home folder. Doing so makes them easy to retrieve later, easier to locate so they can be backed up or copied to another storage device, and less likely to be forgotten or lost in a folder buried deep in the file system. It is extraordinarily easy to lose a file in a computer if you do not implement some method of organization. Files always seem to get lost at the worst possible moment so be consistent and store your files in well-named folders so you can easily find them later.

The Library folder is used to store special files including fonts, sounds, and address books.

When you log into your account the first time, you will see three folders: **Apps**, **Library** and **Mailboxes**. These folders have special use and shouldn't be renamed. The **Apps** folder is used to store applications that you want to use that are not included with NEXTSTEP. The **Mailboxes** folder is used by NEXTSTEP to hold mail messages for the NeXTmail application. The Library folder is used to store *fonts*, sounds Digital Librarian bookshelves, and many other files. In the Library folder you will find three folders named **Addresses**, **Bookshelves**, and **Notebook** (see Figure 3-15). The **Addresses** folder is used to maintain a customizable list of addresses and is typically used when faxing a message from the computer, a feature that will be discussed in more detail in "The Address Inspector" on page 98. The **Bookshelves** folder contains Digital Librarian files, called

Managing Folders

bookshelves, and the **Notebook** folder is for you to place scraps of information that you want to index and retrieve later. The **Notebook** folder works in conjunction with the Librarian command in the Services menu and is discussed in "The Services Inspector" on page 214.

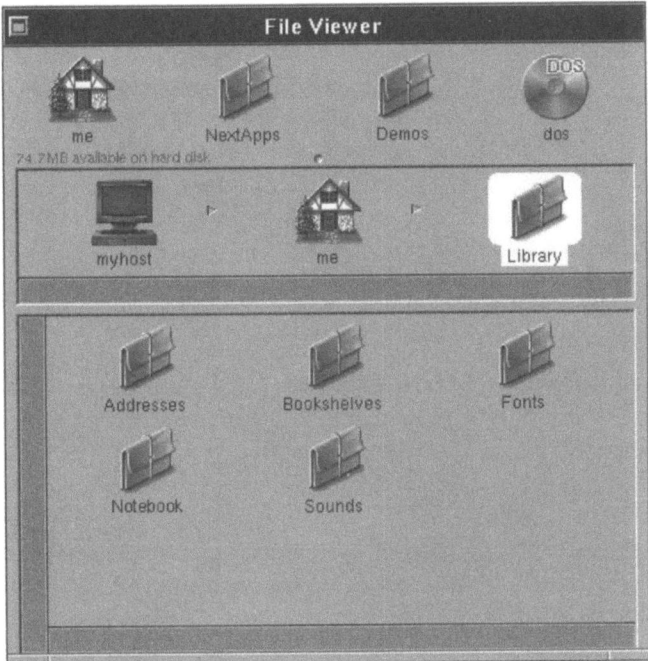

Figure 3-15
The Library Folder

NEXTSTEP places the Addresses, Bookshelves, and Notebook folders in your ~/Library folder for you. You have to create the Fonts and Sounds folder when you want to add fonts or sounds to your system.

When you are ready to add fonts to your computer, they will also go inside your **Library** folder in a folder named **Fonts**. Similarly, sound files should be put inside your **Library** folder in a folder named **Sounds**. NEXTSTEP will look for fonts and sounds only in these folders and make them available to every application automatically.

Many applications also look for the **Library** folder in your home folder to store their preferences files so it is important that the **Library** folder exist. If you rename the **Library** folder, change its location, or delete it, NEXTSTEP will be unable to find the fonts or sounds you've added.

If you want to store applications in your home folder that only you can access, create a new folder named **Apps** in your home folder. NEXTSTEP automatically looks for applications in this folder, so if you don't place your applications there, NEXTSTEP will not know they exist and won't be able to fully integrate them into the other advanced features of NEXTSTEP.

Most users avoid storing documents in the same folder as applications to make backups easier. This is an excellent strategy and should be followed. Applications are rarely modified so once they are backed up, they need not be backed up again. Documents that you create are quite different. They are often modified, sometimes more than once in the same day, and need to be backed up regularly. By placing applications that rarely change in their own folder, you can dramatically decrease the time it takes to locate the files that do change and make backups of them.

The LocalApps folder contains applications that are available to every user.

To save disk space, shared applications should be placed in a special folder named **LocalApps** instead of your **Apps** folder in your home folder. You'll need to have the system administrator create this folder and assign privileges to allow other users to execute the applications it contains. This folder name is special in that NEXTSTEP recognizes it as a folder that contains applications, so its name should not be changed. One major benefit of putting shared applications in a single folder is that only one copy of each application will exist, so locating and upgrading applications will be much easier. In contrast, storing several copies of the same application in every users's home folder will waste a great deal of disk space, and multiply the time required to upgrade the application in the future.

If you are the system administrator, you should exercise caution when placing applications in the **LocalApps** folder, where they can be accessed by every user. The application's user license may restrict its use by more than one user, and you are legally bound to obey the rules of the license. Read the software application's license agreement or call the application's developer to determine the appropriate use of their package.

Another special shared folder is **LocalLibrary**. Like **LocalApps**, its contents are also accessible by every user, but it contains fonts, sounds and other documents, not applications. Like the **Library** folder found in your home folder, the **LocalLibrary** folder should also contain a Fonts and Sounds folder. Fonts and sounds placed in these folders in **LocalLibrary** will automatically appear in every users applications. Placing items common to every user—such as documentation, fonts, sounds, and images—in **LocalLibrary** means they do not have to be duplicated in each user's home folder. Storing these items in a common folder is a more efficient use of disk space.

The root user is responsible for maintaining the contents of the **LocalApps** and **LocalLibrary** folders so you may not have permission to modify them. In this case, notify the administrator to have items you want placed in either of these two folders. If you are the administrator of your own machine, you'll have to log in as the root user to add the items yourself. When NEXTSTEP is installed, the **LocalApps** folder is created automatically but the **LocalLibrary** folder and its Fonts and Sounds folders are not.

The LocalLibrary folder contains fonts, sounds, and other special items that are available to every user.

3.3.4 Organization Strategies

If you are new to computing, you probably have not given much thought to how you will organize the documents you create on the computer. Without a plan, you are certain to cost yourself hours of wasted time looking for things that you might otherwise have been able to find in just a few moments with a little organization and forethought. There are numerous methods for organizing your work, and several are described here to help you determine which is best for you. Organizing your work is not particularly difficult. The key to any organization technique is to make it simple and use it consistently. While it may take some work, you can always change the method you use when a method begins to fail, or you see a better way. Remember that all of these methods refer only to files and folders stored in your home folder.

> Do not change the organization of items in the root folder, or the computer may not start up again after you turn the power off!

Organizing by Project

Many people find their work to be project oriented. Often, several projects are in progress simultaneously and, without proper organization, can become mixed together and confused. If your work is based on projects, you can create a new folder for each project. All documents, graphics, and other electronic files can be saved in the project's folder. This has the advantage of keeping all of a project's documents together so they're easy to find. Saving files this way also makes it easy to make a backup copy of the project's files, transfer them to another computer, or delete them when the project is completed. Using this method also makes it easy for others to find a document. They only need to know the project's name.

Organizing by Document Type

Some computer users prefer to keep all of the documents created by an application together. This was popular with Macintosh users in the early days of the Macintosh. The computer required the application to be on the same floppy disk as the documents it created. When hard disks were introduced, the habit continued even though there was no longer any technical reason to continue it. As long as the application was installed on the hard disk, the Macintosh would find it and open the document. Likewise, NEXTSTEP is also able to find and start an application when you double-click a document, so there is little reason to use this type of organization. In fact, combining applications and documents in the same folder will make it more difficult to backup your computer's files

Organizing by Index

In large offices where hundreds of documents are processed daily by several computer users, files are often coded and stored in coded folders. This is especially true of physical files and folders placed in file cabinets. A master index is maintained that lists the author of the document, the date it was created, who it was created for, perhaps a security code, and where it is located. To find a file, one would search the index by name, date, or author and then find the cross-reference to the location where the item is stored. This method is identical to the library card catalog system in use for over a hundred years. Because it is such a common and familiar system, it can be used with little training by almost anyone, and closely matches printed document storage techniques already in use. To store documents in this fashion on the computer, you would create several folders coded by author, date, project, or other identifying feature, and place documents in the appropriate location. You would then create an index using a database, word processor, or perhaps in written form, to serve as the cross-reference. This method has the advantage of being well understood, extensible to large workgroups, and secure (when secret codes are used to identify documents). The disadvantage is that without the index, you can't find anything at all.

Mixing Organization Methods

In most cases, mixing parts of each of these methods works best. For example, you can store graphic images in folders according to the application that created them, put this folder into a project folder, and put the project folder into a folder that contains projects for the last week. If you have a filing system in place that works well, transferring it to the computer should also work as well. You should consider the storage and retrieval possibilities provided by the computer that can't be duplicated manually. After all, the desire for a faster, more efficient storage and retrieval system is likely one of the reasons you bought a computer in the first place. Transferring a manual system to computer may not be any more efficient than the manual filing system you were using, just more expensive.

3.3.5 Automated Storage and Retrieval

If you routinely handle hundreds or thousands of documents, there are several applications available, such as ElectroFile and Who's Calling, that can assist you in storing and retrieving documents quickly and easily. NEXTSTEP even includes an application named Digital Librarian for just this purpose (see "Digital Librarian" on page 209). These applications generally allow you to create some combination of indexes, project names, client names, and documents tags for documents you wish to store. You can then enter a key word, and the application will present you with the documents that match the key word. These system are designed to be robust, storing thousands of documents and recalling them quickly. You don't have to know how the documents are stored or where they are located, only that they can be found quickly and easily. If you deal with hundreds or thousands of documents regularly, you may want to investigate applications like these to make your document filing faster and easier.

3.4 Finding a File or Folder

As we discussed earlier, the NEXTSTEP file system can grow to be quite large, containing many thousands of files. Normally, the files you need to use are located in just a few folders: **Local Apps**, **LocalLibrary**, **NextApps**, **NextLibrary**, and your own home folder, so finding them in the File Viewer is relatively simple. However, even if you organize your work carefully, you may still have difficulty locating a file. This is especially true when your file system grows, as you attach extra hard disk drives, CD-ROM

Files and Folders

drives, or network your computer to other hosts. NEXTSTEP was designed with large file systems in mind and thus provides numerous ways to find a lost file or folder.

One of the tools NEXTSTEP provides to help you locate files and folders, is the Finder panel (see Figure 3-16). To see the Finder panel, choose Finder in the Tools menu. If you routinely browse many files, you will want to use a keyboard shortcut to present the Finder: use Command-f, or press the Escape key, or press the slash key /. (The more typical Command-f shortcut is often used within an application to open its Find panel, too.)

Figure 3-16
The Finder Panel

The Finder panel can located any item in the file system.

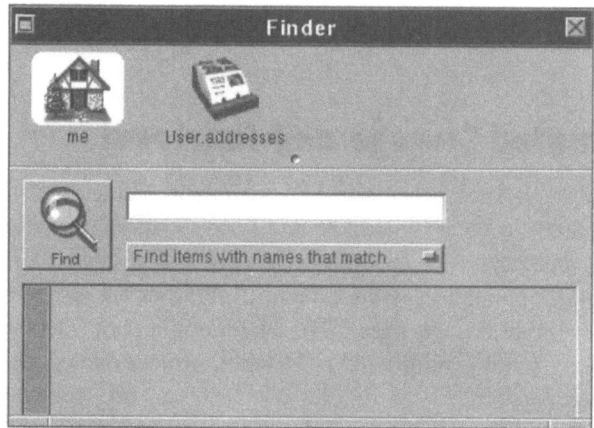

The NEXTSTEP Finder can locate files very quickly, even when the file system is very large. However, you must tell the Finder where to look. On the Finder's shelf are icons called targets. You must highlight a target to indicate where you want the Finder to search. When you click Find, the Finder will look only in the selected target. For example, NEXTSTEP automatically places your home folder and the **User.addresses** icons in the Finder panel's shelf so you can search within these two folders easily. (The **User.addresses** file contains name and address information you enter using the Address Inspector. We'll learn more about this file later.)

To add an icon to the Finder's shelf, drag an icon to the shelf from the File Viewer (see Figure 3-17). If you store documents in a particular folder, you can place the folder's icon in the Finder's shelf so that you can find items within the folder very quickly later on. Often you will have some idea as to where the file might be. In this case, drag the icon of the folder in which it is likely to be from a File Viewer onto the Finder shelf and use it as a target

Finding a File or Folder

to speed the search. If the search list comes up empty, you can search another target or search from the root. Icons you place on the Finder's shelf remain there even after you log out. To remove an icon from the shelf, drag it off the shelf.

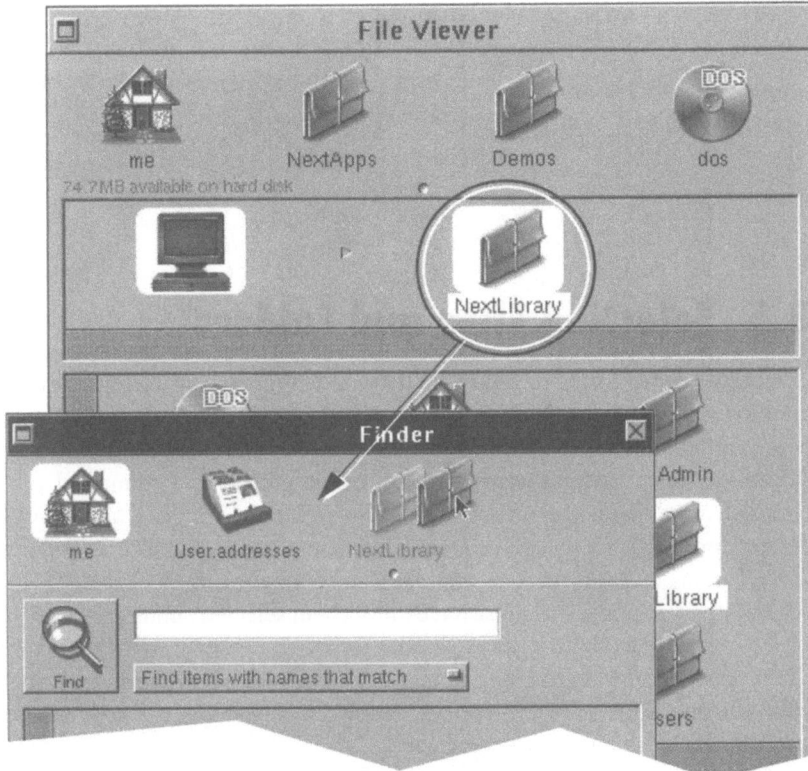

**Figure 3-17
Finder Panel
Target**

Add a target to the Finder panel by dragging an icon from a File Viewer to the Finder panel shelf.

When you click Find in the Finder panel, the Find button becomes STOP. Clicking STOP will cancel a search.

Using the Finder panel, you can search for items according to their names or their contents. A pop-up list in the Finder allows you to choose the method you prefer (pop-up lists are described on page 86). To find a file or folder, type its name or any part of its name in the Finder's text field and click Find. Every item in the file system whose name contains the text you typed will appear in a scrolling list at the bottom of the Finder panel. If you chose "Find items with contents that match" from the pop-up list, the Finder will list all of the files that contain the text you typed in the Finder panel text field. You don't have to wait for a search to be completed in order to manipulate a located file. While the search is in progress, the Find button will become a Stop button. Clicking Stop will stop a search even when it is not yet complete. After you've located the file you're looking for, click its name in the Finder panel to select it and display its icon in the Finder panel. You can drag the icon into the File Viewer to place it on the shelf, copy it to a new folder, or delete it, or you can double-click to open it. If you change your mind, you can click to select another file in the Finder panel to see its icon and manipulate it as well.

> You can type a pathname in the Finder panel to locate a file instantly. Using the Finder panel instead of the File Viewer also allows you to look for the file in the background while you continue working on another project.

3.5 Selecting Files and Folders

Selecting a file or folder in the File Viewer is as simple as pointing to it and clicking a mouse button. Dealing with items one at a time, however, can be not only inefficient and difficult, but a waste of the computer's abilities. When you select several items at once, called grouping, a command you choose from a menu will affect all the selected items. You can also move, delete, and duplicate groups of icons. The computer is able to manipulate several items as easily as it manipulates one. To perform a command on several items at once, you must have all of them selected simultaneously.

There are several ways to group items in the File Viewer, depending on the view you are using: browser, icon, or listing. However, you can only select icons in the same File Viewer. Try each of the following methods to determine which suits you best. When you finally feel comfortable selecting several items at once, take time to learn the other methods, as they will make help make you much more efficient.

3.5.0 Selecting Adjacent Items

In the icon view, you can select icons that are adjacent by holding down a mouse button and dragging a dotted outline around several adjacent icons (see Figure 3-18). The cursor should not be touching an icon when you first press a mouse button, or you will drag the icon instead of creating the outline. Icons inside or touching the outline will be selected when you release the mouse button. If you make a mistake and select too few, too

Selecting Files and Folders

many, or the wrong icons, click anywhere in the icon view except on one of the selected icons to cancel your selection, and try dragging an outline around the icons again.

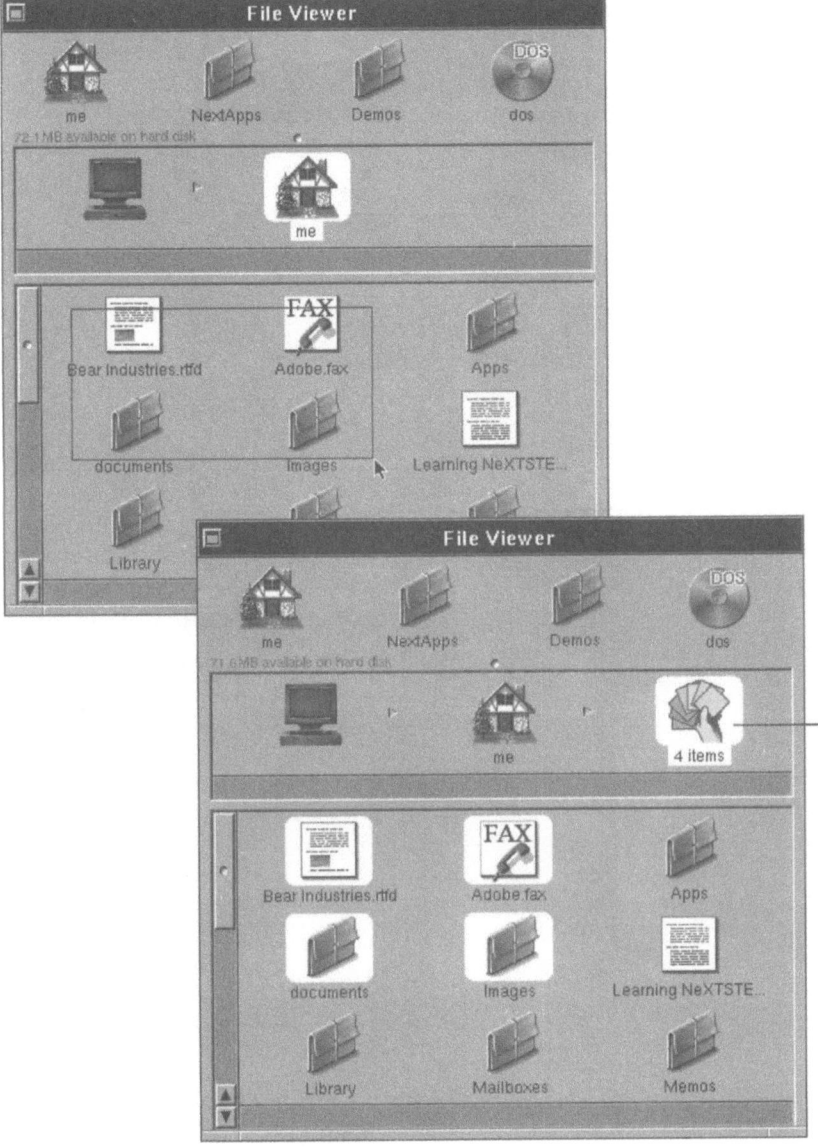

**Figure 3-18
Groups of Adjacent Icons in the Icon View**

In the icon view, you can drag an outline around adjacent icons to select them. Press and hold down a mouse button while pointing to the background of the viewing area, then drag an outline so that it touches or surrounds the files you want to select (top). When you release the mouse button, files in or touching the outline will be selected (bottom).

When you select multiple items, this icon appears in the icon path

Files and Folders

To select adjacent items in the browser or listing view, point to a file name, press and hold down a mouse button and drag up or down to select adjacent files or folders. If you make a mistake, you can click a mouse button while pointing anywhere in the browser or listing view to unhighlight the selected items, and then try again (see Figure 3-19).

**Figure 3-19
Groups of Files in the Listing and Browser Views**

To select adjacent items in the listing view (top) or browser (bottom) point to an item and drag to select adjacent items.

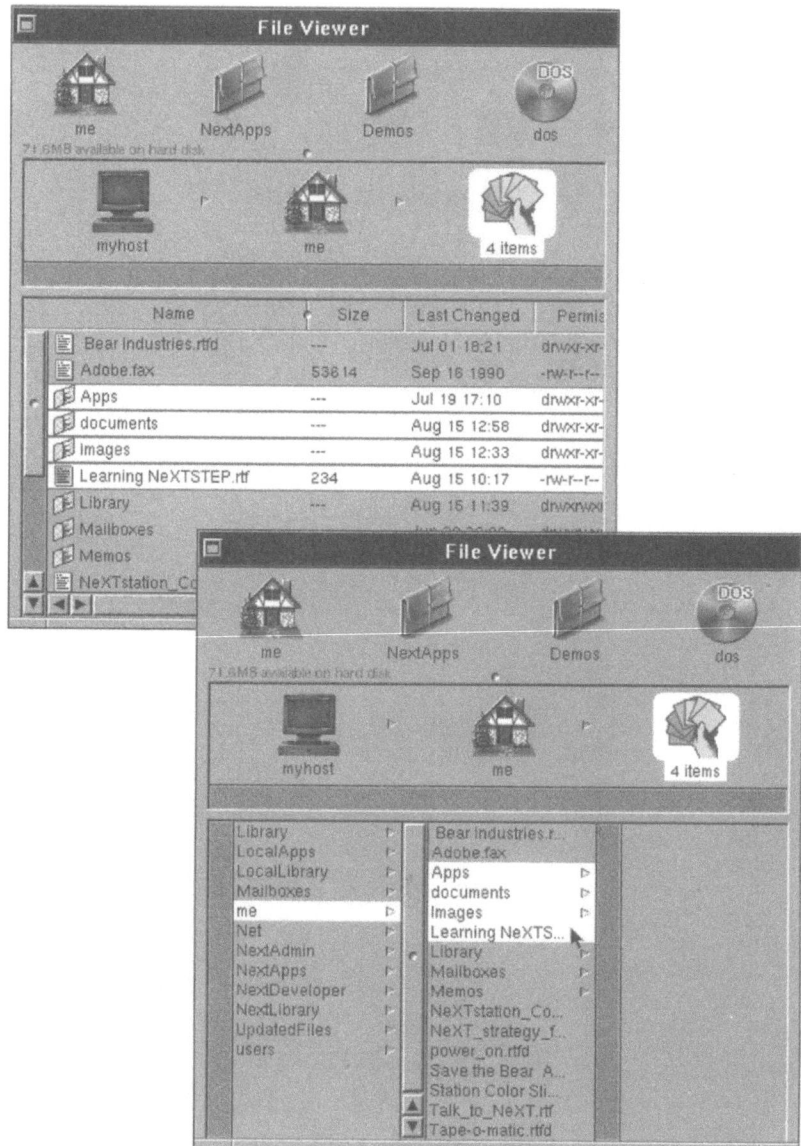

Selecting Files and Folders

If you want to add more items to the selection, press and hold down the Shift key while dragging the mouse to select them. This is called extending the selection. You can add to the selection in this manner as many times as necessary and can remove items from the group by pressing down the Shift key and dragging across items that are already selected.

To group every item displayed in the viewing area of the File Viewer, select the appropriate folder and choose Select All from the Edit menu. You can remove some or all of the icons from the selection by Shift-clicking them or Shift-dragging them.

When you want to select most but not all of the icons in the File Viewer, it is often easier to select them all and unselect those which should not be included, using the Shift-click or Shift-drag method.

3.5.1 Grouping Nonadjacent Items

When the items you want to select are not adjacent, another selection method is needed. In any view you can select nonadjacent items by holding down the Shift key while clicking each of the icons you want to select (see Figure 3-20).

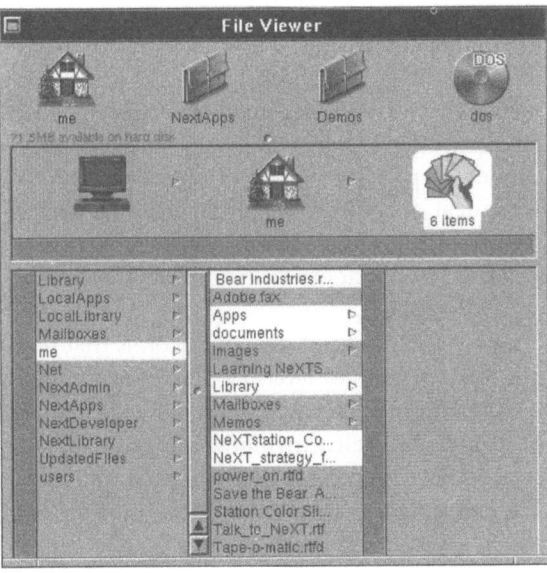

**Figure 3-20
Groups of Nonadjacent Items**

To group nonadjacent items in a File Viewer, hold down the Shift key and click the items you want to select. If necessary, you can Shift-click an item to deselect it.

If you forget to hold down the Shift key, only the last icon you click will remain selected. In this case, press and hold down the Shift key and click the items again to select them and keep them selected. If you select too many items, or accidently select the wrong item, you can deselect it by holding the Shift key and clicking it again. You can combine this method with the drag method to quickly select any number of icons.

3.5.2 Working with the Hand Icon

The hand icon represents a group of selected files that can be treated as a single icon, making it as easy to manipulate many files as to manipulate one.

When more than one item is selected in the File Viewer, a new icon will appear in the icon path, one looks like a hand holding several playing cards. This icon represents the selected group of icons, and any action you perform on the hand icon will be performed on each of the individual icons it represents. For example, if you drag the hand icon to another folder or to a floppy disk, each item the hand icon represents will be copied to the new folder or to the disk.

The hand icon is extremely useful. Dragging a single hand icon is much more intuitive than dragging multiple icons as with Macintosh and Windows systems. For example, when dragging several icons onto a folder to move them, Macintosh users must position the cursor on the target folder, not on the icons being dragged. Visually, this method is also very confusing, as icons scattered all over the screen are moving around making the cursor difficult to see. If a user accidentally releases the mouse button while dragging the group of icons, the icons are scattered all over the desktop or mixed with other icons in another folder. This would be similar to dropping a deck of playing cards on the floor and then looking for the Ace of Spades. Depending on the number of icons you dropped, it can require a great deal of time and effort to clean up such a mess. NEXTSTEP avoids this problem simply and effectively by using the hand icon to represent a group of icons that can be manipulated as one.

Another advantage of the hand icon is that it can be easily placed on the File Viewer shelf for later reference (see Figure 3-21). When you drag the hand icon onto the shelf, the hand icon, not each individual icon, is displayed on the shelf. Any number of hand icons can be placed on the shelf at the same time, each representing a different group of files and folders. You can tell them apart only by the number of icons the hand represents, which appears in the name of the hand icon.

The hand icon can be used in many interesting ways. When you select the hand icon on the shelf, the File Viewer instantly displays the contents of the folder that contains the icons the hand icon represents, and selects each of them, so you can add or remove icons from the selection or simply review it. You can also drag the hand icon onto a folder icon to move or copy all of the files the hand icon represents. The hand icon is a unique and powerful tool for representing a group of selected icons.

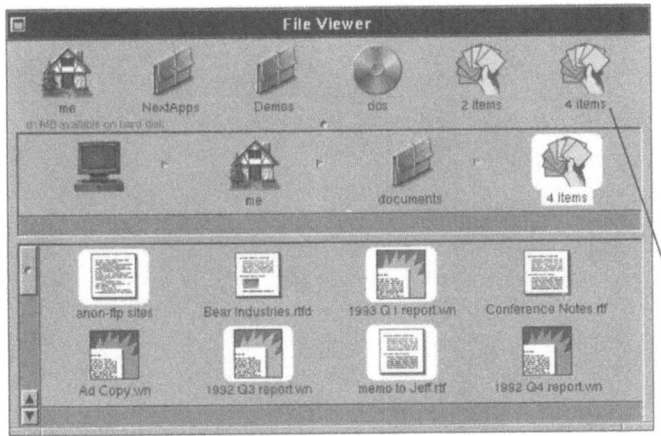

Figure 3-21
The Hand Icon on the Shelf

Any number of hand icons can be placed on the shelf. Clicking a hand icon instantly selects each of the files it represents.

Clicking this icon will display the items you previously grouped

3.6 Compressing Files and Folders

It seems that no matter how much capacity your hard disk has, there is never enough space to store all of the things you want to keep. This is especially true when copying items to a floppy disk. Often, the item you want to copy is larger than a disk can hold. To solve this problem, NEXT-STEP provides a Compress command in the File menu. By compressing files, you can reclaim some of the disk storage space the files used without destroying the files. When you compress a file or folder, NEXTSTEP will re-encode it so that it requires less disk space. The savings you gain with file compression varies, depending on the type of information stored in the file. Generally you'll regain 25 to 75 percent of the size of the original file. To use the file again, you'll have to decompress it which of course takes back the savings in disk space you gained by compressing it. You can compress any number of files or folders into a single compressed file by selecting them in a File Viewer before choosing Compress from the File menu.

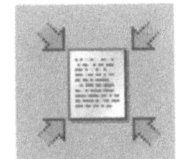

To compress a file or folder, select it in a File Viewer, and then choose Compress from the File menu. NEXTSTEP will compress it in the background so you can continue your work. When a file or folder has been compressed, it will display the compressed file icon (see Figure 3-22), no matter what icon it displayed before. To expand a file back to its normal size, select the compressed file and choose Decompress from the File menu. The Compress command will change to Decompress when you select a compressed file in the File Viewer.

Figure 3-22
File Compression

To compress one or more files, select them in the File Viewer and choose Compress from the File menu (top right). An attention panel will appear to verify that you really want to compress the selected file or files (bottom). When compressed, a file displays a new icon and its name appears with a compressed extension.

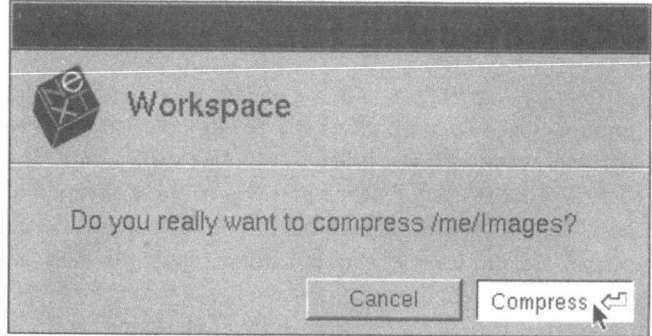

When you are making backup copies of files to floppy disks, you can put more information on the floppy disks by compressing the files first. You won't be able to open the file directly from the floppy disk without first decompressing it, but with backup copies that are used only in case of emergency, this is not a problem. You can also save time when transferring files across a network by compressing them first. This makes them smaller so they can be transmitted faster. If you are transferring files using a modem instead of a network, the savings can be significant in both time and money. Compressing several files into a single compressed file for delivery to another computer prevents the recipient from forgetting to transfer one or more files in a collection. If you were to transfer them separately, there is always a chance that one might be lost, forgotten, or corrupted during the transfer. By compressing them into a single file the chance for error is reduced.

3.7 Moving, Copying, and Duplicating

When you create and save new documents, you will be able to save them in the proper folder. However, if you decide later to move them, you can do so using the File Viewer. If two copies of a document are required, you can also duplicate or copy them using the File Viewer.

3.7.0 Moving Files

To move files from one folder to another, hold down a mouse button, drag the icon on top of a folder, and then release the mouse button. The cursor should change from black to green, and the receiving folder, called the target, should appear to open or sparkle (see margin). If you are using a monochrome display, the cursor will turn from black to white. Conveniently, the procedure for moving many items is identical to moving one item because the selected group of icons is represented by a single hand icon, which you can drag like any other icon.

When you drop an icon onto a folder, if the folder does not open or sparkle, you do not have permission to place items in the folder. Similarly, if an icon you drop into the File Viewer jumps back to its original position on the shelf, icon path, or other File Viewer, you do not have permission to place the icon in that location. To solve the problem, either drag the icon to a different folder or, if you own the folder, change its permissions using the Attributes Inspector, as described in "Attributes Inspector" on page 88. If you move a file to a folder that opens to accept it, but the file is copied instead of moved, you probably have permission to place items in the folder, called Write permission, but do not own the folder. In this case too, you will have to check the permissions of the folder using the Attributes or Access Control Inspector.

When you drop an icon onto a folder, disk, or other special icon, it opens, shines, or sparkles to let you know the item will be placed inside.

Files and Folders

A common problem when moving a file from one folder to another is that there is no room on the shelf to hold the icon you want to move so that you can set it down to select the target folder. If the shelf is full, resize it by dragging the shelf's dimple down to make more room or open a second File Viewer by selecting the target folder and choosing Open as Folder from the File menu, and then drag the icon from one File Viewer to the other.

Table 3-1 How to Move Files and Folders

From	To	Method
Shelf	folder icon	Drag the icon onto the shelf, select the destination folder in the File Viewer and drag the icon from the shelf onto the folder's icon in the icon path.
Shelf	File Viewer	Drag the icon from the shelf to the File Viewer.
Icon path	Shelf	Drag the icon from the icon path onto a folder icon on the shelf.
Icon view	Shelf	Drag the icon from the File Viewer to an icon on the shelf.
Icon view	File Viewer	Drag the icon from one File Viewer to another using any of the techniques described above.
Listing or browser view	File Viewer, shelf, or icon path	Not possible. If you try, you'll select several items instead of drag them.

3.7.1 Copying Files and Folders

When you drag an icon onto a folder you don't own, but to which you have write permission, or when you drag an icon from one disk or disk partition to another, the file is copied rather than moved. This is different from moving an icon because copying creates a new icon, consuming twice its size in disk storage, but does not remove the original one. You can tell when a file will be copied instead of moved as you drag its icon because the cursor will change from an arrow to a copy cursor, also called a double-doc-

Copy cursor

Arrow cursor

Moving, Copying, and Duplicating

ument or copy icon. If you want to copy an icon to a folder that you own, press the Alternate key as you drag the icon to the new folder. The cursor will change into a double-document icon to indicate that the icon is being copied instead of moved. Remember that copying an icon, as compared to moving it, uses up twice the disk space.

3.7.2 Merging Folders

A new feature in NEXTSTEP, called merge folders, allows you to combine the contents of two folders that share the same name. Merging allows you to easily combine folders containing different versions of the same files but keep only the most recent files. For example, to merge two folders named **documents**, drag the first **documents** folder onto the folder icon that contains the second **documents** folder (see Figure 3-23). Because folders of the same name cannot exist in the same folder, NEXTSTEP will display the Processes panel, asking if you want to replace the existing folder with the one you just dragged in, merge the contents of the two folders together, or stop copying. To merge the folders click Merge.

> Do not drop the first **documents** folder directly onto the second **documents** folder as you might be tempted to do or it will be copied into the second folder instead of merged.

When the merge is finished, the remaining **documents** folder, the target, will contain all of the files contained in both folders. Where two files of the same name existed before, only the later version will remain. The merge folders feature is a great convenience when you use floppy disks to transfer files from one computer to another. You can easily maintain up-to-date files with very little effort by merging the folder on the floppy disk with the folder on the hard disk.

3.7.3 Duplicating Files and Folders

To make a copy of an item and store the copy in the same folder as the original, select the icon and choose Duplicate from the File menu. Because no two items can share the same name in the same folder, when the duplicate is created, it will have the name **CopyOf** followed by the name of the original icon. For example, duplicating the file named **MailingLabels** will result in a new file named **CopyOfMailingLabels**. If you duplicate the

Files and Folders

Figure 3-23
To Merge Folders

When you merge folders, drag the folder to be merged directly onto the folder that contains the target (top). When the Processes panel appears (bottom), click Merge to combine the contents of the two folders.

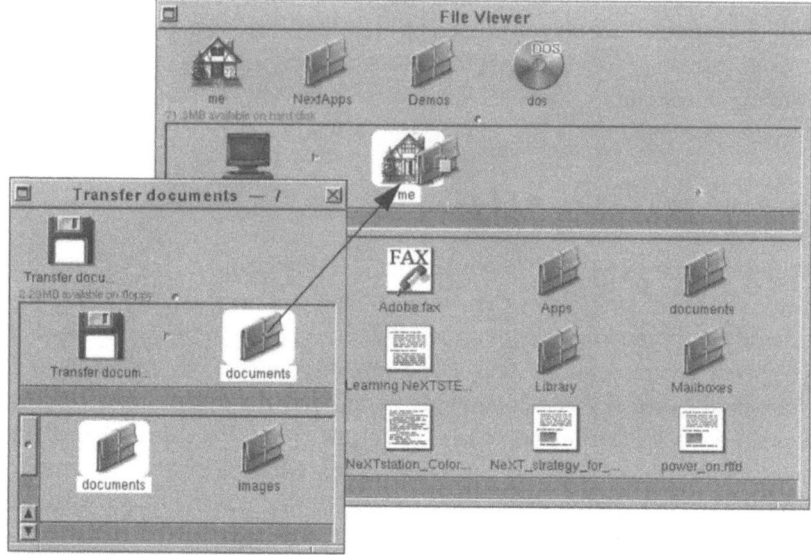

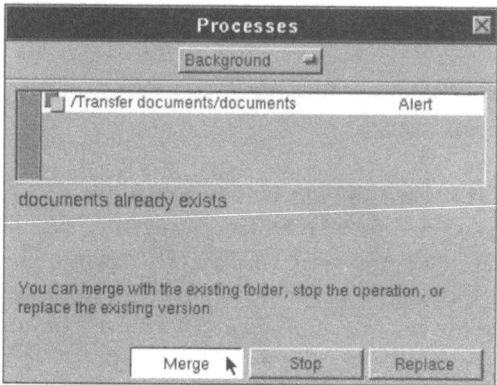

hand icon, each of the items in the group the hand icon represents will be duplicated and each will have the prefix **CopyOf**. Be careful when duplicating the hand icon, because the result could be many files beginning with **CopyOf** intermixed with the originals in the same folder. If this happens accidentally, sort the folder by name to make all of the **CopyOf** documents appear together near the top of the File Viewer display area.

68

3.8 Monitoring Background Tasks

Whenever NEXTSTEP moves, copies, or duplicates an item, it does so in the background. This allows you to continue your work uninterrupted while the files are being moved, copied, or duplicated. In fact, you can move, copy, or duplicate files and folders again while the first task is still in progress. For example, you can drag several file from one folder to another, drag icons from a floppy disk to a hard disk, and duplicate several files concurrently. Each time you ask NEXTSTEP to copy an icon or group of icons, you are creating a process, a task that gets placed in a queue. You can have as many of these processes running as you want. However, the more of these tasks you begin, the slower system performance will become so use prudence when starting several of these tasks. If any problems occur while these tasks are being completed, NEXTSTEP will alert you by displaying a message in the Processes panel.

> You should do everything possible to take advantage of the ability to perform useful work in the background. It is normal to distrust the computer and insist on watching it perform each task until it is completed, but this wastes time. Don't worry that you can't always see what's going on in the background. NEXTSTEP is very trustworthy and will complete the tasks you give it so you can go on to others.

You can check the status of background tasks like copying, moving, and duplicating using the Processes panel. Choose Processes from the Tools menu. The Processes panel can display a list of the currently active background tasks or a list of currently running NEXTSTEP applications. You can choose which list you would like to see using the panel's pop-up list.

To monitor the progress of a particular process, click its name in the Processes panel to select it and observe the messages that appear in the panel (see Figure 3-24). If you select a copy process, the Processes panel will display a pie chart. The pie represents the completed task and is filled in with dark gray slices as the copying progresses. When the pie is completely filled, the copy process is finished. You can stop a copy process at any time by selecting its name in the Processes panel and clicking Stop. You can also temporarily stop a process and continue it later by clicking Pause, and then selecting the item, and clicking Resume. If you have several background processes running, you can pause tasks of low priority until the more important ones have finished and then resume them.

Figure 3-24
Background Processes

You can not only view background processes such as copying using the Processes panel (top) but alter them as well. For example, If you need to temporarily stop copying, select the process in the scrolling list and click Pause. To continue it, select it again if necessary and click Resume. You can also stop a process by selecting it and clicking Stop.

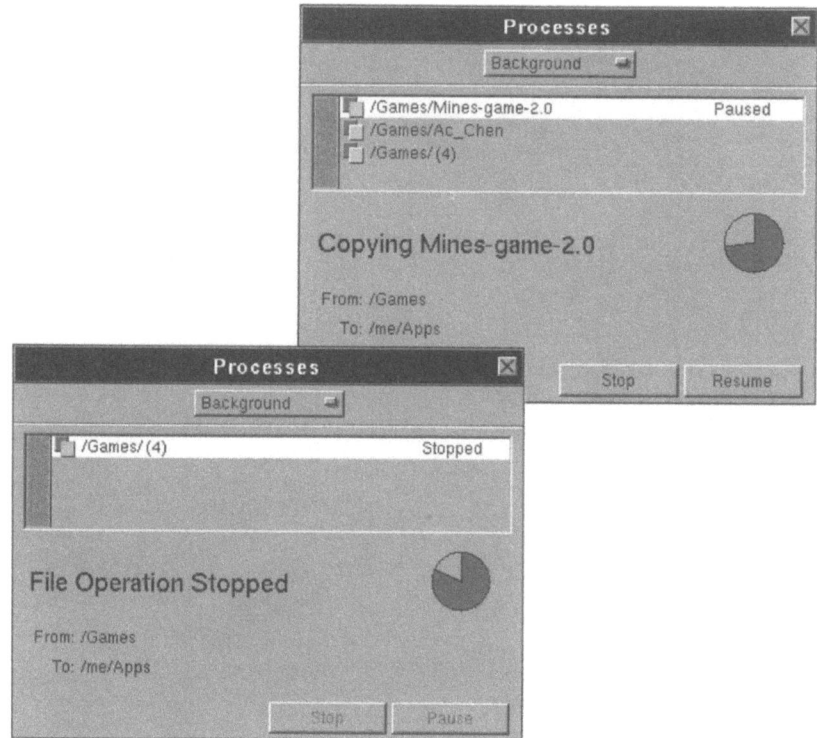

3.9 Using Links

Linking is not limited to images and applications. You can also link files, folders, and applications in the workspace so that they appear to be in more than one folder at a time without having to duplicate them. *Links*, as they are called, are not duplicate copies of an item and so do not take any appreciable space. The link simply makes the original file or folder appear in a different location in the file system. When you double-click the link, NEXTSTEP will act as if you double-clicked the original. Using links, you can customize the file system to suit your needs, making it easier to find the files and folders you use most and saving disk space by avoiding duplicates. You can have as many links to an item as you wish and place them in any folder in which you have permission to write.

Using Links

Linking items in the workspace offers several advantages. Linking items makes them easier find because you can put them where you want them, rather than where they are required to be. For example, many applications are stored in **LocalApps** and in **NextApps** and unless you are the root user, you cannot move them. However, using links, you can make them appear in your own personal **Apps** folder so they are easier to access. You can do the same for items in **NextLibrary** and **LocalLibrary** as well. Also, if you prefer to have an application in a folder along with its documents, but you don't want to move the application, you can link to it so it appears to in both places. Because you link the application instead of move it, NEXTSTEP will still be able to find it in the appropriate Apps folder, place it in the search path, and register its services. If you move the application, NEXTSTEP will not be able to find it and it may be skipped when the system administrator performs backups of the computer's hard disk. If you are sharing your computer, you can place any item where you want it without making it difficult for your colleagues to find it.

A side effect of linking an item to your home folder is that its pathname becomes much shorter. Thus a document located in **/NextLibrary/Bookshelves/Literature.bshlf** could be linked to your home folder and abbreviated **~/Literature.bshlf**. You can refer to an item through its link or original location in the file system, whichever is easier. Being able to refer to an item using shortcuts like links is especially useful when you use the Terminal application.

Several of NEXTSTEP's own folders are actually links. For example, examine the **/etc** folder using the Attributes Inspector. It is actually a link to another folder, **/private/etc**. By linking folders, NEXTSTEP can easily access the information it requires to manage the computer, yet maintain consistency with other UNIX system, which expect to find certain files in standard locations in the file system.

3.9.0 Creating a Link

To create a link, hold down the Control key while dragging an icon in a File Viewer. As you drag the icon, the cursor will become a double-headed arrow to indicate that you are creating a link. To use a link, treat it just as you would the file or folder it represents. If the link is to an application, double-click it to start it running. If the link is a folder, double-click it to view its contents in the File Viewer. If it's a document, double-click it to open it. To destroy a link, drag it into the recycler or select it in a File

When you hold down the Control key and drag an icon in the File Viewer, you will see the link cursor, indicating that you are creating a link.

Files and Folders

Viewer and choose Destroy from the File menu. When you recycle or destroy a link, you do not affect the original item it represents. Only the link is destroyed. However, if you move, rename, or delete the item that the link points to, the link will also be broken. If you destroy an item to which there are links established in the file system, be sure to destroy its links as well. You can identify a link using the Attributes Inspector (see Figure 3-25) and locate links using the Finder panel.

**Figure 3-25
Links Between
Files and Folders**

To create a link, hold down the Control key while dragging an icon onto a folder (top) or into another File Viewer. l inked item acts just like the item it points to, but you can identify it using the Attributes Inspector (bottom).

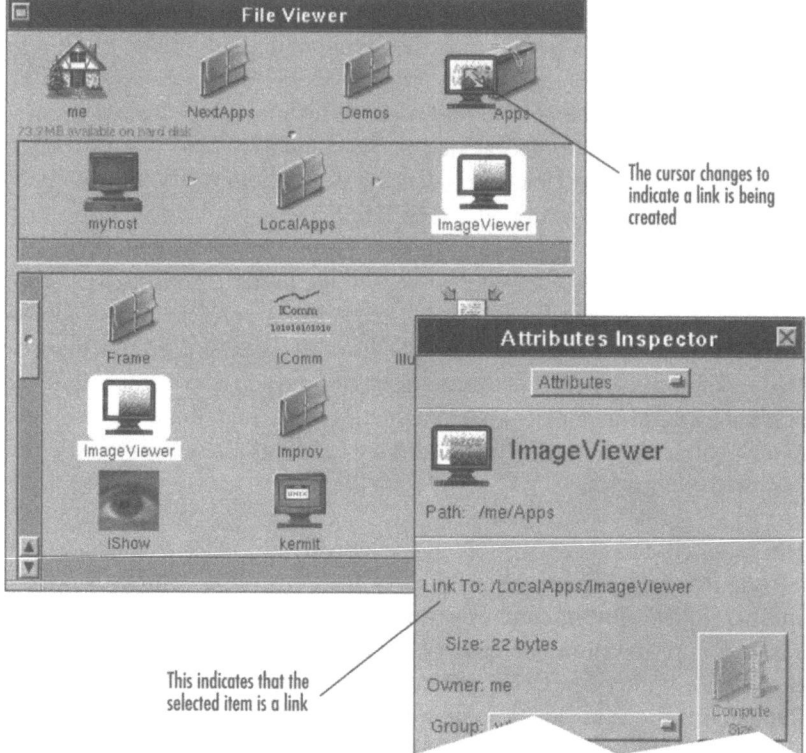

3.9.1 Copying a Link

If you drag a link to another folder, the Processes panel will appear, asking if you want to copy the original item the link points to into the new folder, create a new link, or cancel the copy. Click New Link to create another link to the original item, Skip to bypass copying the item that is linked, Stop to stop copying, or Copy to create a new link in the folder (see Figure 3-26). If you are copying more than one link, and you would like all of the

Deleting Files and Folders

links treated in the same fashion, click the Repeat switch. When the next link is encountered, NEXTSTEP will use your previous selection in the Processes panel instead of alerting you to make a choice. After you make a selection in the Processes panel, the panel will remain visible, so if you don't want to use it anymore, click its close button to make it disappear. (You can tell NEXTSTEP how to handle copied links using the File Copy options in the Workspace Manager's Preferences panel. This is described in "File Copy Options" on page 281.)

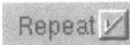

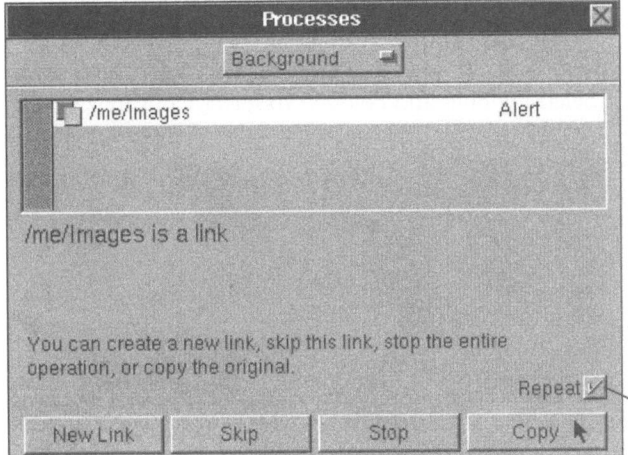

**Figure 3-26
Copying a Link**

When you copy a link, the Processes panel appears to ask how you would like to treat it. You can create a new link, skip over the link as if it didn't exist, stop copying, or copy the item the link points to by clicking the appropriate button.

Turn on to treat every occurrence of a link the same way.

3.10 Deleting Files and Folders

If all you do with NeXTSTEP is create, save, and duplicate documents, it will not be long before you will run out of disk space. To avoid this problem, NEXTSTEP provides two ways for you to delete files and folders, and reuse, or recycle, the disk space they occupied.

3.10.0 The Recycler

The recycler is located in the lower left corner of the workspace or at the bottom of the dock, depending on your computer system, and holds items you want to delete so you can retrieve them at a later time if necessary. To move an item into the recycler, just drag the icon of the item onto the recycler. When the icon touches the recycler, the recycler icon appears to spin. While the recycler is spinning, release the mouse button to drop the

An empty and a full Recycler.

Files and Folders

icon into the recycler. The recycler will display a dot in the center of its icon when at least one item is in the recycler. Items placed in the recycler will remain there, even after you log out or power off the computer, until you choose Empty Recycler from the File menu to erase them. Only after you have emptied the recycler will you be able to recover the disk space used by those files, and use it for other documents.

If the recycler has not yet been emptied, you can recover icons from it by dragging them back into the File Viewer (see Figure 3-27). Double-click the recycler icon to open its window, and drag the icons to be retrieved into the File Viewer. If there are many items in the recycler, scroll to view them. You can use all of the selection techniques described in section 3.5, "Selecting Files and Folders" to select icons in the recycler.

**Figure 3-27
File Retrieval**

If the Recycler has not yet been emptied, you can retrieve items from it by double-clicking the recycler icon to open its window, and dragging the item back into a File Viewer.

NEXTSTEP will *not* display an alert panel before deleting the items in the recycler, so be careful when choosing the Empty Recycler command. Until the recycler is emptied, however, the disk space used by the items placed in the recycler is not available and cannot be used for other purposes.

> Due to the complexity of the UNIX file system compared with Macintosh and DOS, file recovery is impossible. There are no utilities available to recover files, so be very careful when you empty the recycler that you are not destroying an item you will need later.

3.10.1 The Destroy Command

If you want to erase a file or folder immediately, you can do so by selecting the files or folders to be erased and choosing Destroy from the File menu. The keyboard shortcut for Destroy is Command-r. Unlike the recycler, Destroy deletes an item immediately, so you will have no opportunity to

Deleting Files and Folders

retrieve it should you want it back later. For this reason, the Destroy command displays an attention panel to verify that you really want to delete the selected items (see Figure 3-28). Click Destroy in this panel to delete the item, or click Cancel to keep it in the file system and cancel the Destroy command.

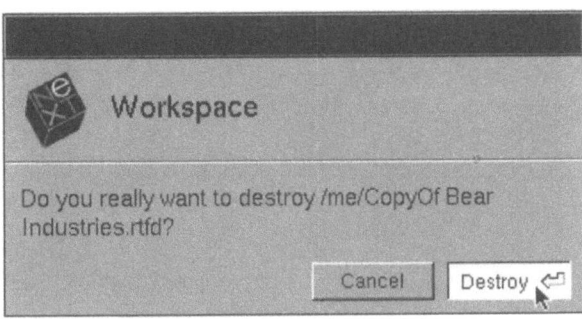

**Figure 3-28
The Destroy Command**

To destroy an item, select it in the File Viewer and choose Destroy from the File menu. An attention panel will appear to verify that you really want to delete the selected item.

It is highly unlikely that you will know in advance whether or not you will want to recover a deleted file before you delete it. If that were the case, you would not delete it. Therefore, when you delete files, folders, and applications, use the recycler instead of the Destroy command so you will have an opportunity for recovery, if necessary. The Destroy command is best used when you need to gain more disk space but don't want to eliminate the items in the recycler until a later time. In this case, select the items you want to delete, making sure you will never need them again, and then destroy them. You will have gained more disk space for other projects, yet kept the items that were in the recycler safe. Later, when you are sure you want to delete them, you can choose Empty Recycler to gain even more disk space.

If after you destroy or recycle files, the File Viewer fails to indicate that you have more disk space available than before, choose Update Viewers from the View menu. If there is no change, the Workspace Manager may still be destroying or recycling files in the background. Wait a few moments and try the Update Viewers command again.

75

4

Removable Disks

With NEXTSTEP you can take advantage of a wide variety of storage devices, including floppy disks, SyQuest and Bernoulli removable hard disk drives, magneto-optical drives, and CD-ROM drives. These disks can be used to transfer information between different computer systems or to store backup copies of important files and applications.

Each of these storage devices has one thing in common. Unlike internal hard disk drives, they all feature media that can be removed while the computer is running. Since they are functionally equivalent, the term floppy disk and removable disk are used interchangeably and include magnetic tapes, magneto-optical disks, and removable cartridges. Differences between the different types of removable media will be noted.

These icons represent fixed and removable disks. From top to bottom: NeXT CD-ROM, DOS hard disk, and Macintosh removable disk.

4.0 Understanding Disk Formats

Personal computer systems running NEXTSTEP and containing high-density floppy disk drives can read, write, and initialize 720 KB and 1.44 MB disks for use with DOS, Windows, and OS/2, 720 KB and 1.4 MB NEXTSTEP disks, and 1.4 MB Macintosh disks. NeXT computers can work with each of these same disks and 2.8 MB Extra Density (ED) disks. If you happen to own one of the original NeXT Computers that were not equipped with a floppy disk drive, you can purchase an external floppy disk drive, such as the Peripheral Land Incorporated TurboFloppy or Digital Information Technologies CubeFloppy external floppy disk drive. These drives can read and write the same disks as the NeXT Computer's 2.88 MB drive and can also read, write, and initialize double-density 800 KB Macintosh disks. See Table 4-1 for a summary of supported disk formats.

Table 4-1 Floppy Disk formats Supported in NEXTSTEP Release 3

Disk Type	DOS	Macintosh	NeXT
Double-Density (DD)	720 KB*	800 KB†	720 KB
High-Density (HD)	1.4 MB	1.4 MB	1.4 MB
Extra-Density (ED)	2.88 MB	Don't exist	2.88 MB

* NEXTSTEP for Intel Processors can read and write 720 KB disks, but not format them.
† Only the PLI TurboFloppy and DIT CubeFloppy drives work with 800 KB Macintosh floppy disks.

4.1 Mounting a Disk

The process of inserting a disk and having the workspace display its contents in a File Viewer is called mounting. When you insert a removable disk into the computer, you need to notify NEXTSTEP that it is ready to be used. This is accomplished by choosing Check for Disks in the Workspace Manager's Disk menu. You can choose how removable disks will appear in the workspace using the workspace's Preferences panel. Choose Preferences from the Workspace Info menu, and then choose Disk Options from the panel's pop-up list. This panel and each of its options is discussed in further detail in the section "Disk Options" on page 280.

If you work with removable disks often, you may want to create a keyboard shortcut to make the Check for Disks command easier to access. To learn how to create a keyboard shortcut, refer to section 11.1.8, "Menu Preferences".

4.2 Unmounting a Disk

The process of ejecting and removing the mounted disk's image from the File Viewer is called unmounting. It is very important to remember that you cannot simply eject a disk at any time. If background programs or processes are running and require the disk, when you attempt to unmount it, the process will fail or hang waiting for a disk that is no longer available (see Figure 4-1). To avoid this undesirable condition, notify NEXTSTEP that you would like to eject the disk before you do so manually. NEXTSTEP will then verify that the drive is no longer in use, unmount it from the File Viewer, and notify you to eject it. (On NeXT computers, floppy disks are ejected automatically by the workspace when it is safe to do so). It is possible to override NEXTSTEP's warnings about ejecting disks that are in use, so be very careful when you unmount them.

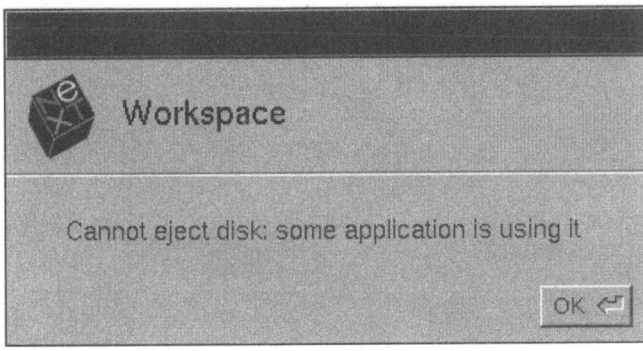

**Figure 4-1
Ejecting a Disk
While it's in Use**

When you attempt to unmount a removable disk while there are background tasks in progress, NEXTSTEP displays this attention panel.

To unmount a removable disk from its drive, select the disk's icon in the File Viewer, and then choose Eject from the Workspace Manager's Disk menu. You can also unmount a removable disk by dragging its icon onto the recycler. This is equivalent to choosing Eject from the Disk menu. If there are no background processes using the disk, it will be ejected in a few seconds. If there are background processes in progress, you will see an attention panel warning you. You can choose to eject the disk anyway or wait until the background process is finished. (To monitor background tasks, use the Processes panel as described in "Monitoring Background Tasks" on page 69.) When the Eject Disk attention panel appears, you can safely eject the disk (see Figure 4-2). Remember that on NeXT computers, floppy disks are ejected automatically.

**Figure 4-2
Unmounting
a disk**

NEXTSTEP displays this attention panel when it is safe to manually eject a removable disk or cartridge.

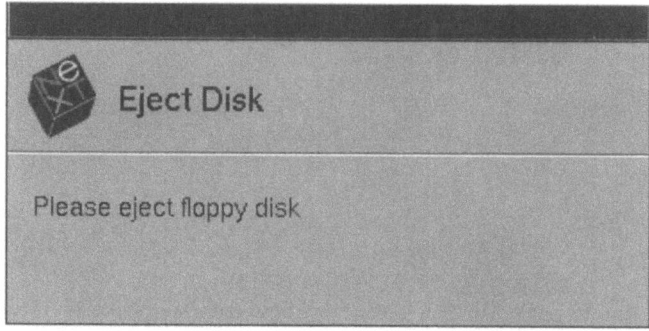

NeXT's Edit application is notorious for refusing to allow floppy disks to be ejected after you open one of its documents. If you were using Edit, and now can't eject a floppy disk, you may have to quit Edit before you will be able to unmount and eject the disk.

If you are unable to determine why you cannot eject a disk, choose Console from the Workspace Manager's Tools menu. The Console window will describe which application is using the disk so you can quit it and eject the disk successfully.

4.3 Initializing a Disk

Every removable disk must be prepared before it can be used in the computer. NEXTSTEP calls this process *initializing* a disk. When you mount a new disk, NEXTSTEP will notice that the disk is not ready for use and display the Initialize attention panel (see Figure 4-3) so you can initialize it. If the disk you inserted was previously initialized and contained data, do not initialize it again. Doing so will erase the information it contains. Click Eject and attempt to mount the disk again. If it fails again, attempt to mount it on a different computer. If it fails to mount on the other computer, you may need to seek assistance to recover the data from the disk. If you don't mind losing the data, you can initialize it again and reuse it.

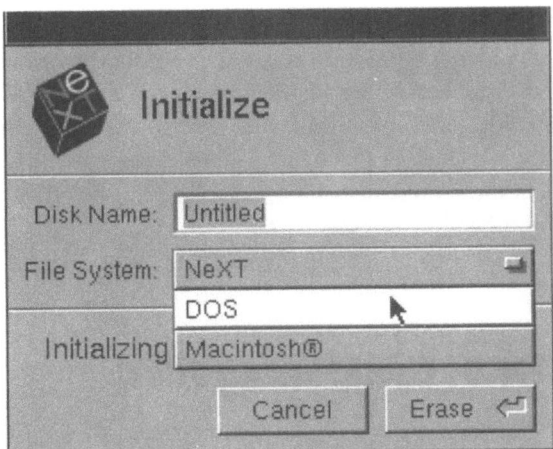

**Figure 4-3
Using The
Initialize Panel**

Using the Initialize panel, you can initialize disks in DOS, Macintosh, and NEXT format.

When the Initialize panel appears, enter a name for the disk (Untitled is the default), and then choose the type of disk formatting you would like to use by selecting the appropriate format in the Initialize panel's pop-up list. To begin initializing, click Erase. As the disk is being initialized, NEXTSTEP will display an "Initializing disk..." message in the lower right corner of the File Viewer shelf. When the message disappears, the initialization is complete, the disk is mounted, and it appears in the File Viewer.

If you tend to use the same removable disk over and over, erasing and loading it up with files again and again, the disk can wear out. Disks that are heavily used, erased, and reused can develop bad sectors, areas on the disk that become unusable. To avoid losing data, you should make a copy of the contents of the disk, and then reinitialize the disk so NEXTSTEP can mark the bad sectors and avoid using them in the future. To reinitialize a disk, mount it, select it in the File Viewer, and then choose Initialize from the Disk menu.

4.4 Copying Files to a Disk

Removable disks wouldn't be much good unless you could move files between them and your system's hard disk. This is very easily accomplished by dragging and dropping a file's icon onto the removable disk's icon in a File Viewer. You can also drag an icon onto a folder icon that belongs to the removable disk. Unlike DOS, when you copy a folder in NEXTSTEP,

copy cursor

every item in the folder, including every item in its subfolders (subdirectories) also gets copied. When you drag an icon, you can know that the file or folder it represents is going to be copied before you release the mouse button, because the icon on which you drop the file will appear to open or sparkle, and the cursor will change into the copy cursor. If the cursor doesn't change, the items you are dragging will be moved instead of copied. If the target doesn't open or sparkle, the item you are dragging will not be moved or copied. In this case, use the Attributes or Access Control Inspector to determine if you have permission to place files in the target.

4.4.0 Compressing Files

When you are copying files to floppy disks, you can put more information on the floppy disks by compressing the files before copying them. To compress files, use the Compress command in the Workspace Manager's File menu. To learn more about compressing files see "Compressing Files and Folders" on page 63.

4.4.1 Using Multi-Volume Copy

Even when you compress a file or folder, it may still be larger than the capacity of a floppy disk, and thus prohibit you from transferring it to another computer or making a backup copy without the use of a network. NEXTSTEP includes a fantastic feature called multi-volume copy that automatically breaks a large file into chunks, and places each chunk on a separate disk. When you copy any of the chunks back onto a hard disk or disk of sufficient capacity, NEXTSTEP will ask for each of the disks containing chunks of the file. After you insert each of the disks containing chunks, NEXTSTEP rebuilds the chunks into the single compressed file. You can then decompress the file to use it. Multi-volume copy works with floppy disks that already contain files as well as those that don't. If the disk contains files, NEXTSTEP will copy as large a chunk as possible, and then ask for more disks until every chunk has been copied. You cannot create a multi-volume set with uncompressed files. Multi-volume copy works only with compressed files.

In the past, if you attempted to copy an item that was larger than the capacity of a floppy disk, the Processes panel would display a message indicating that there was not enough room. Now you can now copy a file of

Copying Files to a Disk

any size onto a floppy disk. When NEXTSTEP discovers that there is not enough room on the disk for the file, it will display the Processes panel asking if you want to create a compressed multi-volume file (see Figure 4-4).

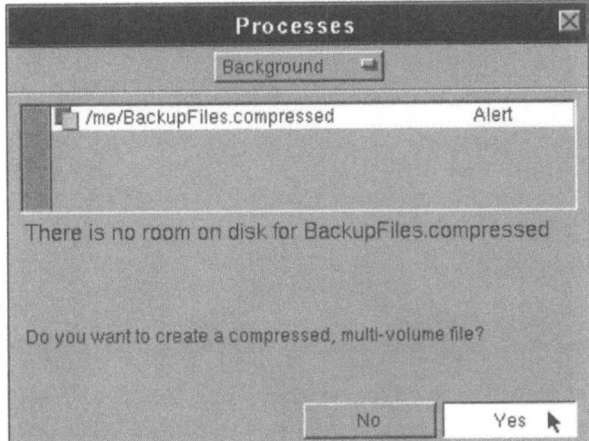
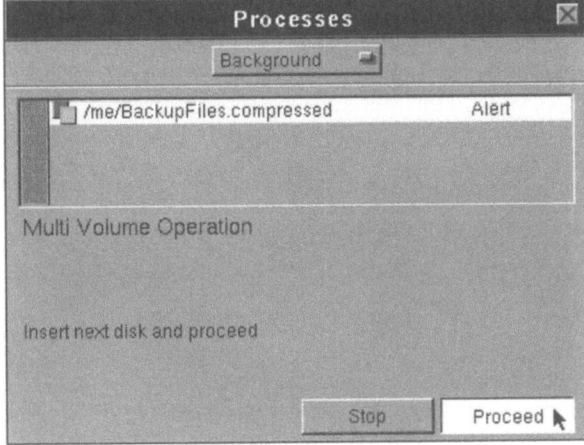

**Figure 4-4
Using Multi-Volume Copy**

When a disk doesn't have enough room for a file, the Processes panel appears to ask if you would like to store the file on several disks (top). If you click Yes, the file will be broken into chunks. When the disk is full, the Processes panel will continue to ask you to insert another disk until every chunk has been copied (bottom).

When the Processes panel appears, you'll have two choices. Click No to stop copying or click Yes to create a multi-volume set, and then insert as many floppy disks as NEXTSTEP requests until all of the chunks are copied, or until you run out of disks. If you click No, the Processes panel will ask again if you want to stop or proceed. Click Stop. If you click Yes and run out of floppy disks before the copying is done, you can click Cancel in the Processes panel to stop copying. Cancelling does not harm other files that may have already been copied to floppy disks.

Multi-volume copy is a powerful feature for copying large files to floppy disks. If you don't have access to a high-capacity backup device, such as a tape drive or removable hard disk drive, multi-volume copy may suffice. Multi-volume copy does not provide the additional benefits of backup applications, such as incremental backups and report generation, and is limited by the relatively small capacity of floppy disks. To create a complete backup, use a tape drive and a backup utility such as SafetyNet, BackupMaster, or enTAR.

4.4.2 Duplicating Disks

PC systems typically have two floppy disk drives, making disk-to-disk copies very straightforward. However, NEXTSTEP currently supports systems with only one 3.5 inch floppy disk drive (you can have others, but not more than one 3.5 inch floppy disk drive) and NeXT computers rarely have more than one floppy disk drive attached to them. This presents a dilemma if you want to duplicate or copy the contents of one disk onto another in NEXTSTEP. The only solution is to copy the disk's contents to a new folder on the hard disk, eject the floppy disk, insert the destination disk, and then copy the files from the folder on the hard disk to the floppy disk. This solution is not simple or quick, but it gets the job done.

> When using a single disk drive to duplicate a disk, don't eject the first disk too soon. Remember that the files are being copied in the background, so it may appear as though the copying is done when it isn't. If you eject the disk too soon, some of the files may not get copied.

5
Inspectors

A unique feature of NEXTSTEP is the Inspector, which allows you to display and modify detailed information about a selected item. For example, to inspect an item in the file system, select it in a File Viewer and then choose Inspector from the Workspace Manager's Tools menu. The Inspector is dynamically updated to display information about the currently selected icon, so each time you change the selection in the File Viewer, you'll instantly see information about the new selection in the Inspector (see Figure 5-1).

The Inspector can be a bit confusing at first because its appearance differs depending on what is selected, but it is not difficult to use. When you want to examine detailed information about two or more files, you might think that you would have to open a separate Inspector window for each of them. This is not the case. The Inspector is either visible or it isn't. You cannot open more than one Inspector. All you have to do is open the Inspector, and then highlight each of the files in turn. As you highlight each item in the File Viewer, the Inspector automatically changes to reflect information about that item. The Inspector can be used to view or change different attributes of the same file. The Inspector provides access to a great deal of information without the need to open several windows

Inspectors

and clutter the workspace. The Inspector is such a compact, powerful tool that many applications make use of one. Let's examine the controls provided in the workspace Inspector and unlock some of its mysteries.

**Figure 5-1
The Inspector Panel**

The workspace Inspector panel displays detailed information about the selected item in the File Viewer. To see the Inspector, choose Inspector from the Tools menu.

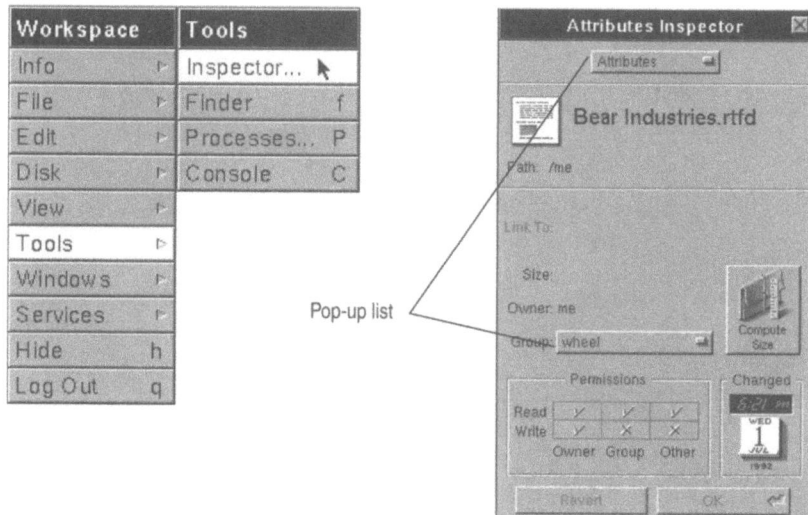

5.0 Inspector Controls

5.0.0 Pop-Up Lists

The Inspector features several interesting controls which that are the key to its versatility. These controls are called *pop-up* and *pull-down* lists. Pop-up lists not only appear in the Inspector panel, but also in many other NEXTSTEP applications. You can identify a pop-up list by the shadowed box that appears next to a button's name (see Figure 5-2). When you position the cursor on a pop-up list and press a mouse button, the list of choices will appear. To select an item in the list, continue holding down the mouse button, drag the cursor to highlight the desired item, then release the mouse button to select it. After you make a selection, the name of the button will change to indicate the item you selected. In general, pop-up lists change the state of something rather than execute a command. For this reason, the button's name is changed to indicate the current state of your selections. For example, when you choose Contents from the Inspector panel, the pop-up list's name changes to Contents to indicate that the Inspector has changed its state from displaying attributes information to contents information.

 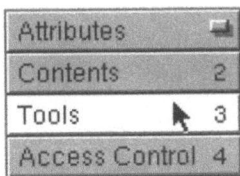 

Figure 5-2
Pop-Up Lists

Drag through the list of items while holding down a mouse button. To select an item, release the mouse button while pointing to it.

The Inspector's pop-up list contains four items that determine the type of information the Inspector will display. For example, when you choose Attributes from the Inspector's pop-up list, you will see detailed information about the attributes of the selected icon in the File Viewer such as its size, pathname, last modification date, and permissions. Choosing Contents from the pop-up list causes the Inspector to attempt to display the contents of the selected item (see page 91 for supported file formats). Tools is used to set the application that will start when you double-click a document and Access Control allows you to view and modify permissions, including execute permission.

Because each Inspector display is different, refer to the Inspector by the item currently selected in its pop-up list. For example, when viewing the Attributes controls, refer to the Inspector as the Attributes Inspector. When viewing the Tools controls, refer the Inspector as the Tools Inspector. This naming convention avoids potential confusion and is used throughout this book.

5.0.1 Pull-Down Lists

A pull-down list is similar to a pop-up list in that they are both identified by icons and they both present a list of choices from which to choose; however, they have a few subtle differences. Pull-down lists are identified by a triangle, not a shadowed box, and the items in a pull-down list always appear below the button (see Figure 5-3). Pull-down lists are used to execute commands rather than change a state or condition, as do pop-up lists, and their names always remain the same no matter which item you select.

Pop-up list
Pull-down list

Inspectors

**Figure 5-3
Pull-Down Lists**

Choosing an item from a pull-down list typically executes a command but doesn't change the button's name.

 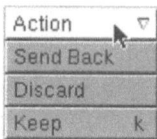 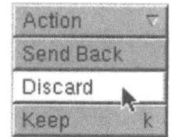 

5.1 Attributes Inspector

The Attributes Inspector displays the pathname, file links, size, owner, group, permissions, and date last modified for the item selected in the File Viewer. Its keyboard shortcut is Command-1. When you want to inspect a different item, simply select it in the File Viewer. The Attributes Inspector will automatically change to describe the item you just selected. You can inspect the attributes of files, folders, and applications.

If you inspect a folder, its size will not be displayed in the Attributes Inspector. Instead, a button named Compute Size appears instead (see Figure 5-4). Clicking Compute Size causes NEXTSTEP to calculate the amount of disk space used by the folder. By calculating the size of large items only when required, NEXTSTEP can display the other information you need in the Inspector much more quickly.

**Figure 5-4
To Calculate a Folder's Size**

When a folder or a very large file is inspected, its size is not immediately displayed. To calculate the item's size, click the Compute Size button.

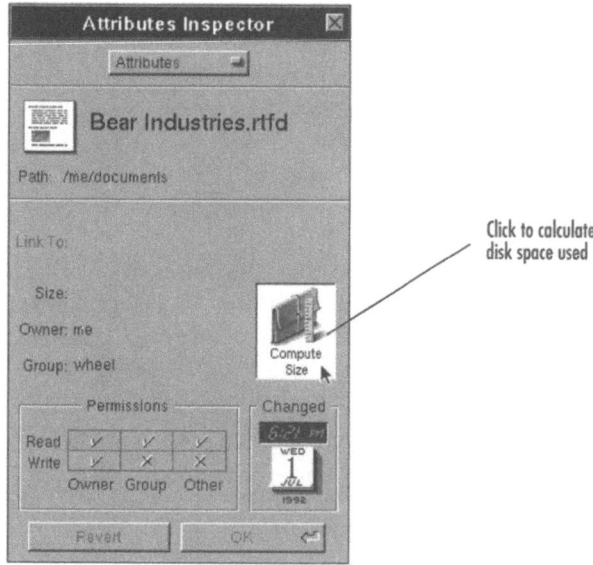

Attributes Inspector

5.1.0 Permissions

One of the most important uses of the Attributes Inspector is to see and modify an item's *read* and *write permissions*. NEXTSTEP secures every item in the file system so that it can only be read or modified by authorized users. These access restrictions, called permissions, are particularly necessary to protect the files owned by the root user from being altered or deleted, as these files are critical to the function of the computer. They also serve to keep other users from seeing your own sensitive information.

The File Viewer's listing view also displays file permissions, but it doesn't allow you to change them.

NEXTSTEP uses the UNIX system's permissions called *read*, *write*, and *execute* (see Table 5-2), each of which apply to three categories of users: *owner*, *group*, and *world*. Owner refers to the user that created the file or folder or application. Group refers to any member belonging to a particular group name established by the root user, and world is anyone who is not the owner and who is not in the specified group. In the Attributes Inspector, world is referred to as other. The listing view also displays file permissions but does not provide titles for owner, group, and other. Until you become accustomed to the UNIX permissions scheme, use the Attributes or Access Inspector (described later) to view and alter permissions.

Table 5-1 File and Folder Permissions

Permission	Description
Read	Allows a user to open and read the contents of the selected file or folder.
Write	Allows a user to make and save changes to the selected file or folder.
Execute	Allows the selected file to be executed as if it were an application. This permission applies only to applications that require this permission in order to be run.

Owner

The owner of an item is the one who created it. If you are the owner of an item, you can reassign the ownership to another user, but once ownership is transferred you may not be able to change the permissions again, unless you are in a group that is allowed to do so. The only way to change the ownership of an item is to use the **chown** command in a Terminal window (see "Basic UNIX Commands" on page 338).

Group

If group names have been configured by your system administrator, you can allow other members of your group access to your files by setting the appropriate permissions using the Attributes Inspector. Users belonging to a group who are not the owner of an item are granted only the permissions provided to the group by the owner.

Only the root user can create and modify groups and assign users to them. If you would like to be a member of a particular group or to begin using groups, contact your system administrator. If you need to use groups to manage access to items in the file system, the root user can create as many as are necessary using the UserManager and NetInfoManager applications located in the **NextAdmin** folder.

Other (World)

Any user who is not the owner of a file or folder and is not a member of the same group as its owner is granted the privileges provided to other.

Assigning Permissions

To examine or modify the permissions to a file, folder, or application, select the item in the File Viewer and display the Attributes Inspector (see Figure 5-5). The lower portion of the Attributes Inspector displays the item's current permissions. To allow a permission, place a check mark in the appropriate location in the permission matrix. When you click a check mark, it will be replaced with an X and deny the permission. After you have set up the permission matrix, click OK to apply the permissions to the selected item in the File Viewer.

Granting write permissions to world means anyone who can log into the computer will be able to read, change, or destroy the file or folder with this permission. This is not something you would often want to do. Be very careful not to provide other write permission to folders containing sensitive information.

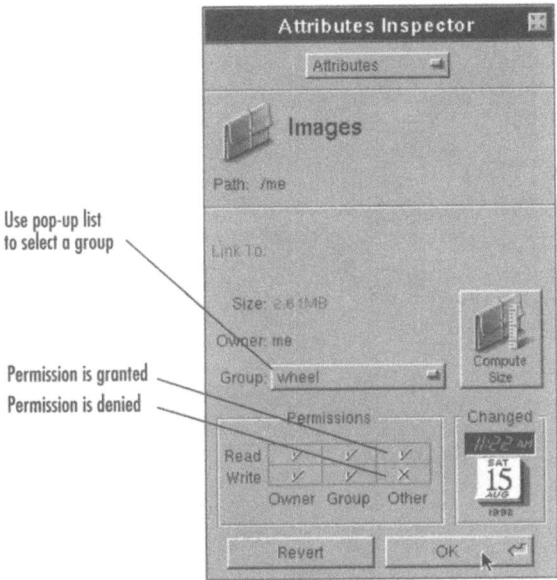

**Figure 5-5
File and Folder
Permissions**

Use the Attributes Inspector to modify access to a file or folder. When you're finished, click OK to save your changes.

You may have noticed that the Attributes Inspector in Figure 5-5 contained a second pop-up list containing group names. When the system administrator includes you as a member of more than one group, the names of each group will appear in a pop-up list. If you're a member of only one group, the group name appears instead of the pop-up list. The pop-up list is used to allow members of a particular group access to the file or folder you are inspecting.

5.2 Contents Inspector

The Contents Inspector can be used to examine the contents of files stored in sound (SND), tagged image file format (TIFF), Encapsulated PostScript (EPS), Rich Text Format (RTF), or Rich Text Format Directory (RTFD) format, and set the sort order for folders. Using the Contents Inspector, you can play a sound file and look at an image quickly without having to start an application. Even if you don't have an application installed that can open the file, you can often use the Contents Inspector to view the file's contents. The sort order you select for a folder determines the way in which items will be displayed in the File Viewer after you choose Sort Icons from the View menu.

Inspectors

To display the contents Inspector, choose Inspector from the Tools menu, and then select Contents from the Inspector's pop-up list. The keyboard shortcut for the Contents Inspector is Command-2. If the Inspector is already open, you only need to select Contents from its pop-up list to examine the contents of a file. Remember that the Inspector displays information about the currently selected file or folder in the File Viewer, so be sure to check the file name (see Figure 5-6).

**Figure 5-6
File Contents Inspection**

The Contents Inspector can preview many types of files, including graphics (top left), folders (top right), sounds (bottom left), and files (bottom middle). When NEXTSTEP is unable to display the contents of the selected item, it displays the No Contents Inspector message (bottom right).

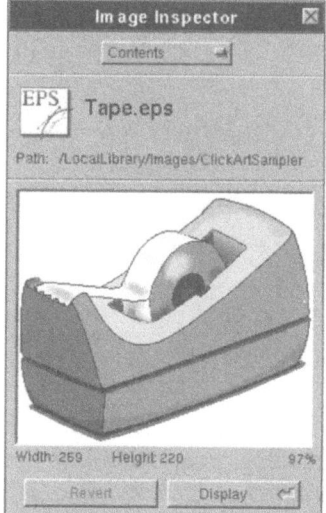
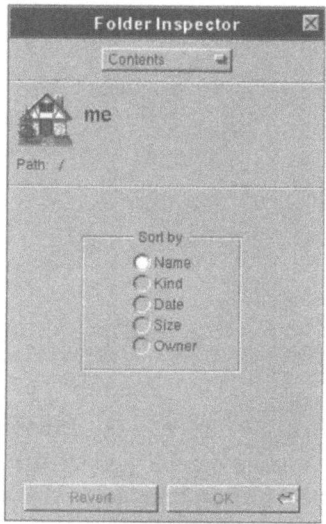
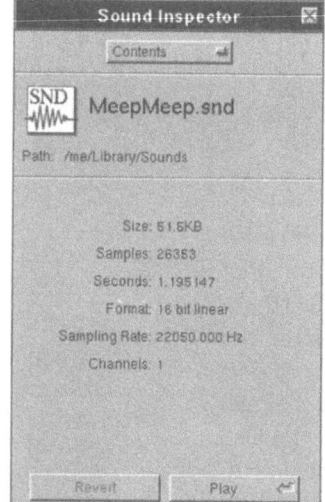
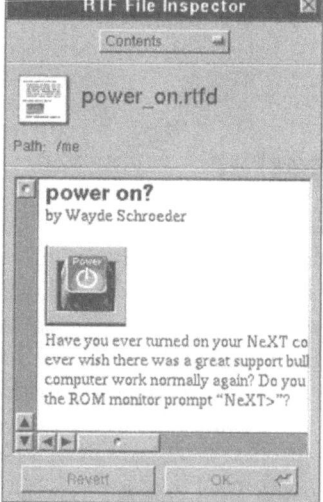
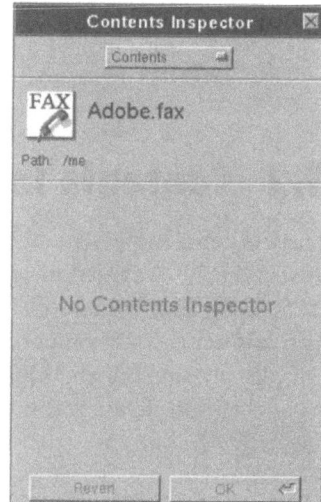

Contents Inspector

To preview an image file, select the file in the File Viewer. If the image is extremely large or complex, or if you have many applications running, it may take a long time for the image to be displayed. Typically, it takes only a few seconds for the Inspector to display an image or play a sound.

> When you are inspecting a text files in RTF or RTFD format, you can scroll to read the entire document in the Inspector and can even copy and paste the text from the Inspector into another document.

If you inspect the contents of a sound file, you will see a button named Play in the Inspector along with information pertaining to the sound. Click Play to hear the sound. If you cannot hear the sound or the sound is too loud, press the speaker volume keys, located to the left of the power key on the keyboard, to adjust the speaker volume.

When you inspect the contents of a folder, the Inspector displays a list of sorting orders you can use to display the folder's contents in the File Viewer. You can have NEXTSTEP sort a folder's contents by name, date, or size, or you can choose Custom to prevent NEXTSTEP from sorting a folder's contents. The Custom option allows you to place the icons in any order and location in the File Viewer you choose (like Windows and the Macintosh). If you later choose to sort the folder's contents, choose a sort order in the Contents Inspector, and then sort the icons using this order by choosing Sort from the workspace's Window menu.

While the Contents Inspector can inspect many file formats, it has limitations. When the Contents Inspector displays "No Contents Inspector," it cannot read the selected file's format. In this case, you will need to open the document using an application. Since you are already viewing the Inspector, you may want to use the Tools Inspector to see which applications on your computer can open the document. You will learn more about the Tools Inspector in section 6.0.3, "Using the Tools Inspector".

> You can extend the Contents Inspector's ability to preview files using a filter service. A filter service allows an application to share its ability to convert files from one format to another. For example, when you install Image Agent by Bäcchus, all of your applications, including the Contents Inspector, will be able to open or import over 40 new image file formats. Filter services are transparent. After installing one, the only way you'll know it's working is that other applications are suddenly able to open or import files they couldn't open or import before.

Rather than take time to start up an application to view a file, you can have NEXTSTEP display it in the Contents Inspector when you double-click the image's icon in the File Viewer. This trick makes browsing files quick and easy. If you decide to edit the image, choose Tools from the Inspector's pop-up list, and double-click the application you would like to open the image. The Inspector is able to display EPS, TIFF, PostScript, RTF, and RTFD files.

To set up Inspector previewing, perform the following steps:

1. Select the an image file's icon in the File Viewer.
2. Choose Inspector from the File menu.
3. Choose Tools from the pop-up list.
4. Select the NeXT icon.
5. Click OK.

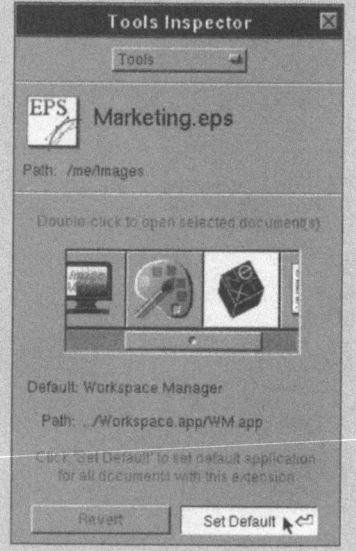

An obvious shortcoming is the Inspector's inability to preview *ASCII* (text with no formatting) files. If you want to preview a lot of documents without opening them into an application, you can work around this shortcoming by renaming text files so that they have an **rtf** extension. Remember that even though you are renaming the document and fooling NEXTSTEP into thinking it contains rich text (text with formatting), the text in the document will remain in ASCII format. After previewing the document you can remove the **rtf** extension.

> If you keep the Inspector open and visible in the workspace at all times, you will have instant access to detailed information about every file you select in the File Viewer. However, don't leave the Inspector in the Contents display unless you want to inspect each file you select, because drawing image files in the Inspector panel can slow performance significantly.

5.3 Tools Inspector

The Tools Inspector is used to set the default application for particular file formats. When you select a file in the File Viewer and open the Tools Inspector, it will display the icons of every available application that can open the file, based on the selected file's extension. We'll find out more about this inspector later when we learn about managing applications. If you want to skip ahead and read more about the Tools Inspector, turn to section 6.0.3, "Using the Tools Inspector".

5.4 Access Control Inspector

The Access Control Inspector is used to extend your ability to assign permissions to a file beyond that provided by the Attributes Inspector. The Access Control Inspector extends the permissions matrix to include a row for execute privileges and provides a check box so you can assign permissions to every item within a folder at the same time (see Figure 5-7).

Inspectors

Figure 5-7
The Access Control Inspector

The Access Control Inspector includes a new row in the permissions matrix for execute permissions and allows you to apply changes in permissions to every item within a folder at the same time.

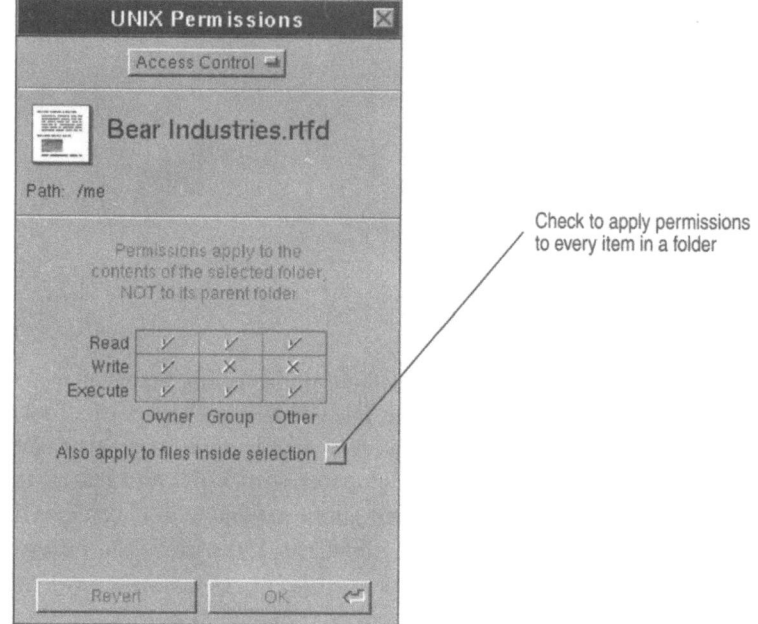

Check to apply permissions to every item in a folder

Often you will want the permissions of items within a folder and its subfolders to share the same permissions. However, when you assign permissions to a folder, NEXTSTEP will not change the permissions of items within the folder unless you tell it do so. In earlier releases of NEXTSTEP, you had to assign these privileges to each item one at a time or use a UNIX command in the Terminal application. Using the switch below the permissions matrix, you can apply permissions to every item within the selected folder in a single step.

You can also change the permissions for several different items at the same time by grouping them in a File Viewer, and then modifying the permissions displayed in the Attributes or Access Control Inspector. When you view the permissions of a group of items, dashes appear in place of check marks and X's in the permissions matrix (see Figure 5-8).

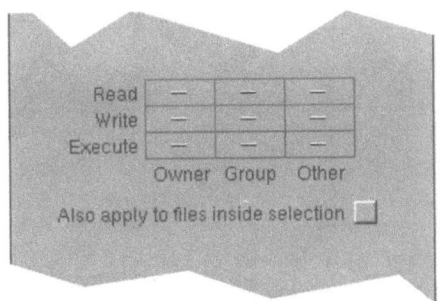

**Figure 5-8
Dashes in the Permissions Matrix**

When more than one item is selected, each permission is displayed as a dash instead of an X or check mark.

To grant a permission to all of the selected files at once, click a dash in the permissions matrix. The dash will turn into a check mark. Click OK to apply the new permission. Similarly, click a check mark to make an X appear and deny a permission for the selected group of files.

You can set the default permissions for all new files and folders you create using the Preferences application as described in "Expert Preferences" on page 297. Setting default permissions wisely can save you time that would be wasted if you had to set permissions for every new file. By default, NEXTSTEP sets permissions so that new files can be read or executed by world, and modified (write permission) only by the owner. These defaults are fine unless you want to prevent other users from reading your files. Several alternative permission settings are illustrated in Table 5-2, with the safest near the top and the least safe settings near the bottom.

Table 5-2 Permissions Settings

Setting	Description
Read ✓ X X Write ✓ X X Execute ✓ X X Owner Group Other	Only the owner can read and change the file. This is the default setting.
Read ✓ ✓ X Write ✓ X X Execute ✓ X X Owner Group Other	Only the owner and group can read the file; only the owner can change it. Group members can also copy it and make changes to the copy, but not change the original file.

Table 5-2 Permissions Settings (continued)

Setting	Description
Read ✓ ✓ ✗ Write ✓ ✓ ✗ Execute ✓ ✓ ✗ Owner Group Other	Only the owner and group can read and change the file.
Read ✓ ✓ ✓ Write ✓ ✗ ✗ Execute ✓ ✓ ✓ Owner Group Other	Everyone can read the file. Everyone can also copy it to their account and make changes to it, but not make changes to the original file.
Read ✓ ✓ ✓ Write ✓ ✓ ✓ Execute ✓ ✓ ✓ Owner Group Other	Everyone can read and change the file.

5.5 The Address Inspector

The Workspace Manager contains a special Inspector that is not in the Inspector's pop-up list. It is called the Address Inspector. The Address Inspector is used to view and modify NEXTSTEP's built-in address books feature. NEXTSTEP address books are normally used to select a fax recipient when using a fax-modem, but even if you don't have access to a fax modem, you can still take advantage of this feature. With the previous version of NEXTSTEP, you had to enter fax numbers, names, and telephone numbers in the Fax panel when you wanted to send a fax. Starting with NEXTSTEP release 3.1, you can now manage an address book in the workspace. Address books are stored in **~/Library/Addresses**. To help you get started, NEXTSTEP provides a sample address book named **Example.addresses**. You can use this address book to learn more about creating, modifying, and removing addresses and to create a new address book of your own. If you don't have a fax-modem, you won't be creating a personal address book using the Fax panel. In this case, duplicate the **Example.addresses** file to create as many individual address books as you want. You

You can use the Address Inspector to maintain telephone and address information for personal or business associates as you would with a rolodex file even if you don't have a fax modem available.

might like one for personal addresses and another for business addresses. There is no "create an address book" command, so duplicating the sample address book is the only way to create one yourself.

Since an address book works just like a file, you can copy and move address books just like every other file in NEXTSTEP to trade address books with other users or back them up on floppy disks. You can also send an address book to another user using electronic mail as described in "Adding Voice Messages" on page 191. Addresses in an address book can be changed, removed, or added using the Fax panel in any application or using the Address Inspector in the workspace.

Inspecting Addresses

Before you can use the Address Inspector, you must open an address book. Double-click the **Addresses** folder in a File Viewer. Don't be fooled by its rolodex file icon. It is still a folder, albeit a special one. When you double-click an address book icon, it will automatically open in a new File Viewer so you can see the names in your address book. To view the information associated with a name, double-click a name in the address book browser. Because you are inspecting an address book, an Address Inspector will appear and display information about the entry, including the name, electronic mail address (if applicable), home telephone number, and work telephone number (see Figure 5-9). The Address Inspector provides a text field in which you can place type information that doesn't belong in the other text fields.

Address book files display this rolodex icon in the File Viewer.

Adding Addresses

To add a name to an address book choose New Address from the File menu. The New Address item will only appear when an address book is the key window. A new icon will appear with the name **Joe Smith**, in the Address book File Viewer. Type a new name and press Return to change it. Typically, you'll want to enter the last name first, a comma, and the first name last. This allows you to view the list in alphabetical order by last name. You can change the name of any member's icon at any time by highlighting it, typing the new name, and pressing Return just as you would to rename any other item in a File Viewer. Finally, enter detailed information in the Address Inspector panel and click OK to save it (see Figure 5-9).

To modify information for an existing address, select it in the File Viewer, open the Address Inspector if it isn't already visible, and change or enter the information in the appropriate text field of the Address Inspector. When you're finished entering the information, click OK to save it.

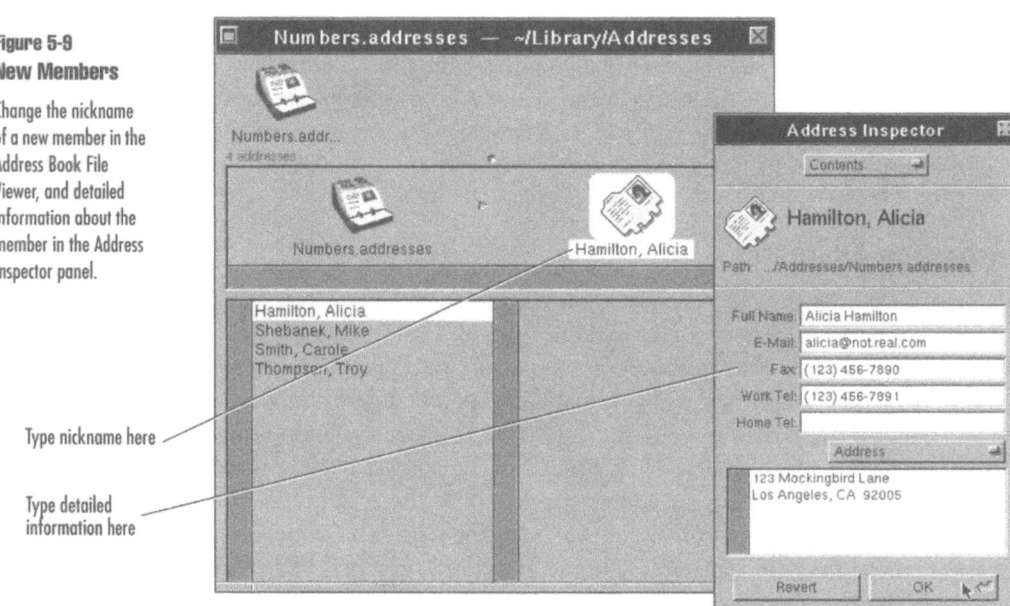

Figure 5-9
New Members

Change the nickname of a new member in the Address Book File Viewer, and detailed information about the member in the Address Inspector panel.

Type nickname here

Type detailed information here

Creating Groups

If you correspond with a particular group of people often, perhaps a team of colleagues at work or school, you can group them together within an address book under a single group name. When you want to send a fax to everyone in the group, you can specify the group name as the recipient instead of addressing and sending a fax to each member individually. This is very similar to sending everyone carbon copies of a letter through the mail. While inspecting an address book, you can create a new group by choosing New Group from the Workspace Manager's File menu (see Figure 5-10). Unless you are inspecting an address book, the New Group command will not appear in the File menu.

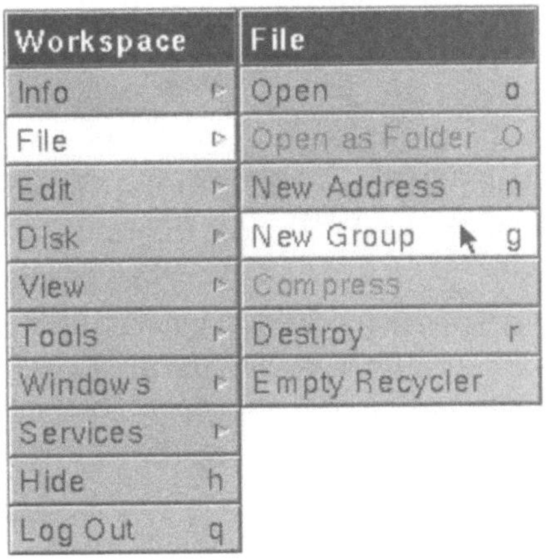

The Address Inspector

**Figure 5-10
Address Book Commands**

Unless you are inspecting an address book, you will not see the New Address and New Group commands in the File menu.

When you choose New Group, you will see a new icon in the address book browser, named Group, that looks like a stack of rolodex cards (see Figure 5-11). NEXTSTEP already selects the entire name when you create a new group so you need only type a new one to replace it. If you happen to click to deselect the name of the group, select it again to change the name, just as you would with any other icon. The name you enter should uniquely identify its members so you can remember who the group name represents when you see it in the Fax panel.

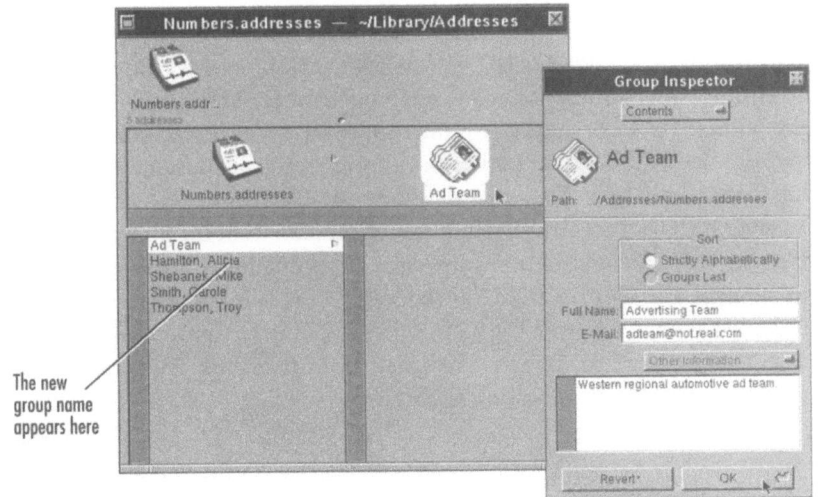

**Figure 5-11
To Create a Group**

To create an address book group, choose New Group from the File menu while inspecting an address book. Name the Group, then type detailed information about the group in the Group Inspector and click OK.

Adding a Name to a Group

A person can belong to any number of groups. You can also place any number or combination of names and groups into a group. First, make the group icon easy to access by dragging it onto the address book window's shelf (see Figure 5-12). You can drag one or more individual or group icons from the icon path onto the group icon on the shelf to add it to the group. NEXTSTEP will link the names to the group list as you drop the icon onto the group icon. Notice how the arrow cursor changes to a link cursor when you drag the icon onto the group icon. The names are only linked, rather than moved, into a group so that you can still address a fax individually when necessary. You can inspect the membership of a group at any time by selecting the group name in the address book browser. The names of group members will appear in italics.

Link cursor

Removing a Name from a Group

To remove a name from a group, open the address book window, select the name (which appears in italics) in the group members list and choose Destroy from the File menu. When the attention panel appears, click Destroy. NEXTSTEP will remove the name from the group but not from the address book. If you change your mind, click Cancel in the attention panel to keep the name in the address book.

Removing a Name from an Address Book

To remove a name from an address book, select the name (which does not appear in italics) and choose Destroy from the File menu. You will see an attention panel asking if you are sure you want to remove the entry from the address book. Be sure you want to remove them before you click OK, because you will have no opportunity to retrieve this information after it has been destroyed. You can also drag an icon from an address book browser into the recycler. When you drag an icon from the address browser into the recycler an attention panel appears asking if you are sure you want to remove this person from the address book (see Figure 5-13). Click Destroy to remove it from the address book, Cancel to leave it in the book, or Silent Destroy to remove the name from the book and prevent the attention panel from appearing again.

If you choose Silent Destroy, the next time you drag an address icon to the recycler, it will be destroyed immediately, with no opportunity for recovery and without a warning. Choose this option carefully!

The Address Inspector

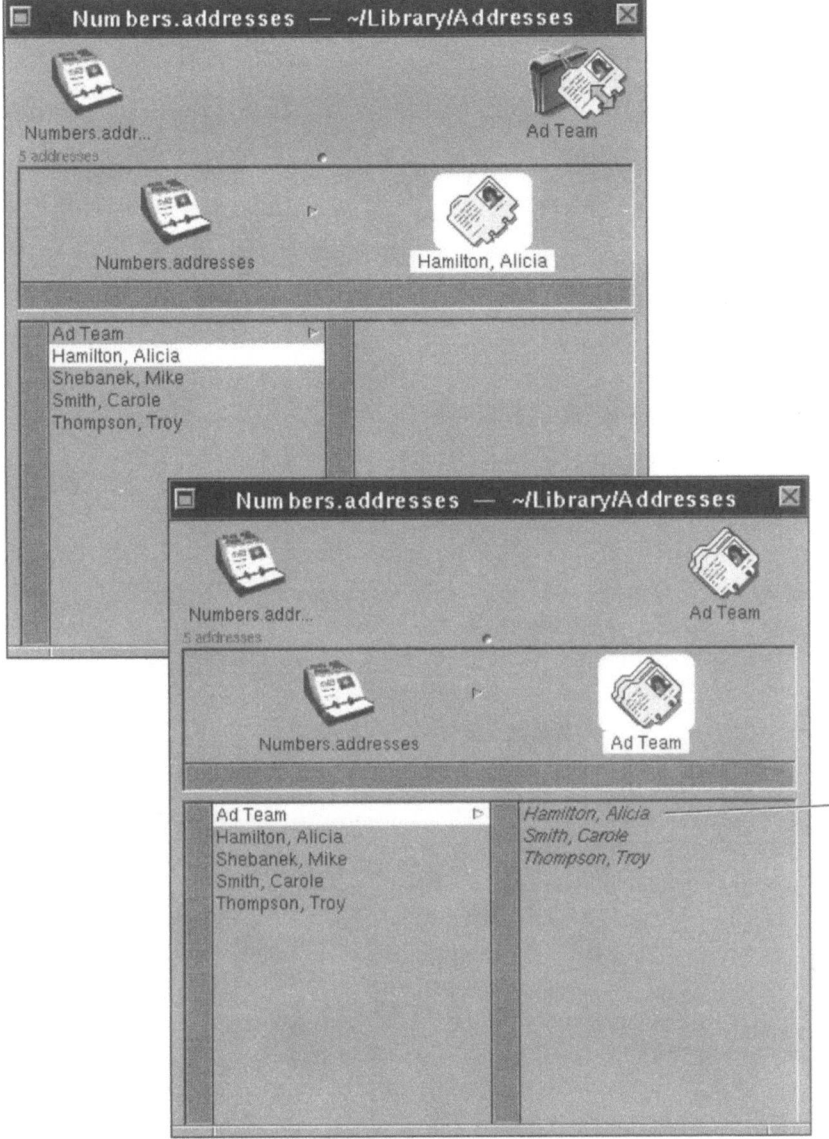

**Figure 5-12
To Add a Member to an Address Book Group**

To add a member to a group, place the group icon on the shelf, then drag a member icon onto it (top). The arrow will change shape to indicate that a name is being added to the group. You will then see the name in the Address Book browser (bottom).

The new name appears here

**Figure 5-13
To Delete a
Name from an
Address Book**

When you drag a member's icon into the recycler, this attention panel appears to verify that you want to remove the name.

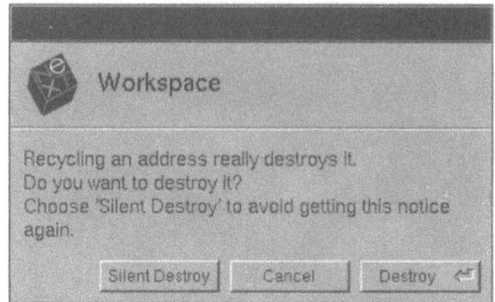

Inspecting an Address Book

When you select an address book icon inside the address book File Viewer, and then open or display the Address Inspector, you will see several interesting features for manipulating the address book. Buttons allow you to sort the names in the address book alphabetically, or alphabetically but with the group names at the bottom of the list. There is also a text field in which you can type notes about the address book. Select Other Information from the pop-up list to enter notes (see Figure 5-14).

Generating an Address List

One of the nicest features of this Inspector is that it automatically create a text document in RTF format that contains information about all of the members in the address book. To generate an RTF File from an address book, select the address book's icon in the Address Book File Viewer, and then click Generate RTF File in the Address Book Inspector panel. The document will automatically appear in the Edit application where you can save it, copy and paste it, or destroy it. The type of information and the order in which it is displayed can be displayed by selecting RTF File Template from the pop-up list in the Address Inspector (see Figure 5-14). Each field name will appear in the text area of the Inspector panel. You can edit this area, adding or removing text as desired, to create a customized listing. When you have completed your changes, click OK to save the changes, and then click Generate RTF File to see the listing using the new template. Changes to the RTF template are saved for as long as you keep the address book browser open.

The Address Inspector

If you make changes you don't want to keep, click Revert. If you make and save changes to the RTF file template, but you want to use the standard template, close the address book browser, and open it again. The original RTF file template will be restored. After you generate an RTF file, you can modify it further, using the Edit application or another word processor, or import the list of names and information into a database application. You can also use this list as a checklist when sending invitations, scheduling a conference, or posting a class roster. You'll find many more inventive ways to use the address list as you work with NEXTSTEP.

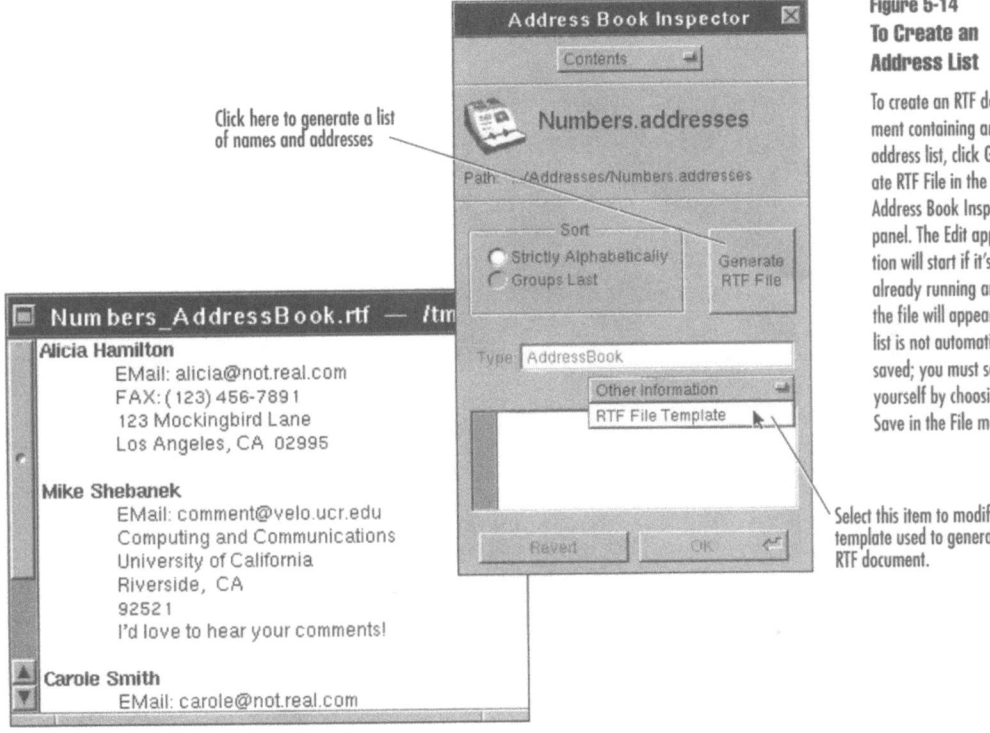

**Figure 5-14
To Create an Address List**

To create an RTF document containing an address list, click Generate RTF File in the Address Book Inspector panel. The Edit application will start if it's not already running and the file will appear. The list is not automatically saved; you must save it yourself by choosing Save in the File menu.

Select this item to modify the template used to generate the RTF document.

Applications
Applications
Applications
Applications
Applications

6

Application Management

Some of the most powerful and innovative applications available today run on NEXTSTEP. They perform such diverse tasks as word processing, three-dimensional imaging, desktop publishing, statistical analysis, image processing, faxing, and financial accounting. NEXTSTEP seamlessly integrates applications so they work together as if you were using a single application. With most computer systems, exchanging data between applications is either impossible or so difficult that using more than one application to accomplish a task is only for computer gurus. With NEXTSTEP, using more than one application is easy, even for the novice.

This chapter describes how to start, monitor, hide, and unhide applications. It even gives a few tricks for starting applications automatically when you log in and setting the application that should open a particular type of document. In following chapters, you'll explore the features common to many NEXTSTEP applications and review the variety of applications included with in the NEXTSTEP user environment.

Application Management

6.0 Starting Applications

NEXTSTEP comes bundled with many applications. Most of these are stored in the **NextApps** folder, and others that you or your system administrator have installed can be found in the **LocalApps** folder or your own **~/Apps** folder. There are several ways to start applications in NEXTSTEP, each with advantages and disadvantages. As you gain experiences with NEXTSTEP, you're certain to find a preferable method. However, don't discount the flexibility provided by other methods; they can save you time and allow you to select an appropriate application with little effort. Any of the following methods can be used at any time in any order.

6.0.0 Starting from the File Viewer

To start an application, double-click its icon in the in the listing or icon view, or its name in the browser view of the File Viewer. When you start an application from a File Viewer, its icon slides into the lower left corner of the workspace to let you know that it is running (see Figure 6-1). This special icon is called a tile and represents the running application. Should an application be placed in the background or made invisible, double-clicking its tile will make it reappear and become the foreground application. Tiles can be repositioned in the workspace by dragging them to another location. This may be desirable to make the icon easier to double-click so you can display its windows should they be hidden.

You can place applications in the dock so you can access them quickly.

6.0.1 Starting from the Application Dock

You can also start an application by double clicking its icon in the application dock. Because only applications can be placed in the application dock, it's often referred to simply as the dock. Each application icon in the dock contains three dots that indicate the application's status. The ellipsis appears when the application is not running and disappears when the application is running. This is an important distinction, because, as we shall soon see, applications can be hidden. The only way you'll know if an application in the dock is running is by looking for the ellipsis.

These dots indicate the application is not running.

The NeXT logo in the dock can be used to control the position of the entire dock. For example, you can drag the NeXT Logo up and down to reposition the dock along the upper or lower right side of the workspace. By dragging the logo down, you can hide all or part of the dock off screen

Starting   Applications

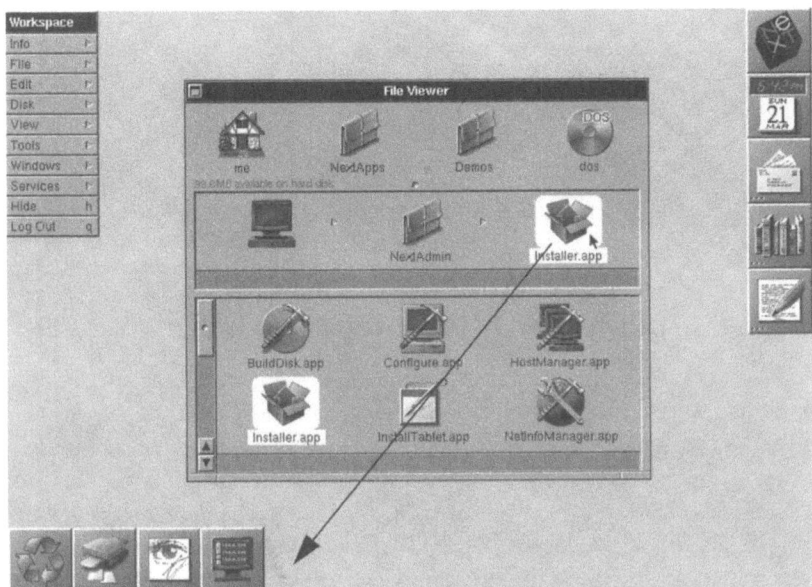

**Figure 6-1
Starting an
Application from
a File Viewer**

When you double-click an application icon in a File Viewer, its icon slides into the lower left corner of the workspace to indicate that it is running.

to gain more viewing area for other items. This can be very useful when you need a little extra room for a very large window, perhaps one that is in landscape (sideways) orientation. To see the entire dock again, drag the NeXT logo icon back up to display more icons in the dock. So that you can always restore the dock to its original position, NEXTSTEP does not allow you to move the NeXT logo off of the screen.

6.0.2 Double-Clicking a Document

Like Macintosh and Windows systems, you can also double-click a document to start an application. When you double-click a document, NEXTSTEP reads its extension to determine which application to use to open it. If more than one application is installed that can open the document, NEXTSTEP starts the application that has been selected in the Tools Inspector to be the default application. If the application that starts when you double-click a document is not the one you wanted to use, you can quit it, open the application of your choice, and then open the document using the application's Open command. To avoid this inconvenience you can set the file's default application using the Tools Inspector, described in the next section.

Application Management

If you can see both the application icon and the document you want to open, hold down the Command key and drag the document icon onto the application icon to start the application and open the document. As you drag the document, the arrow should change into the move cursor before you release the mouse button.

6.0.3 Using the Tools Inspector

The Tools Inspector is used to set the default application for particular file formats. When you select a file in the File Viewer and open the Tools Inspector, it will display the icons of every available application that can open the file, based on the selected file's extension. You cannot add or remove application icons from this list; they are determined automatically by NEXTSTEP. How does NEXTSTEP know which applications are available? It looks for them in the search path described in Table 6-1. If an application is not located in the search path, NEXTSTEP will not see it and its icon will not appear in the Tools Inspector. If you double-click a document whose application is not in the search path, NEXTSTEP will not be able to find and start it to open the document. By installing applications in appropriate directories as described in "Where to Install Applications" on page 269, you ensure that NEXTSTEP can find and open them.

Table 6-1 The Application Search Order

Search Order	Pathname	Description
1	~/Apps	Applications in your home folder.
2	/LocalApps	Applications loaded by the system administrator for use by every NEXTSTEP user.
3	/NextApps	Applications provided by NeXT and included as part of NEXTSTEP.
4	/NextAdmin	NEXTSTEP applications for system administration. Most of these applications are used only by the root user.

Starting Applications

To display the Tools Inspector, type Command-3 while in the workspace. Alternately, you can choose Inspector from the Tools menu, and then Tools from the Inspector's pop-up list. If NEXTSTEP finds more than three applications that can open the selected file, a horizontal scroller will appear in the Tools Inspector so that you can see entire collection of application icons (see Figure 6-2).

When you select an application in the Tools Inspector and click Set Default, it will become the default application for files that share the same file name extension. For example, you can set the IconBuilder application to start each time you double-click a file with a **tiff** extension, or you can have WriteNow start when you double-click a file with an **rtf** extension. When you set a default application, it will remain in effect until you select and set a different one, even after you log out or power off the computer.

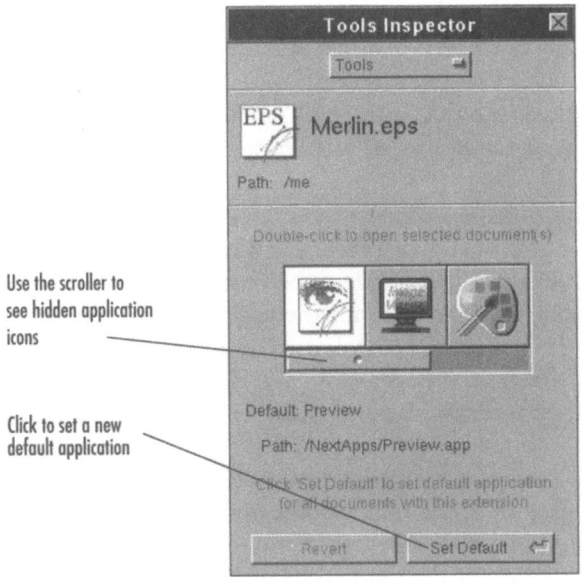

Figure 6-2
The Tools Inspector

The Tools Inspector displays a list of applications that can open the currently selected file. To open the file in a particular application, double-click the application icon in the Tools panel.

The Tools Inspector also allows you to start up an application without setting it as the default. Select a document in a File Viewer, open the Tools Inspector, and double-click the desired application icon in the Inspector panel. This will not change the default application, but it will open the document using the application you double-clicked. Don't worry if you see the Inspector panel disappear. It is normal for it to disappear when the application is started and the workspace is placed in the background. When you return to the workspace, the Inspector panel will appear again in its same location.) Double-clicking an application icon in the Tools Inspector also allows you to open a file in any application without having to locate the application in the dock or File Viewer.

6.1 Monitoring Applications

One of NEXTSTEP's greatest strengths is its ability to work on more than one task concurrently. Tasks that are in progress are called processes and many are hidden in the background so you don't see them. Processes can include tasks you initiate, such as running an application, copying a file, formatting a removable disk, deleting a file, and searching for a document. Even when you haven't initiated a task, there are numerous UNIX processes in progress simply to maintain the computer running. (You can view these using the UNIX command **ps –a** in a terminal window.) NEXTSTEP can perform background activities such as networking, allocating memory, and managing multiple simultaneous logins without user intervention. Such processes, while critical to NEXTSTEP's function, are not generally of interest to the typical NEXTSTEP user. Processes that you initiate are generally referred to as "interesting tasks," and are the subject of this section.

Imagine how cluttered the screen would be if NEXTSTEP displayed every one of numerous processes. While most of these activities occur in the background, they affect the performance of your system and may inhibit your ability to perform other tasks. For example, you cannot eject a disk on which files are being deleted, nor can you move files while they are being copied. NEXTSTEP allows you to monitor interesting processes by viewing their progress, stopping them temporarily, or stopping them altogether.

To monitor background processes, open the Processes panel in the workspace by choosing Processes from the Tools menu, or by using the Command-Shift-P shortcut. If there are background processes, they will be listed in the Processes panel. If there are none, the Processes panel will display a list of running applications. You can choose which list you see by selecting Background or Applications from the Processes panel pop-up list (see Figure 6-3).

Monitoring Applications

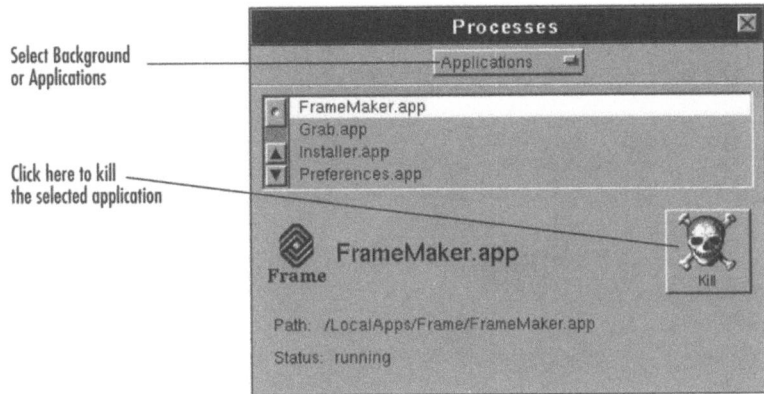

**Figure 6-3
Killing a Crashed Application**

Using the Processes panel, you can monitor the progress of background tasks, kill them, and kill applications that have crashed. To kill a crashed application select its name in the scrolling list and click Kill.

You can use the Processes panel to monitor, pause, resume, or kill (end) background processes, such as copying, deleting, initializing, and computing the size of a folder. The most common background task you will monitor is a copying process because it is such a common task and because it often takes a long time to complete compared with other background tasks. To monitor the progress of background tasks, display the Processes panel and choose Background from the pop-up list, if necessary. You can watch the progress of a particular process by selecting its name in the scrolling list. To kill a background task, select its name in the scrolling list and click Stop (see Figure 6-4). The process will stop immediately, and you will be given no opportunity to continue the process, so be careful when stopping a process. If you would like to temporarily suspend a background process, click Pause instead of Stop. When you click Pause, the button will change to Resume, which when clicked, will allow the background process to continue until completed.

When there are several background tasks in progress, you can force NEXTSTEP to complete one of them first by pausing the others. When the process is finished, you can resume the next process or resume all of the remaining processes.

Application Management

Figure 6-4
Stopping a Process
Click Stop to immediately end the selected background process.

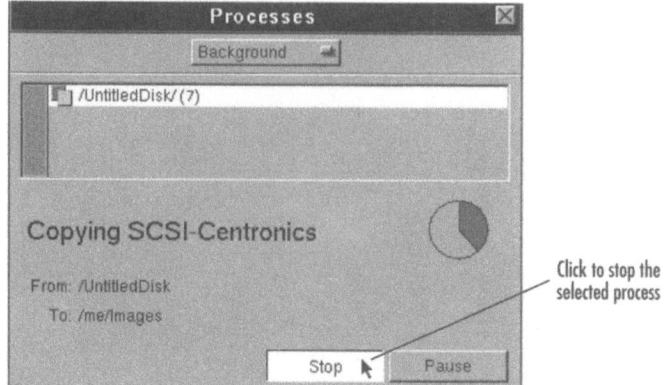

6.2 Hiding and Unhiding Applications

When many applications are running, each with one or more windows, you can easily get confused as to which windows and menus belong to each application and, as a result, accidentally edit or modify the wrong document. To simplify things, NEXTSTEP allows you to *hide* applications including all of their windows and menus. Running applications can be hidden by choosing Hide from the application's main menu, or by using typing Command-h. You can't hide an application that is not running, because it does not have any open windows or active menus. Hiding an application makes all of its menus, open documents, and panels invisible. There is no way to hide only its menus or only a particular window.

Hiding an application makes it invisible but allows it to continue running. If an application is in the middle of an operation, hiding it does not stop that operation. Hiding an application also does not affect its open or unsaved documents. When you make the application visible again, the documents will appear just as they were before they were hidden. You can make some or all of the running applications hidden at the same time. To make an application visible again, double-click its icon in the dock, or the small icon at the bottom of the workspace that was created when the application was started. Hiding an application that you will be using again is much more efficient that quitting it, because it can be recalled within seconds whereas it may a half minute or more to start an application.

6.3 Auto-Starting an Application

As you use your computer, you will find that you often start the same few applications each time you log in as you prepare to work. If this is a routine you repeat often, you can place the applications in the dock and have NEXTSTEP automatically start them for you. To make applications in the dock start automatically when you log in, choose Preferences in the Workspace Manager's Info menu and Dock from the pop-up list (see Figure 6-5). A small representation of the application dock will appear in the panel listing the names of applications located in the dock. Click to place a check mark next to an application's name to cause the application to be started up automatically each time you log in. In Figure 6-5, the Preferences, PrintManager, and SleepPrinter applications are set to start automatically. Workspace Manager is gray because you cannot change its setting. It must always run at login time to provide the workspace.

To turn off the auto-start feature, return to this panel and click to remove the check mark. By default, the Preferences application is set to start up automatically so that you will have a calendar and clock in the dock. You can have any combination of applications in the dock start up automatically, but the more applications that auto-start, the longer you will have to wait before you can begin working.

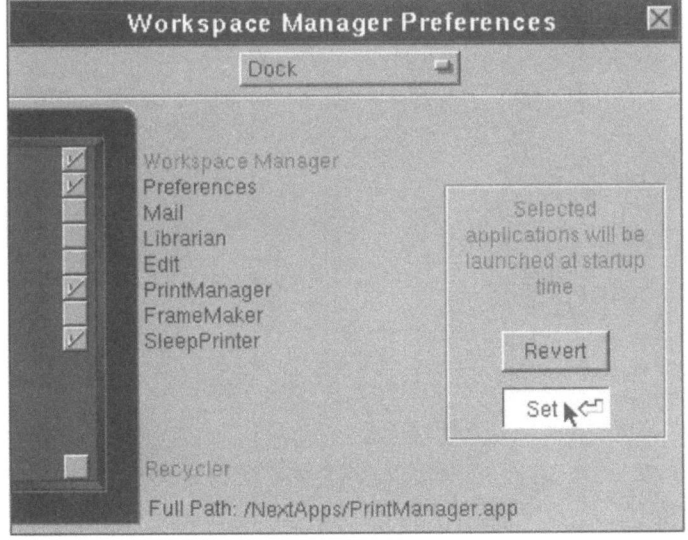

**Figure 6-5
Setting
Dock Options**

To make an application in the dock start up automatically when you log in, click to place a check mark next to its name in the Workspace Manager Preferences panel and click Set.

6.4 Learning Tricks

When you hold down certain keys on the keyboard and click or drag items in the workspace, magical things happen. After a bit of experimentation, you may find even more. Table 6-2 describes several popular tricks.

Table 6-2 Hidden Application Features

Action	Description
Command-double-click a running application icon	Hides all other running applications.
Alternate-double-click a running application icon	Starts application a second time as if it were another application. This is called "creating another instance" of an application.
Command-drag a running application icon	Allows you to reposition the application's icon in the workspace and free space in the dock. This works with the recycler too.

7
Application Features

One of the many advantages of NEXTSTEP is the consistency with which its applications adhere to a well-defined set of interface guidelines. For example, many applications provide on-line help, allow you to open and save documents, select and apply different fonts and colors, and print. To ensure that these features are consistent in every application, NeXT provides developers with code for these features, called software objects. This is extremely advantageous to the programmer, but, even more important, it means these features will always appear and work in the same manner in every application. After you master these common features and commands, you will be able to quickly take advantage of a new application's specific features without having to relearn those they have in common. It sounds very simple but it is a powerful feature of NEXTSTEP.

This chapter describes each of the common features, panels, and commands found in many NEXTSTEP applications. Every one of these common features can be found in the Edit application provided with each copy of NEXTSTEP. If you happen to have a system running NEXTSTEP nearby, you might want to stop after each section and practice the concepts you just learned. Most of the features described in this chapter can be found in NEXTSTEP's Edit application. Features specific to Edit that are not described her will discussed later in Chapter 9, "Bundled Applications".

7.0 Attention Panels

When NEXTSTEP or a NEXTSTEP application needs to present information to you, it places the information in a special window called an *attention panel*. Attention panels are different from other windows in that they display fewer window controls and cannot be miniaturized. Panels always contain urgent information and often require you to click a button within the panel before you can continue working in the application. Figure 7-1 illustrates a typical attention panel reminding you to save changes to documents before quitting an application.

**Figure 7-1
Working with
Attention Panels**

An attention panel presents critical information and often requires you to click a button in order to continue with the current application.

With Windows and Macintosh systems, when an attention panel appears, you cannot continue working unless you click a button on the panel. If the attention panel message is confusing or offers you choices you don't like, you cannot continue until you resolve the situation. NEXTSTEP is much more friendly. If an attention panel appears, you can bypass it by switching to another application. When you can get help or resolve the problem, you can switch back to the application and click an appropriate button in the panel to continue. Meanwhile, you will have been able to use your computer for other tasks. For example, if you run out of disk space while saving a document, you can bypass the attention panel by switching to the workspace, delete a few files to make more space available, and return to the application to try saving the document again.

7.1 The Help Panel

Almost every application provides on-line help in the form of the Help panel. The Help panel has three components: Navigation controls, outline of help topics, and a text area (see Figure 7-2).

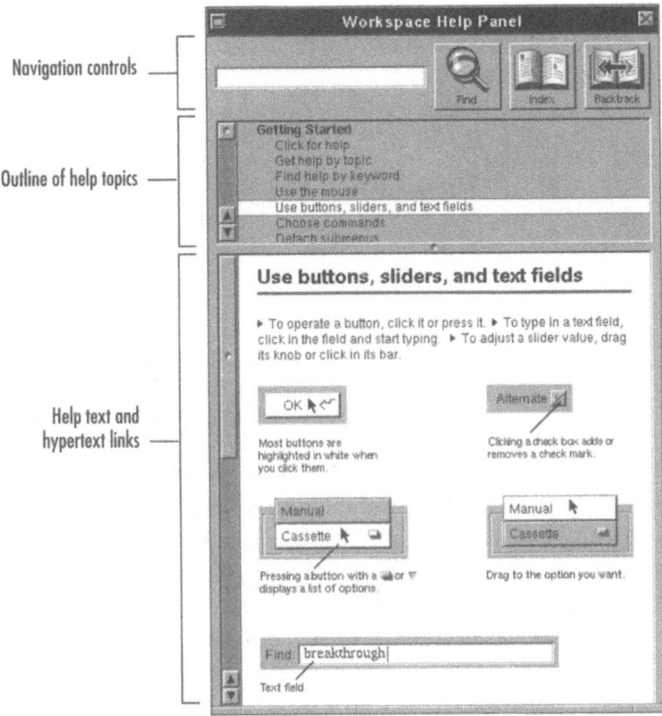

**Figure 7-2
Using the
Help Panel**

The Help panel displays information about the current application's commands and features.

You can use several methods to display the Help panel (see Table 7-1). Choose the method that is easiest to remember or works best for you. Using the keyboard, you can hold down Alternate and Control, and click an item on the screen, you'll see information about that item in a the Help panel. When you hold down Alternate and Control, the cursor will change to a question mark, to indicate that you are about to display the Help panel. Displaying the Help panel this way is referred to as context sensitive help because the Help panel will immediately open to a help item that relates to the item you click on the screen. If you are using a NeXT computer that has the NeXT ADB keyboard, you can press the Help key to change the cursor into a question mark and then click an item on

? Question mark cursor

the screen. The Help command can also be selected using the keyboard shortcut Command-Shift-?. If you prefer, you can choose Help from an application's Info menu to display the Help panel.

Table 7-1 Displaying the Help Panel

Method	Description
Alternate-Control-click	Displays the Help panel and information about the item you clicked on the screen.
Press Help, and then click an item on the screen	Displays the Help panel and information about the item you clicked on the screen. Works only on NeXT computers with ADB keyboard.
Command-Shift-?	Displays the Help panel.
Choose Help from Info menu	Displays the Help panel.

If you use the Help key or Alternate-Control keyboard shortcut to display the Help panel, information about the item you clicked will appear automatically when the Help panel appears. If the information cannot completely fit in the text area, a scroller appears so that you can scroll the text. Information in the Help panel is organized in a similar way for every help item. At the top of the text area is the name of the command or feature in large bold letters. Below the name are directions for using the feature and often an illustration. A thin line separates the description and directions from special notes regarding the feature or command. Finally, at the bottom of the help information is another section separated by a thin line that contains cross-references to related information. These references are linked so that clicking the diamond next to a reference causes the related information to appear in the Help panel. This linking of information, hypertext, makes accessing related information extraordinarily easy.

7.1.0   Help Panel Navigation

If you used the Help command or Command-Shift-? keyboard shortcut to display the Help panel, you'll need to enter a word or phrase in the navigation area text field or select an item from the help topics outline to display help information. To search for a key word, type it into the text field and

The Help Panel

click Find. If the word or phrase exists in the application's Help information, the first page on which it appears will be displayed in the text area with the word or phrase highlighted. To search for the next occurrence of the word or phrase, click Find again. To search for another topic, enter a different word or phrase and click Find.

If while reading information in the text area you see a link button, you can click it to display a related page of information in the Help panel. If you see another link button, you can click it to see still more related information. You can continue to click the link button, search for a word, or choose a topic from the outline in any combination necessary to find the information you are looking for.

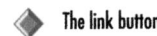

The link button

If you've made several search attempts or are using hypertext links, you may not be able to remember on which help page you started or where to find information you saw previously in the Help panel. The Help panel includes a Backtrack button which traces your steps in the Help panel so you can review every topic you've visited. Each time you click Backtrack, you will see the information from the previous help page until you reach the help page displayed when the Help panel was first opened.

Click Backtrack to revisit a help page you have already read.

At any time while viewing the Help panel, you can review the features of and instructions for using the Help panel by clicking Index. The topic outline will display topics describing how to use the Help panel itself, not the application to which the Help panel belongs.

7.1.1   Help Panel Tips

As you use the Help panel, don't forget that it's a window. You can drag the Help panel by its title bar to place it side by side with another window on the screen so you can read how to perform a procedure while actually performing it in the application's window. If the Help panel is too big, resize it so that you can see more of the application behind it. If you want to keep the Help panel within easy access yet out of the way, miniaturize it into a miniwindow. When you need it, it will be located at the bottom of the screen only a double-click away. You can also drag to select text and graphics in the Help panel text area, copy, and paste the selection into a document of your own for future reference.

Application Features

7.2 The Save Panel

Almost every NEXTSTEP application creates a file, generically called a document, containing information you create. When you create a document, it exists only in temporary RAM. Unless this information is copied from RAM onto a disk, the information is lost when you quit the application, log out, or turn the power off. To *save* a document, choose Save from the application's Document or File menu. The Save panel will appear so you can save the document to disk. You should use the Save command often as you work to minimize the loss of work due to an accident such as a power outage, disastrous editing change, system crash, or other mishap. By saving often, you can always retrieve a recent version of the document from disk and continue your work. In general, you should save your work about every 15 minutes. If you don't save your work from time to time, you accept the risk of losing all of your work since you last saved it to disk should a mishap occur.

The Save panel is similar in every application and contains a browser, Cancel, and OK buttons, and several icons (see Figure 7-3). To save a file, type the name you would like the file to have in the Name field, use the browser to select the folder in which it should be saved, and click OK.

**Figure 7-3
Using The
Save Panel**

The Save panel is used to save a document to disk. It features a browser for selecting a folder in which to save a document, and three buttons for instantly selecting your home folder a removable disk., or ejecting a disk.

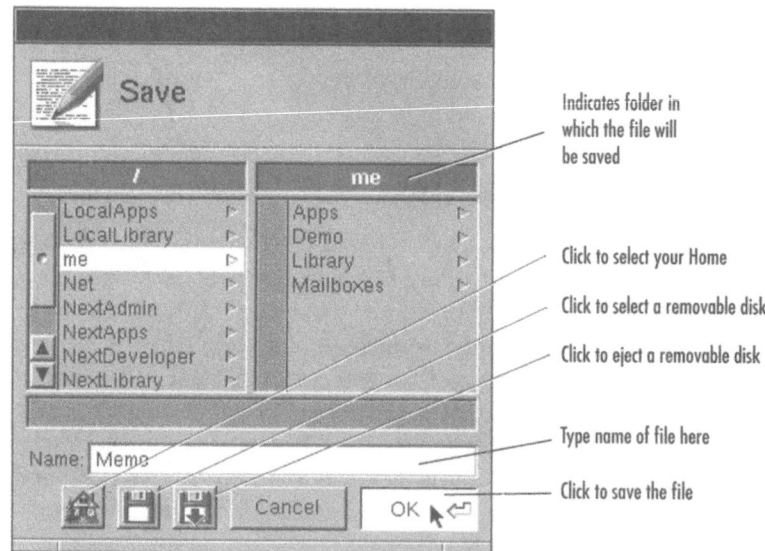

The Save Panel

Unless you have permission to write in other folders, you will always save documents in your home folder or folders within your home folder. So that you can easily select your home folder in the browser, the Save panel provides a home button (see margin). Clicking this button instantly selects your home folder in the Save panel's browser so you can quickly select a location for the document to be saved. The Save panel also contains a floppy disk button that when clicked, instantly selects a mounted removable disk. If more than one removable disk is mounted, subsequent clicks of the button select each disk in turn. If you need to eject a removable disk, click the eject button. If there's more than one removable disk mounted, select it in the Save panel browser and then click the eject button. Clicking Cancel will close the Save panel but not save your work.

 Home

 Removable disk

 Eject

7.2.0   Save Panel Tips

You can use several techniques in the Save panel to select a particular folder in the file system quickly and easily. You may have noticed the return arrow symbol on the OK button in previous illustrations (see margin). This symbol represents the Return key on the keyboard. Whenever you see it on a button in a panel, pressing Return will have the same effect as clicking the button with the mouse. You can also type a pathname instead of just a file name in the Save As text field to select or create a folder and name the file in one step. To save the document, click OK or press Return. This technique avoids using the browser and can save you a great deal of time when you know the pathname to the desired folder. If you want, you can also type a pathname but not the name of the file and click OK or press Return. This will instantly select the folder described by the pathname in the Save panel's browser. You can then type the name of the document, select another folder, or type a different pathname to complete the save process. You can also point and click to select folders using the browser. As you practice these techniques, you will soon develop a favorite method, and saving a file will become quick and easy.

When you save a document, the document's window is also updated. The name and pathname of the file will appear in its title bar, and the close button will display a solid X to indicate the document has been saved. If you forget whether or not a document has unsaved changes, one quick glance at the document window's close button will tell you.

 Saved

 Not saved

When to Use Save As Instead of Save

When you choose Save to save a document for the first time, the application will display the Save panel so that you can name the document and select a folder in which to save it. Each time you save the file thereafter, you will no longer need to enter this information. When you choose Save, the application will simply replace the older version on the disk with the current version on the screen. The Save panel is not necessary in this case because the application remembers the name and location of the document from the last time it was saved.

If you want to save the document using a different name or place it in a different folder, choose Save As instead of Save. The Save panel will reappear and allow you to select a new folder, enter a new name, or both, and save the document again. If you use Save As to change the location or name of the document, the original document will remain in the old folder with the old name.

The Save As command is especially useful when you are about to make a change to a document but want to keep the older version as well. Use it to make a new one with a different name. This way you will have two documents, one with the changes and one without them. If you don't want the old copy, you'll need to destroy it or place it in the recycler.

7.3 The Open Panel

When the application you want to use is already running, but the document you want to work with is not open, use the Open panel to open it. There is no need to close a document or quit the application to open a document. Instead, when the application is already running, choose Open from its File or Document menu to open the document. Almost every NEXTSTEP application allows you to have several documents open at the same time. You can use this feature to your advantage by placing them side by side for comparison or cutting and pasting text between them.

The Open panel (see Figure 7-4) is very similar to the Save panel. It contains a two-column browser, and home, floppy disk, Cancel, and OK buttons as well. To open a document using the Open panel, locate the document by clicking a folder name in the browser. Its contents will be displayed in the browser column to its right. If you click a file name, its name will appear in the text field at the bottom of the Open panel. When you have selected the appropriate file name, click OK to open it. As a shortcut, double-click the file name in the browser to select and open it.

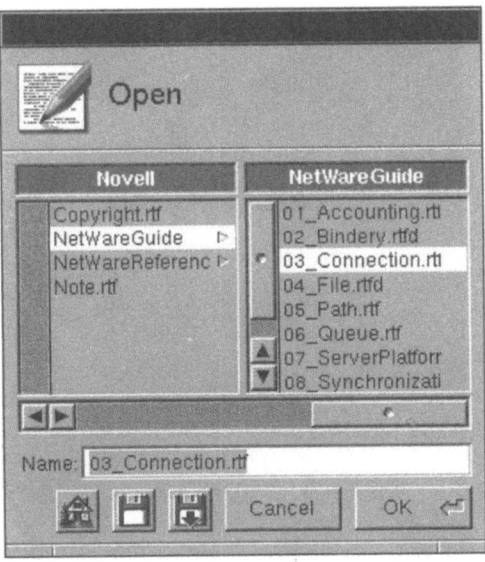

**Figure 7-4
Using The
Open Panel**

The Open panel is used to open a document when its application is already running. Like the Save panel, the Open panel contains a two-column browser and home and floppy disk buttons so that you can easily locate the file you want to open.

The Open panel also provides home, removable disk, and eject buttons so that you can quickly select your home folder or mounted floppy disk without having to retrace your steps back through the file system, and when necessary, easily eject a removable disk. Because most of your documents will be stored somewhere in your home folder or on a floppy disk, these shortcut can save a lot of time. You can also use the same shortcut techniques in the Open panel that you learned for the Save panel.

> NEXTSTEP allows you to drag an icon from a File Viewer onto an application's Open or Save panel instead of clicking home or using the panel's browser to select a file or folder. When you drag the icon onto the panel, the panel's browser will immediately change to reflect the item's location in the file system. Many third-party applications also support this feature. For example, to import a file into a document, drag its icon from a File Viewer onto the document. With a bit of experimentation you may find even more dragging shortcuts.

Application Features

7.4 Basic Text Editing

In almost every application, there is a need for entering and editing text. If not in the application's document, then at the very least, text editing is required in the Save panel to enter the name of the file. If you have used a graphical user interface before such as the Macintosh, Microsoft Windows, or OpenWindows, you'll find NEXTSTEP text editing very similar.

7.4.0 Inserting Text

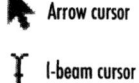

Arrow cursor

I-beam cursor

When you position the arrow cursor over a location that can or does contain text, the cursor changes from an arrow to an I-beam (see margin). Locations that can hold text are called text fields. To begin entering text in a text field, click a mouse button while pointing to it (see Figure 7-5). A blinking bar called an *insertion point* | appears to indicate where text will appear when you type on the keyboard. When the insertion point appears, you can roll the mouse to move the I-beam so that you can more easily see what you are typing. The I-beam is used only to position the insertion point and to select existing text. It does not need to remain in the text field as you type. To reposition the insertion point in another place, point and click the I-beam on that location. To insert text in the middle of existing text, to add a word for instance, click with the I-beam where you want the text to appear, and then type on the keyboard. The text will begin at the location of the insertion point. If you make a mistake while typing, you can delete text to the left of the insertion point by pressing the Delete. Do not use the arrow keys to delete text. They will only reposition the insertion point in the selected text field.

**Figure 7-5
Inserting Text**

To insert text in a document or text field, click the cursor where you want to place the text. When the blinking insertion point appears, begin typing. You can place the insertion point within existing text to insert text into the middle of existing text.

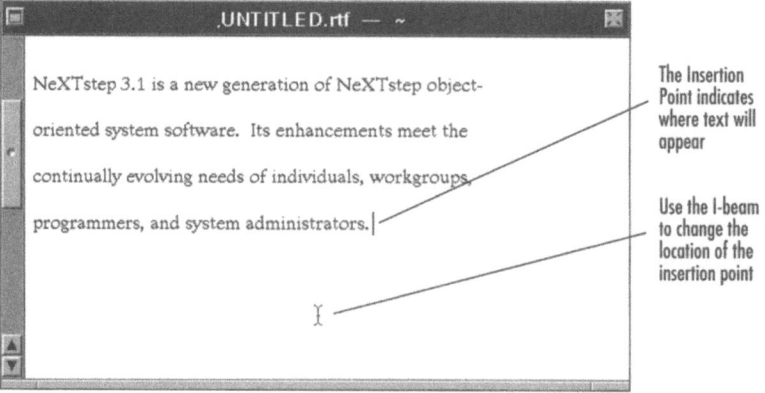

126

Basic Text Editing

7.4.1 Selecting Text

If you could only use the Delete key to delete text to the left of the insertion point, the computer would be little better than a typewriter. Fortunately, you can edit and replace text quickly and easily anywhere in the text. To modify, replace, or delete existing text, you must first select it. Selected text appears highlighted with a gray background (see Figure 7-6). To select text, position the I-beam in front of the first word or character to be selected, press and hold down a mouse button, drag the cursor to the end of the text to be selected, and release the mouse button. You do not have to trace over each character to be selected. NEXTSTEP will only select the text between the location if the I-beam where the mouse button was pressed and where the I-beam was located when the button was released. For example, to select several lines of text, drag the cursor diagonally with the mouse button held down. As you drag down, each line of text will be selected. If you select too much or too little text, release the mouse button, then click it once. This will unhighlight the text you selected so that you can try again.

Selecting text can also be accomplished in several other ways. These other methods can be used in any application that allows text editing in conjunction with or instead of dragging the mouse.

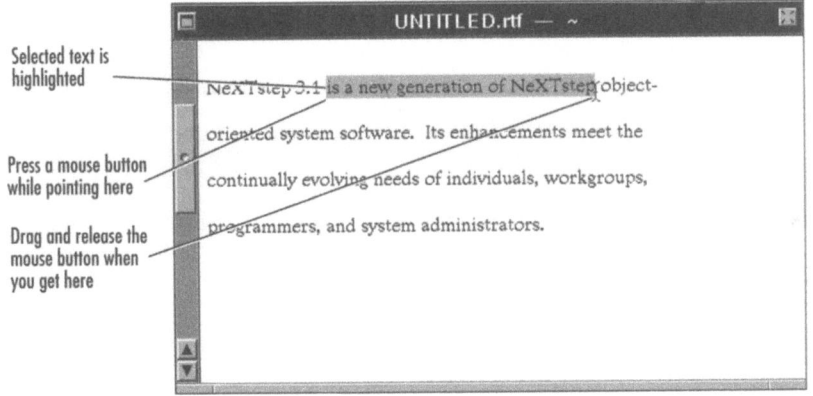

**Figure 7-6
Selecting Text**

To select text in a document or text field, position the I-beam at one end of the text, hold down a mouse button and drag the mouse to the other end of the text. You do not have to trace over each word to be selected. Simply start at the beginning of the text and drag diagonally to the end of the text.

Application Features

Extending a Text Selection

You can extend a selection by pressing and holding down the Alternate key and clicking a mouse button. (Many applications use the Shift key for this purpose as well.) All of the text from the insertion point to the location of the I-beam cursor will be selected. If text is already selected, hold down the Alternate key and clicking a mouse button extends the selection to include the text between the selected text and the position of the I-beam when the mouse button is clicked (see Figure 7-7). If you hold down the Alternate key and click the mouse button while the I-beam is within the currently selected text, the selection is shortened to include only the text from the beginning of the selection to the position of the I-beam when the mouse button is clicked.

**Figure 7-7
Extending the Selection**

If you want a selection to include more text (top), hold down the Alternate key and click again to extend the previous selection (bottom).

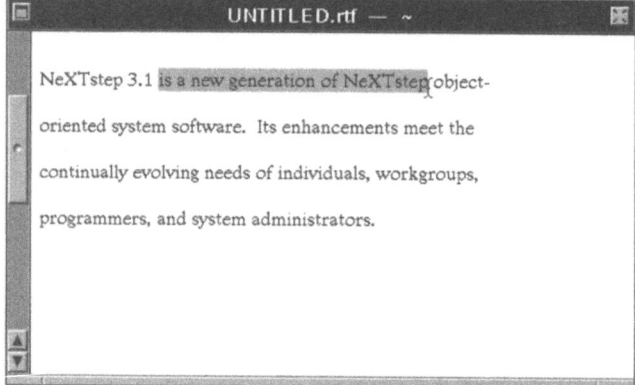

Hold down the Alternate key while clicking here to extend the selection

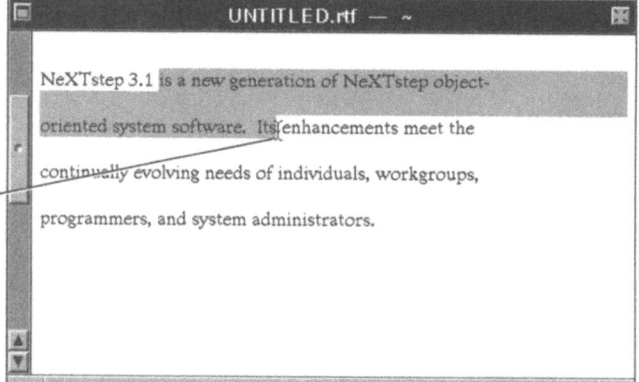

Double-clicking a word selects the word. To extend the current selection a word at a time, click a mouse button twice while pointing to a word but don't release the mouse button on the second click. Instead, drag the mouse to extend the selection a word at a time then release the mouse button to stop selecting text.

Selecting a Paragraph Quickly

Triple-clicking any character in a paragraph selects the entire paragraph. To extend the selection a paragraph at a time, triple-click a mouse button while pointing to a paragraph, but continue to hold down the mouse button after the third click. Drag the mouse up or down to extend the selection a paragraph at a time.

Selecting an Entire Document Quickly

To drag the mouse through an entire document to select it would take a long time. Instead of dragging from beginning to end, you can use the Alternate-click method, but this also requires you to scroll or jump from the beginning to the end of a document. Instead, you can choose Select All from the Edit menu. This command selects the entire document from beginning to end, including graphics, so that you can cut, copy, delete, or change formatting and typestyle characteristics.

7.4.2 Deleting and Replacing Text

If you make a mistake while typing, you can correct it easily by pressing the *Delete key* to delete the character to the left of the insertion point. You can also hold down the Delete key to delete characters rapidly. You can adjust the speed at which it begins to delete characters and how rapidly they are deleted using the Preferences application, as described in "Keyboard Preferences" on page 284.

Using the Delete key works well for removing a word or two of text, but to delete larger selections, such as a paragraph or page of text, you'll need to combine it with one of the selection techniques just described. Pressing Delete while text is selected deletes the selected text (see Figure 7-8). All of the selected text will be deleted, even if the selection crosses page boundaries within a document

Application Features

**Figure 7-8
Deleting
a Selection**

An easy way to delete long phrases or blocks of text (top) is to select the text, and choose Cut from the Edit menu, or press the Delete key (bottom).

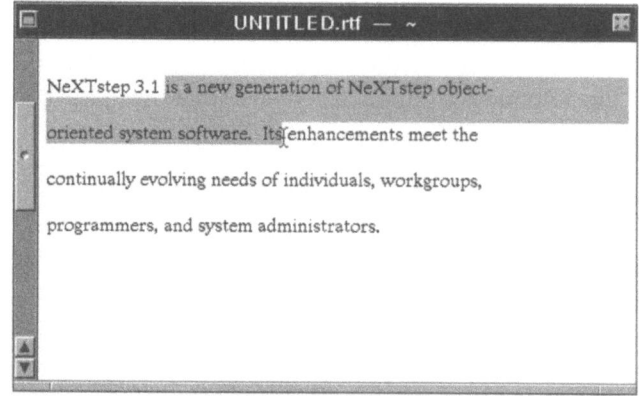

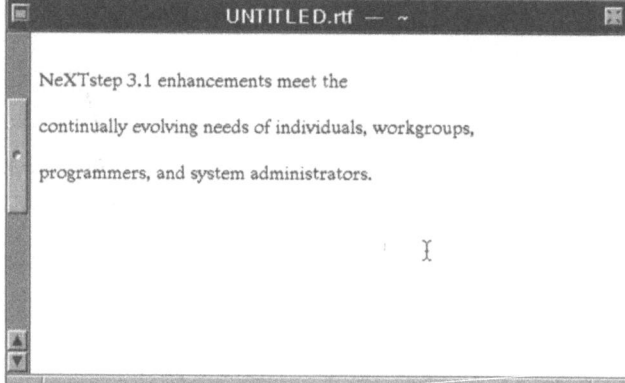

Text can also be deleted using the Cut command in the application's Edit menu. When you cut text rather than delete it using the Delete key, you can paste the text into a different location within the document, paste it into another document, or do nothing with it at all.

Some applications allow text to be undeleted using the Undo command in the Edit menu. Depending on the application, choosing Undo a second time reverses the results of the first Undo command or undoes previous commands so that you can undo every command you performed since you started the application. This latter feature, called multiple undo, is a new and powerful feature in some NEXTSTEP applications.

7.4.3 Copying, Cutting, and Pasting

Text as well as images can be can be moved to a new location in a document by selecting them and choosing Cut or Copy from the Edit menu. This removes them from the document but places a copy of them on the NEXTSTEP *pasteboard*. The pasteboard refers to a place in the computer's memory that stores what you last cut or copied. It can hold only one item: the last item cut or copied from a document. After cutting or copying the selected text or graphic, you can use the Paste command in the Edit menu to paste it any number of times into any open document (see Figure 7-9). If you choose Copy rather than Cut from the Edit menu, the original text or graphic remains in the document, and a copy of it is placed on the pasteboard. The pasteboard does not change from application to application, so you can move information from one to another. The pasteboard is cleared in only three instances: when you copy or cut another selection, when you log out, and when you power off the computer.

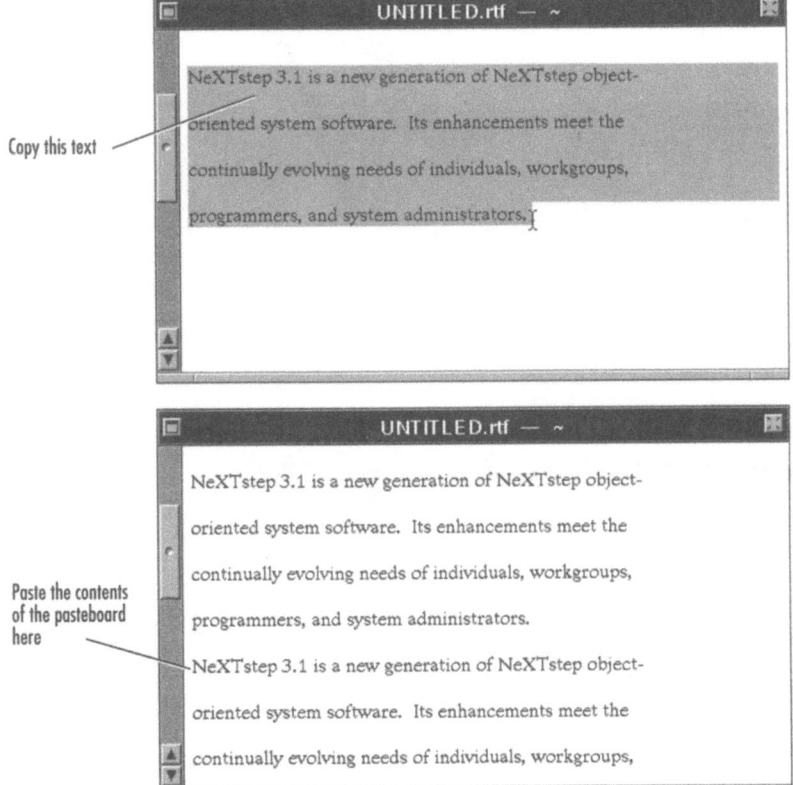

**Figure 7-9
Pasting Text**

Choosing Paste causes the text on the pasteboard to be placed in a document. You can reuse text and images using the Cut, Copy, and Paste commands in an application's Edit menu.

7.5 The Find Panel

The Find panel is different from the Finder panel you use in the workspace in that it is used to find text within a document rather than locate a file in the file system. In every application that uses the standard Find panel, you can display the panel by choosing Find, or Find Panel from the application's Edit menu.

7.5.0 Finding Text

To locate a letter, word, or phrase within the current document, type it in the Find field of the Find panel, click the button next to Entire File, and click Next. If a match is found, it will immediately appear highlighted in the document's window. If you don't see it, you may have to move the Find panel as it sometimes covers portions of the document window in which you are searching. If no match is found, you'll hear a beep and the Not Found message will appear in the message area of the Find panel (see Figure 7-10).

**Figure 7-10
Using the
Find Panel**

The Find panel menu item is usually hidden in the Edit menu of an application (top). When displayed (bottom), you can use the Find panel to locate and replace, or simply find, a letter, word, or phrase within a text document.

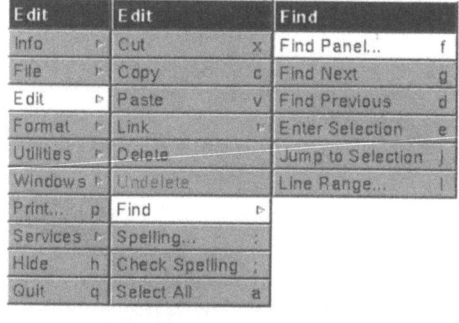

The Find Panel

The Find panel will always begin its search at the location of the insertion point. If it reaches the end of the document without finding a match, it will continue from the beginning of the document until it finds a match or reaches the beginning of the search. You can search backward through the document (from end to beginning) by clicking Previous in the Find panel instead of Next.

In some cases, it may be important to match not only the characters of the text you enter but also their case. For example, when searching for the word *NeXT*, you would use a case-sensitive search to avoid matching the commonly used word *next*. This is accomplished by removing the check mark from the Ignore Case checkbox in the Find Options area of the Find panel. When the Ignore Case checkbox contains a check mark, searching for *NeXT* will also match words such as *next, nExt, NExT*.

If you have experience using UNIX commands, you may be used to specifying a search using a UNIX regular expression. This can also be accomplished in the Find panel by placing an X in the Regular Expression checkbox in the Find panel. With this option checked, the Find panel will interpret the text in the Find field as a UNIX regular expression instead of attempting to match the text as it appears. UNIX regular expressions have a detailed and somewhat obscure syntax, which is described in the UNIX manual pages. To learn more about regular expressions, type **man ed** in a Terminal window. For more about the **man** command, see "The man Command" on page 351.

7.5.1 Replacing Text

Not only can you search for text using the Find panel, but you can also replace the text, too. After finding a match, click the document's window instead of the Find panel to make it the key window, and type the replacement text or enter the replacement text in the Find panel and click Replace (see Figure 7-11). If you prefer, you can type the replacement text in the Find panel before a search and have the matched text replaced automatically when it is found. In this case, you would type the text to be found and the replacement text in the Find panel and click Next to locate the first occurrence in the document. To replace the text, immediately click Replace in the Find panel. If there are other occurrences of the text to be replaced you can speed the process by clicking Find and Replace instead of Find in the Find panel until all of the occurrences are replaced. If you know ahead of time that you want to replace every occurrence of the text within the document, type the text and its replacement in the Find panel and click Replace All. When all of the replacements are complete, the Find panel will display the number of times the text was found and replaced in its message area. Be very careful when you use the Replace All button as not all applications provide an opportunity to undo the Replace All command.

**Figure 7-11
Replacing Text**

Using the Find panel, you can replace text found in the document.

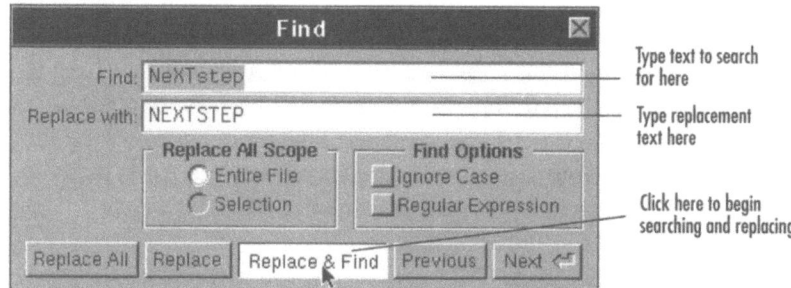

In some cases, you may wish to replace every occurrence of a word or phrase, but only within in a portion of the document, such as a chapter or section. This can be accomplished by selecting (highlighting) the portion of the document in which you want to replace the found text, then highlight the Selection button instead of Entire File in the Replace All Scope area of the Find panel.

7.6 The Font Panel

A point is a unit of measurement used by typographers. There are 72 points to an inch.

Every application that allows you to enter formatted text provides a Font Panel that displays three scrolling lists containing *font family* names, *typefaces*, and point sizes (see Figure 7-12). A preview shows how the type characteristics you select will appear in a document, which saves you the trouble of having to use another application to preview your font selections or create and print font test pages. To display the Font Panel, choose Font Panel from an application's Font menu or type Command-t.

To select a font characteristic, drag the list's scroller to bring it into view, then click it to select it. You can select only one item from each list, but you can choose them in any order or combination. When you click Set, the selected attributes will be applied to the selected text in the document.

The Font Panel

As a shortcut, you can double-click an attribute in the Font Panel to select and apply it to the selected text in a document immediately. Double-clicking an attribute is the same as selecting it and clicking Set.

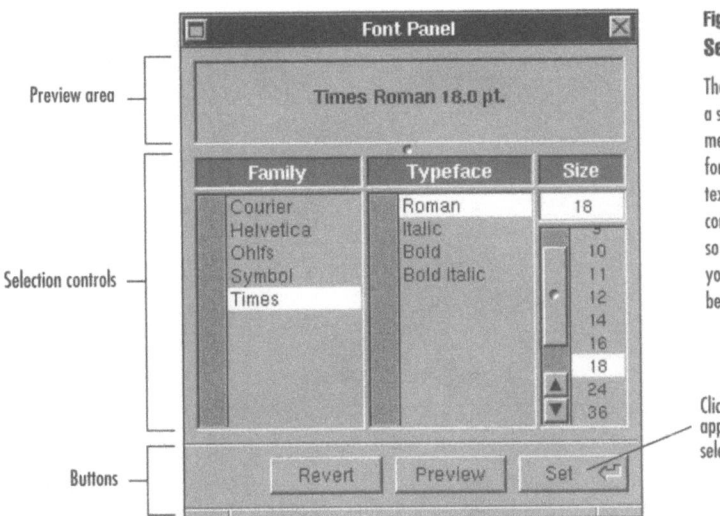

**Figure 7-12
Selecting Fonts**

The Font Panel provides a simple, consistent method for applying font characteristics to text in a document. It contains a previewer so you can see how your selections will look before apply them.

7.6.0 Sizing Text

NEXTSTEP's PostScript fonts can be scaled to almost any size. If you require a size not listed in the size column of the Font Panel, you can drag or double-click to select the point size displayed in the field on top of the size column, and type any size you require. The larger the number you enter, the larger the type will appear in the document. It's rare, but some applications have a maximum size you can enter. You'll have to experiment to see if there is a limit.

The Font Panel allows you to change the size of the selected text based on its current size. This allows you to "tweak" an existing font even when you don't know what size it is, simply by trial and error. To do this, enter a plus or minus followed by a point size in the size field and click Set (see Figure 7-13). For example, after selecting 24-point text in a document, you can type **+10** in the point size field and click Set. The selected 24-point text will become 10 points larger, or 34 points.

Figure 7-13
Sizing Shortcut

You can adjust a font's size based on its current size. Enter a plus or minus and a number in the size field, and click Set to apply it.

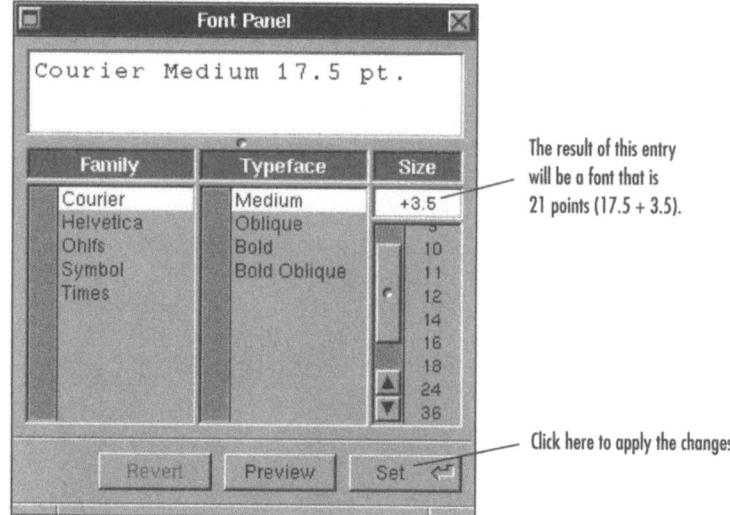

The result of this entry will be a font that is 21 points (17.5 + 3.5).

Click here to apply the changes

You can also resize the Font Panel using its resize bar, to make the list of items longer. This can save time because you'll have to scroll less to see the items you want to select.

7.6.1   Selectively Applying Characteristics

Since the Font Panel appears in almost every application, learning some of the Font Panel shortcuts and tricks can save you a lot of time. You can selectively apply one or two of the three font characteristics without affecting the third. For example, if the selected text contains more than one typeface such as bold and italic, you can change another attribute, such as the font family, yet keep the boldface words bold and the italic words italic. This would be accomplished by selecting only a new font family in the Font Panel. When you click Set, the font characteristic of all of the selected text will be changed, but the typefaces and sizes in the selected text will be left unaltered.

7.6.2 Previewing Fonts

NEXTSTEP makes font previewing easy by allowing you to Shift-click the Preview button in the Font Panel to keep it selected. After you Shift-click the Preview button, changes made to the font characteristic selected in the Font Panel will be instantly reflected in the preview area (see Figure 7-14). This enables you to preview many font characteristics quickly and easily until you find the best combination. When you've found the right combination of font attributes, click Set to apply them or click Revert to return to the selected text's original font characteristics. To turn off automatic previewing, Shift-click the Preview button again.

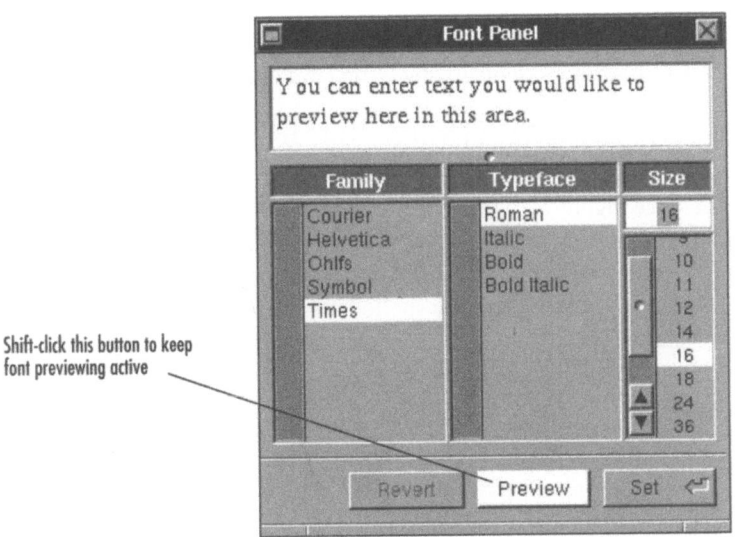

**Figure 7-14
Previewing in
the Font Panel**

By shift-clicking the Preview button, you can preview a font when you select it and avoid having to keep clicking Preview each time.

It is easy to miss, but if you look carefully at the preview area of the Font Panel, you'll notice a dimple that can be dragged up and down to resize the preview area. You can also drag the Font Panel's resize bar to make the panel longer and wider. This enables you too see more font characteristics without having to use the scroller, and also preview text at any size.

Finally, you can edit the sample text in the preview area by selecting it and typing text of your own choosing just as if the preview area were a word processing document. Using this feature, you can preview the exact word or phrase contained in the selected text using different font characteristics. You can even cut or copy the text from the document and paste it into the preview area. Don't type past the end of the preview area. It doesn't respect carriage returns, so the extra text will simply disappear.

7.6.3 Canceling a Font Selection

If after selecting font attributes in the Font panel you decide not to apply them, click Revert instead of Set. This will cause the selected text's font attributes to be highlighted in the Font Panel. Clicking Revert is also helpful when you have changed the attributes selected in the Font Panel but want to start over again with the selected text's original font family, size, and typeface.

7.7 The Spelling Panel

To check spelling, click to place the insertion point in the document where you would like begin checking, and choose Check Spelling from the Edit menu. NEXTSTEP matches words in the document to those in a dictionary containing over 100,000 words. When the speller finds a word in the document not contained in the dictionary, it displays it in the Spelling panel (see Figure 7-15). Examine the word. If it is misspelled, select a word from the scrolling list that closely resembles the word in question. To replace the word in the document with the correct spelling, click Correct, or double-click the correctly spelled word in the Spelling panel's scrolling list named Guess. If the word is spelled correctly, you can click Learn to add it to the dictionary or click Ignore to skip over the word.

If you accidentally enter a misspelled word into the dictionary, you can remove it by typing its name in the Spelling panel's text field, clicking Guess to locate it in the dictionary, and clicking Forget to remove it. After you have corrected a spelling mistake, you can continue checking spelling by clicking Find Next in the Spelling panel.

Don't forget that the Spelling panel can be resized. By making it longer, you will be able to see more words in its scrolling list at the same time. You can also resize the Spelling panel to make it wider to see words that may not completely fit in the scrolling list.

If you routinely use words not found in the standard NEXTSTEP dictionary, you can create or add new ones. When adding a dictionary, place it in the **/LocalLibrary/Dictionaries** folder. To use particular dictionary when spell checking, select the dictionary's name from the Spelling panel's pop-up list before you begin checking.

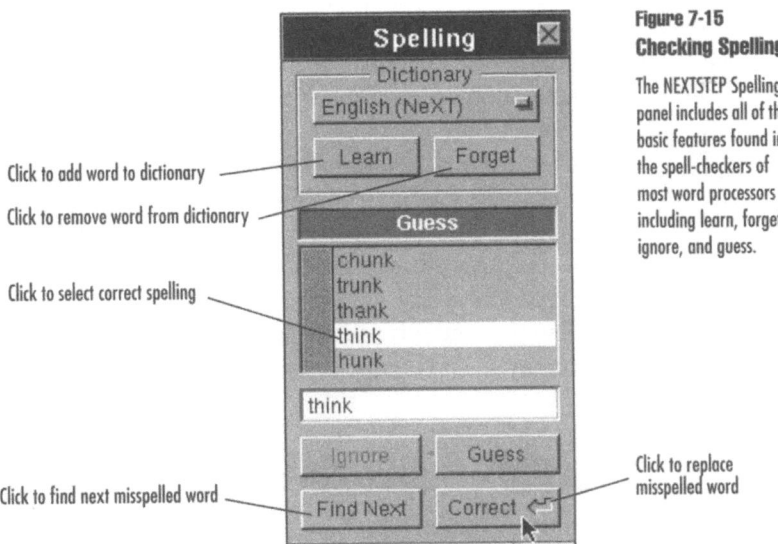

**Figure 7-15
Checking Spelling**

The NEXTSTEP Spelling panel includes all of the basic features found in the spell-checkers of most word processors including learn, forget, ignore, and guess.

You don't have to spell-check an entire document to determine the spelling of a particular word. Instead, choose Spelling from the Edit menu to display the Spelling panel, enter the word you would like to check, and then click Guess. The Spelling panel will display words from the dictionary that resemble the word you entered. If the word is spelled correctly, it will be selected in the scrolling list in the Spelling panel. If not, you can double-click the correctly spelled word to enter it into the document at the insertion point.

7.8 The Colors Panel

Many applications allow you to apply color to text, graphics, and images using a standard NEXTSTEP Colors panel. Even if you are viewing NEXTSTEP in shades of gray, you can still select and apply over 16 million colors although the colors will appear in shades of gray.

Graphic artists, illustrators, and others who design works in color tend to use color descriptions that suit them best, but ones that may not be universally accepted or understood. This caused quite a dilemma for NeXT as it attempted to include color selection in its NEXTSTEP interface. Which of the many colors system should it use? Using a nonstandard or incompatible color description system would not only be confusing, but would result in lost time, wasted money, and a great deal of frustration for its users. The problem is not only NeXT's. In spite of the need for a standard color description technique for all industries, several differing standards still exist and are widely used. To solve the problem, NeXT chose to integrate seven color description methods in its Colors panel. This way you can choose the method you prefer yet still be compatible with the other systems. In the Colors panel, you can use the grayscale, tiff, and Pantone® controls as well as four special collections of controls to select or mix your own colors. These four special groups of controls, called color models, simulate the methods you would use to select a color at a print shop, on your television, and on a computer screen.

7.8.0 Standard Colors Panel Controls

The Colors panel has many faces, (see Figure 7-19), but the changes you make to it in one application carry over to other applications. This allows you to establish color preferences in one application and apply them to another, saving time. This is another example of the seamless interaction between disparate NEXTSTEP applications. Another benefit of a single Colors panel is that you can use the same techniques to select colors in every application. To help you select exactly the color you need, the Colors panel provides several tools, including: a magnifying glass, a color well, color control selection buttons, and color swatches (see Figure 7-16).

The Magnifying Glass

The magnifying glass is used to select a color used in an item on the screen.

The magnifying glass allows you to select a color you see on the screen without having to know how to describe or select it in a color model. To use the magnifying glass, click its icon in the upper left corner of the Colors panel to select it. The cursor will appear as a magnifying glass and as you move it across the screen, will magnify each pixel. Position a pixel in the magnifying glass cross-hairs then click a mouse button to select it. The color panel will change to reflect your choice. You can then apply the color, modify it using the color model's controls, or select a different color. The magnifying glass is best used when you need to match an existing color. Just point and click on the color with the magnifying glass, and it will be selected in the current color model.

The Colors Panel

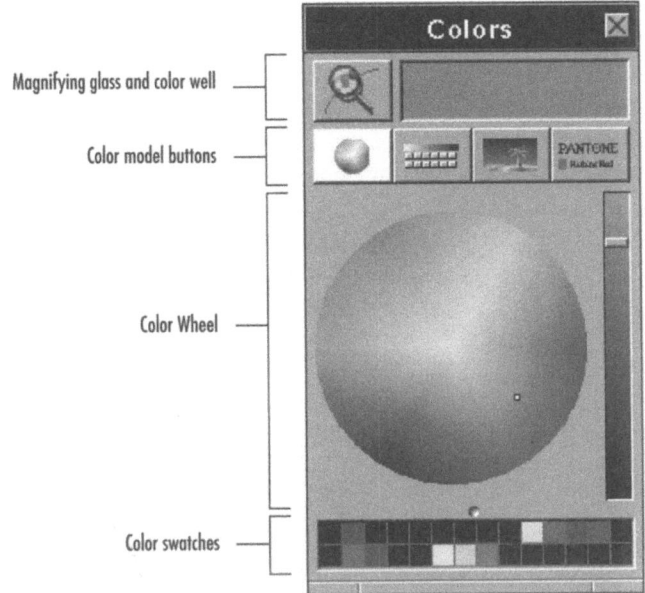

**Figure 7-16
Examining the Colors Panel**

While the Colors panel has many different displays, each contains several basic elements, including a color well, magnifying glass, color model area, and color swatches.

The Color Well

When you have selected a color in the Colors panel, it will be displayed in the color well, a large rectangle, in the upper right corner of the Colors panel. The color well is continually updated to indicate the currently selected color. Depending on the application, you can apply a color by pointing to the color well, holding down a mouse button and dragging the color from the color well onto an object. As you drag, the color a small square color swatch will appear under the cursor to indicate that you are about to apply it. Another method used in many applications to apply a color is to select an object, and then click the color well. For example, in the Draw application included with NEXTSTEP, you would click an object such as a line, box, or circle to select it, and then drag a color from the color well to apply it to the selected object. NEXTSTEP applications may support one or the other or both of these methods.

The color well displays a sample of the currently selected color

Color Model Selection Buttons

Below the magnifying glass icon and color well are the color model buttons. Clicking one of these buttons displays the unique controls for the selected color model. Changing the color model, the description technique, does not change a color, only the way it is described and selected.

Application Features

The color model buttons are used to display each model's color selection controls.

You can switch between color models at any time, even in the same application to select a color in the easiest manner. For example, it is difficult to select a level of gray using the color wheel model, which displays thousands of colors. Instead, to select a shade of gray, use the grayscale color model. Each of the color model buttons looks like a miniature picture of the color model's controls, making it easy to remember which button displays each model. Each of the color models will be described in more detail in "Color Selection Controls" on page 143.

Color Swatches

The color swatches represent colors you want to save for future use

At the bottom of the Colors panel is a bar containing color swatches. Colors you save in the color swatches remain until you replace them even when you switch to another application, log out, or power off the computer. You apply color from a color swatch just as you do from the color well by dragging the swatch onto an object or selecting an object and clicking the color swatch. When you click a color swatch, it becomes the selected color and is also displayed in the color well.

To place a color in a color swatch, drag the color from the color well onto a swatch. If the swatch previously contained a color, it will be replaced by the new color. If you run out of color swatches, you can display additional rows by dragging the dimple just above the color swatches up. If the Colors panel isn't long enough, you may not be able to adjust the number of visible swatches. In this case, drag the Color panel's resize bar to make the panel longer. If you shorten the Colors panel, the additional rows of swatches will disappear, but they will reappear with your color swatches intact when you resize the Colors panel to display the hidden swatches.

7.8.1 Differing Color Panels

Many applications use the standard NEXTSTEP Colors panel as shown in Figure 7-16. However, some applications add additional controls to the Colors panel or make the Colors panel part of an Inspector to save space or make access to them more convenient (see Figure 7-17). Don't worry. The Colors panel controls described here will continue to work in the same manner. Refer to the application's reference manual to determine the use of an application's additional controls.

The Colors Panel

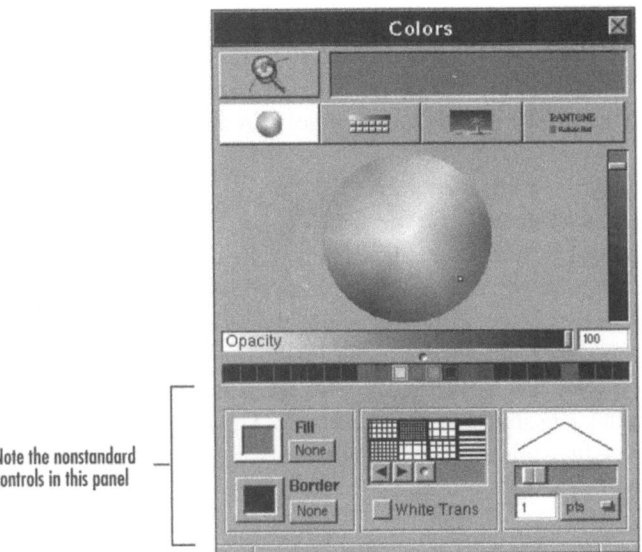

Note the nonstandard controls in this panel

**Figure 7-17
Using Different
Color Panels**

Some Color panels may appear slightly different from the standard NEXTSTEP Colors panel such as this one from Appsoft Draw. However, each of the standard Colors panel controls will continue to work the same.

7.8.2   Color Selection Controls

Depending on your experience in working with color, you will find some color selection controls easier to use than others. Use the one that suits you best. If you are familiar with the Macintosh color picker or have never used color on a computer, the color wheel model is a good model to learn first because it uses a simple point and click method for selecting a color.

The Color Wheel

The color wheel model is usually displayed by default when you first display the Colors panel in an application. If another model was previously selected, click the color wheel button in the Colors panel to display it. The color wheel contains hues of colors that are lighter in the center and darker toward the edge of the wheel. To choose a color, position the cursor over a hue and click a mouse button. The color you select will be displayed in the color well. You can also hold a mouse button down and drag across the color wheel to select and preview colors in the color well. To adjust the brightness of the color wheel, drag the vertical slider to the right of the color wheel. Dragging the scroller up makes the color wheel lighter, while dragging the scroller down makes it darker.

Color wheel

Color Models

Color model and grayscale icons

The second color model button displays buttons for each of the four color models in which you can create or mix your own color (see Figure 7-18). When you click a color model button to see its selection controls, the color model button also changes to reflect the model you selected.

The first color model is called grayscale. Notice that the color models and grayscale icons look the same. To use the grayscale model, click the color model button under the color well, then click the grayscale button as shown in Figure 7-18. A horizontal slider will appear that can be dragged to select levels of gray between black (0%) and white (100%). Seven buttons below the slider contain predefined gray values. Clicking one of these buttons will move the slider to the gray level indicated on the button and place the shade in the color well. The grayscale model is most often used to edit scanned grayscale images or to prepare illustrations for display on monochrome systems.

**Figure 7-18
Using
Color Models**

Clicking the second button displays four color models buttons below.

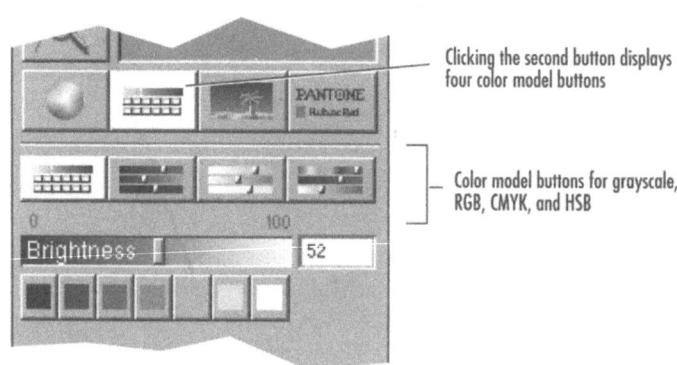

RGB

The Red, Green, Blue (RGB) color model is typically used to adjust color on computer monitors. The colors red, green, and blue when combined in the proper amounts, can produce any color in the spectrum. To select the RGB model, click the color model button under the color well, and then click the RGB button.

Three sliders will appear, each of which controls the amount of red, green, and blue (respectively), mixed to create a single color. Dragging a slider changes the amount of red, green, or blue added to the color in the color well. RGB values range from zero to 255, with zero being minimum brightness, and 255 the maximum brightness of red, green, or blue that can be added to create a color. These values are provided so that you can record the amount of each color required to create the desired hue, particularly when you need to describe a color to someone else.

CMYK (cyan, magenta, yellow, and black) is a popular color model used in the four-color printing process on traditional printing presses. To use the CMYK model, click the color models button under the color well, and then click the CMYK button. Four sliders will appear with which you can control the level of each of cyan, magenta, yellow, and black applied to create a color in the color well. Values for each of these colors range from zero to 100 with zero being none and 100 the maximum cyan, magenta, yellow, or black that can be added to the create a color. These numbers are provided so that you can record the amount of each color required to create the desired shade.

CMYK

The HSB (*hue*, *saturation*, and *brightness*) color model reflects the method often used to adjust color on a television. To use the HSB model, click the colors model button under the color well, and then click the HSB button. Three sliders appear, each of which controls one of the HSB attributes of the currently selected color. The hue attribute is assigned a numerical value from 0 to 360, and the saturation and brightness attributes are assigned values between 0 and 255. These values are provided so you can record them for future reference.

HSB

7.8.3 The TIFF Palette

The third button under the color well is the TIFF palette button. Clicking this button displays the TIFF palette controls. In this model, colors that you can select are limited to those which appear in the specified image file. This model is best used when you are retouching a scanned image. Limiting yourself to the colors contained in the original image prevents you from accidentally introducing new colors to the image while retouching it. An image used to define a collection of colors in this manner is called a TIFF palette. To select a color from a TIFF palette, click the cursor on a color in the palette area just as you would with the color wheel. The default palette is named spectrum and displays the full color spectrum.

Tiff palette

Application Features

**Figure 7-19
Colors Panels**

By clicking the appropriate color models buttons in the Colors panel, you can use any of these color models to select and apply a color in a document. Top row: color wheel, grayscale, RGB. Middle row: CMYK, HSB, TIFF. Bottom: PANTONE.

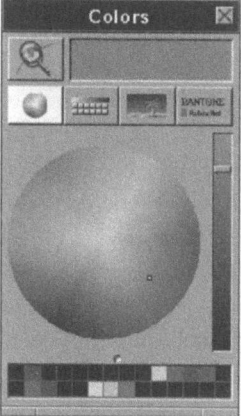
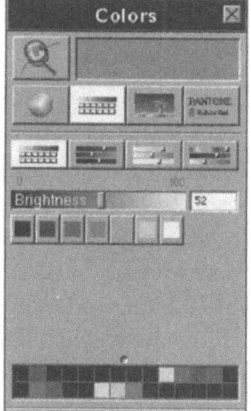
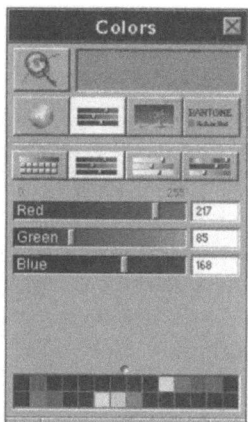

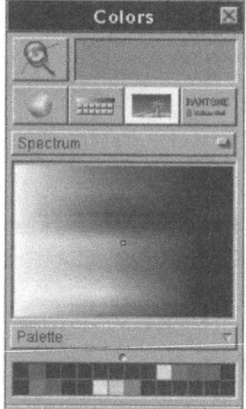

The Colors Panel

Two lists are provided in the TIFF palette, a pop-up list with which you choose the palette to use, and a pull-down list named Palette in which you can add, remove, and rename a TIFF Palette. The commands appearing in the pull-down list, used to customize a palette, are described in Table 7-2.

Table 7-2 TIFF Palette Pull-Down Menu Commands

Command	Description
New from File	Displays an Open panel so that you can select a tiff, ps, or eps file to be used as a palette. Each time you open an image file, its name will be added to the list of available palettes in the TIFF palette pop-up list.
Rename	Presents an attention panel in which you can change the name of a TIFF palette.
Remove	Allows you to delete a TIFF palette from the TIFF palette pop-up list.
Copy	Copies the selected TIFF palette to the pasteboard.
New from pasteboard	Creates a new palette containing colors from the image on the pasteboard. You must have copied or cut an image prior to using this command.

7.8.4 The PANTONE List

NeXT has licensed the PANTONE Matching System (PMS) for inclusion into NEXTSTEP. PANTONE supplies color inks to millions of print shops, and its PANTONE Colors are one of the most widely used and accepted standards in the graphic arts and printing industries. Using PMS eliminates any confusion between the color you specify and the colors used in printing your document. The licensing of PMS and integrating it into NEXTSTEP is an incredible bonus for NEXTSTEP users. Including it in NEXTSTEP saved individual software developers the difficulty, and more importantly, the cost, of licensing PMS themselves. Developers can utilize PANTONE color matching, knowing it is available on every computer system without having to raise the cost of their software to cover the price of a license. This means PMS is integrated into every application, not just available in a few.

PANTONE

Application Features

In contrast, software developers for other computing systems must license PMS themselves. This added cost not only increases the retail price of their software, but does nothing to make PMS available to in every application or to every user, only to those who purchase software that supports it. Because of the cost, many computing system don't support PANTONE Color Matching at all.

PANTONE color swatches can be identified by the small gray square inside their border.

To use a PANTONE list, click the PANTONE button below the color well. A list of named color swatches will appear in a vertical scrolling list, followed by their respective PANTONE numbers (see Figure 7-20). To select a color, drag the scroller until the desired color is displayed, and then point to the color and click a mouse button. As with the other color models, you can drag the selected PANTONE color from the color well onto a color swatch for easy access to it later. PANTONE color swatches are slightly different from others in that they display a small gray square inside to distinguish them for other color swatches.

**Figure 7-20
Using PANTONE Pop-Up Lists**

Using the PANTONE Color options (left) and List options (right), you can create a customized lists of PANTONE colors or use lists that are predefined by NEXTSTEP.

If you happen to know the color's PANTONE number, you can locate it by selecting Find from the pull-down list named Color. A Find panel will appear in which you can type the number or name into the text field, and then press Return or click Next to locate and select it. If you search by name, and the name is used for more than one color, you can use the Find

148

The Colors Panel

panel again to search for the next or previous occurrence of the name in the PANTONE list. Once you select a PANTONE color, it will appear in the color well where you can apply it or save it as a color swatch.

Table 7-3 PANTONE Color Commands

Command	Description
New	Adds a new color to the current PANTONE list.
Rename	Presents an attention panel in which you can rename a PANTONE color. This is especially useful when you add a new color to a PANTONE list.
Remove	Allows you to delete a color from a PANTONE list. An attention panel will appear to verify that you want to delete the selected color.
Find	Allows you to search forward or backward through a PANTONE list for a particular color. You can search by name or number.

There are actually many color lists, each of which is listed in the pop-up list on top of the PANTONE color list. Selecting one of the many lists of colors narrows the selections to colors of a certain hue such as red, green, blue, yellow, or brown, or special collection of colors. You can also create your own list using the commands in the pull-down menu named List.

Table 7-4 PANTONE List Commands

Command	Description
New	Allows you to create a new blank color list.
Open	Allows you to use a list provided to you by another user or software developer. Several color lists can be found in /NextLibrary/Colors.
Rename	Allows you to rename a color list so it is more easily recognizable.
Remove	Allows you to delete a color list from the Colors panel. An attention panel will appear to verify that you want to delete the color list.

Another advantage of PANTONE lists is that you can accurately select and apply colors even when you can't preview them. This is a boon if you are preparing a color document using a monochrome display.

> Many graphic arts supply stores sell PANTONE Matching System quick reference cards for a few dollars. These charts contain color samples along with the appropriate PMS number. Using one of these charts along with the PANTONE panel will allow you to choose colors visually even when you don't have a color display.

7.9 Services

One of the areas in which NEXTSTEP excels beyond competitive systems is in its ability to coordinate tasks and transfer data between applications. Other computing systems—such as the Macintosh, Microsoft Windows, and OS/2—provide very basic tools for moving data between applications so that you can easily process information using the most appropriate program, even when the data did not originate in that program. These systems accomplish data transfer using a simple cut and paste metaphor. NEXTSTEP provides cut and paste, too, but also extends data exchange and application integration through a unique feature named Services.

Simply put, applications can communicate and transfer data through a common menu item named Services. When an application that provides a service is installed in **/LocalApps**, **/NextApps**, or **~/Apps**, NEXTSTEP automatically registers it as a service and places its name in the Services menu. For example, the following NeXT applications shown in parentheses provide services, such as: Search in Quotations (Digital Quotations), Mail Selection (NeXTmail™), Define in Webster (Digital Webster™), and Grab Screen (Grab). Because services are provided by the applications installed in your computer, and in your account, your Services menu may look different from someone else's, even if they use the same computer.

7.9.0 Using Services

Using a service is easy. Select a sound, image, or text, within an application, and then select the desired service from the application's Services menu. Digital Webster, included in NEXTSTEP, is an example of one application that provides a service. To use Digital Webster's service, select a word in any text document, attention panel, window, or workspace and choose Define in Webster from the Services menu. NEXTSTEP will start the Digital Webster application if it isn't already running, the word you selected will be transferred to it, and its definition will appear in the Digital Webster window. You don't have to find the application to start it, or cut and paste the word into its text field, or even ask Webster to start looking up its definition. This is all done quickly and automatically by NEXTSTEP. This seamless integration of applications that know nothing about each other is unprecedented.

Figure 7-21
Using Services

The Services menu provides quick access to the features of many applications and allows them to work together on selected data.

As another example of a service, let's assume you purchase and install HSD's OCR Servant. This application is able to translate images of text such as those received by a fax modem into an editable text document. What you may not realize when you purchase OCR Servant is that it also provides this text recognition service to other applications as well. This means that you can use OCR Servant in any application in which you can select a PostScript, TIFF, or EPS image of text to convert it into an editable text document. The application doesn't even know it exists and doesn't need to know for whom the services performs its work. This is all managed by NEXTSTEP.

NeXTmail is another application that provides a service. At any time and in any application, you can select any amount of text and choose Mail Selection from its Services menu to have the text automatically transferred to NeXTmail, where it will be placed in a new memo so that you can address it and send it on its way to another computer user.

It is difficult to make a mistake when using NEXTSTEP services. Each time you switch to a different running application, the Services menu is dynamically updated so that only services that can be applied to the data you select are made available. Names of services that don't apply appear gray and unavailable in the Services menu so that you can't make a mistake and select a service that doesn't work. This dynamic updating also saves you the trouble of having to learn the types of data each service can process. Services require no installation, other than installing the application as usual, and you are not required to configure them. You don't even have to locate and start the service's application or keep the application running. NEXTSTEP installs, configures, and maintains the Services menu for you and locates and starts the appropriate applications only when they're needed. It's all completely automatic. To learn how to use each of the services in your own Services menu, refer to the reference manual that accompanied the application that provides the service.

Because services are so easy to use, you will find that you use the best features of several applications to complete a project. Many computers provide access to numerous applications, but these applications don't work well together so often only one or two applications are used when four or five would have made the task much faster and easier. You will also begin to find new and unusual ways of solving problems as you move data from one application to another as easily as you move data within the same document until it has been pushed, pounded, rolled out, and massaged just the way you want it. Services, one of NEXTSTEP's most powerful yet easy-to-use features, makes NEXTSTEP unique. After using them a short while, you'll wonder how you ever managed without them.

7.10 NeXTlinks

NEXTSTEP addresses not only the need for application integration but also for data integration with a feature called NeXTlinks. This feature allows you to share a graphic image among several documents. When you make a change to the linked image, each document that shares the image is also updated to reflect the change. This ensures that every document that shares the same image is always synchronized with the others. If you are part of a group project, you can link graphic images to a central document, and as each member of the group completes their illustrations, the centralized document will be updated automatically. Applications that support NeXTlinks have a Link submenu in their Edit menu that contains all of the commands you need to create, inspect, modify, and break NeXTlinks.

7.10.0   Creating NeXTlinks

Using NeXTlinks is easy. You select an image in an open document and copy it to the pasteboard by choosing Copy from the Edit menu. To link the image to another document, open the document, position the insertion point and choose Paste and Link from its Link submenu (see Figure 7-22). The image will be pasted into the document and linked with the original image in the source document. You can link the same image again into another location in the document or link a different image. You can have any number of links to any number images in as many documents as you like. Because the image is linked, not just pasted, it will always be updated whenever a change is made to the original image.

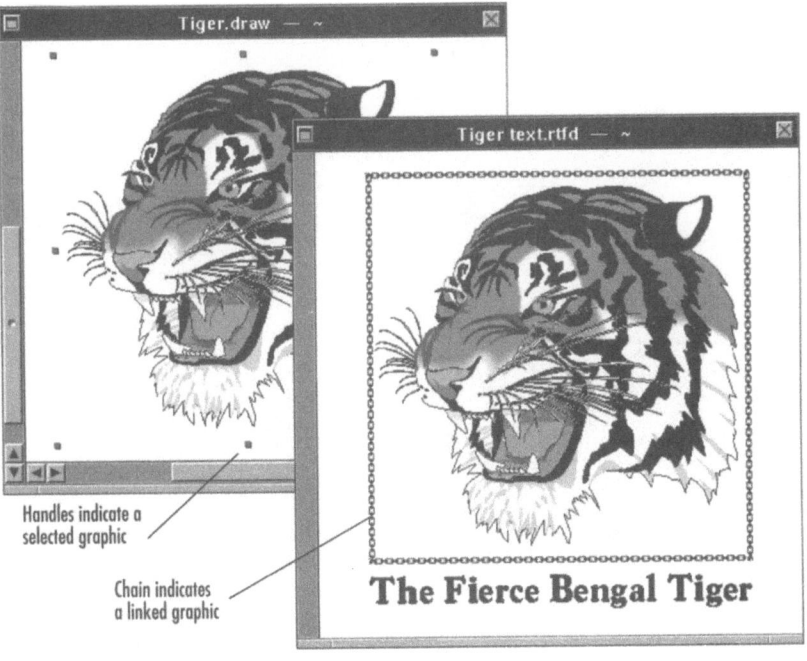

**Figure 7-22
Creating NeXTlinks**

To create a link, copy an image (left), then choose Paste and Link while editing another document. Choose Show Links to see which images are linked (right).

Application Features

7.10.1 Publishing a Link

Published link files look like this in a File Viewer.

You don't always have to have copy an image from an open document to create a link to it. Instead, you can publish the image as stand alone document, and then drag the document's icon from a File Viewer onto an open document to create the link. You must save the document containing the original image before you can publish it. To publish an image this way, select the image in a document, and then choose Publish Selection from the Link menu (see Figure 7-23).

**Figure 7-23
Publishing
a Link File**

To publish a link, select the image in a document (top left) and choose Publish Selection from the Link menu. When the Publish panel appears (bottom left), type a name for the linked image and select a folder in which to save it. When you click OK, a new icon will appear in the File Viewer (bottom right) to represent the link.

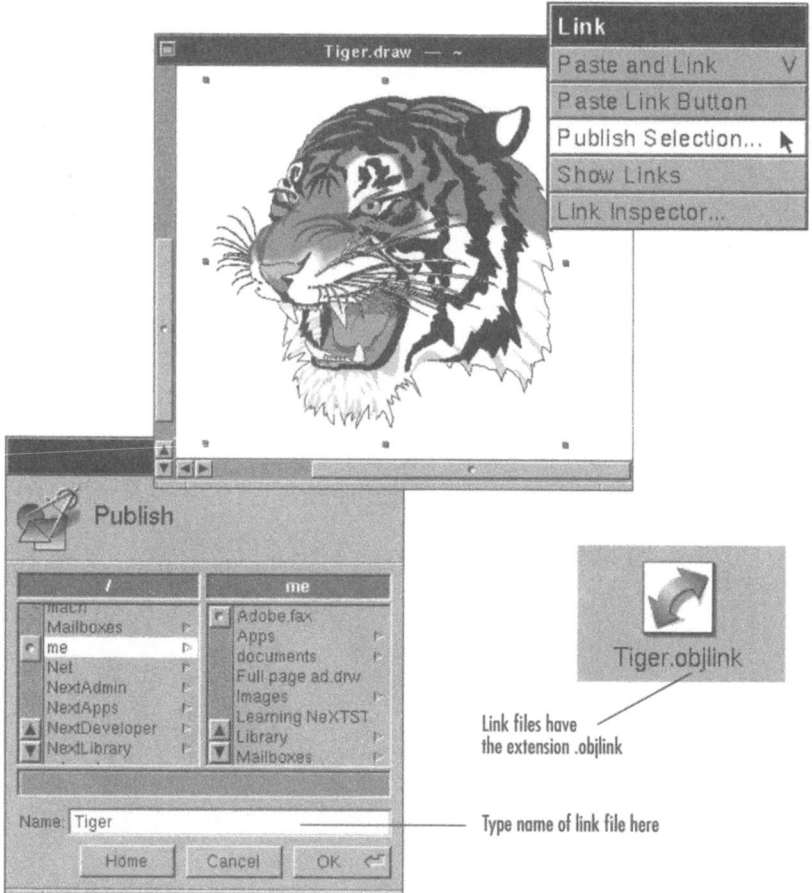

Link files have the extension .objlink

Type name of link file here

154

The Save panel will appear in which you can name and save the published image in the file system. Publishing an image as a stand alone document enables you to drag it onto a document to create a link and also to select and drag several published images onto a document, creating links to each of them at the same time. This can save you time when creating several links and also prevents having to locate and start an application to open the image, copy, and paste it.

7.10.2 Hiding and Showing Links

When you open a document containing graphic images, you may not be able to remember which ones are linked and which are not. To help you identify linked images, NEXTSTEP provides a Show Links command in the Link menu of applications that support NeXTlinks. When you choose Show Links, images that are linked to a source document will display a chain-link pattern around them (recall Figure 7-22). To make the chain disappear, choose Hide Links from the Links menu.

7.10.3 Using the Link Inspector

Applications that support NeXTlinks also provide a Link Inspector so that you can modify how links are updated and can easily open the original image file no matter where it is located in the file system. The Link Inspector, like a workspace Inspector, displays information about the selected item. To inspect a link using the Link Inspector, select a linked image in an open document and choose Link Inspector from the Edit menu. The Link Inspector displays the pathname to the selected (linked) image and four buttons: one each for: Open Source, Update from Source, Break Link, and Break All Links (see Figure 7-24).

Application Features

**Figure 7-24
Working with the
Link Inspector**

The Link Inspector displays the source of the linked image, when the link was last updated, and how it will be updated in the future. Its controls let you open the document containing the original image, update the link manually, break the link, or break the links to every linked image in the document.

To open the document containing the original image, called the source, Click Open Source in the Link Inspector. NEXTSTEP will automatically locate and open the source document using the application specified in the Tools Inspector. As a shortcut, you can double-click a linked image while holding down the Control key to open the source document. This is useful when you want to make a change to the original image. If a change has been made to the original, but it doesn't show up in the current document, click Update from Source in the Link Inspector. This may be necessary if you have set the link's update mode to Manually. The Break Link button keeps the image in the current document, but breaks the link to the original image. When you break a link, changes made to the source document no longer affect the image in the current document. To re-establish a link, you must copy the image again from the source document, open the document to be linked, and choose Paste and Link again. You may want to break a link when a change to the original or linked image is required but you don't want the change in one image to alter the other. If there are several linked images in a document, you can break the links to all of them by clicking Break All Links in the Link Inspector.

The Update area of the Link Inspector displays the date when the source (original) image was last modified so that you can determine when changes may have been made to it. The Update area also displays a pop-up list through which you can choose how a link will be updated (see Figure 7-25). Selecting Manually in the pop-up list will prevent the selected linked image from being updated even when the original image is changed. To update this kind of link, click Update from Source in the Link Inspector. The most commonly used update method is When Source Saved. When the source document is saved to disk, the link is updated. Finally, you can set the link to update Continually. This causes the linked image to be updated at the same time a change is made to the source image, even if the changes to the source image have not been saved. This is extremely useful when the source and linked images are side by side in two open windows so you can see how changes to the source affect the linked image.

**Figure 7-25
Updating a Link**

Using the Link Inspector, you can control when a NeXTlink is updated.

> When practicing how to use the NeXTlinks feature, open two documents side by side and create a link between them. Set the link to update continually using the Link Inspector so that when you make a change to the source image, you'll be able to see instantly how the changes affect the linked image.

7.10.4   Using The Link Button

Some applications that support NeXTlinks also support link buttons. Instead of displaying an image when you create a link, you can display a small diamond-shaped link button. When you click a link button, the document containing the source image will be opened. Using link buttons, you can create hypertext documents. For example, you could see a mechanical drawing by clicking a link button next to a technical description, or you could click an item in an index to display detailed information about that entry. The possible uses of link buttons are endless.

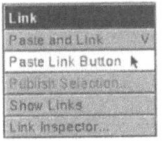

To create a link button instead of a linked image, choose Paste Link Button from the Link menu.

 The link button

Link buttons are created, inspected, modified, and broken much like linked images. The only difference is that instead of choosing Paste and Link from the Link submenu, choose Paste Link Button to create a link button. To inspect a link button, select it and choose Link Inspector from the Link submenu.

7.10.5 Repairing a Broken Link

Links work only when NEXTSTEP knows the source document's name and location in the file system. If either of these is changed, or the source document is destroyed, the link will be broken. When you attempt to update a link that is accidentally broken this way, an attention panel will appear with a message that the source document could not be found and asking if you would like to use another document instead. If you want to break the link, click Cancel in the attention panel. If you want to locate the source document or choose another, click OK. When the Open panel appears, select the document you would like to use as the source for the link, and then click OK.

8

Printers and Fax Modems

On most systems, printing is rather one dimensional, with few options and output that rarely identical to that shown on the screen. NEXTSTEP's print feature is far more robust, offering you a multitude of useful, easy-to-use options that produce output just like the images you see on the screen. You might have expected a discussion of the Print panel, standard in every NEXTSTEP application, in the previous chapter. However, printing from NEXTSTEP is so robust, it merits a chapter of its own. The standard NEXTSTEP Print panel not only allows you to print, as you might expect, but integrates several other capabilities as well: printer selection, document previewing, faxing, and saving a document as a PostScript file. In this chapter, we'll examine each of these Print panel features, and then look at how to configure a new printer and fax modem using the PrintManager application. For your convenience, a complete list of printers that are supported in the NEXTSTEP user environment is provided in Appendix A.

8.0 Getting Ready to Print

Before you print, you should review the settings in the Page Layout panel, provided in most applications. This panel is intended for you to match the page layout to that of your printer. If you mismatch the settings, you'll get misaligned printed pages. Using the Page Layout panel, you can select a paper size, orientation (portrait or landscape), number of pages to place on a printed sheet, and the ability to scale an image to any size (see Figure 8-1). Normally you won't have to review the Page Layout panel before printing, only when you want to make a change. The Page Layout panel is typically found in an application's main or Format menu.

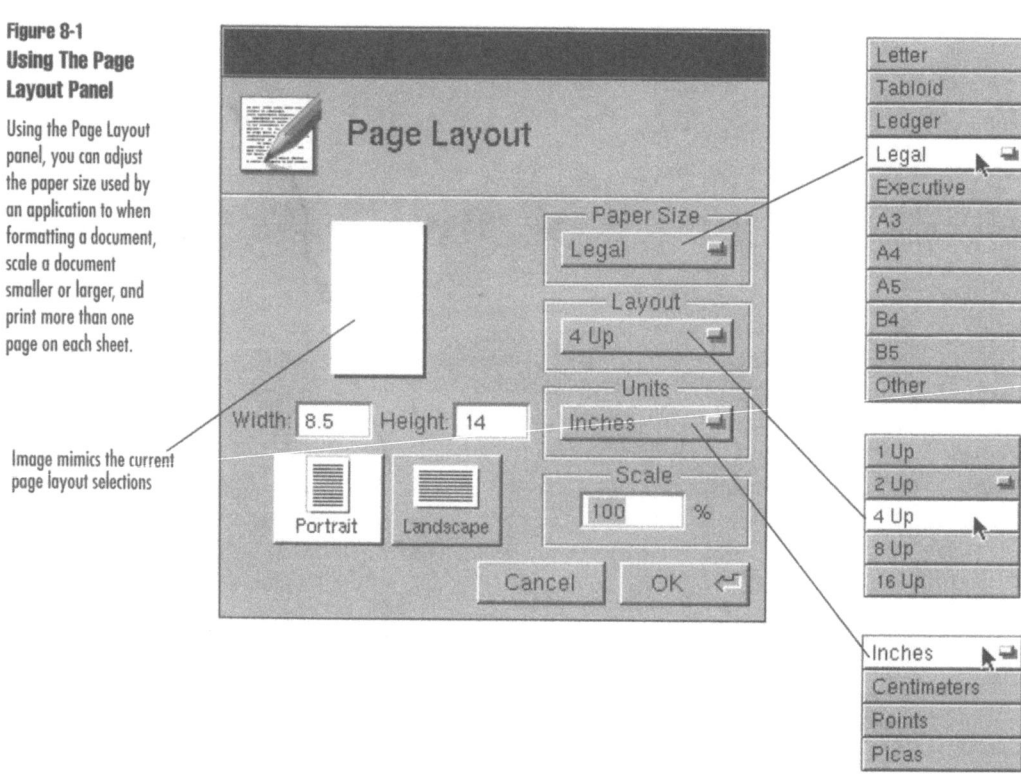

**Figure 8-1
Using The Page Layout Panel**

Using the Page Layout panel, you can adjust the paper size used by an application to when formatting a document, scale a document smaller or larger, and print more than one page on each sheet.

Image mimics the current page layout selections

To modify the settings in the Page Layout panel, make a selection from the Paper Size, Layout, or Units pop-up lists. Paper sizes include letter, legal, ledger, tabloid, and more (see Figure 8-1). Layout refers to the number of pages in the document that should be printed on a single piece of paper: 1,

2, 4, 8, or 16. This option is very helpful when you want "thumbnails" of a document for proofing a layout or to review a multipage document without wasting a lot of paper (see Figure 8-2).

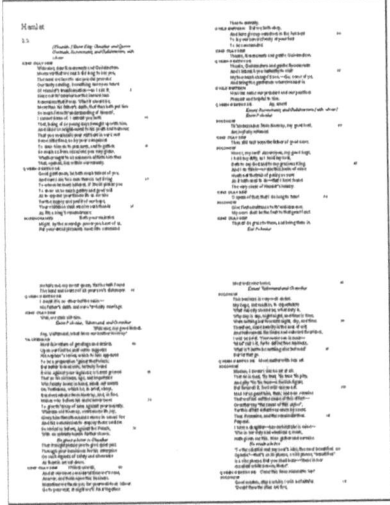

4-up layout

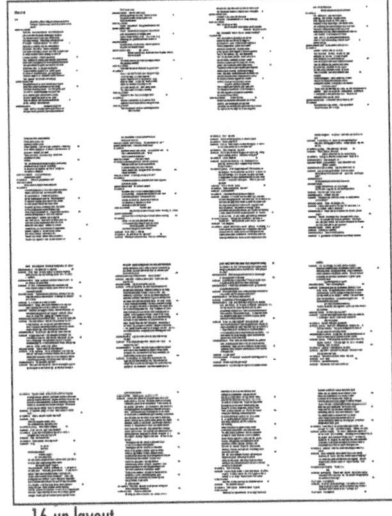

16-up layout

Figure 8-2
Print Layouts

Using the Layout option in the Page Layout panel, you can print more than one page of a document on a single piece of paper. Notice how the 2- and 8-up layouts are printed landscape on the sheet of paper. This is normal. Changing the paper orientation in the Page Layout panel has no effect on these layout options.

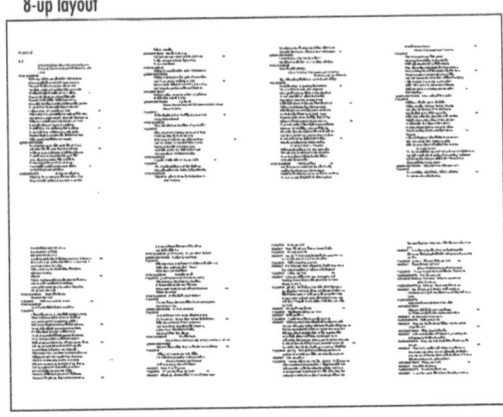

2-up layout

8-up layout

If you don't like the predefined paper sizes available in the Page Layout panel, you can type in your own in the width and height fields. The numbers you enter are assumed to be in the units of measurement selected in the Units pop-up list. Your choices in this list are inches, centimeters, point, and picas.

Finally, you can scale the entire page so that it fills more or less of the paper by entering a size in the scale field. For example, entering 80 would generate an image of the page that is only 80% of its original size. Entering 135 would create an image 135% of its original size.

When you are satisified with your changes, you can save them by clicking OK, or leave them as they were by clicking Cancel. In the next section, you'll learn how to preview the changes you made using the Print panel. This way you can experiment without wasting time or paper.

8.1 Printing

To print a document in any application, choose Print from an application's main menu. The Print panel will appear, allowing you to customize your print request (see Figure 8-3). The Print panel contains three text fields, one each for the number of times the document should printed, and the beginning and end of the page range to be printed. To select a field and its contents, double-click the field or press Tab. Pressing Tab selects each field in order from left to right and is a technique that can be used in every NEXTSTEP panel that contains text fields. If you prefer to print every page of the document, click the All button. If you click the From button, NEXTSTEP will automatically enter **First** in the From field, and **Last** in the To field. You can keep these settings or enter a different page range as described. To print only one page, enter the same page number in both the To and From fields.

For example, to print page five, type **5** in the To field and **5** in the From field. You can also choose to use manual or automatic (cassette) paper feed using a pop-up list. You would choose Manual when you want to feed special paper, perhaps color paper or paper printed with a letterhead, and Cassette for paper loaded in the printer's paper tray. The other Print panel pop-up list is used to select the resolution of the printed page, which can be either 300 or 400 with the NeXT Laser Printer, and 300 or 600 for several Hewlett-Packard LaserJet printers. If the printer provides several options, use the higher resolution for final prints, and the lower resolution for drafts. When you are printing a document containing a scanned image, print at the same resolution as the scan for best results. For example, when a 300 dpi image is scaled to 400 dpi, the image can be degraded instead of enhanced. The Options button displays a panel in which you can select

Printing

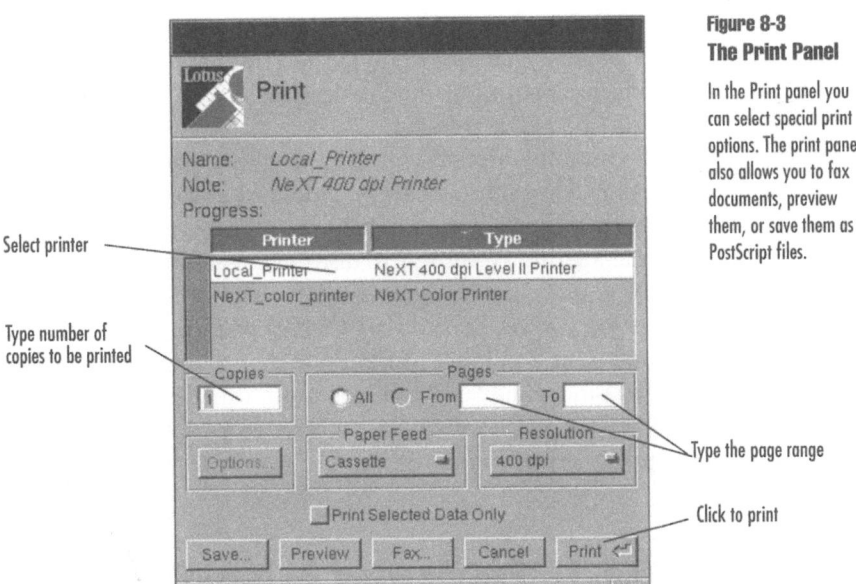

**Figure 8-3
The Print Panel**

In the Print panel you can select special print options. The print panel also allows you to fax documents, preview them, or save them as PostScript files.

special print options available with a particular printer models, such as resolution enhancement in the HP LaserJet III, or PhotoGrade in the Apple LaserWriter IIg® or LaserWriter Pro 630®. After you have selected and entered the appropriate print settings, click Print to print the document. NEXTSTEP will save the PostScript code used to print the document in a queue and allows you to continue working while the print request is processed in the background.

8.1.0 Saving a Document as a PostScript File

Clicking Save in the Print panel will save a document in a PostScript file instead of print it. When you click Save in the Print panel, the standard Save panel will appear. Select the appropriate folder in the file system in which to save the PostScript output, enter a file name, then click OK. Saving a document from the Print panel is different from using the Save command in the File or Document menu of an application. Saving a document using the Save command saves the document so that it can be edited later using the same application. Saving a file using the Print panel creates a PostScript file that generally cannot be edited by the application that

Click Save to save a document as a PostScript file instead of printing it.

created it. Only applications that can edit PostScript files will be able to edit a document saved using the Print panel. Two examples of PostScript editing applications are Preview and Adobe Illustrator.

Because the files generated by the Print panel's save command are PostScript, they can includes graphics just as easily as text, and the fonts used in the document are not required to view it on another computer system, making this a great way to distribute read-only documents to other NEXTSTEP users. Every edition of NEXTSTEP includes the Preview application, which can be used to read PostScript files. Using Preview, you can read and print PostScript files but not change them. Many other computer systems including Sun® and Macintosh can also read PostScript files, making the PostScript format a great way to distribute documents to other computer users as well.

8.1.1 Previewing Before Printing

Click Preview to inspect a document in the Preview application before printing it.

Clicking Preview in the Print panel displays the printed pages in a window in the Preview application. If the Preview application is not running, it will be started automatically. Because Preview utilizes the same PostScript code that is used to render the document on the printer, what you see in Preview is exactly what you will see on paper. WYSIWYG makes the Preview application invaluable for avoiding lost time and costly printing mistakes. No longer will you have to print a document to see if text is aligned, page breaks are correctly place, or fonts applied correctly.

Preview can be started either from the workspace or from within the Print panel. It displays PostScript files, allowing you to browse forward and backward a page at a time or zoom in to view the document at up to four times its original size. If everything looks as it should, you can print the document from the Preview application without having to return to the original application. Because the Preview's Print command uses the standard Print panel, you once again have the opportunity to print the document, save it as a PostScript file, or cancel and return to the original application to implement more changes. Using Preview's commands, you can magnify the image to inspect it more closely, review the pages to be printed, and save the document to a file, print it (using the Preview application's Print command), or close the Preview document without saving it.

8.2 Faxing

Clicking Fax in the Print panel faxes a document through an attached fax modem to any compatible fax machine instead of printing it. You must have a combination fax modem attached to your computer, either directly or through a network, in order to fax a document. The ability to fax a document directly from the computer without first having to print it saves you time, trouble, and wasted paper. It also avoids image degradation that accompanies scanning a document into a fax machine. Faxes sent directly from NEXTSTEP are extraordinarily clear and easily to read when compared with traditional faxes, a feature everyone can appreciate.

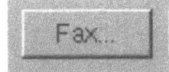

Click Fax to transmit a document through an attached fax modem to another fax machine.

To send a fax instead of print a document, click Fax in the Print panel to display the Fax panel. This panel may look intimidating at first glance, but it's actually quite friendly. The upper two-thirds of the panel is used to enter the name and telephone number of person you are sending a fax to, and the lower third of the Fax panel is used to select fax options, the pages to be faxed, and the time the fax should be sent.

You'll learn how to read incoming faxes in the next chapter. If you want to skip ahead, read the section titled "FaxReader" on page 197.

8.2.0 Selecting a Fax Modem

Before you can send your first fax from the Fax panel, you must select an appropriately configured fax modem. If several are available, you can only use one at a time. To select the fax modem you want to use, click Modem in the Fax panel (see Figure 8-4). A new panel will appear listing the available fax modems. Click to select the one you want to use, and then click OK. After selecting a fax modem once, you need not select it again unless you want to use a different modem.

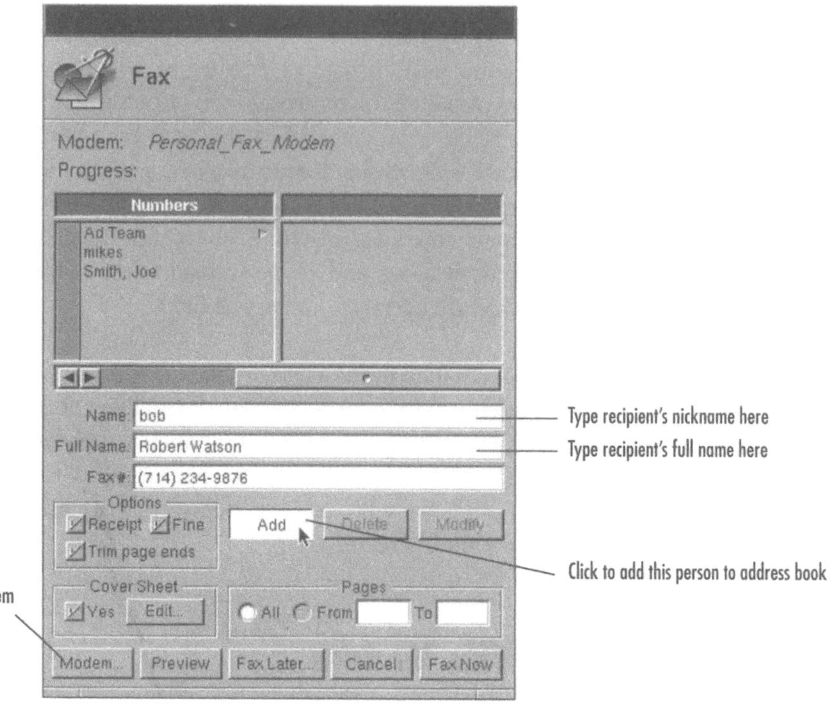

Figure 8-4
The Fax Panel

The Fax panel allows you to address a fax and control several transmission options.

8.2.1 Addressing a Fax

To enter a person's name and fax telephone number, position the insertion point in Name field and type a short name, alias, or nickname. The name you enter in this field is the one you will use to locate the fax number in the future. Enter the person's first and last names in the Full Name field. This information is automatically placed on the cover sheet so it contains a more formal version of their name. Finally, enter the telephone number of the fax machine where the person receives faxes. Do not enter any punctuation, such as parentheses, commas, dashes, or slashes in this telephone number. Instead, enter spaces in place of punctuation. For example, do not enter a fax number like **1, (714) 853-1212**. Instead the fax number should be entered **1 714 853 1212**. When you have entered all of the information for a fax recipient, click Add to enter the information into the fax address book (see Figure 8-4). The text you entered in the Name field will appear in the Numbers column in the Fax panel so you can locate

Faxing

it easily later. You can add as many fax numbers as you want to your Address book and even create and use other address books. See "The Address Inspector" on page 98 for more information.

To delete an entry in an address book, select it in the Numbers field of the Fax panel and click Delete. The item will be deleted immediately, so be sure you really want to delete this person before you click Delete. Should you need to modify an address book entry, click the entry in the Fax panel browser. The entry will appear in the text fields so you can edit it. When you have made the appropriate corrections, click Modify to save the changes. If you click Add by mistake, you will create a new entry in the address book instead of modifying the old one. In this case, select the incorrect entry and click Delete to remove it.

Don't forget that you can also add, change and remove users in an address book using the Workspace Manager's Address Inspector.

Information you add to the fax address book is saved on disk and can be used again in the future. You need only enter a person's fax information once. In the future, when you want to send that person a fax, simply select his or her name in the Numbers column of the Fax panel, select the fax options described below, and click Fax to send it.

If at any time before you send a fax you would like to stop, click Cancel. You will return to the application where you can continue working, editing the text, drawing an image, printing, or faxing again. You can also preview a fax just as you would a print request by clicking Preview. The Preview application will be started if it isn't already running, and you will see the fax as it will appear on the remote fax machine. One difference between previewing a fax and a print request is that the last page of the Preview document contains the fax cover sheet.

8.2.2 Selecting Fax Options

The Fax panel offers several controls to modify the way a fax is transmitted. You can select several fax options, including when it is sent, the pages to be faxed, and the cover sheet template to be used. Many of these options are predefined so you don't often have to change them. However, if your fax requires special attention, you have to opportunity to specify the particular options necessary (see Figure 8-5).

Figure 8-5
Fax Options

In the lower left corner of the Fax panel are options that provide you additional control over fax transmissions.

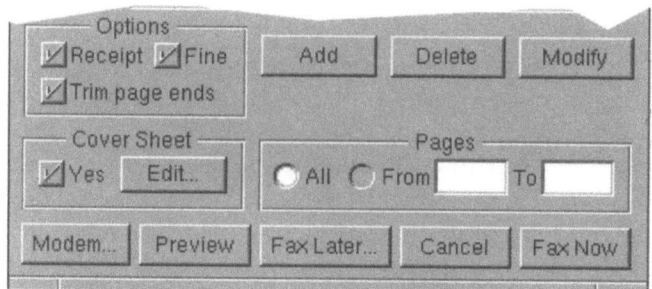

Receipt

Not all faxes are successfully transmitted. Fax attempts can fail due to poor-quality telephone lines, dialing a wrong telephone number, a fax machine not answering your call, or incompatibility between the sending and receiving fax machines. To help you monitor the success or failure of a fax attempt, you can have NEXTSTEP send you an electronic mail message indicating the results of your call. Simply turn on the Receipt option. The mail messages you receive will indicate if the fax was sent successfully, or, if not, will give a description of why the transmission failed so you can make corrections and try again.

Fine

If you want your fax to be sent with the best-quality resolution, turn on the Fine option. Sending a fine-resolution fax may take longer and possibly incur a greater cost for the telephone call but will look much better than standard-resolution faxes. If the person you are faxing to happens to own HSD's OCR Servant application and is receiving faxes through a fax modem, you may want to use the Fine setting when sending them a fax. This enables OCR Servant to more easily convert the fax into a word processing document so that they can edit the text it contains.

Trim Page Ends

If you attempt to fax a document that has unusual page dimensions, portions of it may be lost when it is recreated on standard size paper by the receiving fax machine. To avoid this problem, turn on the Trim page ends option. This will cause the document to be broken into pieces that can be accurately transmitted and received.

Faxing

Cover Sheet

Although it is not required, you should always include a cover sheet to ensure that all of the pages are received and that the fax is forwarded to the correct person. Most fax machines are shared, so including a descriptive cover sheet may be the only way to ensure the recipient receives the fax. To include a cover sheet when sending a fax in NEXTSTEP, turn on the Yes option. A standard cover sheet template includes name of the recipient, the date of transmission, number of pages, sender, and comments is provided in NEXTSTEP and used to create the cover sheet.

Pages

If you had entered the pages to be printed in the Print panel, or if you had clicked the All button, the Fax panel will reflect these selections. However, in the Fax panel you also have the opportunity to set or reset the number of pages to be faxed.

8.2.3 Creating a Cover Sheet Template

You can create as many customized fax cover sheet templates as you want using the Draw application located in **/NextDeveloper/Demos**. It is called a template because the cover sheet is primarily used to indicate where NEXTSTEP should place the information regarding your fax, such as the sender name and address, recipient, number of pages being sent, notes, and other information on the cover sheet. You don't actually enter this information on the cover sheet, but merely place special boxes, called fields, where the information should appear. This information changes each time you send a fax, so unless you use fields, you would have to draw a new cover sheet for each fax you send. This is much too tedious. Using fields in a Draw document, NEXTSTEP will enter the information for you when you send the fax.

8.2.4 Selecting a Cover Sheet Template

To select a particular cover sheet template, or modify the information it contains, click Edit in the Fax panel. The Cover Sheet panel will appear, displaying a miniature of the cover sheet for your inspection and text fields in which you can modify the name of the sender and recipient that appears on the cover sheet or add comments to it (see Figure 8-6). To select a particular cover sheet, select its name from the Cover Sheet's pop-up menu. When you have finished making these modifications, click OK. You can create and install customized cover sheets using the Draw application included with NEXTSTEP (see "Draw" on page 230).

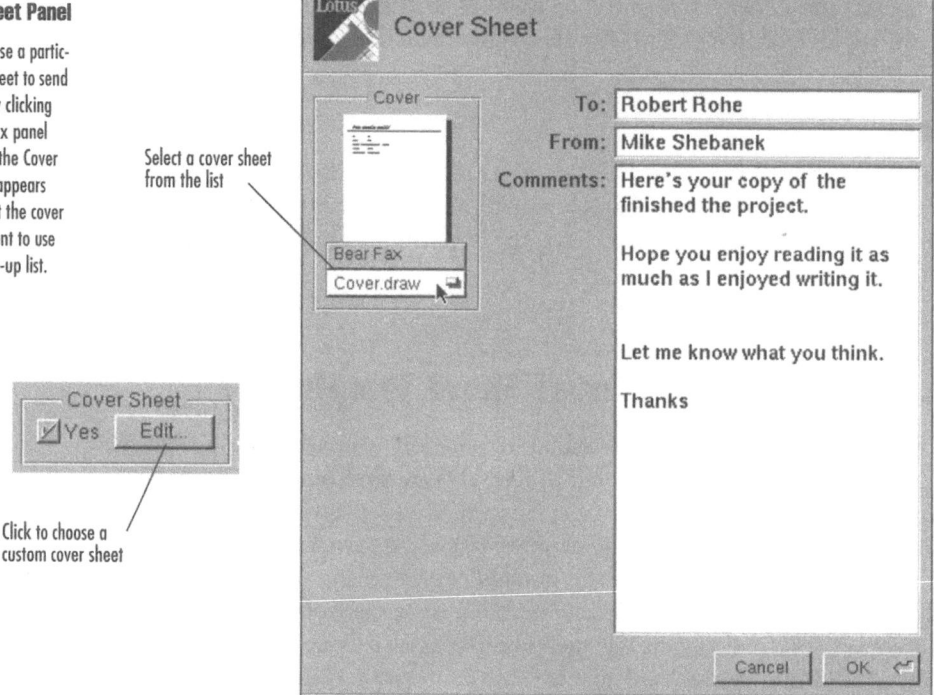

**Figure 8-6
The Fax
Cover Sheet Panel**

You can choose a particular cover sheet to send with a fax by clicking Edit in the Fax panel (left). When the Cover Sheet panel appears (right), select the cover sheet you want to use from the pop-up list.

Select a cover sheet from the list

Click to choose a custom cover sheet

8.2.5 Sending a Fax

You have two choices for when to send a fax, now and later. To send a fax immediately, click Fax Now in the Fax panel. The fax will be prepared and placed in a fax queue and delivered as soon as the fax modem becomes available. You can place as many fax requests in a queue as you like. Each will be sent in the order it was received.

If you choose to send a fax at a later date, click Fax Later (see Figure 8-7). A panel will appears that looks very much like the clock and calender in the application dock. This particular calendar is used to set the day and time for the fax to be sent. Click the hour, minutes, or day number to select it and then click the arrows underneath the calender to select the proper data and time. When the calendar and clock display the proper time, click OK. The fax will be placed in the queue but will not be sent until the specified date and time. Why delay a fax instead of sending it right away? Perhaps it is Sunday night and you are leaving on a trip but need to send a fax to an associate. The problem is that his fax machine will not be turned on until Monday morning to receive the fax. In this case, you could delay sending the fax until Monday morning when there will be a fax machine available to answer the call.

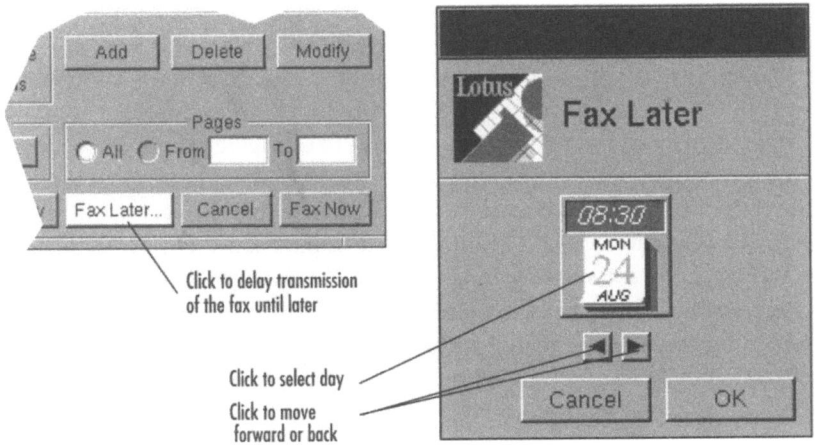

**Figure 8-7
The Fax Later Panel**

You can delay sending a fax until a specified time by clicking Fax Later (left). In the Fax Later panel that appears, select the day and time when the fax should be sent, and click OK to set it.

Each time you print or fax a document, NEXTSTEP quickly and automatically places your request in a queue so that you may continue working. When the printer or fax modem becomes available, NEXTSTEP automatically processes the request in the background. The print and fax queues consist of requests that are serviced in a first-in-first-out (FIFO) fashion. There is no way to send a print job directly to a fax modem or printer without having it pass through a queue and no way to reorder or reprioritized fax or print requests in a queue. The only control you have over the queue is to remove a request and disable the queue so that all requests are kept in the queue and not processed. This is accomplished using the PrintManager application described in "PrintManager" on page 207.

8.3 Configuring a Printer

Having examined the many features of the Print panel, we can appreciate the power NEXTSTEP provides you in controlling your printer. However, before you can begin printing for the first time, NEXTSTEP must be made aware of the printer so that it knows what type of printer is being used, how it is connected to the computer, and the special features it contains so you can take advantage them from the Print panel. During this process, NEXTSTEP will create a print queue, a storage area for print requests that have yet to be serviced by the printer. You will recall that each time you print a document, it is sent quickly to this queue so you can continue working. When the printer is ready to process the request, the document is sent from the queue to the printer. You don't have to be the system administrator to create a print queue and define a new printer although the system administrator often does this during the initial setup of the computer.

Unlike many other systems, you don't have to configure printer or fax drivers for each individual application, only once for all applications, To add a printer or fax modem, you need only configure it once. Every application will then be able to take advantage of it immediately. This procedure is very easy to do for single printers attached to single workstations and is often performed by the system administrator. If the printer attached to your computer is to be shared with other users, there are a few more considerations, and the task should be handled by the system administrator.

8.3.0 Configuring a PostScript Printer

Print Manager

Before you print for the first time, you must create a printer definition. To create a new printer definition you'll need to start the PrintManager application and click Create in the Printers panel (see Figure 8-8). The Create New Printers panel will appear in which you type a name for the printer, and a short description and select its model name from the scrolling list of printers supported in NEXTSTEP. You'll also need to select communication settings that match your printer's. Do not attempt to use a serial port speed over 19,200 unless you have a very high-speed serial port in your computer. When you have finished selecting the appropriate settings, click OK and quit PrintManager. The next time you chose Print from an application's main menu, the printer's name will appear in the Print panel and you can print to it. If an application was already running when you created the new printer definition, it will not recognize the new definition until you quit and restart the application.

Configuring a Printer

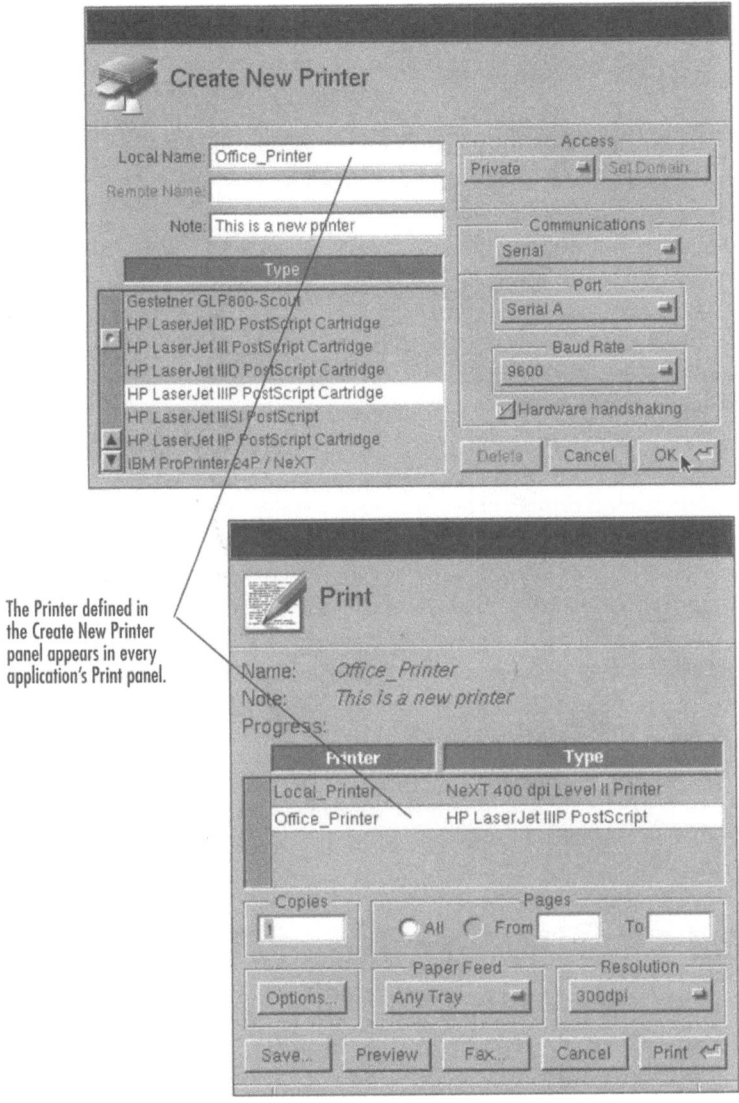

**Figure 8-8
Create a New
Printer Definition**

Using the Create New Printer panel, you can define new printers (top). Each printer you define will appear in every application's Print panel (bottom).

The Printer defined in the Create New Printer panel appears in every application's Print panel.

NEXTSTEP supports a wide variety of PostScript printers from many manufacturers, but what if the printer you want to use is not in the Create New Printer panel's list? NEXTSTEP solves this problem by allowing you to add new printers quickly and easily. For every PostScript printer in the list matching file exists in **/NextLibrary/PrinterTypes/English.lproj**. These files are called PostScript Printer Definition (PPD) files and contain descriptions of each printer's unique characteristics and features. The format of these files is defined by Adobe, the maker of the PostScript language, and is available to printer manufacturers. To obtain a PPD file for your printer, contact the manufacturer. When you receive it, have the system administrator place it in **/NextLibrary/PrinterTypes/English.lproj**. The system administrator must do this for you because the folder's security privileges prevent anyone else from doing so. As soon as the file is copied, the printer it describes will appear in the PrintManager. If the PrintManager was running when you copied the new PPD file, you will have to restart it for it to recognize the new printer file.

If after configuring a printer you need to change its definition, select its name in the Printers panel and click Modify. The Modify Existing Printer panel will appear so that you can alter an entry. This panel looks identical to the Create New Printer panel and its controls and features are the same.

If you create a printer definition accidentally, no longer utilize a particular printer, or need to remove a printer for any other reason, select the printer's name in the Printers panel, click Modify, and then click Delete. An attention panel will appear to verify that you want to delete the printer. Click Delete to remove its queue from the computer. If you need to disable the printer but you don't want to remove its definition, choose Unavailable from the Access pop-up list instead of clicking Delete. This will prevent you and other users from using it, but make it very easy to restore. Deleting a printer definition in this manner does not remove its PPD file, so you'll be still able to create another new definition using the same printer model in the future.

8.3.1 Configuring a Non-PostScript Printer

NEXTSTEP provides printing support for two non-PostScript printers, with many more to follow soon. These two printers are the 24-pin IBM ProPrinter and Epson 510 printer. They offer lesser-quality output, but can provide a low-cost solution until a laser printer can be purchased or made accessible. Should you choose to printer to a non-PostScript printer, you'll also need to purchase a license from NeXT. This is required because the printer will take advantage of the built-in PostScript rasterizer provided in NEXTSTEP, and printers which use this feature must be licensed by Adobe.

Configuring a Printer

If you already own a printer and it's not a ProPrinter or Epson 510, there is another solution. A third-party software package named DOTS allows you to use several popular non-PostScript printers with NEXTSTEP. Be aware that without PostScript, the printer may not be able to scale images correctly or print rotated or scaled text, and image resolution may suffer. Check the manual that came with your printer to determine its capabilities. DOTS may not be the best possible printing solution, but it does provide a reasonably inexpensive alternative to a PostScript laser printer.

Table 8-1 *Non-PostScript Printers Supported by DOTS*

Manufacturer	Printer Name
Canon	BJ10 BJ300 BJ330
Epson	24-pin 24-pin wide
HP	DeskJet 500 DeskJet 500C DeskJet Plus LaserJet II LaserJet III PCL 2, 3, and 5
IBM	ProPrinter X24 AGM ProPrinter X24 AGM wide
NEC	24-pin 24-pin wide
OKI	Microline Microline wide OL 800

8.3.2 Configuring a NetWare Printer

NetWare Manager

As we'll see in Chapter 12, NEXTSTEP has built into it, the ability to access files on a Novell NetWare file server. In fact, it's also able to take advantage of Novell NetWare printers. With NetWare, as with NEXTSTEP, print requests are sent to a queue before being processed by a printer. Therefore, when you configure NEXTSTEP to use a NetWare printer, you are actually configuring NEXTSTEP to send its print jobs to a NetWare print queue where they will in turn be processed along with other NetWare print requests.

Configuring a NetWare printer in NEXTSTEP is easy to do, but before you can begin, you must log into to the NetWare file server that supports the printer (as described in the section "Novell NetWare" on page 320). After logging into the NetWare server, start the NetWareManager application located in **/NextAdmin** and choose NetWare Printers from the Server menu. In the NetWare Printers panel, click Create to display the Create Printer panel (see Figure 8-9). Enter the name by which you would like to refer to the NetWare printer in the NEXTSTEP Print panel and select the printer model in the scrolling list that matches the printer being served by the NetWare print queue. Note that the printer should be PostScript capable, or many NEXTSTEP applications may not be able to print to it. Next, click Set to view a list of the available NetWare print queues supported by the NetWare file server to which you are logged in. Click to select the print queue to which you would like your NEXTSTEP print requests sent, and then click OK. The Create Printer panel will display information about the printer you selected. If any of the information is incorrect, repeat the appropriate steps to correct it. When all of the information is properly entered, click OK to create the NEXTSTEP printer definition. The printer's name will then appear in the Print panel of every application. To use it, you must be logged into the NetWare file server that supports the print queue.

8.4 Configuring a Fax Modem

PrintManager

Before you can fax a document, you must first configure a computer to manage a fax modem. Fax modems combine the ability to dial a telephone and convert digital to analog signals and back again with the ability to transmit scanned images. In NEXTSTEP, fax modems can be shared or used by a single user. This and other fax modem options are defined using the PrintManager application.

Configuring a Fax Modem

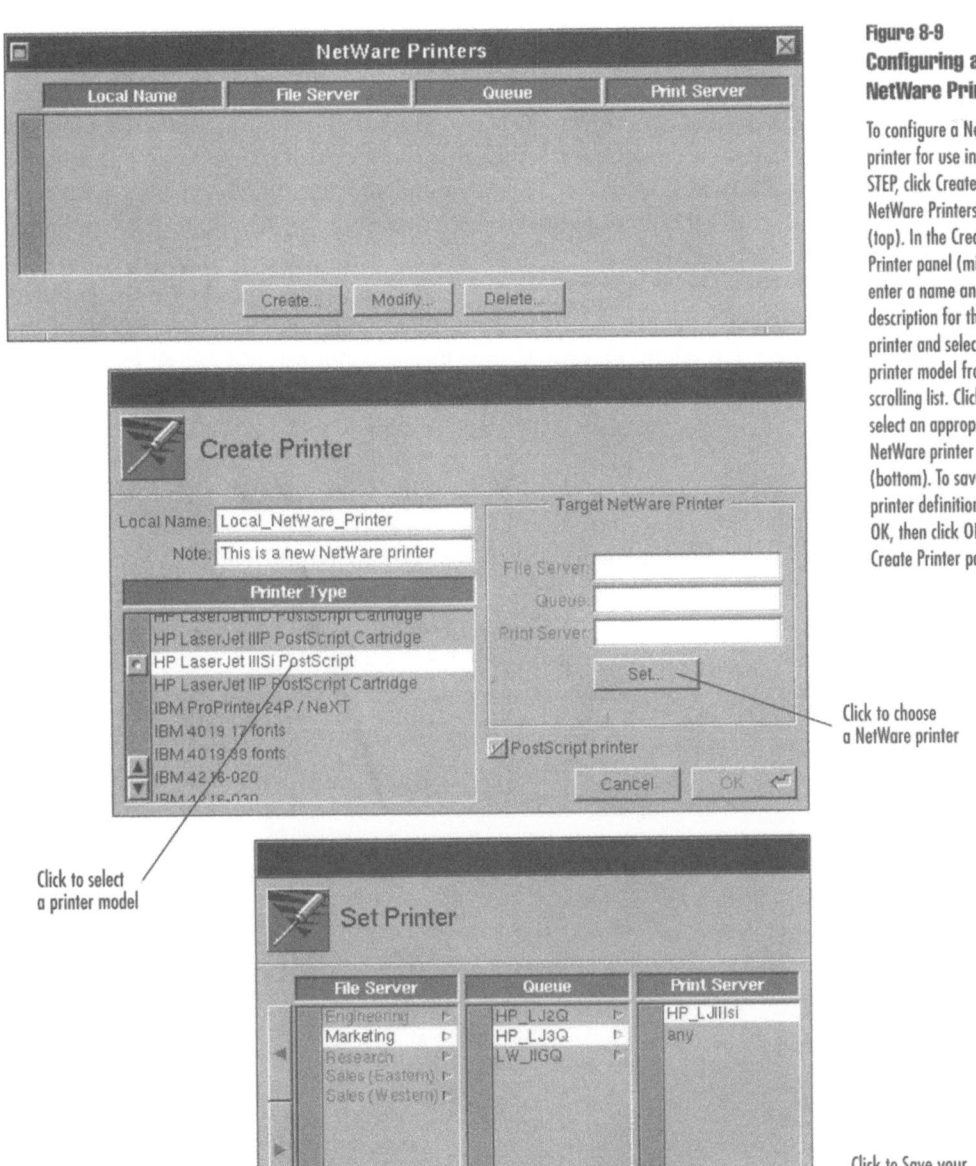

**Figure 8-9
Configuring a
NetWare Printer**

To configure a NetWare printer for use in NEXTSTEP, click Create in the NetWare Printers panel (top). In the Create Printer panel (middle), enter a name and description for the printer and select a printer model from the scrolling list. Click Set to select an appropriate NetWare printer queue (bottom). To save the printer definition, click OK, then click OK in the Create Printer panel.

Printers and Fax Modems

8.4.0 Fax Modem Definition

To create a new fax modem definition you'll need to start the PrintManager application, select Fax Modems to display the Fax Modems panel, and then click Create (see Figure 8-11). The Create New Fax Modem panel will appear in which you can enter a name for the fax modem, and a short description and select its model name from the scrolling list of supported fax modems. When naming a fax modem, you can only use letters, the underscore character _ , and periods. You will also need to select Public or Private from the Access pop-up list to determine who will be able to use the fax modem. Private means only you can use it. Choose Public if you also want to allow other users to send faxes through this fax modem. When you choose Public, you also need to select a NetInfo domain from the second pop-up list to identify a group of users you would like to have access to the fax modem. NetInfo domains are created and managed by your network administrator. (To learn more about NetInfo domains, use Digital Librarian to search the **SysAdmin** bookshelf located in the folder **/NextLibrary/Bookshelves**.) The third option, Unavailable, prevents anyone from using the fax modem and is used to temporarily turn it off.

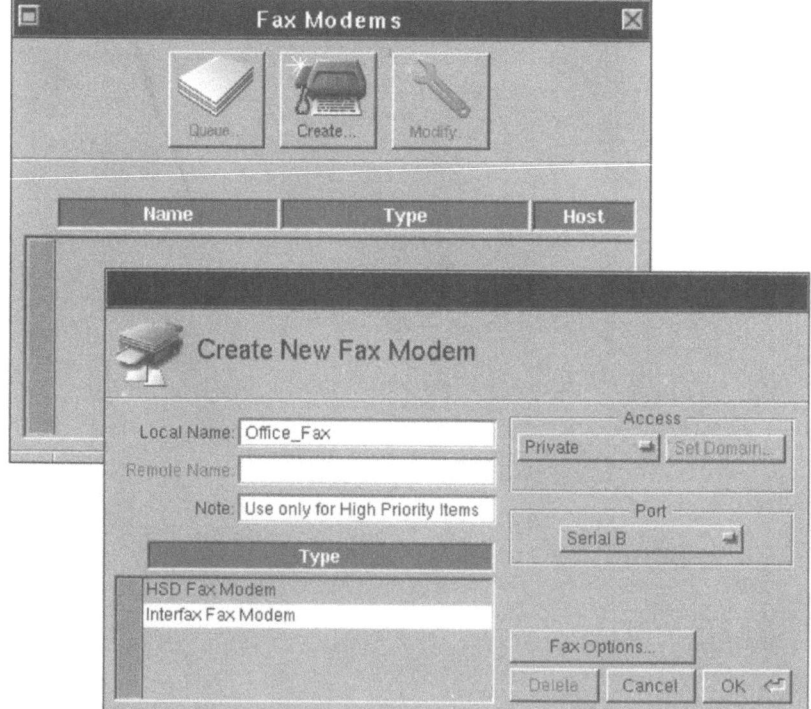

**Figure 8-10
Creating a Fax Modem Definition**

To configure a new fax modem. click Create in the Fax Modems panel (top) and enter the appropriate information in the Create Fax Modem panel (bottom).

178

Before you click OK to save these settings in the Create panel, you will want to review some of the options provided for the fax queue. This is accomplished using the Fax Options panel. To see it, click Fax Options in the lower left corner of the Create a New Fax Modem panel. The Fax Options panel has a pop-up list, rather like an Inspector panel, that allows you to review different collections of options. The pop-up list contains four items: Modem Options, Recordkeeping Options, Permissions Options, and Printing Options. Let's examine each of these individually.

8.4.1 Modem Options

Using the Modem Options, you can configure how your fax modem will handle incoming and outgoing telephone calls. Under the "If no answer, retry" heading (see Figure 8-11), choose the number of times you would like the fax modem to attempt a fax transmission before it quits trying. You can select 1, 2, 3, 4, 5, 6, or 10 times. Using the pop-up list under the "Answer calls after" heading, you can choose the number of rings that must occur before your fax modem answers an incoming call. You can also set this option to Don't Answer to effectively make the fax modem a transmit-only device and avoid receiving incoming faxes. Other options include speaker volume control and activity (typically used to troubleshoot problems), and the type of dialing used with your telephone line: pulse or tone. At the bottom of the Fax Modem Options panel is a field that contains the telephone number of your fax modem. When you enter number in this field, it is transmitted to other fax machines so they, or the person to whom you are sending a fax knows how to send a fax back to you. Note that you should not enter any parentheses or slashes to separate the area code from the telephone number. For example, you would enter **714 123 4567** instead of **(714) 123-4567**.

Figure 8-11
Fax Modem Options Panel

Using the Modem Options controls, you can configure how your fax modem will handle incoming and outgoing phone calls.

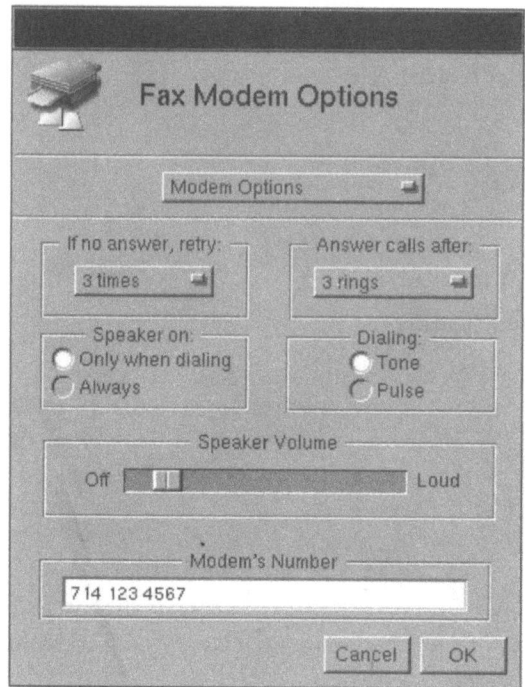

8.4.2 Recordkeeping Options

Faxes by nature are often more time-critical than information sent via surface mail. For this reason, it may be important to keep a record of when faxes are sent and received, and even keep a backup copy of the fax itself. This can be accomplished using the Recordkeeping Options controls. To see them, choose Recordkeeping Options from the Fax Modem Options panel's pop-up list. There are three options you can configure for Recordkeeping: how long to keep (archive) copies of old faxes, how long to maintain a log of incoming and outgoing fax transmissions, and where to store this Recordkeeping information. Use the pop-up lists provided (see Figure 8-11) to configure these options. Typically, faxes are archived for three to six months and a transmission log is kept for three months (one quarter of a fiscal year), six months (half a fiscal year), or one year.

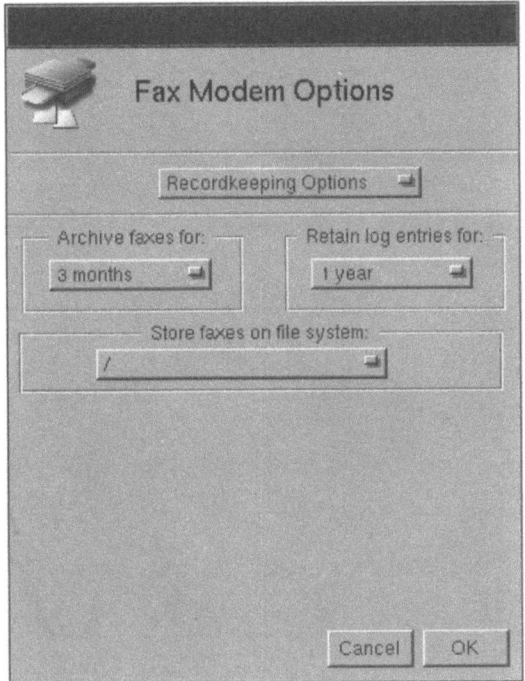

**Figure 8-12
The Recordkeeping Options Panel**

Using the Recordkeeping Options controls, long to keep faxes, how to log transmissions, and where to store your records.

8.4.3 Permissions Options

If you want to allow other users to view incoming faxes, you must identify add their user names to the Fax Modem Users list (see Figure 8-13). To see the list, choose Permissions from the Fax Modem Options panel's pop-up list. Initially, you will see only your own user name in the list of fax modem users. Notice that your user name appears bold and italicized. This indicates that you are an unrestricted user. There are three types of permissions you can allow users of a fax modem: unrestricted, trusted, and restricted. These settings determine which faxes users will be able to read. Unrestricted users can read any incoming fax. They are also responsible for distributing incoming faxes to the intended recipient by assigning faxes. (You will learn more about assigning faxes in "Assigning a Fax" on page 201.) Trusted users, whose names will appear in italics, have the same access as unrestricted users, but are not notified by NeXTmail when a new fax arrives as are unrestricted users. Assign users who only need to read faxes restricted access.

**Figure 8-13
The Add Fax Modem User Panel**

Using the Add Fax Modem User panel (left), you can select users who should have access to incoming faxes. If necessary, you can assign the user unrestricted or trusted permission to the fax-archive (right).

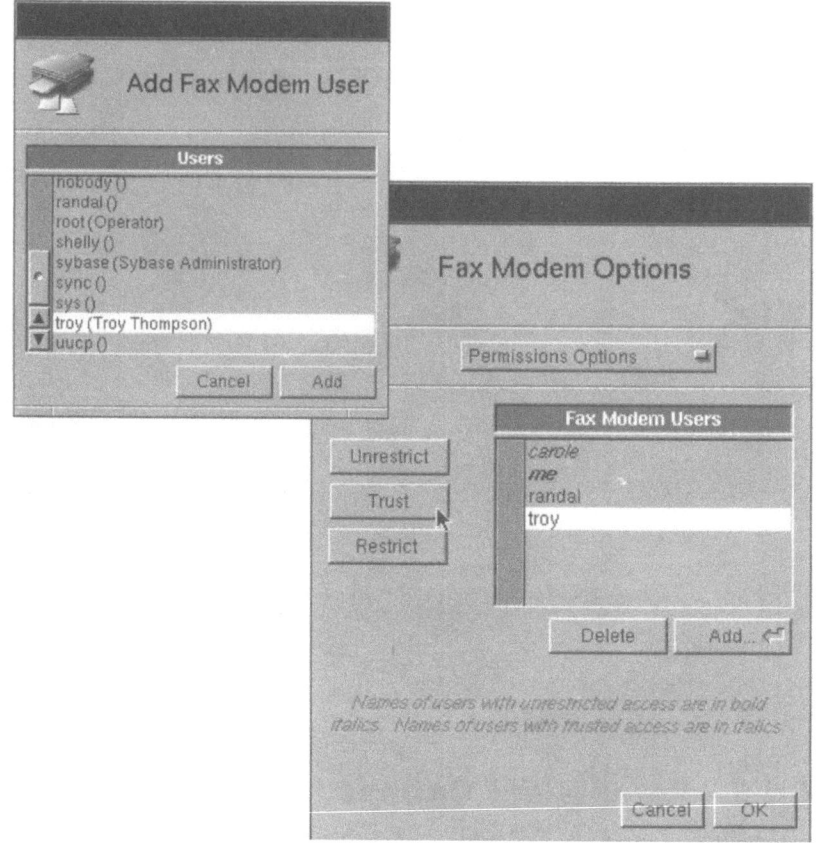

To add a new fax modem user, click Add, highlight the name in the new Add Fax Modem User panel that appears and click the new **Add** button in the Fax Modem Options panel (see Figure 8-13). The list of names reflects the names of users that have accounts on your computer or are part of your NetInfo domain. When you add a new user, he or she is automatically assigned restricted access to faxes. To assign a different permission, select the name in the Fax Modem Users list and click Unrestricted or Trusted. The user's name should appear in bold italics (unrestricted) or italics (trusted) if the permission was assigned correctly. Repeat this procedure to add and assign permissions to every user you want to have access to faxes. To remove a user from the list, highlight the name in the Fax Modem Users list and click Delete.

Table 8-2 **Fax User Permissions**

Permission	Description
Unrestricted	This user is responsible for assigning faxes to users when notified by NeXTmail that a fax has arrived. This user has access to every fax that arrives and to all faxes in the fax archive. There must be at least one unrestricted user per fax modem.
Trusted	This user has the same privileges as an unrestricted user but is not notified by NeXTmail when a new fax arrives.
Restricted	This user can only read faxes that have been assigned by a trusted or unrestricted user.

8.4.4 Printing Options

On occasion, the unrestricted user may not want to take the time to direct incoming faxes to each user. In this case, you can direct the fax modem to print faxes on paper automatically just like a regular fax machine. In this case, someone will have to search through the regular printer output for faxes or users can be left to look for their own faxes. To set up automatic printing, choose Printing Options from the Fax Modem Options panel's pop-up list. First click Choose and select a printer, then select a paper size from the Paper Size pop-up list to match the paper loaded in the printer, and finally, turn on the Print switch to activate automatic printing.

8.4.5 More on Fax Modem Configuration

To save the changes you have made to a fax modem configuration, click OK in the Fax Modem Options panel, and then click OK in the Fax Modems panel (see Figure 8-10). If an application was already running when you created the new fax modem definition, it will not recognize it immediately. Quit and restart the application to have it recognize the new fax modem.

To modify an existing fax modem configuration, open the Fax Modems panel, select a fax modem in the list, and click Modify. The panels for modifying are the same as when creating a new configuration.

If for some reason you need to remove a fax modem from operation, you can delete its configuration. This is necessary so that users won't attempt to send a fax using a device that no longer exists. To remove a fax modem configuration, open the Fax Modems panel, select the fax modem in the list, and click Modify. When the Modify Existing Fax Modem Panel appears, click Delete. An alert panel will appear to inform you that read and unread faxes and the fax archive belonging to this fax modem will also be deleted. If you need to retrieve unread or archived faxes, click Cancel and do so, otherwise, click Delete to remove the archive and the fax modem configuration.

9
Bundled Applications

NEXTSTEP is one of the few system software packages that include a wealth of productivity applications as a standard feature. Applications included with NEXTSTEP are said to be bundled. There are numerous bundled applications in the NEXTSTEP user environment for productivity, demonstration, system administration, and more. This chapter presents a brief description of the unique aspects of each of the bundled applications. Every user and system administration application runs on both NeXT hardware and Intel-based computer systems. However, certain demonstration applications run on only one or the other system. For you convenience, a table describing every application bundled in the NEXTSTEP user environment is provided on page 259. Demonstration applications which run on only one type of hardware are marked clearly in this table.

The use of bundled NEXTSTEP applications for programming and network and system administration are beyond the scope of this book. If you need to know more about a particular application than is provided in this chapter, read the on-line help available in each application. You can also learn more about network and system administration from on-line documentation in the **/NextLibrary/Documentation/NextAdmin** folder, and the NEXTSTEP *User's Guide*. To learn how to program NEXTSTEP applications, read *NEXTSTEP Programming, Step One: Object-Oriented Applications* by Simson Garfinkel and Michael Mahoney, published by TELOS: Springer-Verlag, 1993 or *NEXTSTEP Programming: Concepts and Applications* by Alex Duong Nghiem, published by Prentice Hall, 1993.

9.0 Edit

Edit is a graphical text processor that can be used to create and modify ASCII and RTF files. While it is not intended to replace word processors such as WordPerfect or WriteNow, it can be used to edit and view text files and contains a surprising number of advanced features, such as a text ruler for tabs and text alignment, multiple fonts, search and replace and the inclusion of graphic images. What differentiates it from a word processor is the lack of basic features such as multiple-column formats, stylesheets, footnotes, headers, and footers. For these reasons, Edit is commonly used to examine and modify ASCII files such as those found in the **/etc**, and **/lib** folders, as well as dot files in your own home folder, and to write simple letters or reports. To start Edit, double-click its icon in a File Viewer or the dock. When Edit starts, it will present a new blank document in which to work. You can use all of the techniques for editing and modifying text described in "Basic Text Editing" on page 126 to create a document. If you need to open an existing document, use the Open command in Edit's File menu to select and open the file.

If you are a programmer, you may find Edit lacking in basic features, such as the ability to locate a particular line of code containing an error or the ability to expand and contract sections of code. These features are include in Edit, but are deactivated so as not to confuse a typical user. To activate these features, start Edit and choose Preferences from its Info menu. In the Preferences panel, select Developer Mode and click Set. When you quit and start Edit again, you'll see many new menus containing commands particularly useful to programmers.

A useful discussion of Edit's Developer Mode can be found in *NEXTSTEP Programming, Step One: Object-Oriented Applications* by Simson Garfinkel and Michael Mahoney, by TELOS: Springer-Verlag, 1993.

9.1 NeXTmail

The NeXTmail application allows you to exchange electronic mail messages with other users of the same computer, or with computer users on the same network, compatible with SMTP (Simple Mail Transfer Protocol), which is supported by most UNIX-based mail systems. Mail can be useful even if your computer is not attached to a network. If you share your computer, you can send messages and documents to other users so that when they log in, they can receive your message. You can also mail messages to yourself so that you will remember important events or meetings.

9.1.0 Creating and Addressing a Message

To create a mail message, start Mail, located in the **NextApps** folder, and click Compose. A new window will appear (see Figure 9-1) in which you can enter the text of your message using the techniques described in "Basic Text Editing" on page 126.

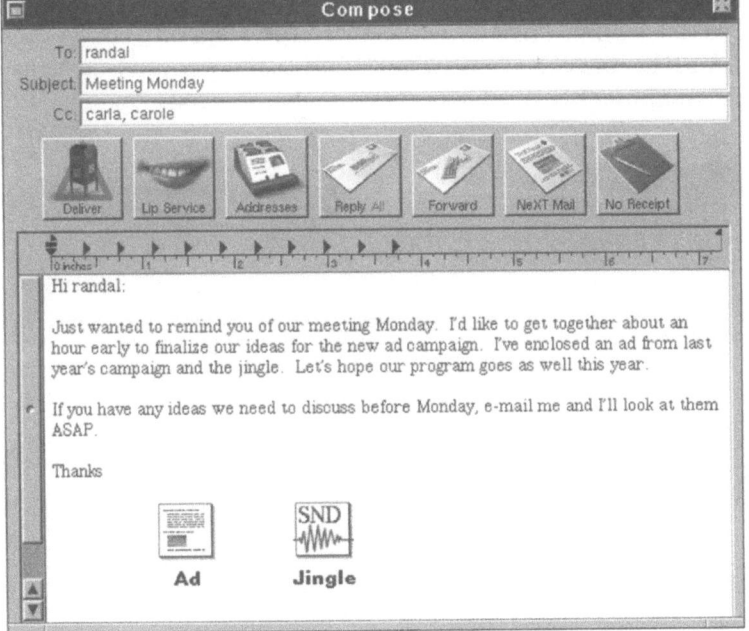

Figure 9-1 The Compose Window

Use the Compose window to create and edit a mail message.

Bundled Applications

Before you can send a mail message, you must first address it to someone. To address a mail message, you can type the recipient's user name in the To: field of the Compose window or double-click an address in the Addresses panel (see Figure 9-2). You can enter as many names as you want in the To: field, although some may not be visible if you add too many. Typically, a person's e-mail name is not the same as their real name. For example, a person named Diana Jones may have the user name **djones**. In this case, you would enter **djones** instead of Diana Jones. Your user name is the same as the name you entered in the upper field of the login panel to begin your NEXTSTEP session. Next, position the insertion point in the Subject: field by clicking the cursor on that field, or pressing the Tab key. Enter a short phrase as the subject of your message so that the recipient can preview the message when a copy of it arrives. The Cc: field is used to hold the names of users who should receive the message but to whom the message is not directly addressed.

If you prefer, you can point and click to enter user names. A list of users to whom you can send mail is available by clicking Addresses in the Compose window. Names in the Addresses panel are grouped into several categories: Users, Groups, Login Names, Private Users, and Private Groups. You can alter the Private Users and Private Groups lists, but the others are defined by the system or network administrator responsible for configuring electronic mail.

**Figure 9-2
Addresses Panel**

You can use the Addresses panel to address a mail message. Just double-click the name of each person you want to receive the message.

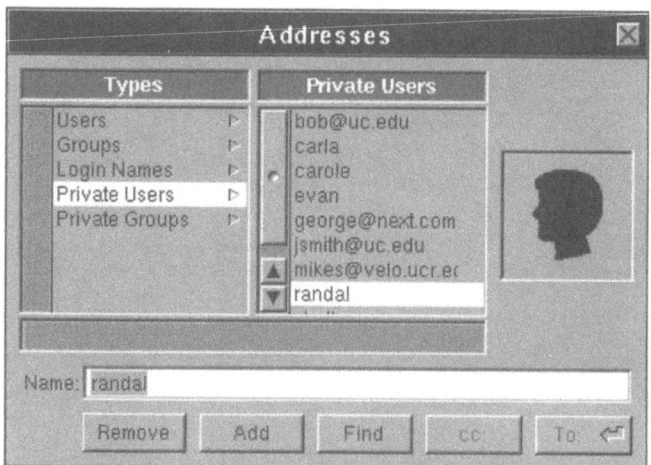

If you need to send a copy of the message to someone but you don't want them to know who else received it, you can do so using a feature called blind carbon copy. Blind carbon copy, or Bcc, can only be accessed when you use the Send Options panel (see Figure 9-2). To see this panel, choose Send Options from the Tools menu.

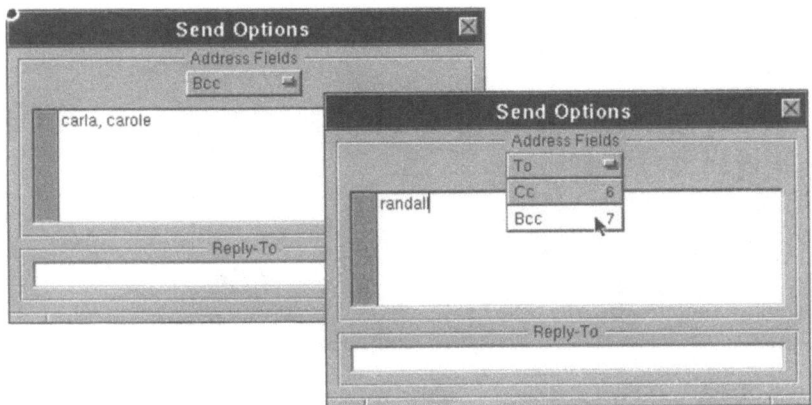

**Figure 9-3
Blind Carbon
Copies**

You can only send a blind carbon copy using the Send Options panel. Be sure to separate each name with a comma.

The Send Options panel's pop-up list can be used to see the names of all recipients of the message, including those who are carbon copied and blind carbon copied. To add a user to the Bcc list, choose Bcc from the pop-up list. Type the names of users who should receive a blind carbon copy of the message in the text field of the panel, separating each name with a comma. When you are ready to send the message, click Deliver in the Compose window. The Send Options panel also has a text field named Reply To. If you would like replies to your message to be sent to a different user account than the one you are using to send the message, enter the user name of that account in this field. When the recipients use their Reply button, their return mail will be sent to this other user account.

9.1.1 Customizing the Mail Addresses Book

If you want to send a message to a person whose name does not appear in the Addresses panel, you can add it yourself. To enter a new address, type it in the text field of the Addresses panel, then click Add (see Figure 9-4). You can add as many names as you wish, but enter only those people to whom you send mail often so that the list doesn't become too long and cumbersome to search through. To delete a member in the Addresses panel, select his or her name from the appropriate list and click Remove.

Figure 9-4
Add a Name to Addresses Panel

Using the Addresses panel, you can add and delete users from the Private Users and Private Groups lists.

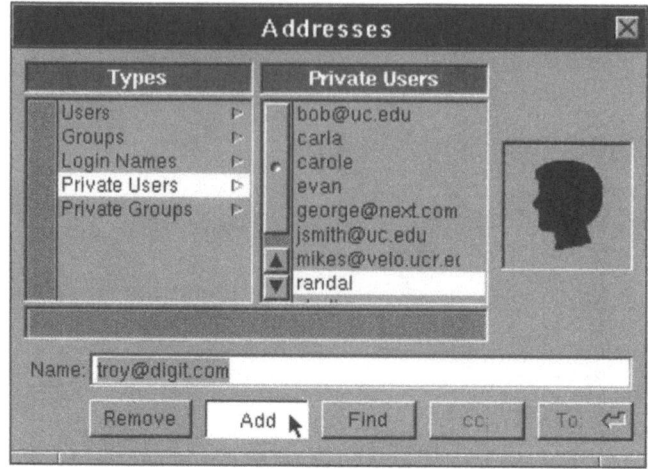

If you routinely send the same message to a collection of users, you can group them together and refer to them with a single name. Such a collection of users is called a group. When you want to send a message to the group, you only have to select the group's name as the recipient, not every member of the group. This saves a great deal of time that would otherwise be wasted addressing the letter to each user individually.

To create a group, select Private Groups in the Addresses panel, enter a group name in the text field, and then click Add. Group names should not include a space or comma. To add user names to a group, select the group name in the Addresses panel scrolling list, then type a user's name in the text field and click Add to make them a member of the group. You can repeat this procedure to make as many groups as necessary and add members to the groups.

9.1.2 Attaching Documents to a Message

If you are sending a mail message to another NeXTmail user, you can include graphic images, documents, folders, applications, and even sounds as part of your message. Non-NeXTmail packages often do not support such attachments to mail, or if they do, do not share the same mail format and thus cannot accept the attachments. To include documents from other applications such as WriteNow, Draw, or Edit into your mail message, drag

NeXTmail

the document's icon from a File Viewer and drop it into the text area of the Compose window (see Figure 9-1). The documents will appear as icons at the insertion point. If you drag a TIFF, EPS, or PS image file into the Compose window, the image will appear instead of an icon.

9.1.3 Adding Voice Messages

To include a prerecorded sound, drag its icon from a File Viewer onto the Compose window just as you would with an image. The sound will appear as a set of lips. When the message is received by other NEXTSTEP users, they can double-click the lips icon to hear the sound. You can also record a voice message or sound if your computer supports microphone input. This is accomplished using the Lip Service™ panel in the Compose window (see Figure 9-5). A Lip Service panel will appear with controls for recording and playing back your voice. To place a sound created with Lip Service in the mail message, click Insert in the Lip Service panel. To send the message, click Deliver in the Compose window.

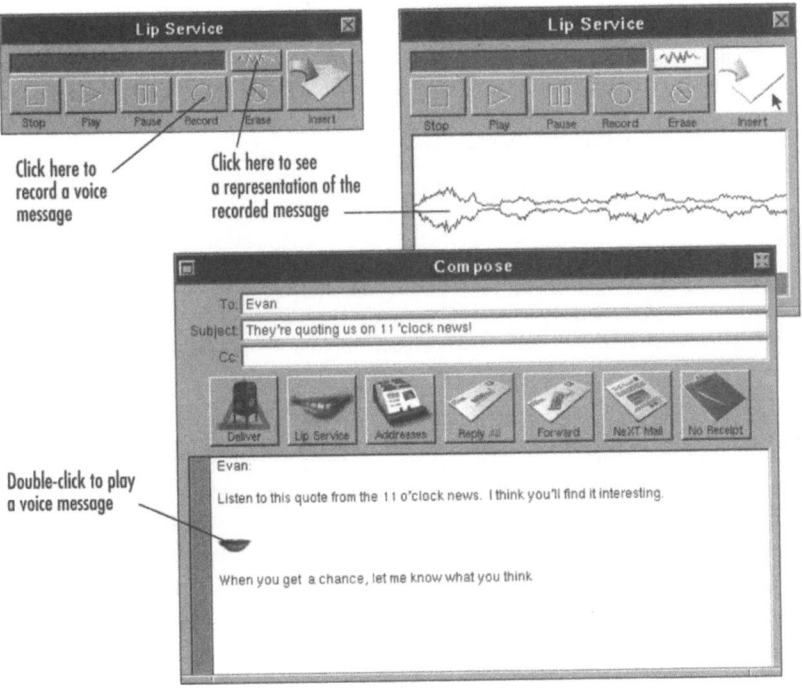

Figure 9-5
Lip Service

To create and enclose a voice message, use the Lip Service panel. Recipients of your voice message can then double-click the lips icon to display the Lip Service panel and play the message aloud.

9.1.4 Reading Mail Messages

 **Unread Message**

 **NeXTmail Message**

If Mail is running and you receive a message, its icon will become animated, indicating a message has arrived. To view the message, display the **Active.mbox** window (see Figure 9-6). This windows lists all of the mail messages you have received, including new messages. Unread messages are identified by a small bullet symbol next to the date and sender's name. Messages that are sent in NeXTmail format have a triangle symbol and may contain images, sounds, or attachments, as well as text.

**Figure 9-6
Incoming
Mail Messages**

To read an incoming mail message, select it in the scrolling list at the top of the active.mbox window.

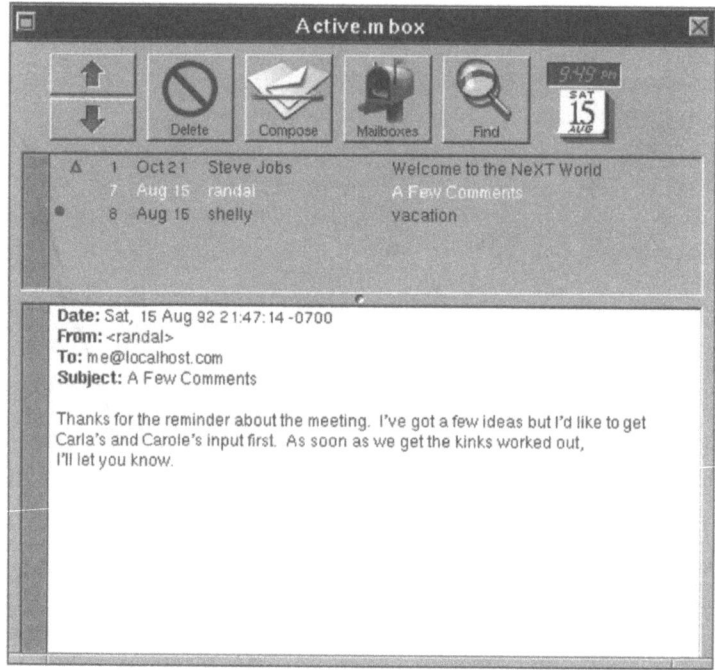

To read a message, select it in the **Active.mbox** window. Its contents will then appear in the lower area of the **Active.mbox** window. If you click Reply, NeXTmail will create a new Compose window and automatically address it to the sender of the selected message. To copy the sender's original text click Forward. If you click Forward only, a new Compose window will appear including the message from the previously selected mail, but with no address. You can then make changes or additions to the message and readdress it to whomever you wish.

9.1.5 Sorting Mail

Mail can be sorted by the date it arrived, name of the sender, its number, or its subject by choosing an option from Mail's Utilities menu. Sorting mail may make it easier to find an old message that you wish to see again, or new messages just arriving. You can also sort your mail into different mailboxes to make messages easier to find. For example, you can create separate mailboxes to store personal mail, business mail, mail regarding a project, and mail messages to yourself. To create a new mailbox, choose Mailboxes from the Tools menu to see the Mailboxes panel. This panel will list each of your personal mailboxes by name. When you first use Mail, only the **Active.mbox** will exist in the list. To create a new mailbox, type a name in the Mailboxes text field, then click New. The name you entered will be added to the list in the Mailboxes panel and a new mailbox will be created. To open it, select its name in the list and click Open, or double-click its name in the Mailboxes panel. A new window will appear having the same name as the mailbox you opened.

 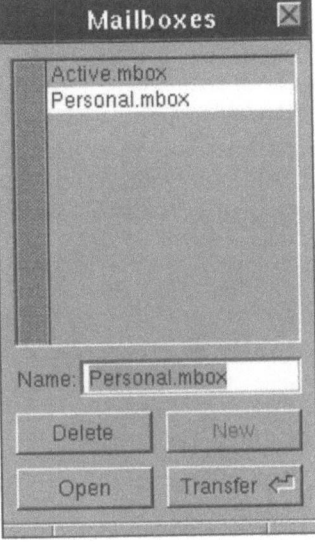

**Figure 9-7
Creating a New Mailbox**

To create a new mailbox, enter a name in the field and click New (left). The mailbox will appear in the list (right).

Each mailbox works just the same as the original **Active.mbox**. Your new mail will always arrive in **Active.mbox**, but you can transfer a message to another mailbox very easily. Select the mail message you want to transfer, or several of them at once, in the **Active.mbox** window. Then display the Mailboxes panel, select the name of the mailbox the messages belong in, and click Transfer in the Mailboxes panel. The messages will be transferred

Bundled Applications

to the selected mailbox. To read them, you'll have to open the mailbox's window. After a mailbox has served its purpose, you can delete it by selecting its name in the Mailboxes panel and clicking Delete. This will delete all of the mail messages in the mailbox, and you cannot recover them, so be very careful when you delete a mailbox.

9.1.6 Deleting Old Mail Messages

To keep your mailbox from using too much disk space, you should delete old messages. To delete a message, select it in the appropriate **.mbox** window, click Delete. If you should want the message back later, you can choose Undelete from Mail's Edit menu to recover the last message you deleted. Choosing Undelete again recovers the next previously deleted message and so on until there are no more messages to undelete. This is just like the recycler in that when you delete a message, it is not really deleted, and thus recovers no disk storage space.

To regain the disk space that deleted mail was using, choose Compact from the Utilities menu. When you compact mail, you will not be able to recover or undelete previously deleted messages. Mail messages that you delete in the future will again remain on the disk until you choose to compact your mailbox again. Therefore, it's a good idea to compact your mailbox from time to time to recover disk space for other uses. Be sure to save mail that you want before compacting.

> Mail messages are not really removed from the disk when you delete them. This allows you to retrieve them later if necessary. You should periodically reclaim the disk space deleted messages are using. Choose Compact from the Utilities menu.

9.1.7 Using NeXTmail Options

Mail includes several options for customizing the way messages are handled and received. To see these options, choose Preferences from Mail's Info menu, and be sure Normal is selected in the Preferences panel's popup list (see Figure 9-8). In the Preferences panel, you can select a sound to be played when mail arrives, the interval at which Mail checks for new messages, and whether message retrieval should be automatic or manual. Most users prefer to have Mail check for new messages automatically. You can also use the Preferences panel force Mail to save a copy of every outgoing mail message in a special mailbox called **Archive.mbox**. This mailbox is created automatically when you turn on this option. You should use this option so that you have a record of the mail you have sent should it be lost in transmission or in case you need to refer to it later. You can also have mail attach a receipt to outgoing messages so that you receive a brief message when the message is read. If you send mail to many users, return receipts can overwhelm you and make messages from other users more difficult to find. It is best to attach such a receipt only to very important mail messages. Finally, if you routinely send mail to someone not using NeXTmail, you may want to turn on the Non-NeXT Mail option. This option prevents you from including graphics, sound, and formatted text which other mail systems cannot interpret. If you have this option turned on, you can still send NeXTmail to other NeXTmail users by clicking the Non-NeXT Mail button in the Compose window. This button will change to NeXT Mail, reformatting the message and allowing you to drag in sounds and images and create formatted text in your message.

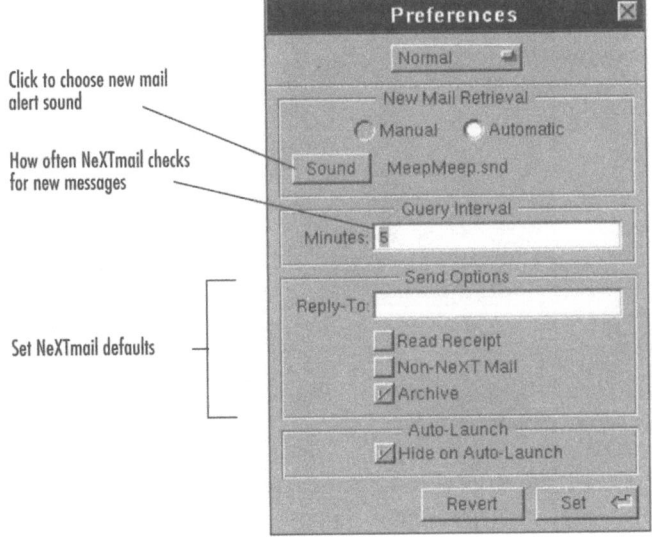

**Figure 9-8
NeXTmail
Preferences**

Use the Preferences panel to select an alert sound, set the query interval and NeXTmail defaults.

9.2 Preview

Preview is a simple application that allows you to see the contents of a PostScript, EPS, or TIFF file as they would appear on paper when printed. Preview does not provide any drawing tools for creating or modifying doc-

Bundled Applications

uments; it is strictly a viewer. Preview is started automatically when you click Preview in any application's Print or Fax panel, or you can start it yourself by double-clicking its icon in a File Viewer. Preview interprets and displays the same code that is sent to the printer so what you see in Preview is exactly what you see on paper when the document is printed.

To help you examine a document more closely than may be possible in individual applications, Preview provides several viewing controls in a Display menu (see Figure 9-9). The Zoom In and Zoom Out commands increase and decrease the magnification of a document in the Preview window. When you use these controls, you are changing only your view of the document, not the document itself. When you print a document while it appears in a magnified view, it will still print at its original size. At close magnification, you may have to use the Preview window's horizontal and vertical scrollers to position a particular portion of the document within the window. To view a document at a further magnification, choose Zoom Out from Preview's Display menu. Preview does not allow you to zoom in or out to a particular magnification.

**Figure 9-9
Preview Display Commands**

Preview's Display menu contains commands for viewing different pages of a document and viewing pages at different magnifications.

Preview		Display	
Info	▸	Page Backward	b
File	▸	Draw Page	d
Edit	▸	Page Forward	f
Format	▸	Cancel	k
Display	▸	Zoom In	[
Windows	▸	Zoom Out	]
Print...	p	Disable Image Caching	B
Services	▸		
Hide	h		
Quit	q		

You can also display a particular page in the Preview window. To see the next page of a document, choose Page Forward from Preview's Display menu or the Command-f shortcut. To view the previous page, choose Page Backward from Preview's Display menu or type Command-b. If you want to go to a particular page, double click the page number shown in the lower right corner of the Preview window, type the number of the page you would like to see, and then press Return. Note that the page number you type may not match the page number shown in the document. For example, if you choose to preview pages 8 through 21 of a document, then to see page 8 of the document in the Preview window, you would enter 1 and

FaxReader

press Return. This would display the first of page of the Preview document. To see page 9 of the document, you would enter 2, and so on. Preview's page numbers are relative to those pages visible in the Preview window.

Preview is great for viewing pictures as well as text. You can set the Preview application to start up any time you click a PostScript, EPS, or TIFF file in the a File Viewer using the Tools Inspector (see "Access Control Inspector" on page 95). This enables you to see images saved in these formats even when you don't have the application that created it installed on your computer. To make previewing even faster, start Preview automatically each time you log in and hide it so it's not in the way of other windows. When you select Preview in an application's Print or Fax panel, Preview will already be running, so you'll see the document quickly.

9.3 FaxReader

The FaxReader application allows you to see fax messages received by a fax-data modem attached to your computer and those attached to computers on the same network as your computer. Of course this application is useful only if you have a fax-modem available. If you have a fax modem and use it often, you may want to keep the FaxReader running in the background. Like NeXTmail, when a fax arrives, the FaxReader icon will become animated to indicate a new fax has arrived.

9.3.0 Reading a Fax Message

If you are an unrestricted fax modem user and a fax arrives, a NeXTmail message is automatically sent to notify you. If not, you can check for new faxes from time to time using the FaxReader application located in the **NextApps** folder. If you happen to have the FaxReader running already, the FaxReader icon will change to display a fax document arriving on the fax machine (see margin) instead of receiving a mail message. If you routinely receive faxes, it is a good idea to place the FaxReader in the dock and have it start up automatically each time you log in. This way you can read your faxes as soon as they arrive without wasting time waiting for the FaxReader application to start up.

When FaxReader is running and a fax arrives its icon changes (top) to show a fax arriving (bottom).

Bundled Applications

After opening or unhiding the FaxReader application, select the fax modem queue you would like to investigate from a list of available fax queues (see Figure 9-10). If you are able to receive faxes from more than one fax-modem, you'll want to check each queue. The list of faxes is displayed in a window when you choose Fax Modem from the main menu.

**Figure 9-10
The Fax
Modem Panel**

The Fax Modem panel lists each of the fax queues to which you have access. To display the contents of a particular fax queue, double-click its entry in the list.

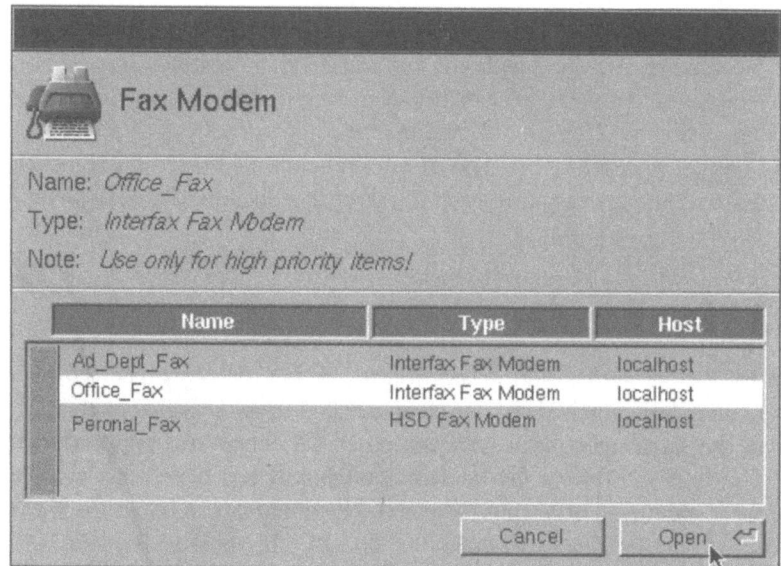

■ Unassigned fax
● Unread fax

To display the contents of a fax queue, double-click the name of the queue in the window or select it and click Open (see Figure 9-11). In the list of faxes, you'll notice special symbols next to each item (see margin). These symbols indicate when a fax has been read or if the fax has not yet been assigned. To read a particular fax, double-click its entry in the list or select it and click Open.

FaxReader

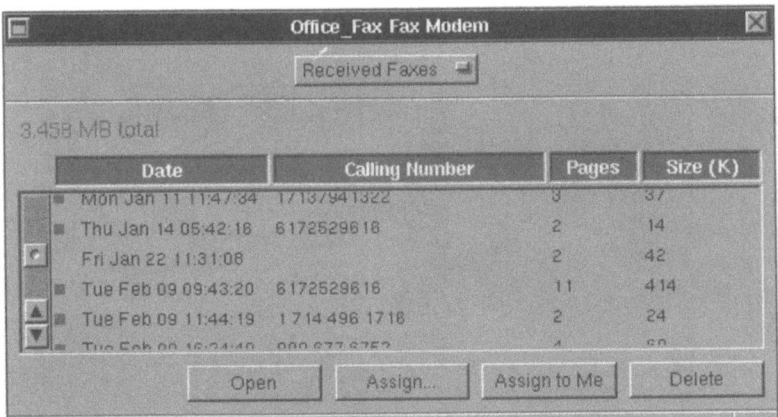

**Figure 9-11
The Received
Faxes Panel**

This panel displays each of the incoming faxes that you are permitted to read.

Remember that a fax is actually a scanned image of the original and cannot be edited. If you need to send an editable version and the recipient uses NEXTSTEP on a networked computer, you may be able to include it as part of a NeXTmail message. For this reason, you may notice that faxes appear grainy, or with low resolution. This is normal as most fax machines significantly degrade an image when it is scanned in preparation for transmission. To help you better view a fax, the FaxReader provides an Inspector. The Fax Inspector can be used to increase or reduce the size of the image, rotate it and trim (crop) an oversize fax to fit a single piece of paper so you can print it (see Figure 9-12). Oversized faxes can also be printed on several sheets of paper or simply scaled to fit using the Inspector panel. To view the Inspector and make these changes to the way a fax is displayed, choose Inspector from the Display menu.

> You can save a fax as a file using the Save command. This allows you to send a fax along with a NeXTmail message to those who don't have access to the fax modem.

Bundled Applications

Figure 9-12
The Fax Window

When you open a fax message, it is displayed in its own FaxReader window. If the fax is longer than one page, page up/down arrows (see inset) allow you to view each page.

Some faxes consist of several pages. Rather than have several windows clutter the screen, each with a single page, each page can viewed in the same window. This is accomplished by clicking the up and down arrows in the lower right corner of the FaxReader window (see Figure 9-12). If a fax is larger than the window, scrollers will appear, which you can use to view each of its corners. A page indicator appears next to the arrows to let you know how many pages make up the fax.

To view a particular page of a multipage fax, double-click the page indicator to select it, enter the number of the page you want to view, and press Return.

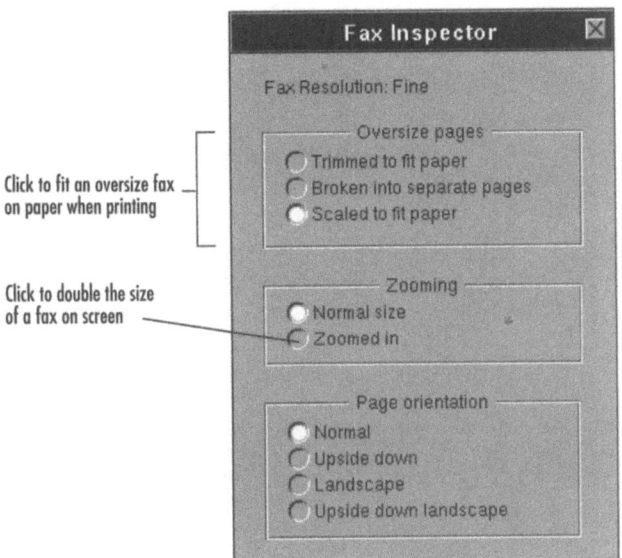

**Figure 9-13
The Fax
Inspector Panel**

Using the Fax Inspector panel, you can control how faxes are displayed.

9.3.1 Assigning a Fax

Normally, fax modems are shared on a network so that many users can take advantage of a single fax modem. In this case, the owner of the fax queue, the one who sets it up, controls who is able to read faxes. The fax queue administrator can also list other users as a trusted member or an unrestricted member of a fax queue, so that you can control who is able to read incoming faxes or have unrestricted access to read every fax in the queue. If you are the only person using the fax modem, you will have unrestricted access to faxes in the queue and won't need to worry about assigning them to others. However, when you assign a fax to a user, it will show up only in their FaxReader panel and only they, and others to whom it has been assigned, can read the fax. Be sure to include yourself when assigning faxes if you also want to read the fax or it will disappear from the fax list and you won't be able to view it.

To assign a fax to another user, select the fax in the Received Faxes panel and click Assign. The Assign Fax panel will appear with a list of user names. Select the names of the users to whom the fax should be assigned and click Assign. Only users whose names were selected will be able to read the fax. You can assign any fax assigned to you, to another user.

9.3.2 Accessing the Fax Archive

Every fax queue has an archive that maintains a record of every fax received. The length of time a fax is kept in the archive is determined when the fax queue is configured. When a fax has been held longer than this time, it's deleted automatically. If you delete a fax or assign it to another user, you can often retrieve it from the fax archive (assuming it's still in the archive). To view the fax archive, choose Archived Faxes from the pop-up list that appears at the top of the Fax Modem panel (see Figure 9-14). This is the same panel that displays the received faxes, and the fax log (as we'll soon see). If you have only restricted access to a fax queue, you won't be able to see fax archives. Unrestricted and trusted access to a queue can only be granted by the person who configures the fax queue.

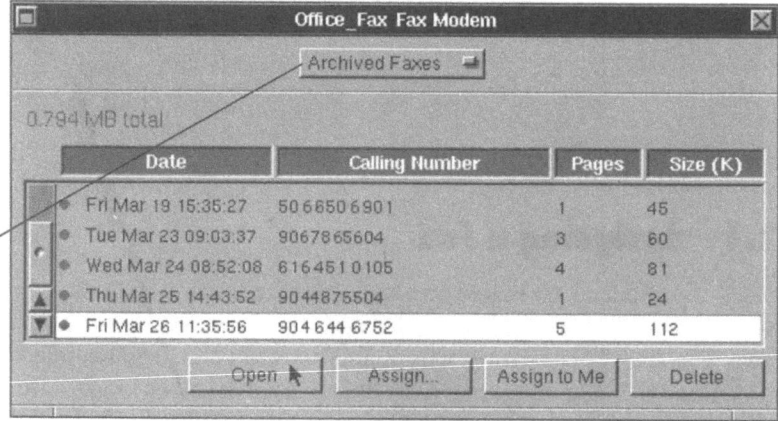

**Figure 9-14
The Archived Faxes Panel**

Double-click a fax in the Archived Faxes panel to open it.

Choose Archived Faxes from pop-up list

To retrieve a fax from an archive, double-click it as you would for a new fax that just arrived. If you delete the fax however, you'll not be able to get it back unless you have saved it as a file (using the Save As command from the Fax menu).

9.3.3 Reviewing the Fax Log

The FaxReader can also be used to view the status of faxes you have sent. To view a record of fax transmission attempts and their outcome, choose Log from the fax modem panel's pop-up list (see Figure 9-15). A record of each fax transmission will appear in the panel. An S at the beginning of a record indicates the local fax modem was attempting to send a fax. An R at the beginning of a record indicates a fax being received. For each transmission, the log indicates the date and time, duration, number of pages, the result of the transmission, and the name of the remote fax machine. This display is especially useful in determining problems when you set up a fax modem for the first time, and in tracking faxes you were told were sent to you but that you did not receive.

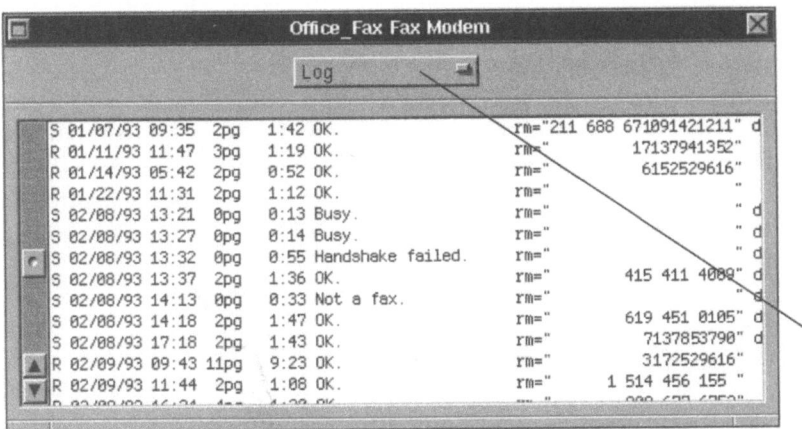

Figure 9-15
The Fax Modem Log Panel

Each entry in the fax log represents a sent (S) or received (R) fax, and includes detailed information about the transmission.

Choose Log from pop-up list

9.4 Preferences

The Preferences application allows you to customize many aspects of the NEXTSTEP environment to your liking. You can find the Preferences application in the **/NextApps** folder, but by default, the Preferences application icon also appears under the NeXT logo in the application dock for easy access. To open the Preferences application, double-click its icon in the dock or in a File Viewer. This section describes how the Preferences application works. A detailed description of each individual Preferences display is provided in the Preferences application and can be found in "Customizing the User Environment" on page 282.

While the Preferences application is running, its icon displays a working clock and calendar. When you quit Preferences, they disappear. By default, NEXTSTEP starts Preferences when you log in so the clock and calendar are visible, but hides its window so it doesn't clutter the screen.

The active Preferences icon (top) and inactive Preferences icon (bottom).

Hide the Preferences application instead of choosing Quit, so that you can still see its clock and calendar in the dock.

When you open or unhide the Preferences panel, you'll see several icons in a scrolling list underneath which are preferences controls and options relating to the currently selected icon (see Figure 9-16). Each time you click an icon in the scrolling list at the top of the panel, controls and options relating to the icon are displayed in the panel. By adjusting these controls, you can review and modify many NEXTSTEP attributes. To see other icons in the list, drag the scroller horizontally. You can rearrange the icons in the scrolling list to make those you use often easier to access. To rearrange these icons, hold down the Control key while dragging an icon. Place the icons you use most at the left end of the scrolling list so that you don't have to scroll the list to select the icon each time you open the Preferences panel. You cannot add or remove these icons or the controls they represent, but some applications, such as IPT's Partner software, do install their own preferences icon.

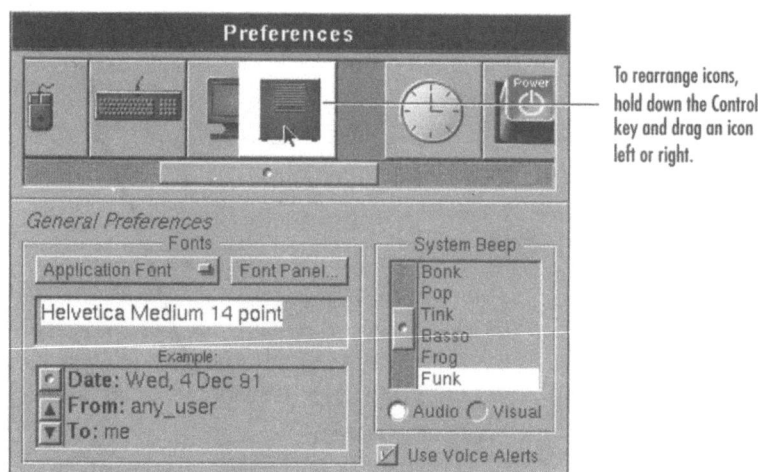

**Figure 9-16
Preferences
Panel Icons**

You can rearrange the icons in the Preferences panel by holding down the Control key and dragging the icons to the positions you prefer.

To rearrange icons, hold down the Control key and drag an icon left or right.

When you make a change to a Preferences option or control, the change takes effect immediately unless otherwise noted in the panel. You can change as many or as few options as you wish at any time. Changes you make in the Preferences application continue to apply even after you log out or power off the computer until you change them.

9.5 Terminal

The Terminal application is your portal to the UNIX command-line interface of NEXTSTEP. Using the Terminal application, you can enter UNIX commands by typing them just as you would type commands on a computer running DOS. You may rarely use the Terminal, as you can accomplish just about everything you need to do using the Workspace Manager. However if you want to program applications, log in to remote computer systems using **telnet** or **rlogin**, or learn UNIX, you will need to use Terminal. Often, system administrators will use a terminal window to log in as the root in order to perform maintenance, without first having to log out of the NEXTSTEP workspace. You may use Terminal to log in to a remote computer, transfer files, or run UNIX commands an utilities not available in the workspace. A detailed description of UNIX commands and jargon is provide in Chapter 13, "UNIX Commands You Should Know".

When you start Terminal, a new shell window will appear named **ttyp1** (see Figure 9-17). In a shell, you can enter UNIX commands such as **ls**, **cd**, **ps**, **cat**, and **man** (you may want to skip ahead and browse "Often-Used UNIX Commands" on page 338). You can have many shell windows open at a the same time, each representing a unique session on the computer. You can run various UNIX utilities and commands in each of the windows and close them at any time to log out from a session.

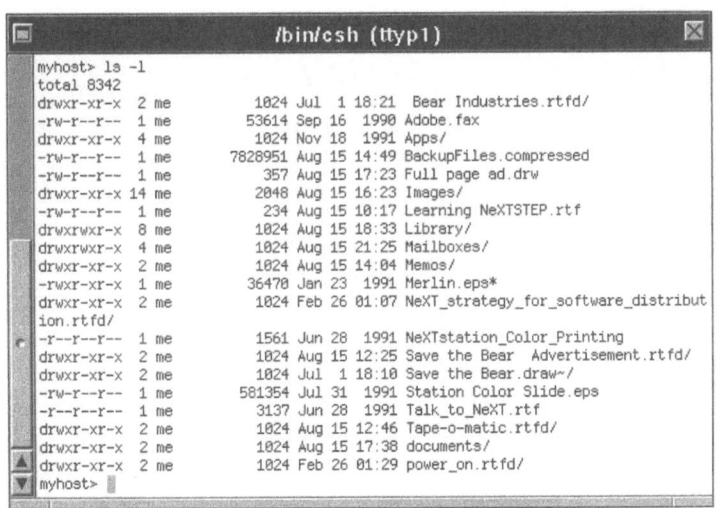

Figure 9-17
The Shell Window

Terminal windows, called shells, represent unique login sessions. In the shell window, you can use only UNIX commands, such as the ls command shown here.

Bundled Applications

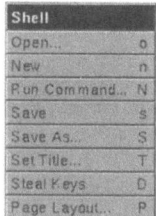

The Shell menu contains Terminal's most commonly used commands.

Terminal's shell menu allows you to customize the shell in many ways. Choose Open to open a customized shell that has been configured for a special purpose or New to open a new standard shell window. You can customize a shell's characteristics using the shell Preferences panel, and then save the shell using the Shell menu's Save and Save As commands so you won't have to reconfigure the window each time you want to use it. The Shell menu even offers a Run Command option, which allows you to run a UNIX command in the background without having to open a new shell window (see Figure 9-18). When the command has finished executing, the results are displayed in a new shell window, leaving the other shell windows undisturbed. If you have many shell windows open at once, you may want to change their titles to make it easier to remember the activities being performed in each window. This prevents you from entering a UNIX command in the wrong window and spoiling a session. To rename a shell window, make it the key window by clicking anywhere on it, and then choose Set Title from the Shell menu. Enter a descriptive title in the Set Title panel, then click Set to set the title. The Shell menu's Steal Keys command is used by application programmers for debugging.

**Figure 9-18
The Run Command Panel**

If you want to run a UNIX command without creating a new shell window, use the Run Command panel (top). Commands entered in Run Command work in the background. If they need to display results, a new shell (bottom) will automatically appear.

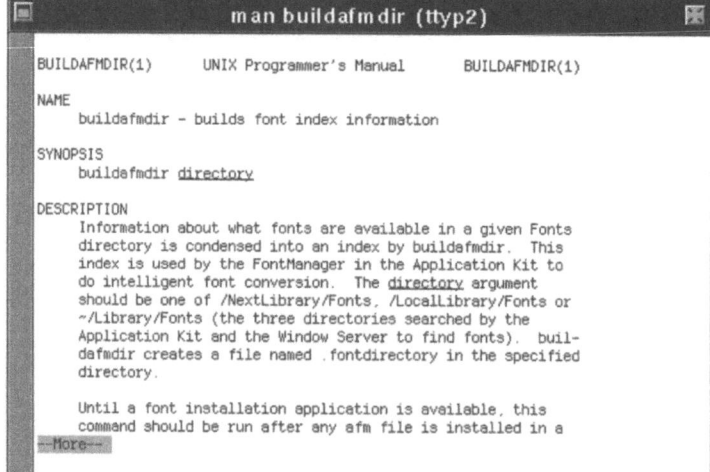

You can customize the font and font size a shell displays using the Terminal application's Font menu commands. To make the text in a shell window larger, choose Larger from the Font menu. To make the text smaller, choose Smaller. You can also choose to have the text displayed in bold and italic using commands in the Font menu, and even select a different font using the Font panel. Remember that the Terminal window relies heavily on text to provide you information so choose a font that is easy to read.

9.6 PrintManager

The PrintManager application, also located in the **/NextApps** folder, is used to create, monitor, and control print and fax modem queues. If you fax or print often, you may want to place the PrintManager icon in the dock or on the File Viewer shelf so you can monitor print and fax requests. For even faster access, have the PrintManager start automatically each time you log in. When you need to see a print queue, you can double-click the PrintManager icon in the dock and its panels will appear instantly.

9.6.0 Managing Print and Fax Queues

When you print or fax a document, it's saved in a queue along with other print and fax requests so that you can continue working. There is a queue for each device you configure. If you have three printers and two fax modems defined, one queue will exist for each of them for a total of five. Because you can submit requests much more quickly than a fax or printer can process them, there will often be several items in a queue. When requests are backed up in this way, you can examine the queue to see which job is being processed, which are in line, and mentally calculate how long it will be until a particular job is processed. All of this is accomplished with the PrintManager application.

After starting PrintManager, choose Printers or Fax Modems from its main menu to display the appropriate queue panel. Each of the fax modems and printers configured for use on your machine will appear in their respective Printers or Fax Modems panel (see Figure 9-19). To see the requests in a particular queue, select the fax modem's or printer's name, then click Queue. The Queue panel will appear and list the documents in the queue that have not yet been processed, the name of the applications that created them, their owner, number of pages they contain, and their size.

Bundled Applications

**Figure 9-19
The Fax Modems and Printers Panels**

The Printers and Fax Modems panels list the names of printers and faxes configured to work through your computer.

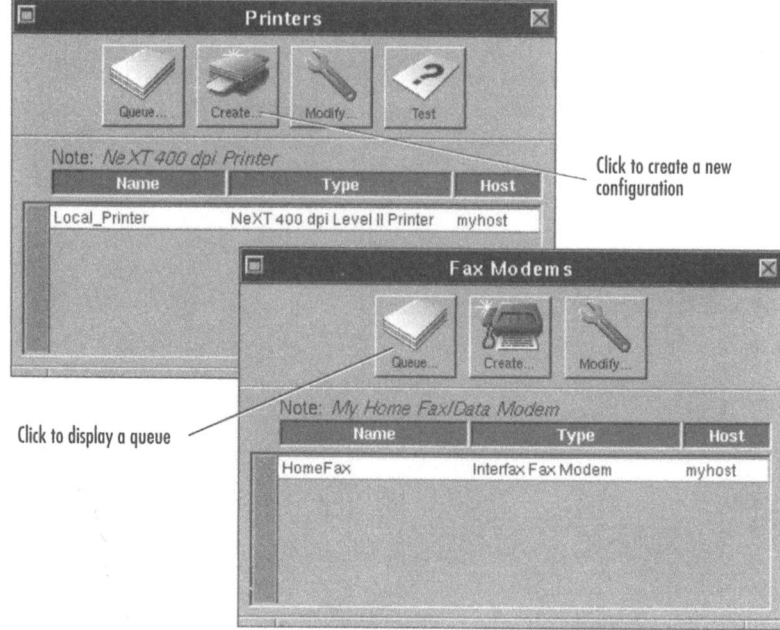

The Printer Queue panel, unlike the Fax Queue panel, contains an extra column to indicate documents that require manual paper feeding. If the document requires paper to be fed manually into the printer, an M will appear in the Feed column of the Printer Queue panel. When the printer is ready to process the document, NEXTSTEP will automatically alert you to feed the required paper using an attention panel, voice message, or both, depending on your selections in the Preferences Application (see "General Preferences" on page 288).

**Figure 9-20
The Printer Queue Panel**

This queue reveals several print requests waiting for the printer. If the job has begun printing, there is no way to stop it before it finishes.

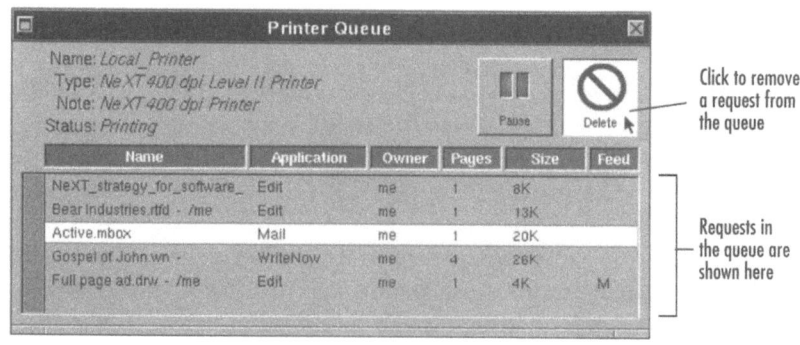

Both the Printer and Fax Queue panels include two buttons, one each for Pause and Delete. Clicking Delete removes the currently selected print request from the queue (see Figure 9-20). Clicking Pause, however, does not pause the request currently being printed as you might expect. Instead, it disables the selected queue, stopping all of the other requests in the queue from being processed until you click Continue. The only way to stop the currently printing job is to select it in the queue and click Delete. Even deleting the current request doesn't stop it immediately. The printer or fax modem will continue to print or fax a few pages after you delete the request being processed while NEXTSTEP deletes it from the queue. You can easily locate the next document to be processed because requests appear in reverse order in the queue with the oldest request at the top of the list and the most recent at the bottom. Queues are always processed in a First In First Out (FIFO) manner so the oldest jobs in the queue get processed first. If you cancel a request but later want to process the remaining pages, you will have to open the document in an application and print or fax it again. There is no way to continue a cancelled job.

9.7 Digital Librarian

The Digital Librarian is a tool for finding and viewing specific information contained in a collection of on-line documents. With it, you can search for every document that contains a particular word or collection of words without knowing the name of the document. Librarian provides several tools for specifying how you would like your search performed and where the search should look. Librarian is very similar to the Finder panel (see "Finding a File or Folder" on page 55), in that they can both search a target folder for a matching file name or for a match in the contents of a document. The difference lies in the detailed control Librarian provides in finding a match. In many cases, the Digital Librarian can also display the document it finds without opening another application, and is also accessible as a Service from other applications.

Pre indexed system administration and Literature bookshelves are provided in NEXTSTEP.

If you're like most computer users, you were probably so excited to get your computer and set it up that you began using it before you read its manuals. If you haven't purchased your computer yet, don't skip the chapter on Digital Librarian. Librarian is extremely important because it's the tool you will use to read on-line documentation, and in the future, FAQs and Questions and Answers. (For more details, see " Frequently Asked Questions (FAQs)" on page 378, and "Questions and Answers" on page 371.) Two bookshelf files are provided in **/NextLibrary/Bookshelves** containing targets relating to system administration and, for your entertainment, the complete works of Shakespeare. These items are pre indexed and ready to use. Many applications also provide on-line documentation and reference manuals pre-indexed for use in Digital Librarian. These are usually installed automatically when the application is installed.

9.7.0 Digital Librarian Targets

Before you can search the contents of a folder with Digital Librarian, you must create or open a bookshelf file, and then make the folder a target. Bookshelf files contain collections of related targets. To create a new bookshelf, choose New from the Bookshelf menu. Each time you add or remove a target from a bookshelf, you'll need to save your changes just as you would with any other document using the Save or Save As command in the Bookshelf menu. To open an existing bookshelf, choose Open from the Bookshelf menu and select the bookshelf you want to open. Bookshelves are typically saved in **~/Library/Bookshelves**, a folder you create. Bookshelves are also typically stored in **the /NextLibrary/Bookshelves** and **/LocalLibrary/Bookshelves** folders. When the Bookshelf window appears, drag a folder icon from a File Viewer onto the Bookshelf's shelf area, just as you would in the Finder panel or a File Viewer window (see Figure 9-21).

**Figure 9-21
Digital Librarian
Bookshelf Window**

A Digital Librarian bookshelf is used to organize related targets to perform searches based on a document's name or contents.

Sorted list of matching documents

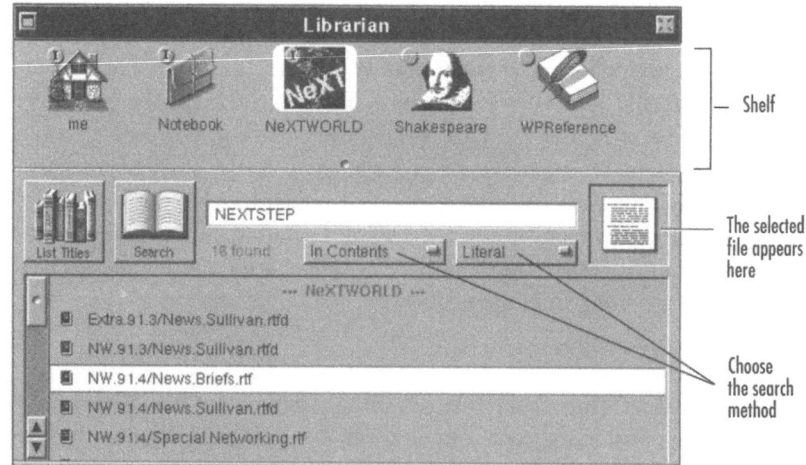

Shelf

The selected file appears here

Choose the search method

9.7.1 Digital Librarian Searches

To search for documents that contain a particular word, type the word into the text field in the center of the Digital Librarian window, and then select the appropriate options using the two pop-up lists to establish the criteria for a match. In Figure 9-21, a search is performed for the literal string NEXTSTEP 3.1 in the contents of the documents contained in the folder named **NeXTWORLD** (the highlighted target). The left pop-up list is used to select where matches will be found. Choosing In File Names will find matches only in the names of documents contained in the target. If you would like to search for the name of a document manually, click List Titles. The names of every document in the target will appear in the lower half of the Librarian window. If you choose In Contents from the pop-up list, Digital Librarian will only find matches that occur within the text of the documents in the target, not in their names.

You can search for matches in the contents of documents or in their names.

The item selected in the right pop-up list determines how, not where, matches will be found. For example, choosing Word will only match when the word appears by itself and not as part of a larger word. If you enter multiple words, only documents that contain all of the words will be found. A match is found even when the words do not appear together. Choosing Prefix will result in a match when the word is found and when the word appears at the beginning of another word such as *an* and *another*. Choosing Within will find a match when the word is found and when the word appears anywhere within another word, such as *hovel* and *shovel*. Choosing Literal will only match the word or words you entered when they appear together in that order. For example, if you enter *mouse button*, Digital Librarian will only list documents where the phrase *mouse button* appears. It will not match *button mouse* or *mouse* or *button*. The Expression option is used to match UNIX regular expressions. To learn more about regular expressions, type **man ed** in a Terminal window. For more about the **man** command, see "The man Command" on page 351.

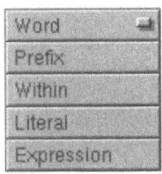

Use this list to change the way Digital Librarian finds matches.

After selecting the search method, click Search to begin finding matches. While Librarian is searching the target, the Search button will change into a Stop button. You can stop a search at any time by clicking Stop. If you let the search continue to normal completion, the Stop button automatically reverts to Search. This button's change of name is the only indication that a search is complete.

While it is possible that a search may find no matches, typically it will find many. When Digital Librarian finds a match, its lists the names of documents in which a match occurred in the lower portion of the Librarian window and sorts them according to the method selected in the Searching Inspector (described in 9.7.3, "The Searching Inspector").

9.7.2 Document Inspection

To inspect a document in Digital Librarian, double-click its name or its icon in the icon well. Librarian, or an appropriate application, will open it and display the page on which the search string was found. The application that will open the document is indicated by the icon that appears in the Librarian icon well when the document is selected. A default application is set to open documents of a particular type (to review how to set the default application, see "Using the Tools Inspector" on page 110). The search string will also be selected so you can identify it easily. To inspect another document, return to the Librarian window and double-click another document in the list. Repeat this procedure as many time as necessary to find what you are looking for. When you find interesting text, images, or sounds, you can move or copy the information using the Copy and Paste commands as usual. To copy the entire document or import it into another document, drag its icon from the Librarian icon well into a File Viewer or document window.

9.7.3 The Searching Inspector

Normally Digital Librarian lists the items it finds in alphabetical order. However, you can change the sort order using the Searching Inspector. To display the Inspector, choose Inspector from the Target menu, and then select Searching in the Inspector panel's pop-up list. There are four methods: by description, by weight, by date, or unsorted (see Figure 9-21).

Digital Librarian

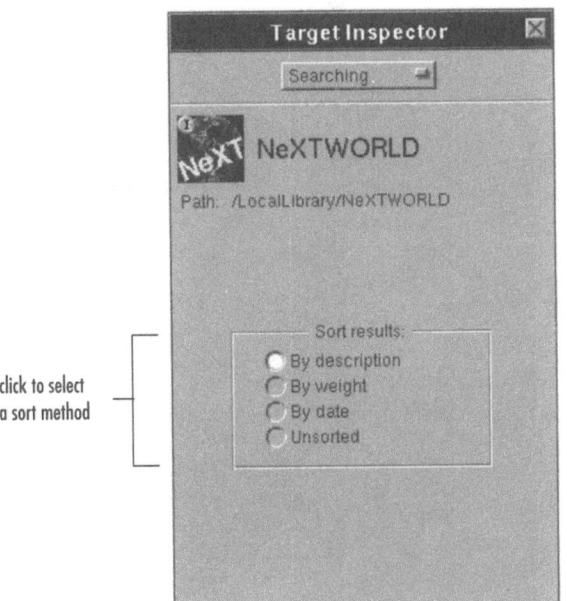

**Figure 9-22
The Searching Inspector**

The Searching Inspector is used to select the method Digital Librarian uses to sort the documents it matches. Only one method may be selected at a time.

click to select a sort method

The By description option sorts the found items alphabetically. Sorting By weight places the documents with the most matches near the top of the list and those with the fewest at the bottom. Sorting By date places the items in reverse chronological order with items modified most recently near the top. The Unsorted option lists items in the same order in which they were found.

9.7.4 The Indexing Inspector

Although you don't have to index a target in order to search it, doing so will dramatically increase the speed of a Digital Librarian search. The Finder panel can also make use of Digital Librarian indexes (see "The Finder Option" on page 279). To index a target, double-click the target, or select the target and choose Inspector from the Digital Librarian Target menu. Either method will cause the Target Inspector panel to appear. To create or update a target's index, choose Indexing from the pop-up menu, then click Set Up or Update (see Figure 9-21). When a target has been indexed, an index symbol will appear in the upper left corner of its icon on the Digital Librarian shelf.

 Unindexed

 Indexed

**Figure 9-23
The Indexing
Inspector**

To create or update a target's index, use the Indexing Inspector. Digital Librarian can be set to automatically update a target's index or to wait for you to update it manually.

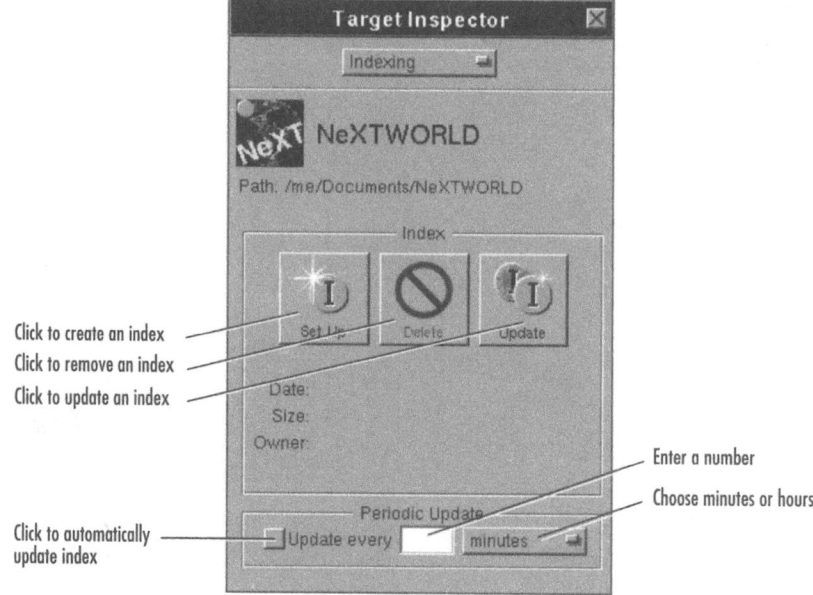

Digital Librarian does not continually update a target's index so if you make changes to documents within the target, the index may be out of date, and a search may fail to turn up a match. To have Librarian update a target's index automatically, select the target, display the Indexing Inspector, and turn on the switch next to Update every. In the text field enter a number and choose minutes or hours from the pop-up list (see Figure 9-21). Note that the Digital Librarian must be running for automatic indexing to occur. To keep it running but out of the way, hide it after it starts or miniaturize its window.

9.7.5 The Services Inspector

The Services Inspector provides two switches, Jot in and Search in (see Figure 9-24). These apply to the currently selected target so be sure you have the appropriate target selected before turning them on or off. Turning on the Jot in switch makes the currently selected target appear in the Services menu item of other applications. The purpose of this option is to allow you to store bits and pieces of information or whole documents from other sources in a single place, index, and retrieve quickly. For example, every new NEXTSTEP account contains a folder named **Notebook** as a Jot in item so scraps of information can be saved easily. To use the Notebook target, select a portion of text in any other application, and then choose the Jot selection in Notebook to save the text in the Notebook folder. The text is automatically saved in a text document in the Notebook folder without having to open the Edit or Digital Librarian applications. If you want to save an entire document, choose Jot document in Notebook.

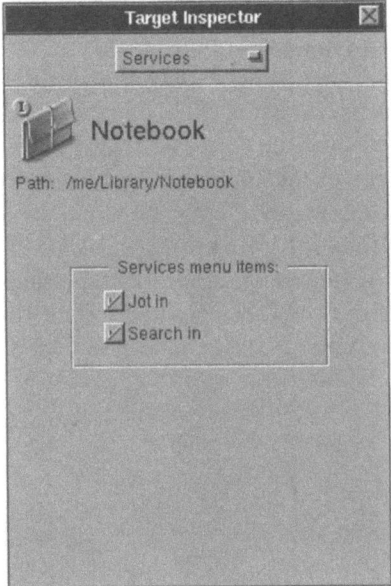

**Figure 9-24
The Services Inspector**

Using the Services Inspector, you can make a target appear as an item in the Services menu of other applications.

The document containing the text is named using the date, and then numbered sequentially so that if the service is used again, the second document doesn't overwrite the first. Don't worry that the name of the document may not describe the information it contains; you'll be using the Librarian to search for the information according to its content, not its file name. This may be a radical change if you're used to visually searching a DOS or Macintosh file system for a file name, but you'll quickly get used to it. Using the Jot in service, you can very easily keep track of odd pieces of information that might otherwise get lost. By the way, you can add any number of targets to the Services menu as Jot in items. So for example, you could create several folders to store information such as Personal, Things to Do, Do Today, Action Items, Review, and Pending, then place scraps of text into each one to keep them organized.

Turning on the Search in switch places the currently selected target into the Services menu, too, but as a place in which to search for information rather than record it. For example, suppose you need to retrieve an important product announcement that you saved in the Notebook folder (the target) using Jot in. Now you're using another application, perhaps the WriteNow word processor and you need to place a quote from the announcement into the report you're writing. To search the **Notebook** folder from WriteNow, you highlight a key word with which to search, perhaps the name of the product or the name of the person you want to quote, and then simply select Search in Notebook from the Library item in the Services menu. The Librarian will open, the Notebook target will be selected, the text you highlighted will be entered and a search will be performed, all automatically. You can then double-click the appropriate document in the Digital Librarian to open it, copy the text, and return to WriteNow to paste it. NEXTSTEP's ability to multitask makes this tight integration of applications possible and greatly simplifies the work you must do to not only find information, but make it useful. As with Jot in, you can make any number of folders Search in items in the Services menu.

You can open Digital Librarian from any application by choosing Search from the Librarian item in its Services menu. You can also make any folder a target by selecting it in a File Viewer and choosing Target from the Library item of the Services menu.

9.7.6 The Languages Inspector

Several language modules are bundled with NEXTSTEP. Digital Librarian will index documents differently depending on the language being used. To assist Digital Librarian in indexing targets optimally, use the Languages Inspector to indicate which language is being used for each target. You can use different languages for each target if necessary.

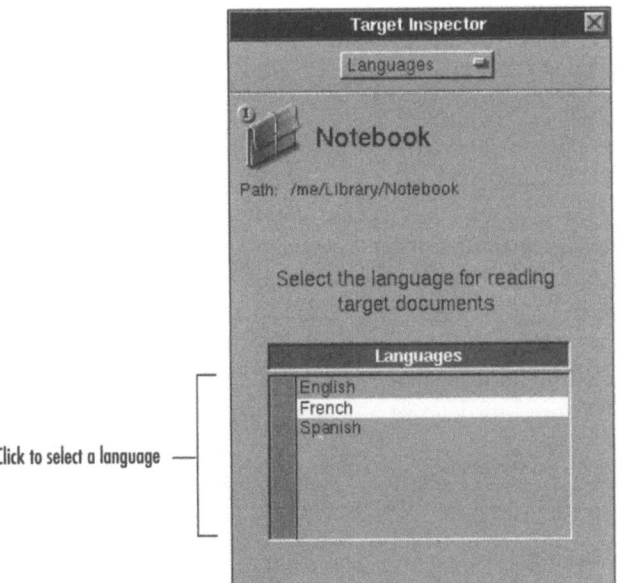

**Figure 9-25
The Languages
Inspector**

Use the Languages Inspector to tell Digital Librarian how to best index a target.

9.8 Digital Webster

NEXTSTEP includes an on-line dictionary and thesaurus called Digital Webster, based on *Webster's Ninth New Collegiate Dictionary*, and *Webster's Collegiate® Thesaurus*. Webster is easy to use as a stand alone application, and is also available to other applications via the Services menu (see "Services" on page 150). To find the meaning of a word, double-click the Digital Webster icon in a File Viewer or in the application dock, type the word into the text field in the Digital Webster panel, and then click Define. If the word is contained in the dictionary or thesaurus, the complete listing from both of these works will appear in the information area at the bottom of the Digital Webster panel. You can copy and paste this information into other text documents or simply read it as a reference. If you choose to copy and paste a reference into another document, remember to obtain permission in writing, as the dictionary and thesaurus are both copyrighted.

If you want to search only the dictionary, or only the thesaurus, you can close them by clicking their icons in the Digital Webster panel (Figure 9-26). The dictionary and thesaurus icons, which appear as open books, will appear as closed books when you click them. When they are closed, Digi-

Bundled Applications

tal Webster will not search through them to match the word entered into the text field. Be sure to have at least one of the two book icons open before attempting to define a word. If both are closed at once, Digital Webster will ask you to open one or the other or both before it will attempt to look up a word.

If the definition is long, you can locate the word you entered in the Digital Webster panel within the definition by clicking Find. When you click Find, the word is located within the text area and highlighted so you can see it easily. If you click Find again, the next occurrence of the word will be highlighted. You can repeat this procedure to locate all occurrences of the word within the definition. To look up another word, enter a new word in the text field and click Define. If the word is found in the dictionary or thesaurus, its definition will be displayed.

Figure 9-28
Digital Webster

To find the definition of a word, type it in the text field and click Define. If the Thesaurus icon is an open book, synonyms for the word will appear below its definition.

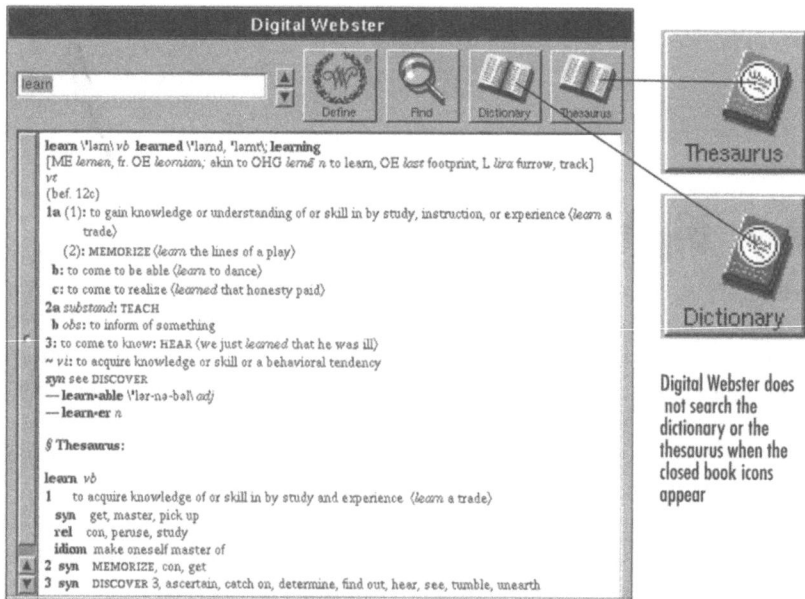

Digital Webster does not search the dictionary or the thesaurus when the closed book icons appear

There are several advantages to having the Webster's dictionary and thesaurus on-line compared to having them in paper form. One of greatest advantages is that you can easily cross-reference words contained in a definition. For example, if you don't know the meaning of a word used in a definition, you can select it using the mouse, then click Define to look up the meaning of the word. In this manner you can quickly learn the meanings of words that you want to know, as well as the words used to define their meaning. A second advantage of Digital Webster is that it maintains a record of the words you have defined so that you can revisit their definitions quickly. To the right of the text field in the Digital Webster panel are two arrows (solid black triangles). Clicking the up arrow displays the word previously defined, and clicking the down arrow displays the word previously defined. Clicking these arrows repeatedly reviews all of the words you have defined since you started running Digital Webster. To see a previous definition click the appropriate arrow button until the desired word appears, then click Define. When you quit Digital Webster, the list of words is cleared and a new one begun. Last, but certainly not least is that the computer can look up the definition of a word while you work on another task. For example, begin a search in Digital Webster then continue working in another application. While you are working, Digital Webster is looking up the definition. When it is convenient, you can return to Digital Webster to read it.

9.9 Digital Quotations

A digital version of the *Oxford® Dictionary of Quotations* is included with NEXTSTEP to help you when writing speeches, historical research papers, and even documentation. To start Quotations, double-click its icon in a File Viewer or the application dock. The Quotations panel looks and operates very much like Digital Librarian (see Figure 9-27). You enter a word or phrase that is contained in a famous quotation, click the Quote button to make the dialog bubble on the button turn white, and then click Search to see a list of quotations that contain the word. If you want to see a list of quotations by a particular person, enter their name in the text field, click Quote to make the silhouetted image of the speaker turn white, then click Search. If several quotes are listed, click Find to have Quotations highlight the next occurrence of the word in the Quotations panel.

Bundled Applications

**Figure 9-27
Digital Quotations**

To find a quote, enter a word or phrase and click Search. To search by author, click the Quote button to turn the silhouette white and click Search. To search for a quote, click the Quote button to turn the dialog bubble white, and then click Search.

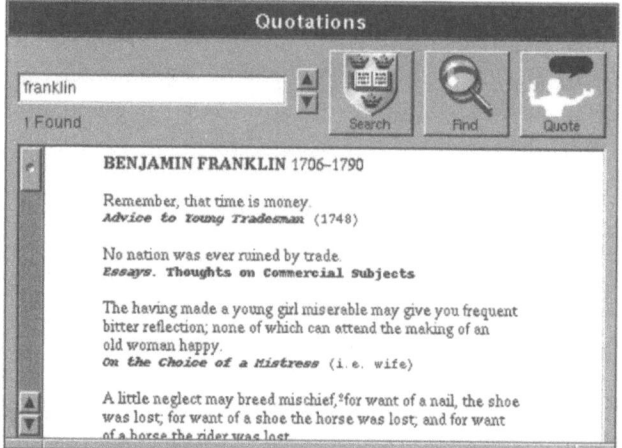

Like Digital Webster, Digital Quotations remembers the words you have searched for since it started running. You can review these words and the listings they generated by clicking the up and down arrows next to the text field. When you find a quote you like, you can copy and paste it from the Quotations panel into another document. Be sure to give the author of the quote credit by including his or her name along with the quote when you copy and paste it into another document. Quotations is also available from other applications using the Services menu. To learn more about services, see "Services" on page 150.

9.10 Grab

NEXTSTEP includes a handy little application named Grab, that enables you to take a picture of the screen and save the image in a TIFF file or copy it to the pasteboard. This is commonly referred to as grabbing a portion of the screen, hence the name of the application. Grab is wonderful if you need to document NEXTSTEP applications or procedures, or want to record a message that appears in an alert panel or a menu choice. You can save a picture of anything that appears on the display and import it into another application, such as WriteNow, FrameMaker, or Appsoft Draw. To capture an image on the display, start the Grab application by double-clicking its icon in a File Viewer or in the dock.

Grab

Grab provides several options for taking a picture. To photograph a window, choose Window from the Grab menu. Grab will include the title bar, scrollers and other window parts, as well as the contents of the window in the picture. The NeXT logo in the application dock will become a camera icon to indicate that Grab is running and ready to take a picture. If you need to display a particular window or application, open it and position it on the screen as required. To take the picture, click the camera icon in the application dock. The arrow cursor will become the pointer cursor, which you use to select the window to be photographed. When you click any portion of a window, you will hear the camera's shutter click, the window will be photographed, and it will appear in a new window. It is normal for the mouse to freeze for a moment or two while the picture is being taken, so don't be alarmed if this happens.

Pointer cursor
Arrow cursor

If you choose to photograph the screen, the NeXT logo in the dock will again become a camera icon. Open and position windows on the screen to prepare for the picture. When you are ready, click the camera, and then click anywhere on the screen. A picture of the entire screen will be taken and presented in a new window.

345, 587

When you choose Selection in the Grab menu, the arrow cursor becomes a right-angle (see bottom image in margin). Point to the upper left portion of the screen you wish to grab and hold down a mouse button. You will see in pixels, the coordinates you have selected. As you drag the mouse, the coordinates will change to indicate the size of the area you are selecting in pixels. A black box will surround the selection so that you can see what will be included in the picture. When you have selected the desired area, release the mouse button to take the picture.

Grab will display the picture it takes in a new window. You can save the picture as a TIFF file by choosing Save in Grab's File menu, or choose Copy from Grab's Edit menu to copy the image to the pasteboard. Select a location for the file in the file system using the Save panel, then enter a name for the file and click OK. If you don't like the picture, close its window and click Don't Save when the Save attention panel appears. The window will disappear and the picture will be lost. Take another picture or continue with your work.

Normally, the cursor is not included in a picture so that it doesn't appear in the image. To have the cursor appear in a picture, choose the Choose Cursor command in the Grab menu. The Choose Cursor panel will appear (see Figure 9-28), displaying the various NEXTSTEP cursors that can be photographed, including a selection for no cursor, which is used to make the cursor invisible during photographs. Click a Cursor to select it. When you take a picture, the cursor you selected will replace the arrow cursor in the picture.

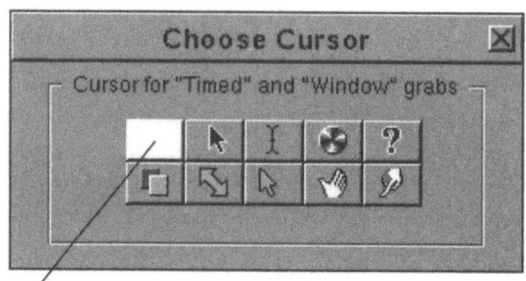

**Figure 9-28
The Choose
Cursor Panel**

Use this panel to choose the type of cursor you want to appear in the picture (clockwise from the upper left corner: none, arrow, I-beam, spinning disk, Help, pointer, hand, copy arrow, link, and copy).

This selection means no cursor will appear

9.11 Demonstration Applications

NEXTSTEP contains many more applications in **/NextDeveloper/Demos** on an "as is" basis with no documentation, support, or explanation. These demonstration, or demo, applications can be interesting, useful, or simply entertaining. They are included with NEXTSTEP to showcase unique features, serve as examples to software developers, and provide entertainment. Very little documentation exists for these demos except in their help and info panels. However, most of their features are obvious and can be easily learned after using them a short while. To help you get started, this section offers a description of the unique or interesting features of each these demos.

9.11.0 Billiards

Billiards is a fun and fascinating electronic pool table. It can be played by one or more players and offers variations on play, such as pool, eight-ball, nine-ball, and slop. Billiards works very much like a real pool table. After selecting the type of game you want to play from the Game menu, position the cursor behind the cue ball and drag the mouse to extend the cue stick (see Figure 9-29). The further you drag, the harder the resulting shot. You can also change the angle of the cue stick by dragging in various directions. When you release a mouse button, the cue stick will strike the ball

Demonstration Applications

and set the shot in motion. To win the game, follow the standard rules of play for the game you selected. The rules for each game are provided in the Help panel available by choosing Help in Billiard's Info menu.

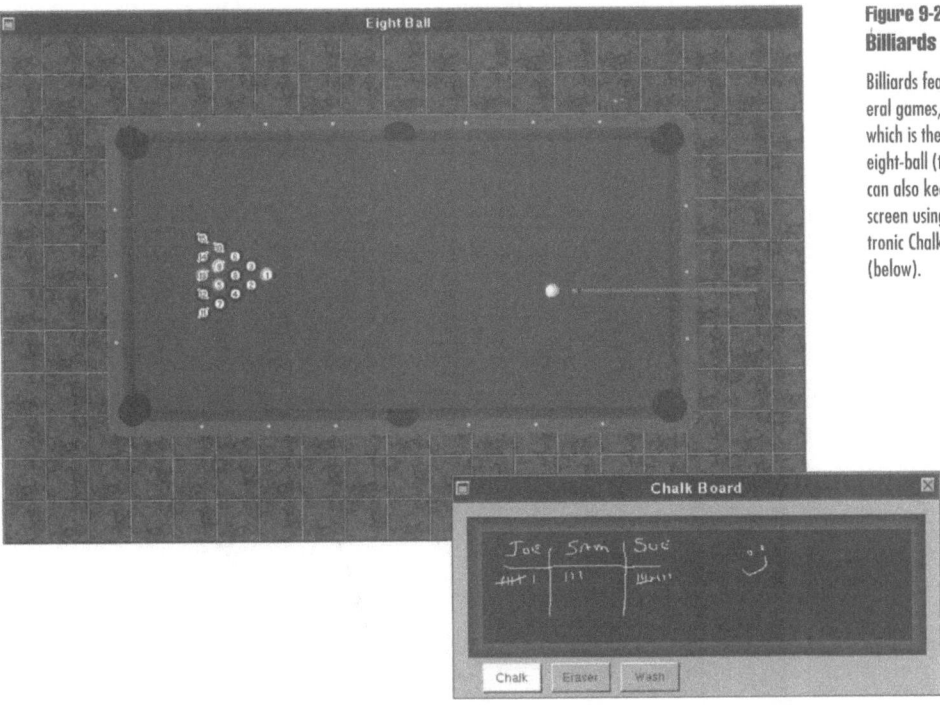

Figure 9-29
Billiards

Billiards features several games, one of which is the popular eight-ball (top). You can also keep score on screen using the electronic Chalkboard (below).

For added realism, you can turn on sound effects and keep score using an electronic chalkboard. If you're in need of practice, you can replay a shot, stop a shot in progress, and undo a shot. If you need extra help, you can even turn on the X-ray feature which acts as a laser sight and helps you line up your shots. Finally, if you enjoy watching rather than participating, you can turn on auto-play and watch as the computer attempts to clear the table. All of these options are provided in Billiard's Tools menu.

> If you want to practice trick shots, you can drag the balls to better position them on the table, then shoot as usual to test your skill. If you want to remove a ball from the table, drag it into a corner pocket. The ball will appear below the table in a "rack". To put a ball back on the table, drag it from the rack and drop it in position on the table. Don't worry about dropping the ball. You won't hurt the felt!

9.11.1 BoinkOut

BoinkOut is a NEXTSTEP rendition of the popular BrickOut arcade game in which the object is to knock out all of the bricks by hitting them with a colorful and changing ball, using an on-screen paddle (see Figure 9-30). One of the most enjoyable features of this game is its use of sound. Unlike most video games, BoinkOut plays very subtle sounds when bricks are hit by the bouncing ball, the ball strikes the paddle, and the paddle misses the ball. This application is an outstanding example of NEXTSTEP color, animation, and sound.

Figure 9-30
BoinkOut

BoinkOut is a fun game in which you try to eliminate every brick on the screen by hitting it with the bouncing balls. Use the paddle to deflect the bouncing ball back toward the bricks.

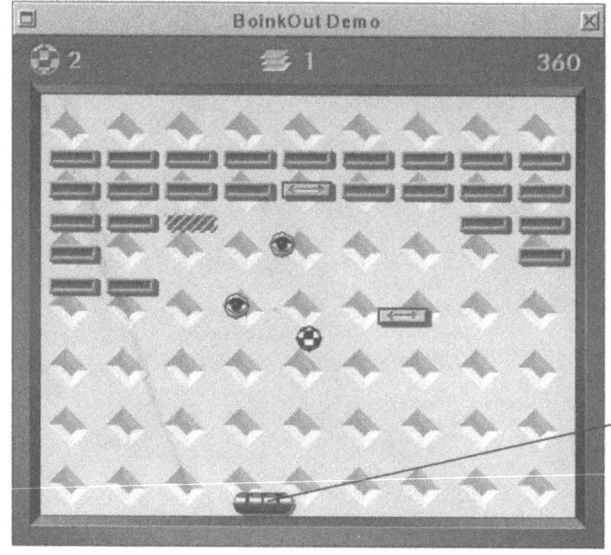

Position the paddle to deflect the bouncing balls

9.11.2 BugNeXT

If your computer is able to send Internet mail, you can use the BugNeXT application to send NeXT a comment, suggestion, or bug report. BugNeXT allows you to create a message and helps you describe the problem by providing a collection of topics and automatically routing your message, along with information about your computer system, through the NeXTmail application. You may not get a personal reply from NeXT, but you can feel satisfied that your suggestions and reports of problems are received. To prevent NeXT from being overburdened with unnecessary or false bug reports, do your best to find a solution from every other possible source before sending NeXT a message.

Demonstration Applications

Before you send your first report, use the BugNeXT Preferences panel to enter information common to every report, and to verify NeXT's e-mail address and your return e-mail address. To do this, choose Preferences from the Info menu. When the BugNeXT Preferences panel appears, type the name of your company, a description of your computer, your e-mail address, and the e-mail address for NeXT (see Figure 6-31).

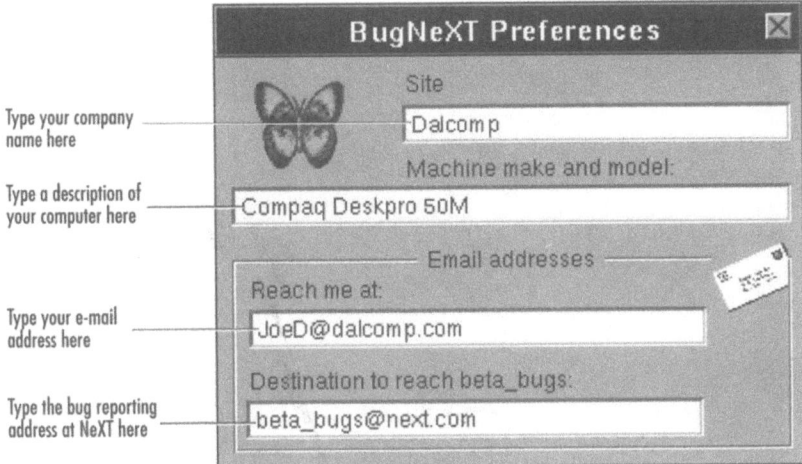

**Figure 6-31
BugNeXT
Preferences
Panel**

Use this panel to set the default information for every report.

To submit a report, select a topic using the browser in the Submit panel. Type a title for your bug report or suggestion in the Title field, then press Return and type your report or suggestion (see Figure 6-31). Be as descriptive as possible so that the problem or suggestion will not be misunderstood. You can check the spelling of your report by choosing Spelling from the Edit menu. Finally, select the item from the Severity pop-up list that best describes your report and click Submit to send the report to NeXT. If you make a mistake and want to start your message over again, click Clear. To send another message, choose New from the Submit menu.

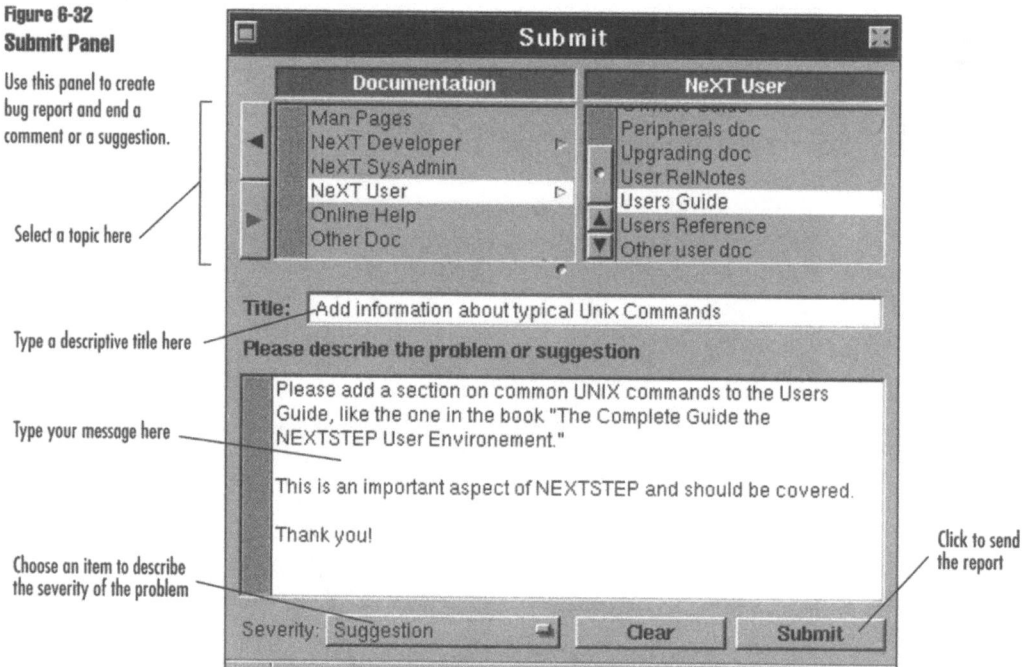

Figure 6-32
Submit Panel

Use this panel to create bug report and end a comment or a suggestion.

Select a topic here

Type a descriptive title here

Type your message here

Choose an item to describe the severity of the problem

Click to send the report

9.11.3 CDPlayer

If you purchased a NeXT CD-ROM drive, you can play audio CDs as well as read data from CD-ROM discs. The trick is to use the CDPlayer application in **/NextDeveloper/Demos**. You'll also need to use walkman-style headphones in the headphone jack or self-powered speakers such as Acoustic Research's AR-570 Powered Partners. CDPlayer allows you to select a particular track, skip tracks, and play tracks in random order. If you have a NeXT CD-ROM drive, don't miss out on this feature. Drives from other manufacturers may work, but many use different signals for playing audio CDs and will not respond to CDPlayer, so be careful when purchasing a CD-ROM player for your computer.

Demonstration Applications

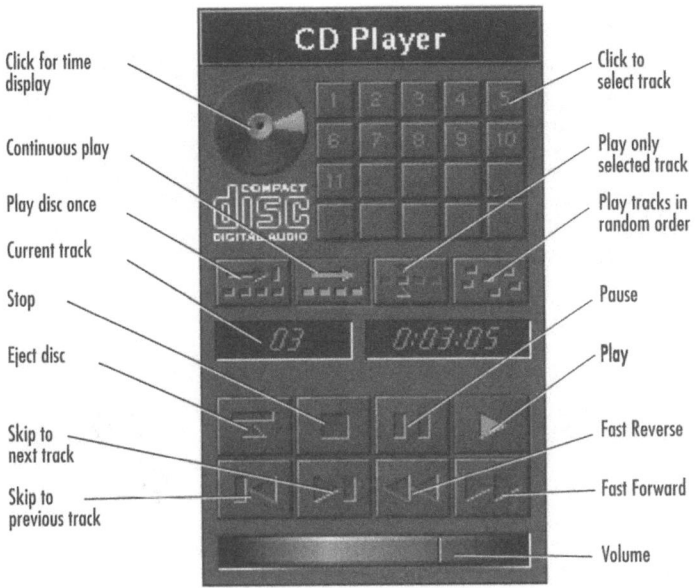

**Figure 9-33
CDPlayer
Application**

The CDPlayer demo application provides all of the controls associated with a standard CD-player remote control and works in conjunction with the NeXT CD-ROM drive.

9.11.4 Chess

One of the more beautiful demonstration applications is Chess. As its name implies, Chess is an electronic version of the popular board game. It is based on the publicly available GNU chess, but employs a NEXTSTEP graphical interface. You can view the board in two dimensions, as it appears in chess books and newspapers that illustrate brilliant moves, or in three dimensions as you would see it when playing with real chess pieces (see Figure 9-34). By default, you will be assigned the white pieces and be allowed to start the game. To begin a game, move any piece on the board by dragging it. (In the three-dimensional view, each square on the chess board will display a white border as the piece touches it.) To place a chess piece on a particular square, release a mouse button. If you make an illegal move, the computer will beep and reposition the piece in its original location so you can move it again. After you move a chess piece, the computer will calculate an appropriate counter move and position a black piece. The game continues until one either the black or white king is in checkmate.

Figure 9-34
Chess

This figure illustrates the three-dimensional view of the chessboard. By default, the human player controls the white chess pieces.

Chess also provides two panels with which you can view and alter a game. The Controls panel allows you to view the computer's progress as it analyzes the board and attempts to choose its next move. As the computer completes its analysis, it displays a white bar (see Figure 9-35). When the white bar fills the box, the computer will make its move. You can force the computer to move a piece before it is ready by clicking Force Computer to Move. This can be useful if you are short on time or if you are losing and want to prevent the computer from making the best possible move. Also using the Controls panel, you can change the color of each set of chess pieces. For example, click the frame of the color well (see Figure 9-35), then select a color from the Colors panel that appears. As you select a color, the sample chess piece (the knight) in the Controls panel will change so you can preview your selection. When you have made your final color choice, click Set Color Pieces to apply the new color to the pieces on the chessboard. Be sure to choose easily distinguishable colors for each

Demonstration Applications

player's pieces or you may confuse them. The colors will only apply while Chess is running. When you quit and restart Chess, the chess pieces will revert to their normal colors.

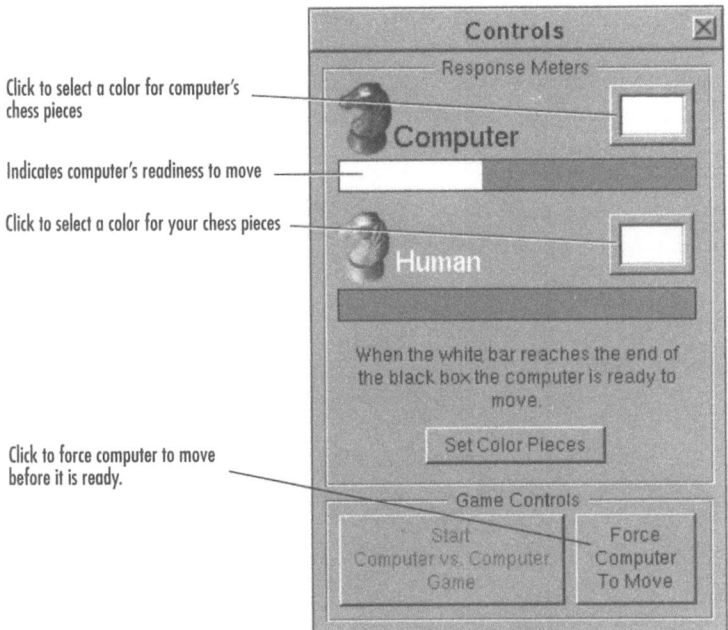

**Figure 9-35
Controls Panel**

Using the controls panel, you can watch the computer "think" and force it to move before it is ready. Before a game begins, you can also choose to make the computer play against itself.

Using the Preferences panel, you can make the computer opponent more or less challenging, ranging from 60 moves in 5 minutes (less time to "think"), to 1 move in 600 minutes (more time to "think") as shown in Figure 9-35. You can also use this panel to set the default for who is to play and what color pieces they will have. For example, you can set the default to computer vs. computer, human vs. human, or human vs. computer. When you have made you selections, click Set to make them the default for each new game.

If you choose to have the computer play against itself, you won't be able to move the first piece to begin the game as you normally would. Instead, click Start Computer vs. Computer Game in the Controls panel.

One of the advantages of playing computer chess is that you have the opportunity to play and replay any number of moves. This allows you to see how one move affects another and to pursue several possible outcomes to the same game. To undo a move, choose Undo from the Move menu.

You can undo any number of moves back to the first move of the game. If you happened to miss the computer's last move, you can have the computer point it out to you by choosing Show Last Move from the Move menu. Finally, if you are stuck and can't figure out which piece you should move, you can ask the computer for help. Choose Hint from the Move menu. The square containing the piece that should be moved will blink, then the square to which the piece should be moved will blink. Choosing Hint several times will not reveal different possible moves, only the same suggested move over and over.

**Figure 9-36
Preferences Panel**

Using the Chess Preferences panel, you can determine the game's level of difficulty and the type of opponent you wish to have play.

Drag to set level of difficulty

Click to set opponents

Type to enter names for opponents

Click to make these the choices default for all new games.

9.11.5 Draw

The Draw application is used to create images, diagrams, illustrations, fax cover sheet templates, and just about any other drawing you might care to create. Draw is an excellent tool with which to learn about NEXTSTEP because it features many of the standard NEXTSTEP panels, such as Open, Save As, Font, Spelling, Link, and Color found in many NEXTSTEP applications. Draw does not include extensive documentation, but is easily learned with only a little practice. To learn more about Draw, review the Help panel displayed by choosing Help from its Info menu. Some of the more interesting and unintuitive aspects of Draw are described below.

Draw Tools

To create an image in a Draw document, click a tool in the Tools panel, then drag the mouse to apply the tool to the drawing (see Figure 9-37). For example, to draw a rectangle, click the rectangle tool, then drag the mouse with a mouse button down diagonally across the Draw document to create a rectangle.

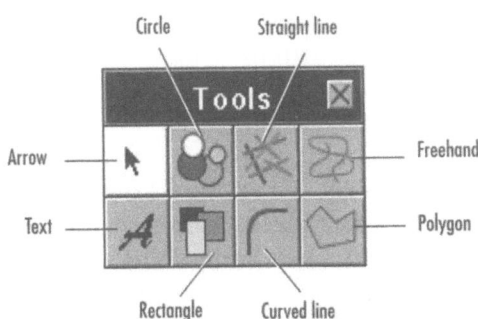

**Figure 9-37
Draw Tools**

Use the Tools palette to select a tool with which to draw. Each tool is used to create a new object, except the arrow which is used to select, move, or resize an object.

To add text to a drawing, click the Text tool, then click on the document to position the insertion point, and type the text you would like to have appear. The result is an invisible rectangle containing the text called a text object. To change the appearance use the Font panel as described in "The Font Panel" on page 134. Draw's Font menu also includes common font menu commands which include Bold, Italic, Underline, Subscript, Superscript and Unscript. Two unusual Font commands, Copy Font and Paste Font, allows you to copy the font characteristics of a text object and apply them to another text object without changing the text. To use these commands, create a text object apply desired font characteristics and choose Copy Font. To apply all of the font characteristics, select text in another text object using the Text tool and choose Paste Font.

Draw also features a grid which can be made visible or invisible, to assist in aligning items. Draw's Snap to Grid command forces items you draw to align with the nearest grid mark. There are also alignment commands to group graphic images and to align text. You can even groups several items together to create more complex drawings and preserve each item's relative spacing when moving them around a document. To change line weight, apply color, and apply special effects to a selected item, use the commands located in the Draw Inspector panel.

Fax Cover Sheet Templates

An interesting use for Draw is to create fax cover sheet templates (see Figure 9-38). A cover sheet template can include a company logo, photograph, as well as the fax text fields. Special commands are contained in Draw's Fax Cover Sheet menu to automatically enter the special fax fields. These commands allow you to insert a text field for the current date, notes, sender (From), recipient (To), number of pages, and the address of the sender. When a fax is sent using this cover letter, the fields are replaced automatically with the information you enter when you prepare the fax. The border around the field does not print, nor does the title of the field; only the contents will appear.

To insert a fax text field in a Draw document, select the field name from the Fax Cover Sheet submenu. A light gray box containing the name of the field will appear in the document; it can be resized and relocated anywhere in the document. You can change the way text will appear in a field by selecting the field and choosing font characteristics from the Font panel or Format menu. If you would like to alter the name of a field in the document, double-click the field to select its name, and then edit the name. When you click anywhere outside the selected field, the field's name will be unselected and the field will again appear as a gray box. You can rename a field using any name you want. NEXTSTEP will remember the type of information it's supposed to contain and will substitute the proper information when you use it to send a fax. You can always preview the fax and cover page to verify that everything looks as it should. When you have finished creating a new fax cover sheet template, give it an easily identifiable name and save it in **~/Library/Fax**, **/NextLibrary/Fax/English.lproj**, or **/LocalLibrary/Fax**. Fax covers sheets placed in any other folder will not be seen by NEXTSTEP.

Demonstration Applications

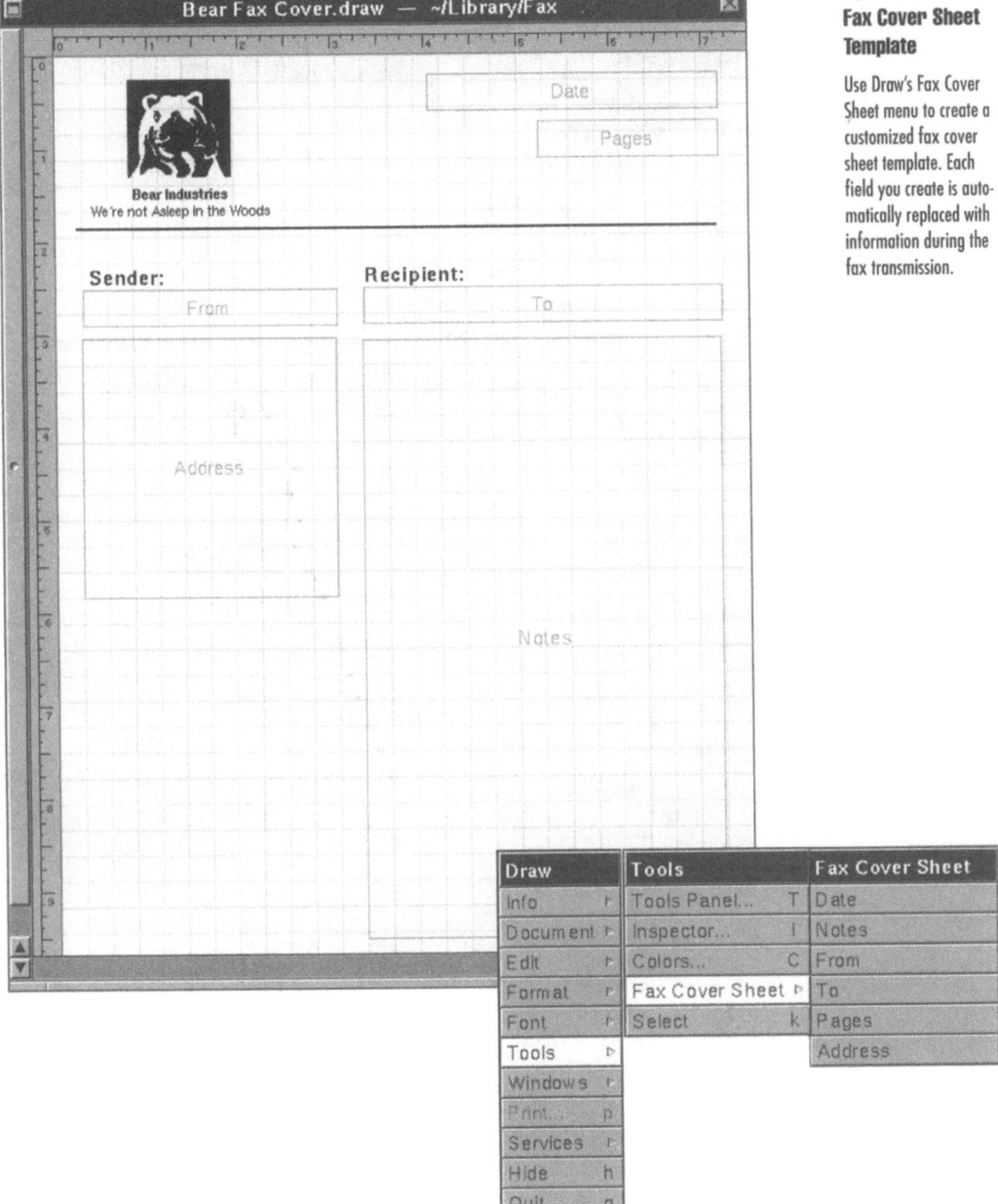

**Figure 9-38
Fax Cover Sheet Template**

Use Draw's Fax Cover Sheet menu to create a customized fax cover sheet template. Each field you create is automatically replaced with information during the fax transmission.

When creating a fax cover sheet template, consider the following:

❖ Don't make a fax cover too detailed or intricate. Fax machines are not high resolution, and small details are easily lost or unreadable.

❖ Use large simple type. If the type you choose is too fancy or small, it may not be readable after being printed by the receiving fax machine. Use at least 14 point type for best results.

❖ Don't put too much on the fax cover sheet. The more text, graphics, and artwork you place on the cover sheet, the longer it will take to image, send, and print. This increases the cost of the transmission, uses up ink, and wastes time on the recipient's fax machine. Remember, the pages behind the cover sheet contain the important information. Keep the cover simple.

When you save a Draw document that contains fax text fields, Draw will display an attention panel asking if you are sure you want to keep these fields. If you're not intending to create a fax cover sheet template, do not save the document, as these fields will not appear when the document is printed. Replace the fax fields with rectangles created using the rectangle tool and save the document again. If you want open, print, or modify an image created with Draw in another application, you'll need to save the image using a format other than Draw's native file format, signified by a **.draw** file extension. Choose Save To instead of Save or Save As. When the Save To panel appears, you will have the option of selecting TIFF or EPS as the file format. These file formats are supported by many other NEXTSTEP applications.

9.11.6 Keyboard

When you press a key on the keyboard, NEXTSTEP identifies the key you pressed and refers to a keymap to determine the character it should display on the screen. The Keyboard application can be used to customize a keyboard map so you can produce characters for which there is otherwise no keyboard equivalent or to make special characters easier to access. For example, you can modify the keyboard so that pressing Alternate-a creates the Adieresis Ä character, or so Control-p creates the π symbol. To assign a special character to a key, drag the character symbol from the matrix at the top of the Keyboard panel to the keyboard key at the bottom of the panel that you would like to use to create the character (see Figure 9-39). If you want to use a modifier key, such as Shift, Alternate, or Control, click the modifier key in the keyboard on-screen, and then drag the character onto the key to set it. Modifier keys will stay on, so you can easily assign additional characters to modifier key combinations. To turn of the modifier key, click it again. When a modifier key is on, it turns white in the on-screen keyboard. When it is off, the key turns gray. If you want to assign symbols, rather than the characters found in the standard character set, choose Symbols from Keyboard's Table menu. Symbols will appear instead of standard characters so you can assign them to key combinations.

If you want to try out your new key assignments, choose Use from the File menu, and the customized keys will be ready to use immediately. If you want to use your new keymap each time you log in, save the keymap into your **~/Library/Keyboards** folder. This folder is not normally created by NEXTSTEP, so you will have to create it. You can also save the keymap into **/LocalLibrary/Keyboards** or **/NextLibrary/Keyboards** to make it available to every user on the system. After you've saved the keymap, quit the Preferences application if it is running and restart it. Then click the Localization Preferences icon (see "Localization Preferences" on page 286) and select your customized keyboard map from the list of keyboard definitions.

If while modifying a keyboard map you make a mistake, you can choose Revert to reload the keyboard map that was last saved, or choose Defaults to restore the keymap to its original state as provided by NeXT.

**Figure 9-39
The Keyboard Application**

In this example, the Alternate modifier key has been selected (notice white key) and the pi character is being dragged onto the p key. When this keyboard map is in use, pressing Alternate-p will produce the pi character.

Currently selected character

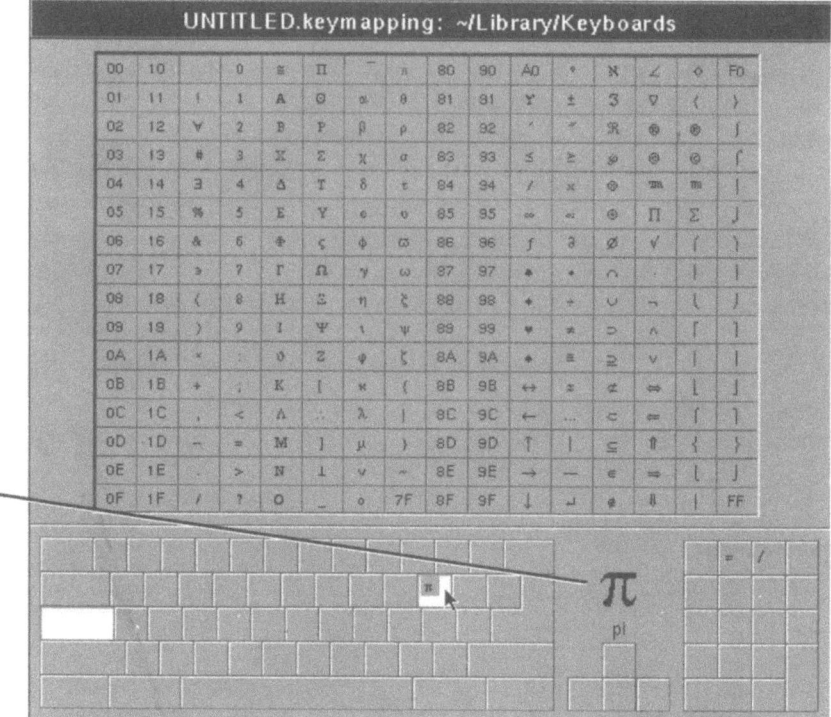

9.11.7 Mandelbrot

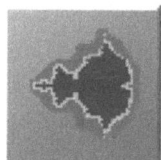

The mathematician Mandelbrot explored mathematical equations that can be used to represent naturally recurring patterns in nature. The resulting visual images based on these formulas are often referred to as fractals. Fractals have great meaning to mathematicians, but those not mathematically inclined, can still enjoy beautiful fractal images using the Mandelbrot demonstration application.

To create a fractal image, start Mandelbrot, and then enter values in the text fields at the bottom of the Mandelbrot window. It may be easier to begin with preset values and make modifications to them. Several preset values are provided in the Places menu. You can think of particular images as places in a Mandelbrot world. When you have selected a place to visit, click RUN to create the fractal image (see Figure 9-40).

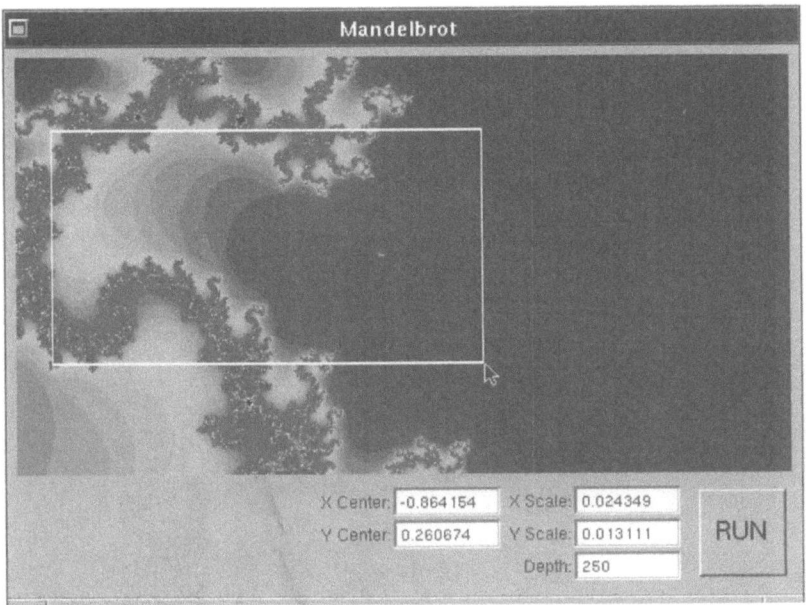

**Figure 9-40
Mandelbrot**

The Mandelbrot window allows you to explore an infinite number of fractal images resulting from Mandelbrot sets.

One of the unique features of a Mandelbrot world is that it contains an infinite number of worlds to visit. For example, to visit a new place, select a smaller portion of a fractal image (see Figure 9-40) and click RUN. The new resulting image will be based on the area you selected. You can repeat this process as many times as you like to visit different places in the Mandelbrot world.

To make fractal images even more interesting, you can adjust the colors used in the image. Select a predefined color scheme from the Colors menu or manipulate the controls in the Color Map panel (see Figure 9-41).

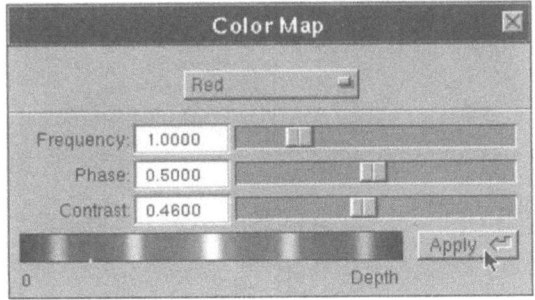

**Figure 9-41
Color Map**

Using the Color Map panel, you can customize the colors used to create a fractal image.

9.11.8 Molecule

Molecule is a dynamic viewing application that graphically displays the structure of a molecule in three dimensions. There are several molecular structures preconfigured for you to view. To open them, choose Open Molecular File, then select a molecule from those contained in the **Molecule.app** app wrapper. The Molecule window will display the structure, which you can then manipulate using the sliders and buttons at the bottom of the window (see Figure 9-42).

You can only display one molecule at a time, but there are several to choose from including aspirin, methane, methanol, benzine, nitroglycerin, TNT, octane, and water.

Figure 9-42
Molecule

Using the sliders and buttons, you can view a molecular structure from any angle and at any magnification.

9.11.9 NeXTtv

NeXTtv is an application specifically designed for use with the NeXTdimension™ video adapter card and NeXTcube™ computer. Using NeXTtv and this hardware, you can import video signals and display them on the computer screen. In simple terms, NeXTtv allows you to watch television on your computer screen. You can simply watch or capture a single frame and modify it with some rudimentary painting tools.

After attaching a video cassette recorder (VCR), laser disc player, or other video source to the NeXTdimension card, start NeXTtv. To view the video images, click the power button in the lower left corner of the NeXTtv window, and then click the button representing the port to which the video source is connected, such as line one, line two, or line three (see Figure 9-43). To freeze the image on a particular frame of video input, click the camera icon. Click the camera icon again to continue viewing live video.

Figure 9-43
NeXTtv

Using the NeXTtv application you can view video images from a video cassette recorder or other video source. Several controls are also provided for fine tuning the image.

If you need to adjust the hue, saturation, brightness, or other image qualities, click the appropriate button at the bottom of the NeXTtv window. When you click one of these control buttons, a digital display will appear on the NeXTtv television screen (see Figure 9-44). Continue clicking the + or - button to adjust the control to your liking. A few moments after your final click, the display will disappear from the screen.

Figure 9-44
NeXTtv Controls

When you click a + or - button, on screen digital display appears. Click a + or - button again to increase or decrease the effect of that control on the image.

9.11.10 Open Sesame

NeXTSTEP includes an application named Open Sesame that allows you to run an application located on a networked computer from another machine. For example, there may be applications on a NeXT computer which do not run on the Intel-based system you are using, but to which you have access through a network. In this case, you can run the application on the NeXT computer, but have it displayed on yours. The application will appear to run on your local computer, but will actually be processed, and use resources on the remote system. If your computer is not connected to a network or you don't want to start remote applications, you can use Open Sesame to start system administration or other applications on your own computer, such as the Installer, NetWareManager, and NFS-Manager, as if you were the **root** user. If you perform system administration for your own computer, this feature allows you to configure your computer without having to log out of your current session and log back in as **root**.

Configuring Open Sesame

Before you can use Open Sesame, you must perform a few simple steps. First, you must have an account on the remote machine. If you don't, you won't be able to start an application on it. Contact the system administrator of the remote computer to obtain a user account. Second, you'll need to create a file named **.rhosts**, and place it in your home folder on the remote machine. This file should contain the name of every computer, one per line, from which you would like to start an application remotely. For example, if you are logged in to a machine named **Larry**, and you want to run an application on the computer named **Moe**, then you should have a **.rhosts** file in your home folder on **Moe**, containing the name **Larry**. If you also want to run applications on Moe from the machine named **Curly**, then the second line of the **.rhosts** file should be **Curly**. Third, you'll need to turn on the Public Window Server option using the Preferences application (see "Expert Preferences" on page 297).

> Turning on Public Window Server is a potential security risk as this potentially allows any remote application access to your account, not just the one you are starting on the remote computer. After you are finished using a remote application, turn off the Public Window Server option in the Expert Preferences panel of the Preferences application to restore your account's security.

To run an application on your own computer as if you were **root**, your user name must be added to the group **wheel** by the system administrator.

Table 6-1 Configuring Open Sesame

Step	Description
1	Create an account on the remote computer
2	Create a .rhosts file containing the names of the remote machines from which you want to run an application.
3	On the remote machines, turn on the Public Window Server using the Preferences application.

You can configure Open Sesame with a list of often used computers so you don't have to type their name each time you want to start an application. To do this, start Open Sesame, and then choose Hosts from it's menu. A Select Hosts panel will appear in which you can add often used remote hosts. Type the name of a host in the field at the bottom of the panel and click Add (see Figure 6-45). Do this for each of the hosts you want to add to the list. To delete a host name from the list, select its name in the panel and click Remove. If there is one host that you use more often than the others, or only a single host that you use, select its name in the Select Hosts panel and click Set Default. This will cause its name to be typed automatically each time you attempt to run a remote application so you don't have to. When you are finished customizing the Select Hosts panel, click its close box to make it disappear.

**Figure 6-45
The Select
Hosts Panel**

To add a host to this panel, type the name of a host and click Add. To remove a name from this panel, select a host name and click Remove.

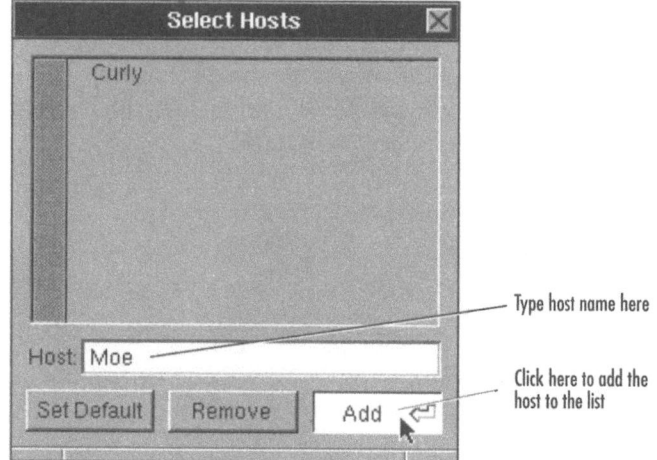

Type host name here

Click here to add the host to the list

Starting Remote Applications

You can use Open Sesame whether it's running or not. If Open Sesame is not running, you can still access it from the Services menu. To use Open Sesame this way, select an application on a remote computer. This is typically accomplished using NFS as described in "Network File System (NFS)" on page 308. After selecting an application, choose Open Sesame from the Services menu (see Figure 6-46). It's best to select an application instead of a document. If you select a document and attempt to open it using Open Sesame, your computer may not be able to determine which application on the remote computer is able to open it. To open a document using a remote application, open the remote application first, then, after the application is running, open the document using the application's Open command.

If you configured host names as described in section , these hosts will appear in the menu as well (see Figure 6-46). For example, if you configured the Select Hosts panel to include the names Larry, Moe, and Curly, then you'll see Open On Larry, Open On Moe, and Open On Curly, in the Open Sesame menu. To run the selected application on Moe, choose Open Application On Moe from the Open Sesame menu.

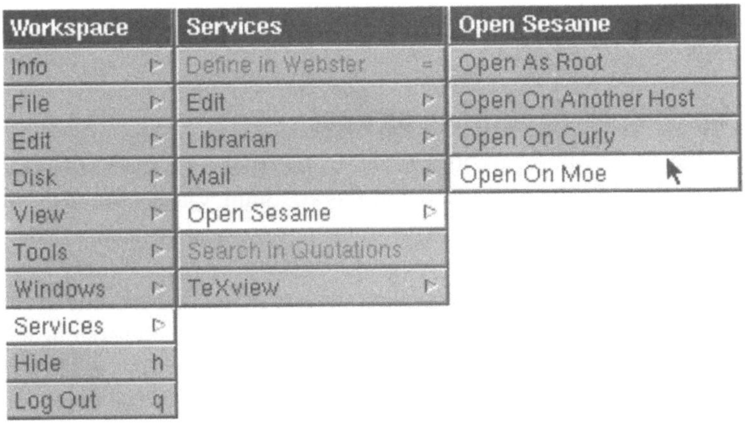

Demonstration Applications

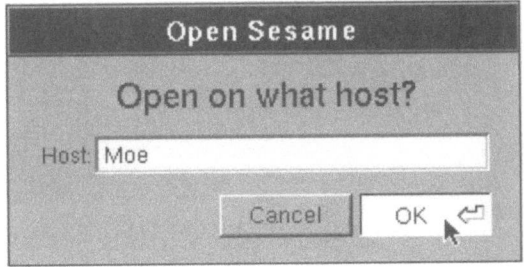

**Figure 6-46
Open Sesame Menu**

The Open Sesame menu provides command for starting applications as the root user, or on a remote computer. Host names configured in Open Sesame also appear in this menu.

If the name of the machine you want does not appear in the menu, choose Open On Another Host. The Open Sesame panel will appear in which you can type the name of the host (see Figure 6-47). After typing the name, click OK to start the application. If you change your mind and don't want to run the selected application, click Cancel. If you typed the name of a host that does not exist, was incorrectly spelled, or for which Open Sesame has not be correctly configured, an attention panel will appear to inform you, and request that you review Open Sesame's Help Panel. In this case, review the instructions in section .

**Figure 6-47
Open Sesame Panel**

When you choose Open Application On Another Host, this panel appears. Type the name of the host on which to run the application and click OK.

If Open Sesame is running, you can use the previous method to start a remote application, or use the drag and drop method. To use drag and drop, hold down the Command key, drag the remote application's icon and drop it on the Open Sesame tile in the workspace. This will cause the Open Sesame panel to appear so that you can enter the name of the remote host on which it should run. Type the name of the remote host in the panel and click OK. The application will appear as if it is running on your own computer.

Opening an Application as Root

Some applications can only be run by the **root** user, such as NetInfoManager and NFSManager located in **/NextAdmin**. Others, such as NetWareManager and Installer, don't require you to be logged in as **root** to run them, but doing so allows you more flexibility. If you're already logged in, it may be inconvenient to stop what you are doing, log out, log in as root to run an application, then log out and log back in to continue working. To avoid this inconvenience, use Open Sesame to open an application as if you were logged in as the **root** user. To do this, select the application in a File Viewer, then choose Open Sesame from the Services menu. In the Open Services menu, choose Open As Root. An authentication panel will appear in which you type the password to the **root** account. If you type the correct password, the application will open as usual, but while you are in the application, you'll have the privileges of the **root** user. Remember, you won't be able to open an application as root unless your user name is a member of the group **wheel**.

**Figure 6-48
User Authentication Panel**

When you run an application as root, this panel appears, requesting the root password. Type it in the empty field and click Login.

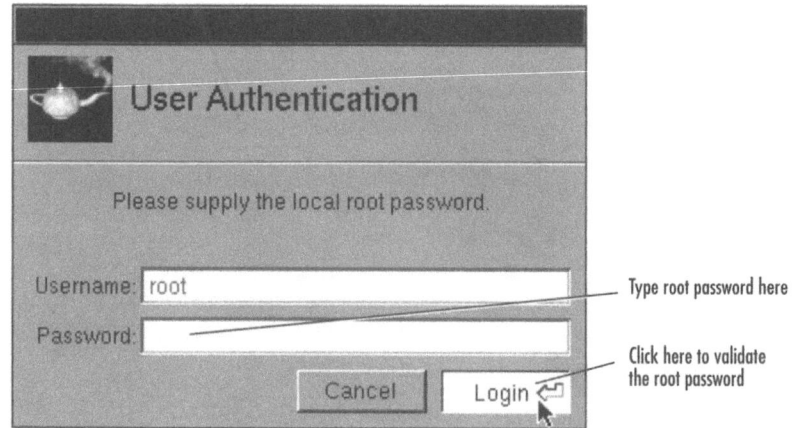

Type root password here

Click here to validate the root password

9.11.11 PhotoAlbum

PhotoAlbum is designed for use with Kodak PhotoCDs. PhotoCD refers to a compact disc containing numerous images that are developed from regular 35 mm film, but placed on a compact disc instead of printed on paper. Using PhotoAlbum and a PhotoCD compatible CD-ROM drive, you can view images from a PhotoCD, crop them, paste them into other applications, save them as TIFF files, and print them. Not only can PhotoAlbum manipulate these images directly, it also provides a special feature called a filter-service, that allows PhotoCD files to be dragged directly into applications from a File Viewer.

Each image stored on a PhotoCD is actually recorded five times at various resolutions, each one four times larger than the previous one. The collection of five files that represent a single image is called an ImagePac and appears in the File Viewer with a .pcd extension. Because of the size of these images, some are compressed to allow more images per disc. Images are organized as follows:

ImagePac file

Table 8-2 ImagePac Contents

Name	Size	Compressed
Base16	128x192	No
Base4	425x384	No
Base	512x768	No
4Base	1024x1536	Yes
16Base	2048x3072	Yes

Viewing an Image

To view an image from a PhotoCD, double-click its icon, start PhotoAlbum and choose Open PhotoCD, or select a PhotoCD file in a File Viewer and display the Contents Inspector. In the first two instances, PhotoAlbum will be started and an Overview window (see Figure 9-49) will appear displaying small versions of each image on the disc called thumbnails. To view a particular image in more detail, double-click it's thumbnail. A Photo window will appear in which you can view any of the five files that represent the image.

Bundled Applications

**Figure 9-49
Overview and
Photo Windows**

PhotoAlbum displays thumbnails of every image on a PhotoCD in the Overview window. To view a particular image up close, double-click it's thumbnail. The image will then appear at the default size selected in the preferences panel.

Exporting an Image

PhotoCDs wouldn't of much use if you could only view images. Using PhotoAlbum, you can also copy and paste all or part of an image into another application. To select an entire image, display it in a Photo window, then choose Copy from the Edit menu. To copy only a portion of an image, drag to select a rectangular portion of the image, then choose Copy. To place the image into another document, open the document, select the location where you want the image to appear, and choose Paste. You can also save all or part of an image as a TIFF file by choosing Save instead of Copy. If you want to conserve disk space, you can compress the image as you save it using the JPEG compression method. When a PhotoCD file has been saved in TIFF format, you can edit it using IconBuilder, or edit it with a commercial application such as Appsoft Image or TIFFany.

When you import the image into another application, it may not appear in the size you expect. PhotoAlbum is able to save images in Photo Print size (approximately 3.5 x 5 inches) and Full Page size (approximately 7 x 10 inches). If you prefer you can also save the image using the 1:1 option, where one pixel equals one PostScript point. This option saves the image in exactly the same size it is currently being viewed in the Photo window. If you drag and drop the image from a File Viewer into another application, PhotoAlbum will automatically convert the image into a Photo Print size (3.5x5 inch) TIFF file before it appears in the document. If you need a different size, you'll need to use the PhotoAlbum application.

You can adjust several default settings for PhotoAlbum by choosing Preferences from the Info menu. A panel will appear (see Figure 9-50) in which you can adjust the gamma correction, set the resolution of an image when you double-click its thumbnail, and the size at which an image will appear when you drag it from a File Viewer into a document. Gamma correction is used to adjust the image intensity so it looks correct on your particular computer. Higher settings make the image more intense.

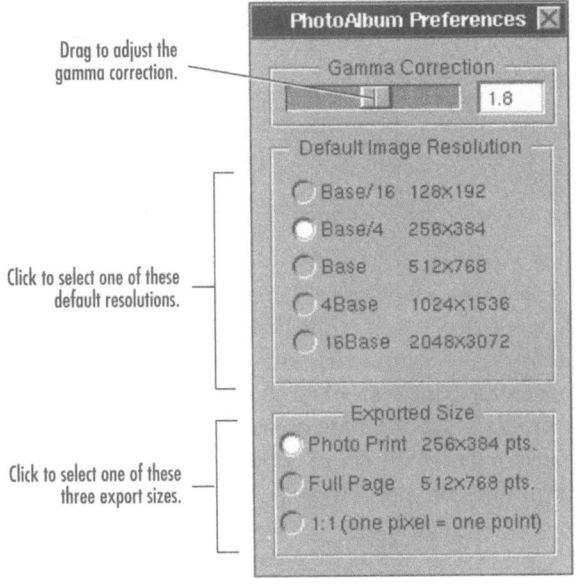

Figure 9-50 Preferences

Using this panel, you can set PhotoAlbum's defaults for gamma correction, image resolution in the Photo window, and the size at which an image is displayed when exported to another document.

Multi-session drives are not supported in NeXTSTEP 3.1. Multi-session refers to the ability of the CD-ROM drive to read PhotoCD discs that have been recorded onto more than once.

9.11.12 RenderManager

Using RenderManager, you can reduce the amount of time it takes to render an image by using the power of several cooperating computer systems. This coordination of computer systems is performed by RenderManager. To make your computer available for rendering images, click Configure in the RenderManager window (see Figure 9-51). This makes your computer a rendering server.

**Figure 9-51
RenderManager**

The RenderManager window displays a list of computers available to render an image.

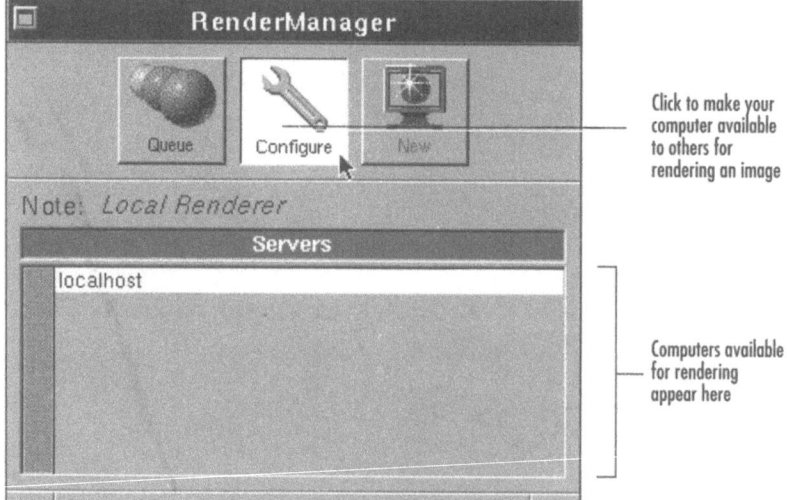

To make your computer a rendering server, click Public, and then click Where to select a NetInfo domain (see Figure 9-52). Only computers on a network and within the same NetInfo domain can work cooperatively to render an image. Contact your network administrator if you need help selecting an appropriate domain. If you want to include a note describing your computer system to others, you can enter it in the text field named Note. To save your settings, click OK.

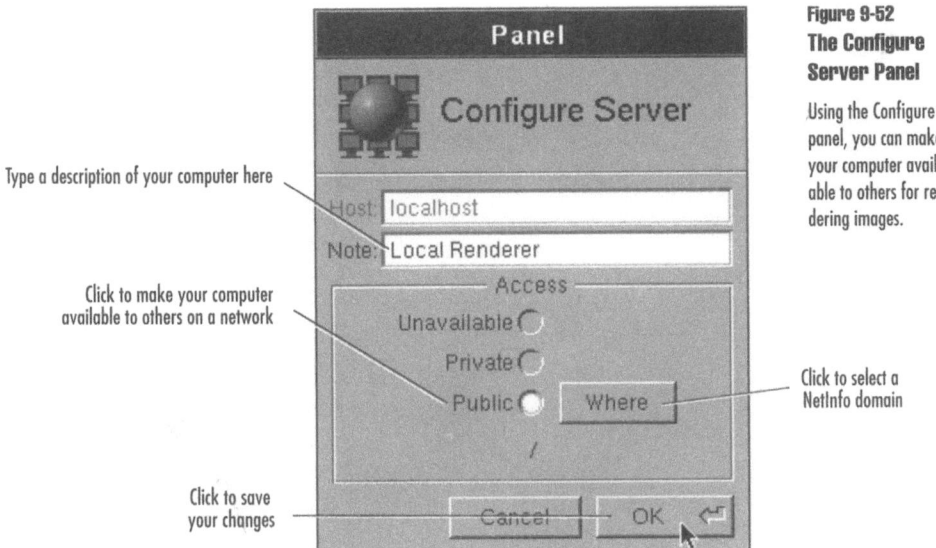

**Figure 9-52
The Configure
Server Panel**

Using the Configure panel, you can make your computer available to others for rendering images.

To begin rendering an image, print or render the image as usual. You can place several images to be rendered in a queue at the same time so that they can be processed without further intervention. To examine the queue, click Queue in the Render Queue panel. The requests are placed in the queue in reverse chronological order with the most recent request at the bottom. You cannot reorder the requests in the queue, but you can remove a request by selecting it and clicking Delete.

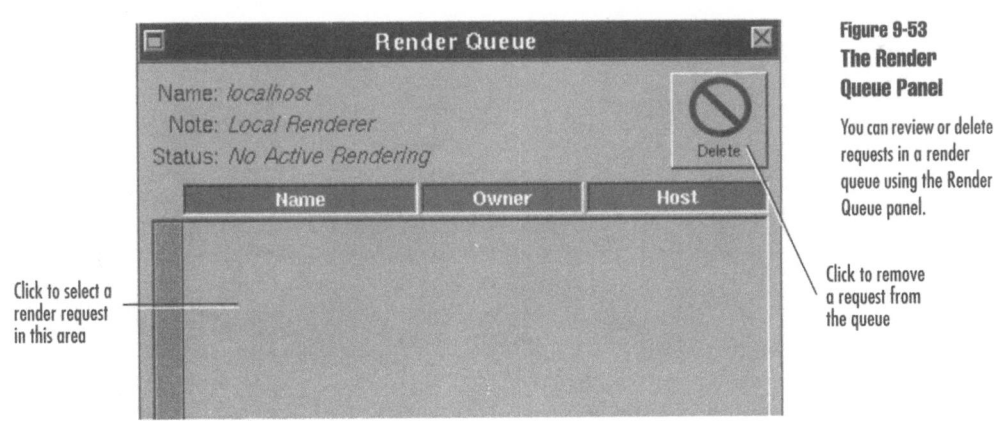

**Figure 9-53
The Render
Queue Panel**

You can review or delete requests in a render queue using the Render Queue panel.

Bundled Applications

9.11.13 ScreenScape

ScreenScape is another application designed for use with the NeXTcube computer and NeXTdimension video adapter card. This application outputs a rectangular area of the screen, called the video frame, through the NeXTdimension card to a monitor or video recording device, such as a VCR, so you can display or document a procedure performed on the computer for others. Output begins as soon as ScreenScape is started. Typically, a rectangular area of 640 x 480 pixels will be displayed. As you move the cursor, the area displayed will follow. You can also freeze the output area by choosing Freeze Position from the Video Frame menu, or using by using its shortcut, Command-f.

A ScreenScape Controls panel is provided so that you can adjust the positioning of the video frame, how it tracks the cursor, and other output signal characteristics (see Figure 9-54). These settings can be saved to a file and recalled later, allowing you to save different collections of settings for different uses. This is accomplished using the pull-down menu in the lower right corner of the ScreenScape Controls panel.

**Figure 9-54
ScreenScape
Controls**

Using this panel, you can adjust the position of the output rectangle and the output signal characteristics.

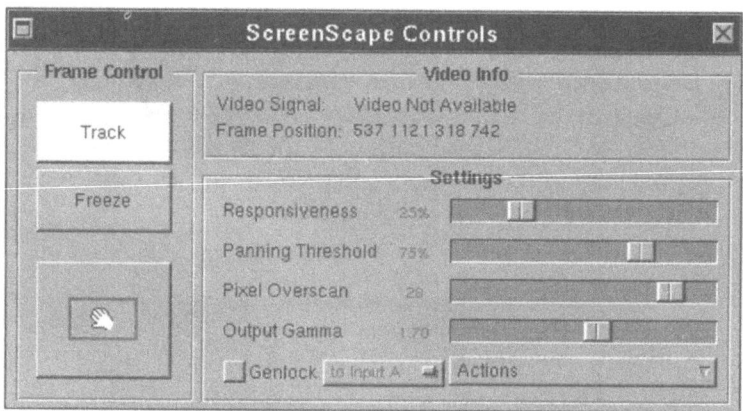

To freeze the video frame in a particular location on the screen, click Freeze. To allow the video frame to follow the cursor again, click Track. If you aren't able to monitor the output on another screen, you can view and set it using the hand icon. When you drag the hand icon, an orange rectangle will appear, which you can position on the screen. This orange rectangle represents the video frame. Dragging the orange rectangle places the video frame in a particular location. This way you'll know exactly what portion of the screen is being transmitted.

Sliders are provided so you can adjust several other ScreenScape features. Each of these is described in Table 9-3:

Table 9-3 ScreenScape Settings

Setting	Description
Responsiveness	Controls the speed at which the output rectangle tracks the cursor. Slower speeds are smoother but less reactive, while faster speeds are more jerky but quicker.
Panning Threshold	This control defines a margin near the video frame in which the cursor must enter for the video frame to move. A larger area makes the video frame move more quickly while a smaller area requires the cursor to come nearer the edge of the video frame before it will move.
Pixel Overscan	Most television equipment discards 10-15% around the edge of an image. By selecting a small Pixel Overscan number, you can reduce the size of the video frame so that it fits completely on a television monitor. The Pixel Overscan number represents the number of pixels from the edge of the video frame.
Output Gamma	This controls the contrast of the output image.
Genlock	When this is on, you can synchronize the output signal to that of an input signal. A pop-up list is enabled from which you can select the appropriate input signal.

9.11.14 Sound

You can open and listen to prerecorded sound files using the Sound application. Double-click a **.snd** file or choose Open from Sound's File menu. Opened sounds will appear in their own sound panel (see Figure 9-55) where you can re-record over them, copy and paste them into other sound panels to create new sounds, edit them, or just play them back. If you want

Bundled Applications

to know more about a sound, choose Inspector from Sound's Info menu. An Inspector panel will appear in which is displayed detailed information about the selected sound, such as its duration in seconds, its size on the disk, and notes that you can type to describe the sound.

Using Sound, you can also record sounds and include them in the documents of many applications, such as NeXTmail, FrameMaker, and Improv. Of course you'll need to have a sound card installed in your computer that is capable of recording from a microphone. If you happen to have a NeXT computer, a microphone is built-in.

When you start the Sound application, an untitled sound panel appears with which you can control the recording and playback of sounds. To record a sound, click Record in the Untitled panel that appears. Sound will record using the microphone built into the MegaPixel display, or the Sound Box attached to systems with color monitors. Other sound adapters such as the SoundBlaster card may be supported on PC systems. To stop recording, click Stop.

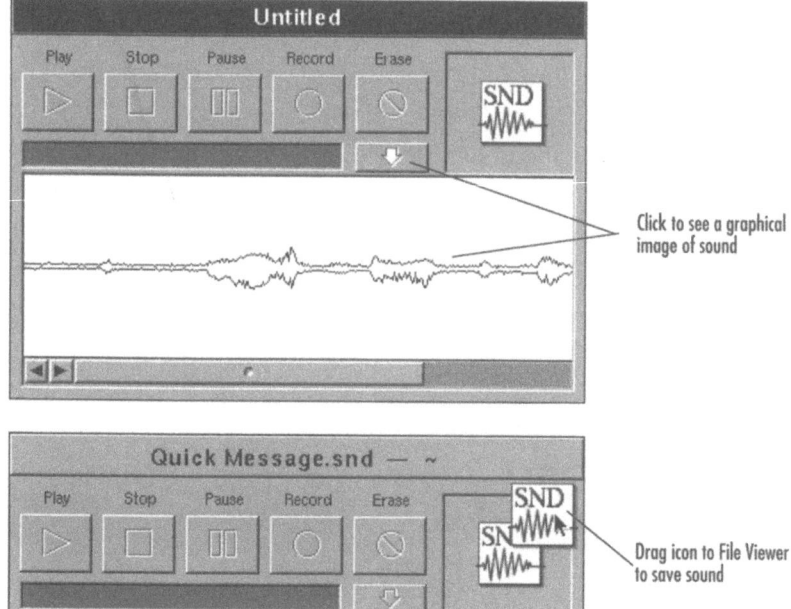

**Figure 9-55
The Sound
Application**

Sound displays controls for recording sounds, similar to an audio cassette player. You can also see a graphical representation of the recorded sound by clicking the arrow button (top). To save a sound, use the Save command or drag the .snd icon from the Sound panel (bottom) into a File Viewer.

You can play back your recording by clicking Play. You may have to record, play, and re-record several times to obtain the recording you want. To help you edit your recording, click the down, below the Erase button. This will extend the Untitled panel to reveal the sound editing area (see Figure 9-55). A line graph will appear in this area after you have recorded a sound. By copying, cutting, pasting, and deleting portions of the line graph, you can edit the recorded sound. Typically, you will delete the long silence normally found at the beginning and end of a recording to make it smaller to minimize dead air time when playing back the recording. If you want to play back only a portion of a recording, select an area of the line graph by dragging the mouse with a mouse button held down, and then click Play. If the selection is not desirable, click Erase to delete it.

When you are ready to save the sound, choose Save or Save As from Sound's File menu. Enter a name and select a folder for the sound file in the Save panel and click OK to save the sound. You can also save a sound by dragging the **.snd** icon from the Untitled panel onto a File Viewer. The sound file will be copied to the appropriate folder in the File Viewer after which you can rename the sound file so that it's no longer called Untitled. When you have named the sound, its panel's name will also change to reflect the sound's new name.

9.11.15 3View

NEXTSTEP, unlike any other system software, includes support for Pixar's RenderMan three-dimensional photo-realistic image format known as RIB. Developers will soon take include photo-realistic rendering as a standard component of NEXTSTEP applications. Meanwhile, you can use 3View to preview RIB files provided in **/NextDeveloper/Examples/RenderMan**. Remember that this is a demonstration application, and not all of its controls work as well as they could.

When you view a RIB file in 3View, you are viewing the image from a camera perspective (see Figure 9-56). Several tools are provided to enable you to change the camera's position, or view. Note that when you select a tool, dragging the 3View window changes the position of the *camera*, not the image, so you have to drag in the direction opposite from what you might expect. For example, to move the image down, drag up. To move the image left, drag right. To help you understand how better to control the view of a RenderMan image, each of the tools is described here.

Bundled Applications

**Figure 9-56
3View Rendering**

With 3View, you can view RIB files. Lower resolutions such as dot (top) and wireframe (middle) can be manipulated much faster than fully rendered images (bottom) and are used when positioning an object. Today 3View is a tool for developers, but it allows you to take a peek at the amazing image quality soon to be available in NEXTSTEP applications.

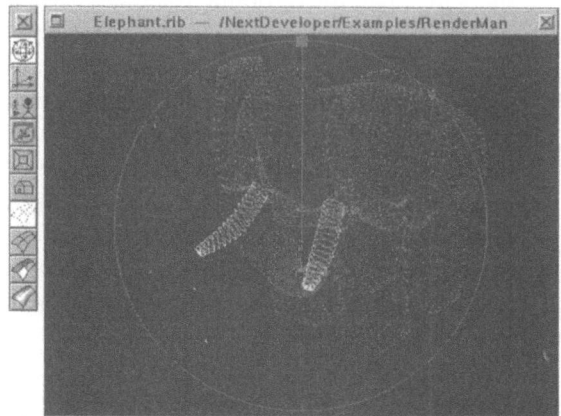

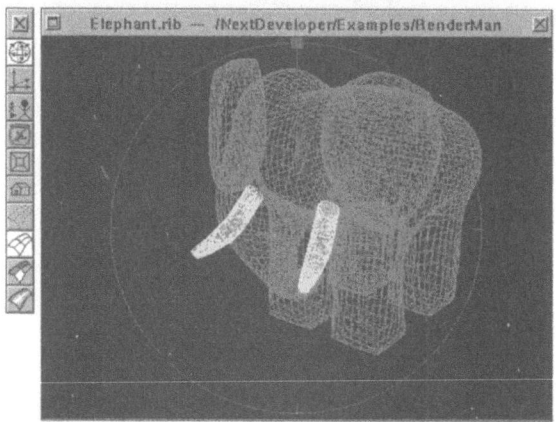

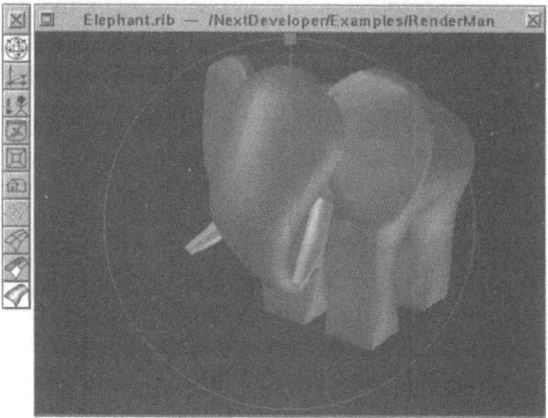

Translate

Translates the camera in space. There are three control sticks in this view and two sticks are active at all times. On each stick is a square. To enable a particular stick, click its square. When the two 90-degree sticks are selected, the camera will move in the XY plane. When the third stick is selected, motion will be in the XZ plane.

Rotate

Rotates the camera about the view point. Drag the square on the edge of the circle to tilt the camera.

Zoom

Makes the image larger or smaller just like a zoom lens on a camera. To make the image larger, drag an outside stick toward the center stick. Drag an outside stick away from the center stick to make the image smaller.

Screen Aides

Toggles the screen aides: circle, sticks, squares, and so on, on and off. The default is for screen aides to be visible.

Projection

Toggles between perspective and orthographic projection. The default is perspective.

Home

Returns the camera to its home position. (This does not work well with the images provided by NeXT.)

Point Cloud

Changes the rendering style to point clouds, having no "fill."

Wire Frame

Changes the rendering style to wire frame.

Flat Shading

Changes the rendering style to flat shading, in which a flat "fill" appears between wires in the wire frame.

Smooth Shading

Changes the rendering style to smooth shading, in which the edges that appear in flat shading are smoothed to provide the most photo-realistic representation of the image.

9.11.16 Zilla

Zilla, like RenderManager, is used to coordinate several computers on a network to work together, thus increasing the speed at which a problem can be solved. Unlike RenderManager, Zilla is not used strictly for rendering images, but rather for any type of processing. Here's how Zilla works. Another user configures their computer to be used by Zilla when they are not using it. You start Zilla, select their machine, enter your user name and password for their machine and the command or application you want to run. Zilla then performs your task using their idle computer. Your computer isn't slowed down because it's using the other computer's CPU. Because Zilla only runs when the other user isn't using their computer, they don't notice any reduction in processing speed either.

Configuring Your Computer as a Zilla Server

If your screen has been dimmed from lack of activity Zilla assumes your are not using your computer and allows another user to take advantage of your computer's idle CPU.

To make your computer available to others, start Zilla and enter your NEXTSTEP user name and password. Choose Permission from the Info menu click Partial Permission, and then OK. If you quit Zilla, your computer will be available to others when you're not using it. (Other users who wish to use your computer with Zilla will have to have a user name and password for your computer, too.) If you want to initiate a task that utilizes Zilla, keep Zilla running.

Running a Task on a Remote Computer

The following example, taken from Zilla's Help panel, shows how to start a simple UNIX command on one remote machine. Before you begin a task, you'll need to create a Zilla document containing a collection of computers, called hosts, that will process it (see Figure 9-57).

Demonstration Applications

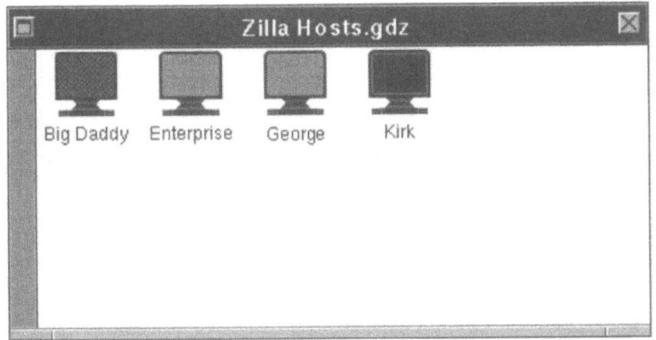

**Figure 9-57
A Zilla Document**

A Zilla document contains icons that represent a collection of Zilla hosts. This collection is called a Zilla network. You can save a Zilla document so that it can be recalled for use later.

To add a host to your Zilla document, choose New from the Hosts menu to view a network window, and then select Add Hosts from the Hosts menu. A new panel will appear in which you can select a host. Add as many hosts as necessary. If you want to save this collection of hosts, choose Save from the Network menu. This way you can recall a collection of hosts, called a Zilla network, without having to select each of them again.

For each host you add, Zilla will display an icon in the Hosts window. Hosts that have been set to partial permission will display a light gray icon, and those set to total permission will display a dark gray icon. The icons will also be updated, albeit slowly, to reflect the status of the host they represent. To see a description of the icons that can appear in this window, choose Legend from the Hosts menu (see Figure 9-58).

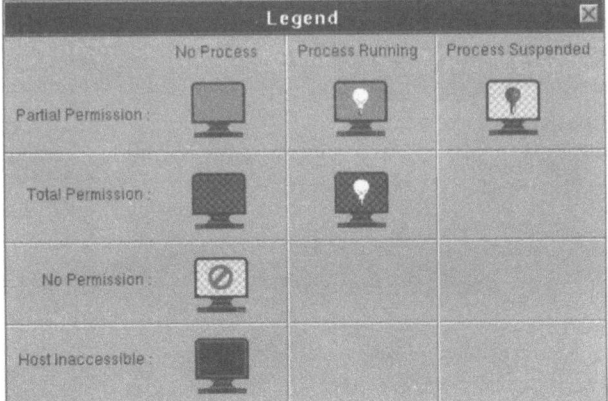

**Figure 9-58
The Legend Panel**

The Zilla Legend panel describes each of the icons that may appear in a Zilla document.

Bundled Applications

To begin a task, double-click a host icon in the Zilla document. This will display the Host Inspector panel (see Figure 9-59). In the Host Inspector, you'll enter information such as your user name and password and the UNIX command your want to run on the remote host computer. The Login and Password fields will contain the same user name and password you used to start your Zilla session. If your user name and password on the remote computer are different, enter the correct ones in the Host Inspector panel. Without a user name and password for the remote host, you will be unable to use it even though it has been made available to Zilla. In the Command field, enter the command required to start the task. In our example, we'll enter a simple UNIX command **cal 1993 > calfile**

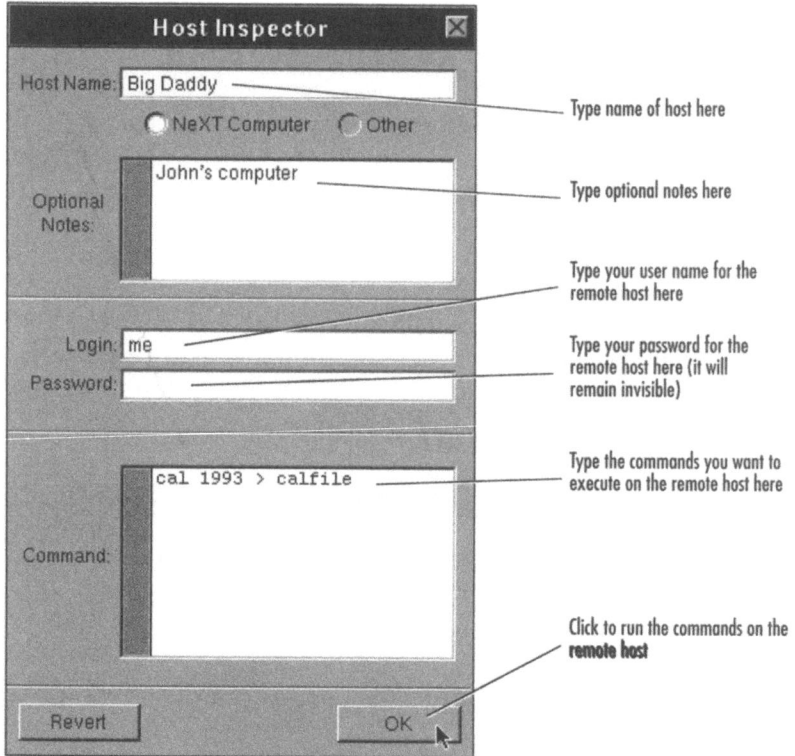

**Figure 9-59
The Host
Inspector Panel**

Use the Host Inspector to enter your user name and password and the commands you want to execute on the remote computer.

When you have entered all of this information, click OK. The UNIX command you just entered runs a calendar program. To start it running, choose Run from the Control menu. A panel will appear to confirm that you want to use all of the hosts in your Zilla window in Individual mode. Individual mode means that you have entered the command you want to run in the

Host Inspector for every host icon in the Zilla document. Other modes are available and can be investigated using the Advanced Features portion of the Zilla Help panel.

When you confirm that you want to begin the task, the host's icon will briefly display the word Launch. This means that the task is being started. When the task is fully running, the icon will change to a light bulb (see Figure 9-58). If the host you selected has granted only partial permission, Zilla will only process your request when that machine's screen is dim. If the host's icon is white, the screen is not dim and the process must wait to run. If the icon is gray, the host's screen is dim, and the process will run immediately. If the host you selected has granted total permission, the process will start running immediately regardless of the state of its screen.

Once the process is running, the bulb will quickly go away in our example. This is because we have started up a very small program which should run to completion in a few seconds.

When the task has been completed, the light bulb icon will disappear. Since our task was to create a file containing a calendar of the current year, you will also find a file in your home folder named **calfile** containing the output of the calendar program you ran.

You can use Zilla to run many different types of programs and applications, and even run the same one on several machines to achieve the effect of multiprocessing. Zilla's Help panel describes advanced features like this in more detail.

9.12 Summary of Bundled Applications

The following three tables list and describe the applications bundled with the NEXTSTEP user environments. The first table describes fully supported NEXTSTEP applications. The second table describes demonstration applications. These applications are fully functional, but do not include printed documentation. They are provided "as is." The third table describes applications that are often used by system administrators, although non administrators can find their features useful from time to time. Administrative applications are described in more detail in the on-line NEXTSTEP system and network administration documentation (see "NEXTSTEP Manuals and References" on page 363).

Table 9-4 User Applications

Application	Description
Edit	Text editor featuring a graphical user interface. Edit is used to read, modify, and print ASCII and RTF files.
FaxReader	Used to read incoming fax messages from a fax modem. FaxReader also maintains a log of incoming and outgoing transmissions and an archive of received faxes.
Grab	Photographs, or grabs, a portion of the screen and saves it to the pasteboard or as a TIFF file. Grab is often used to create illustrate NEXTSTEP applications or procedures.
Librarian	Searches and retrieves documents using a keyword or phrase. Used to locate on-line documentation as well as documents you create.
NeXTmail	Application for sending and receiving multimedia electronic mail with other NEXTSTEP users on a network, and text-only mail with non-NEXTSTEP users on a network. NeXTmail can also be used to send mail to computer users sharing the same computer.
Preferences	An application for customizing the NEXTSTEP user environment, such as background color, sound, language, or mouse speed.

Summary of Bundled Applications

Table 8-4 User Applications (continued)

Application	Description
Preview	Used to preview output from an application before printing or faxing it. Preview also allows you to view TIFF, PS, and EPS files.
PrintManager	Used to configure new fax modems and printers, and monitor and manage fax and print queues.
Quotations	Searches and retrieves quotations from the electronic edition of *The Oxford Dictionary of Quotations* included with NEXTSTEP.
Terminal	Allows you to enter UNIX commands using a command line interface. Terminal is used primarily by the root user, programmers, and other UNIX users.
Webster	Searches and retrieves entries from the electronic edition of *Webster's ninth New Collegiate Dictionary and Thesaurus* included with NEXTSTEP.

Bundled Applications

Table 8-5 **Demonstration Applications**

Application	Description	System
Billiards	An electronic billiard table featuring billiards, pool, eight-ball, nine-ball, and slop.	NeXT, Intel
BoinkOut	A colorful game in which you attempt to remove walls of bricks. Similar to Breakout.	NeXT, Intel
BugNeXT	Allows you to easily report a NEXTSTEP bug or offer a suggestion or comment to NeXT via NeXTmail.	NeXT, Intel
CDPlayer	Allows play of audio CDs but only with NeXT's CD-ROM drive.	NeXT, Intel
Chess	Computer chess game based on GNU chess. Features both two- and three-dimensional graphical interfaces.	NeXT, Intel
Draw	Basic drawing application for creating and editing image files.	NeXT, Intel

Summary of Bundled Applications

Table 9-5 Demonstration Applications (continued)

Application	Description	System
Keyboard	Allows you to create customized key maps so that you can easily create or enter special characters.	NeXT, Intel
Mandelbrot	A tool for creating and studying fractals.	NeXT, Intel
Molecule	Displays rotatable 3D views of molecular structures. Several sample molecule structures are provided as examples.	NeXT, Intel
NeXTtv	Allows you to view and capture live video but works only with the NeXTdimension video adapter card.	NeXTcube with NeXTdimension adapter
OpenSesame	Allows you to run an application on a remote computer but allow input and display output on your own. Also allows you to run an application on your own computer as root.	NeXT, Intel
PhotoAlbum	Tool for coordinating the use of several computers running NEXTSTEP, to render a photo-realistic image.	NeXT, Intel
RenderManager	Tool for coordinating the use of several computers running NEXTSTEP, to render a photo-realistic image.	NeXT, Intel

Bundled Applications

Table 8-5 Demonstration Applications (continued)

Application	Description	System
ScreenScape	Captures frames of video input from NeXTdimension video adapter and saves them as image files.	NeXTcube with NeXT-dimension adapter
Sound	Records and plays sounds recorded through an attached microphone and speaker	NeXT, PC with sound adapter
3View	Used for viewing three-dimensional images saved in RenderMan format.	NeXT, Intel
Zilla	An application for coordinating the use of several computers to render a photo-realistic image.	NeXT, Intel

Table 8-6 Administrative Applications

Application	Description
BuildDisk	Administrator's tool for formatting and installing NEXTSTEP onto a new disk drive.

Summary of Bundled Applications

Table 9-8 Administrative Applications (continued)

Application	Description
Configure	A tool for configuring Intel-based computer system peripherals such as mice, video display, keyboard, serial and parallel ports, and more.
HostManager	Administrator's tool for configuring computers running NEXTSTEP for use on a network.
Installer	Utility for installing software packages.
Install Tablet	Utility for installing and configuring a WACOM digitizing tablet.
NetInfoManager	Administrator's utility for accessing the database of users, printers, servers, services, and other system information of a NEXTSTEP network.
NetWare Manager	Application to manage the access to Novell NetWare file servers and print queues.
NFS Manager	Administrator's utility for configuring NFS file sharing with other computers on a network.

Bundled Applications

Table 9-8 Administrative Applications (continued)

Application	Description
Simple NetworkStarter	Administrator's tool for configuring a NEXTSTEP computer on a network.
User Manager	Administrator's tool for managing user accounts.

10

Application Installation

NEXTSTEP includes numerous useful applications, but you will also want to add other applications to your system as well. In typical NEXTSTEP manner, a simple installer application, called the Installer, is provided to make installations easy. This chapter will show you how to use the installer, and provide guidelines for choosing where to install applications.

NEXTSTEP applications are typically composed of numerous individual program files, icons, interface descriptions, and other items. To keep all of these files from cluttering up your file system, they are stored neatly hidden within a single icon. This icon, called an app wrapper, short for application wrapper, acts just like the application it contains. In fact, you may have been using app wrappers without even knowing it. To see inside an app wrapper, select an application in the File Viewer and choose Open as Folder from the Workspace Manager's File menu (see Figure 10-1). Not all applications utilize app wrappers so you may have to experiment until you find one. Without app wrappers, installing all of the files that make up a NEXTSTEP application correctly might be difficult to do, but NeXT has made it easy by storing all of an application's files in a single folder.

Application Installation

**Figure 10-1
Opening an
App Wrapper**

You can see inside an app wrapper by selecting it in a File Viewer and choosing Open As Folder from the File menu. Each of the files it contains, will appear inside a new File Viewer.

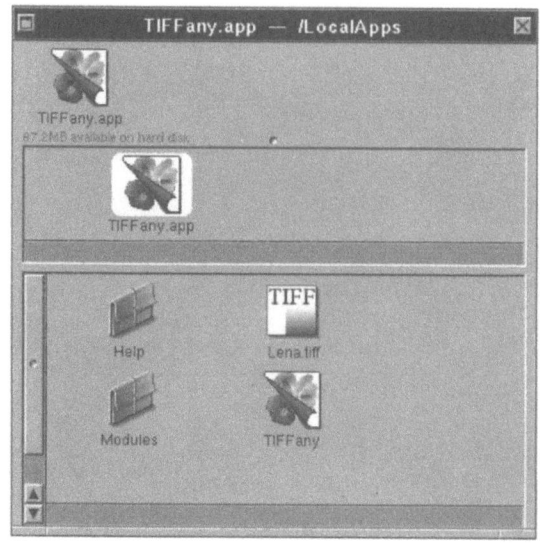

The Installer is used to install large applications compressed into a package.

Not only are there often many files within an app wrapper, but many application include auxiliary files, such as documentation, samples, and tutorials—which are not saved within an application's app wrapper. For this reason, applications and other large collections of software are often delivered in a special compressed form called a package. If the application is not compressed, you can drag its icon from a floppy disk directly onto your hard disk to install it. If the application is in the form of a package, you can install it almost as easily using the Installer.

NeXT encourages its software developers to use the Installer to simplify software installation and shield you from the technical details of performing an installation. The primary reason for file packages is that many applications include sample documents, fonts, dictionaries, tools, and other files. Having an installer program to manage the installation of all of these files provides many benefits:

❖ You only need to learn one method for installing software.

❖ Installations are much faster.

❖ Automation means fewer mistakes are likely to made.

❖ No technical expertise is required.

10.0 Where to Install Applications

One of the biggest decisions, perhaps the only decision to be made when installing a file package is where to put it. If you're not acting as the system administrator, you can only install it in your **~/Apps** folder. (It is possible to install it elsewhere, but the application will not be found in the standard search path). If you are the system administrator, you have several choices. Applications that should be accessible to every NEXTSTEP user should be installed in the **/LocalApps** folder (see Figure 10-1).

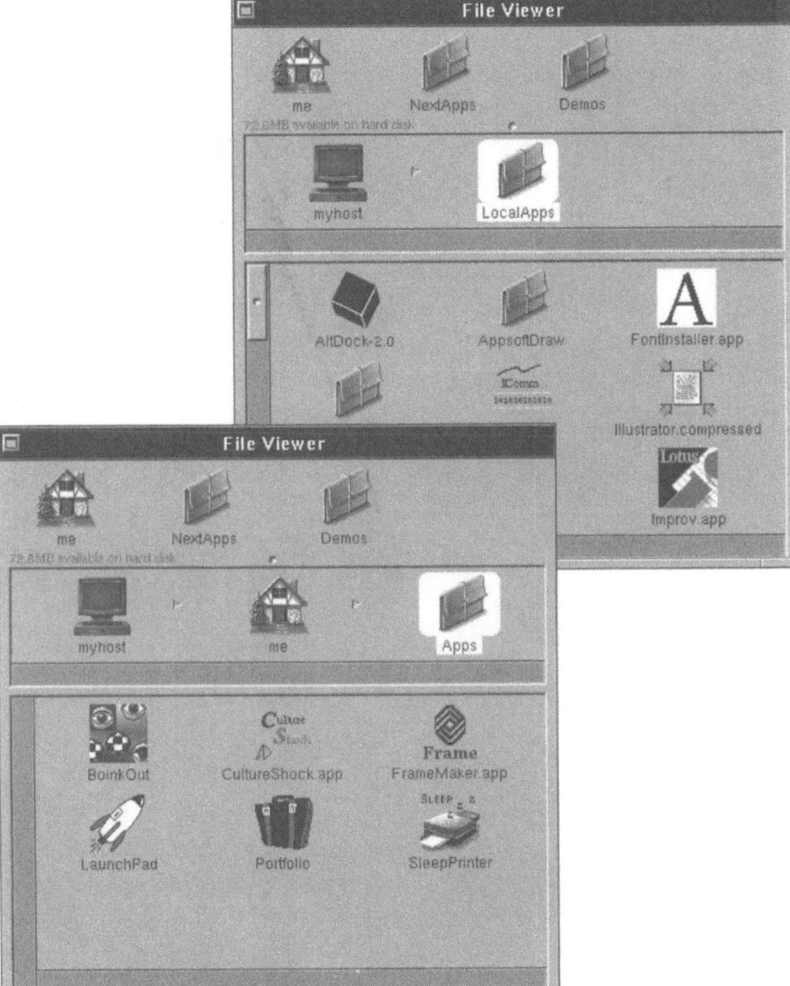

**Figure 10-2
Deciding Where to Install Applications**

Applications installed in /LocalApps (top) can be used by every NEXTSTEP user. Applications installed in a user's own ~/Apps folder (bottom) can only be accessed by that user.

Applications installed in this folder can only be read and executed by users other than **root**, but cannot be changed or deleted. Some applications may not work when placed in **/LocalApps** because they require a multi-user license. You can only install the application in one user's **~/Apps** folder. If you want to install the application in **/LocalApps**, purchase a multi-user license for the application. If you are not sure if an application is licensed for multiple users, read the license agreement included with the software or call the application's developer. The **/LocalApps** folder is not created when NEXTSTEP is installed, so the system administrator may have to create it and assign world, read and execute permissions to it.

Adobe PostScript fonts, the most widely used with NEXTSTEP, are licensed for use on a particular printer, not to individual users, so you can make them accessible to every user without breaking the license agreement.

If the package you're installing contains fonts, install it in **/LocalLibrary/Fonts** to make them available to every user of the computer. If the fonts are to be accessible only to a single user, install the fonts in a user's **~/Library/Fonts** folder. Note that the **~/Library/Fonts** folder is not automatically created so you may have to create it yourself.

Likewise, if the package you are installing contains system beep sounds, place them in **/LocalLibrary/Sounds** to make them available to every user of the computer, or in a user's **~/Library/Sounds** folder so that only that user can access them. The **~/Library/Sounds** folder is not created by NEXTSTEP either, so you will have to create it yourself.

The **/NextLibrary** and **/NextApps** folders are reserved for fonts, sounds, and applications provided by NeXT, Inc. supplied with NEXTSTEP. Don't place or install anything in these folders that isn't provided by NeXT.

10.1 The Installer

Using the Installer is relatively simple. When you buy software, you will receive among the various manuals, registration cards, advertising, and quick-reference sheets, floppy disks containing the application software and its associated files in one or more file packages. The Installer will decompresss the file packages, separate the files, and install them in the appropriate folders in the file system. To start the Installer, double-click a file package in the File Viewer, or double-click the Installer application in the **/NextAdmin** folder. If you choose the latter, you'll have to open the file package by choosing Open from the Installer's package, then locating the file package in the file system, and clicking Open.

Initially, the Installer will display the status of the package as uninstalled, its size decompressed and compressed, its version, location on the disk if it has already been installed, and a description of what is in the file package. This display is called the Info view (see Figure 10-3).

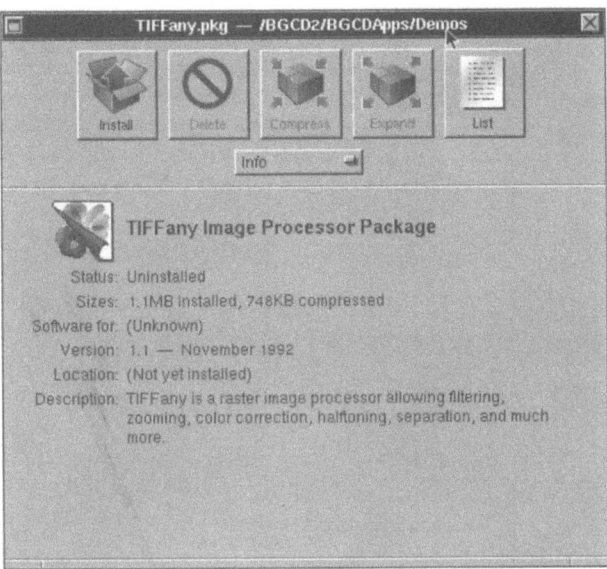

**Figure 10-3
Displaying
Package Status**

When you start the Installer, you will see the Installer Info panel, which displays detailed information about the package you are installing.

To install the contents of a file package, first open it in the Installer, and then click Install. The Installer will ask you where in the file system you want to install the package by presenting an Install In panel containing a browser (see Figure 10-4). Select a folder in the panel and click OK. Another panel will appear to verify your selection. If you made a mistake by selecting the wrong folder, click Cancel and begin the installation again by clicking Install in the Installer Info view. If the application is designed to run on more than one platform, NeXT and Intel computers for example, another panel will appear. In this panel, you can choose to install the application so it can run on one, two, or more systems. This is only necessary if you plan to allow users to access this application from other computer systems. If you are installing it only for users of your computer, click to remove the check marks next to every system but your own. This prevents extraneous code from being installed and reduces the amount of disk space the application consumes on the hard disk.

Application Installation

**Figure 10-4
Installing an
Application**

To begin an installation, click Install (top), select a folder in which to install the software and the type of system(s) on which it will run (middle), and click Install. You can monitor the Installer's progress by watching the Progress display (bottom).

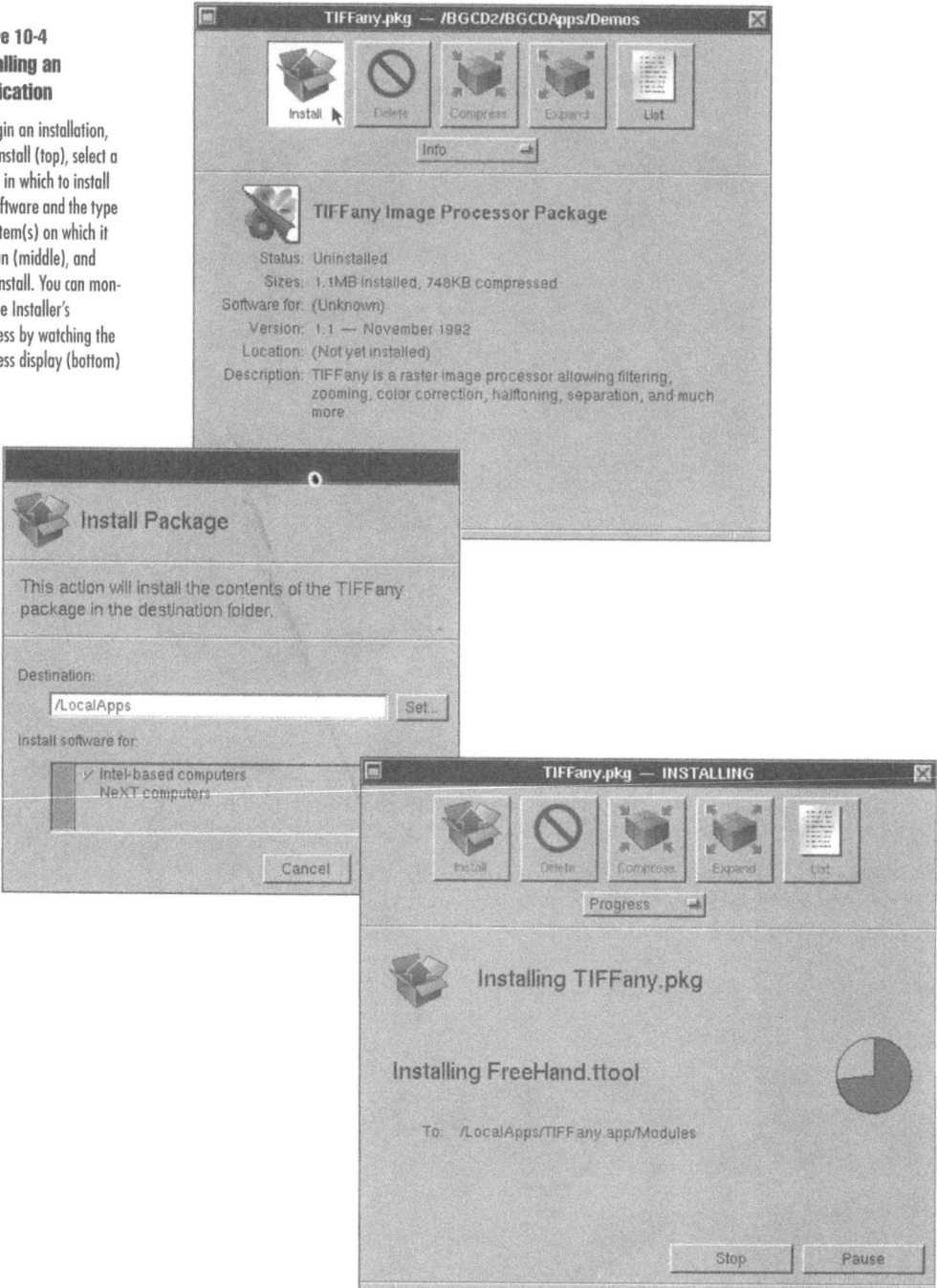

The Installer

When you click OK, the Installer will verify that you have permission to write in the selected folder, and then it will determine if any of the files contained in the file package has been previously installed. If so, an attention panel appears informing you that some of the files already exist and that continuing with the installation will overwrite these files. Click Continue to overwrite the existing files with those in the file package or click Cancel to begin the installation again.

During an installation you will see the Progress view display the names of each file as it is installed. If necessary, you can pause or even stop an installation by clicking Pause or Stop respectively (see Figure 10-4). If you pause the installation, the Pause button will become Resume, which, when clicked, continues the installation. If an installation is stopped instead of paused, it must be restarted from the beginning.

After an installation has been completed, choose Log from the Installer's pop-up list to see a detailed description of what took place, errors that were encountered, and the final location of the package's files. If any files could not be installed, the Log panel will indicate this too.

If you're too eager to get started with a new application, you may install it in the wrong folder and then spend hours looking for it, or give up looking and install it again a second time. Be patient! If you install an application in the wrong place, you'll spend at least twice as much time finding and moving it, than it would take to install it correctly the first time. Making such a mistake can be even more bothersome if there are auxiliary files installed in several other locations that must also be moved. Before you quit the Installer, look at the Installer's Log view to determine where in the file system the file package's parts were installed. If, after quitting the Installer, you can't find the application, start the Installer again. When you install a package, a record of the installation is kept in the **/NextLibrary/ Receipts** folder. If necessary, you can open the empty file package and click List to recreate the installation log. When the log has been recreated, choose Log from the Installer's pop-up menu to view it and determine where the file package was installed.

You can also remove installed file packages using the Installer. Using the Installer to remove an installed package ensures that all of the files associated with the original file package are also removed from the file system. If you want to use it again later, you will have to install it again from the original disks. If you know you ahead of time that you'll want to use the

Application Installation

package again later, you can compress the application back into its file package instead of deleting it. This makes the application use less disk space, but keeps it on the disk so you don't need to bother inserting floppy disks to reinstall it To delete or compress an installed application, start the Installer and open the application's file package in **/NextLibrary/Receipts** or double-click the file package in **/NextLibrary/Receipts**. When the Installer panel appears, click Delete or Compress (see Figure 10-5).

**Figure 10-5
Compressing
and Deleting
an Application**

Using the Installer to compress or delete an application ensures that all of its associated files are compressed or deleted along with the application.

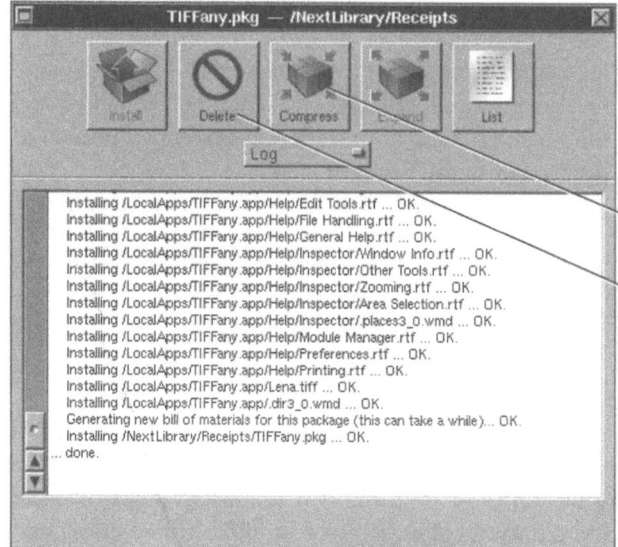

Click to compress an installed package

Click to delete an installed package

So You Want To Know More

```
/bin/csh (ttyp1)

124 ?   SW    0:00  (cron)
128 ?   S     7:09 - console (WindowServer)
129 ?   SW    0:02 - console (loginwindow)
130 ?   SW    0:00  (WindowServer)
156 ?   S     0:04  /usr/etc/pbs -a
158 ?   S     0:04  /usr/lib/NextStep
159 ?   S     0:00  appkitServer
160 ?   SW    1:07  /usr/lib/NextStep/Workspace.app/Workspace -LoginW
161 ?   SW    0:03  /NextApps/Preferences.app/WM.app/WM -NXA
188 ?   S     0:01  /NextApps/Edit.app/Edit -NXOpen /users/mikes
189 ?   S     0:16  /LocalApps/WordPerfect/WordPerfect.app/Word
195 ?   S     0:07  /NextApps/Grab.app/Grab -MachLaunch 12 380
197 ?   S     0:02  /NextApps/Terminal.app/Terminal -MachLaun
  2 co  S     0:00  (mach_init)
198 p1  S     0:00  -csh (csh)
209 p1  R     0:00  ps -0
localhost> ls -l
total 21
drwxr-xr-x   4 root          1024 Jun  1 13:50 Adaptors/
drwxr-xr-x   3 root          1024 Jun  4 21:57 Addresses/
drwxr-xr-x   2 root          1024 Jun  5 10:30 Bookshelv
drwxr-xr-x   5 root          1024 Jun 12 11:28 Documen
drwxr-xr-x   8 root          1024 Jun  4 21:27 Fax/
drwxr-xr-x   3 root          1024 Jun 12 11:27 Fonts
drwxr-xr-x  20 root          1024 May 30 19:11 Keyb
drwxr-xr-x   2 root          1024 May 31 17:59 Mus
                             1024 Oct 30  1990 Mus
```

11

Customization

No matter how well a product is designed, we all enjoy changing things to suit our own preferences. NeXT recognized that users would want to customize NEXTSTEP and provided many ways to do so. Two of these ways are through the Workspace Manager's Preferences panel and the Preferences application. If you want to make more radical changes to NEXTSTEP than these allow, several utilities are also available that make NEXTSTEP even easier or more fun to use. This chapter gives details about the Preferences panel, Preferences application, and several popular utilities. It concludes with a discussion of other modifications, such as adding fonts and system beeps and customizing the login panel.

11.0 Customizing the Workspace

Many features of the NEXTSTEP workspace can be modified to suit your taste. To display the Workspace Manager Preferences panel, choose Preferences from the Workspace Manager's Info menu. The panel provides a pop-up list from which you can choose the features you would like to modify. Changes that you make to workspace Preferences will take effect immediately, and you can change as many or as few features as you want at any time. When you are finished making changes, click the close button to

Customization

make the Workspace Manager Preferences panel disappear. Modifications to the workspace remain in effect until you change them again, even after you log out or power off the computer.

11.0.0 Dock Options

Choosing Dock displays the dock options (see Figure 11-1). These options determine which of the applications in the application dock will be started automatically each time you log in. To make an application start automatically, turn on the switch next to the application's name. When you have set the desired number of switches, click Set or press Return on the keyboard to make these changes take effect. The next time you log in, the applications you selected will start up. If you don't see the name of an application you want to start up automatically, close the panel, drag the application's icon from a File Viewer into the dock, then open the Workspace Manager's Preferences panel. The application's name will appear in the list in the same order as it appears in the dock. Note that if you set many applications to start automatically, you will have to wait after you log in as NEXTSTEP starts each application before you can begin working. It's best to select only those applications that you use each time you log in.

**Figure 11-1
Dock Options**

You can set applications stored in the dock to start automatically each time you log in.

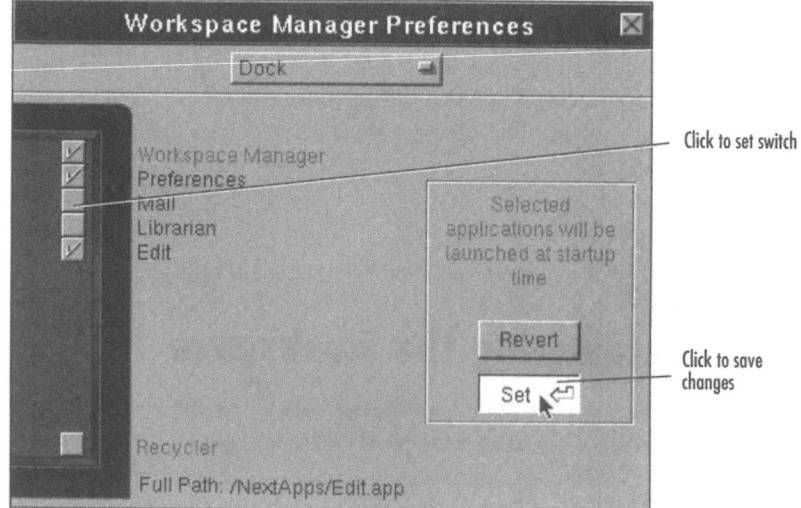

Customizing the Workspace

11.0.1 Shelf Options

The shelf options in the Workspace Manager Preferences panel allow you to modify two aspects of the File Viewer shelf. To view the shelf options, choose Shelf from the pop-up list. Clicking the Resizable Shelf switch makes the shelf dimple appear so that you can resize the shelf in the File Viewer. If the dimple doesn't appear, you will not be able to resize the shelf (see Figure 11-2).

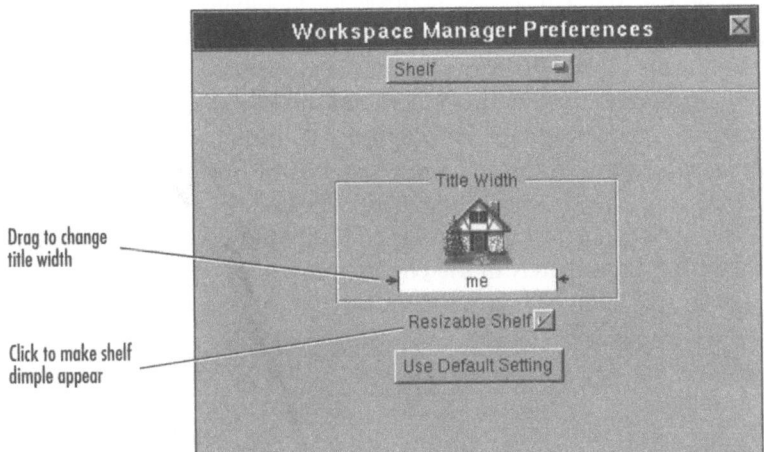

**Figure 11-2
Shelf Options**

Dragging one of the arrows allows you to extend or shorten the space provided for file and folder names in File Viewer shelves.

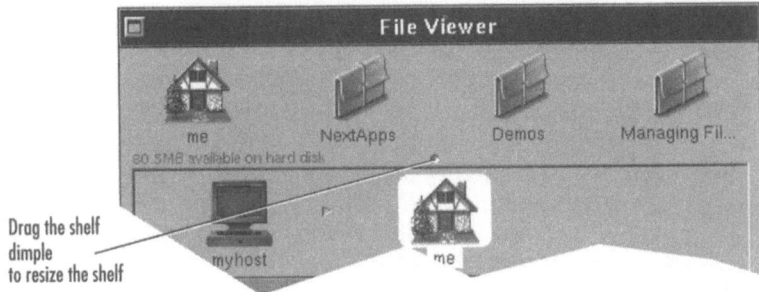

You can also adjust the number of characters used to display an icon's name, called the title width. To adjust the title width, drag either of the two arrows horizontally (see Figure 11-2). When the title width is very short, icon names are abbreviated in the File Viewer's icon view making them more difficult to read. When the title width is very long, fewer icons are displayed (in icon view). Experiment to find the best setting. If you

Customization

have changed the title width and wish to return to NEXTSTEP's normal setting, click Use Default Setting. Note that changes made in the shelf options panel affect every File Viewer.

11.0.2 Browser Options

When you choose Browser in the Workspace Manager Preferences panel pop-up list, you will see the controls for modifying the browser's column width. To change the browser's column width, drag the arrow horizontally (see Figure 11-3). When the column is too narrow, file and folder names are abbreviated making them more difficult to read. When the column is too wide, fewer columns are displayed in the browser. Again, trial and error will help you determine the best setting. You can speed this process by placing the Workspace Manager Preferences panel next to a File Viewer. As you adjust the browser column width, you can see the changes take effect immediately in the File Viewer.

Figure 11-3
Browser Options

You can extend or shorten the column width in the Browser View by dragging the arrow. Every browser column is changed to this width.

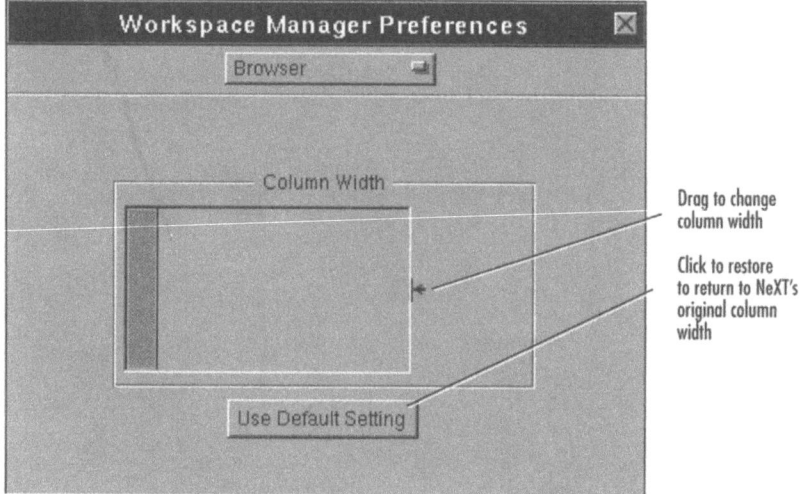

Drag to change column width

Click to restore to return to NeXT's original column width

Because every column of the browser must be the same width, setting the column width changes the width of every column. You cannot customize each column of the browser individually. If you have modified the browser's column width and want to set it back to NEXTSTEP's original setting, click Use Default Setting.

11.0.3 Icon View Options

The Icon View options are almost identical to the shelf options, but adjust the number of characters used to display icon names in the File Viewer's icon view instead of the shelf. Like the shelf control, you can adjust the number of characters used to display an icon's title width by dragging either of the two arrows horizontally (see Figure 11-4). If you have changed the title width and wish to return to the standard setting, click Use Default Setting.

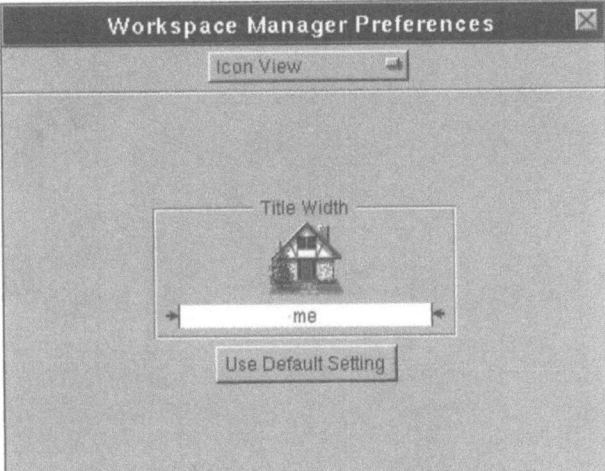

**Figure 11-4
Icon View Options**

Dragging one of the arrows in the Icon View preferences extends or shortens the space provided for file and folder names in File Viewer icon view. Changes made here affect every File Viewer.

11.0.4 The Finder Option

There is only one Finder option in the Workspace Manager Preferences panel (see Figure 11-5). When it is on and you are using search in contents mode in the Finder panel, the search matches only whole words. When this switch is off, partial words that match the search text will be considered successful, but uppercase and lowercase will be ignored.

Figure 11-5
The Finder Option

Turn on this switch to use Digital Librarian indexes when searching for a file or folder in the workspace.

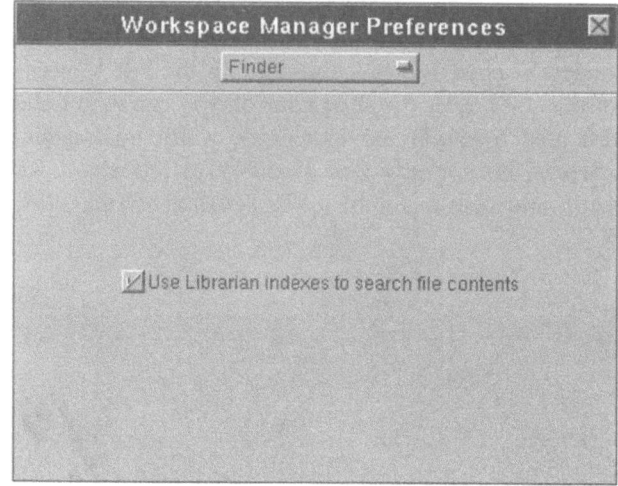

11.0.5   Disk Options

You can change the way in which disks, both removable and nonremovable (fixed) appear in a File Viewer. Removable disks include CD-ROMs, floppy disks, optical disks, and removable hard disk cartridges. Fixed disks include magnetic hard disk drives, RAM drives, and others that cannot be removed while the computer is running. To select an option, click the button next to the description. It will turn highlight to indicate that it is selected (see Figure 11-6). Only one option can be selected at a time for removable and fixed disks but you can change your selection as many times as you wish. When you select "place icon on shelf if there is room," the icon for the disk will appear on the shelf when the disk is inserted (removable disks), or when you log in (fixed disks). When you select "open new folder window," removable disks will appear in their own File Viewer when they are inserted, and fixed disks will appear in their own File Viewer when you log in. Selecting "select the disk" causes a removable disk to become the selected item in the File Viewer when it is inserted, and a fixed disk to be selected in the File Viewer when you first log in. The "do nothing" option prevents NEXTSTEP from selecting or displaying the disk. Regardless of the options you select, fixed and removable disks always appear in the root of the file system and can be viewed in any File Viewer.

Customizing the Workspace

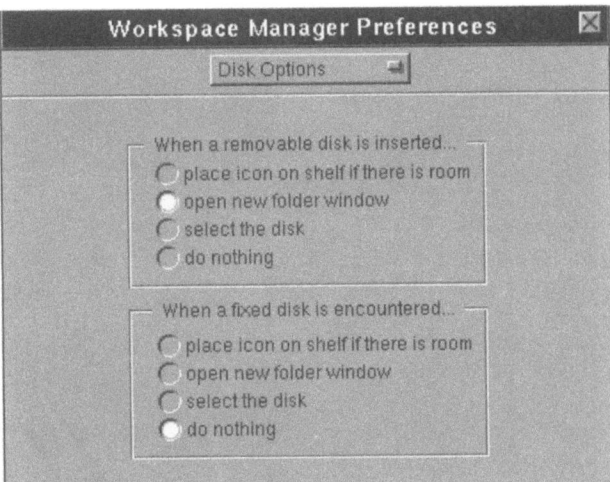

**Figure 11-6
Disk Options**

When NEXTSTEP encounters a disk, it will present it in the workspace according to the choices selected in this panel. Only one item from each group may be selected at a time.

If you are new to NEXTSTEP, you may find the "open new folder window" selection is preferable because disks you insert open in their own File Viewer, making them very easy to locate and use. If you select "place icon on the shelf if there is room," and there are no empty positions on the shelf of the File Viewer, you'll have to navigate the file system to work with the disk. If you forget that this option is selected, you may think NEXTSTEP failed to recognize and mount the disk when you insert it, and might mistakenly attempt to mount or re-initialize it. Fixed disks are not as transient as removable disks, and always appear in the same location in the file system so they are easier to find. Therefore, it is not as critical to have NEXTSTEP handle them in a special manner when you log in. The option you choose for fixed disks is strictly one of personal preference, and none of them has any significant drawbacks or advantages.

11.0.6 File Copy Options

Each time you attempt to copy a linked item in workspace (see "Copying a Link" on page 72), the Processes panel will appear asking you how the link should be treated. You can avoid this bother using the File Copy Options panel (see Figure 11-7). For example, if you are not familiar with links, or you do not copy links often, you may want to select "ask" so that you can see what NEXTSTEP is doing and decide at the moment how to handle the link. Only one item may be selected at a time.

281

Customization

**Figure 11-7
File Copy Options**

To prevent NEXTSTEP from asking you what to do each time you copy a linked item, select an item other than "ask."

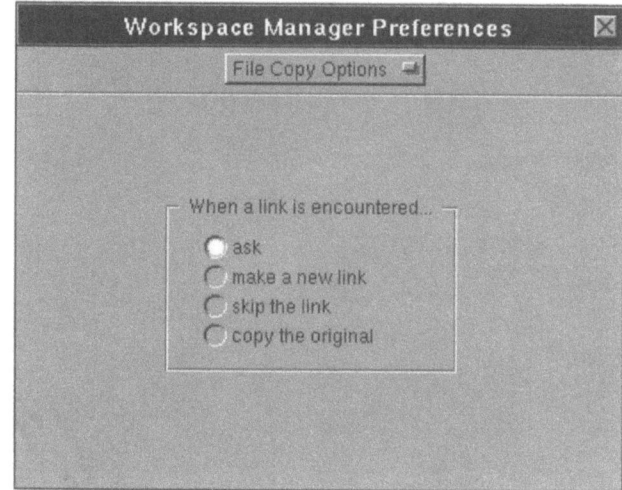

11.1 Customizing the User Environment

Using the Preferences application, you can modify your working environment to suit your liking. Items that can be modified include mouse speed, background color, beep sound, time zone, menu positions, password, and items listed in the Services menu. This section describes each of the Preferences panels provided in NEXTSTEP. You may see other panels in your Preferences depending on the software you have installed.

By default, the Preferences application is set to start automatically from your dock each time you log in. If it isn't in your dock, or it isn't running, you can find it in the **/NextApps** folder. Double-click the Preferences icon to start it running. If you can't see the Preferences panel, double-click its icon in the dock to make it visible

11.1.0 Mouse Preferences

When you click the mouse icon, you will see controls for customizing the mouse's attributes (see Figure 11-8). The upper left corner of the mouse options panel presents four icons for mouse speed, ranging from slow on the left, to fast on the right. If the cursor moves too quickly when you roll

Customizing the User Environment

the mouse, select a slower speed. If you feel you have to roll the mouse too far in order to move the cursor across the screen, select a faster setting, farther to the right.

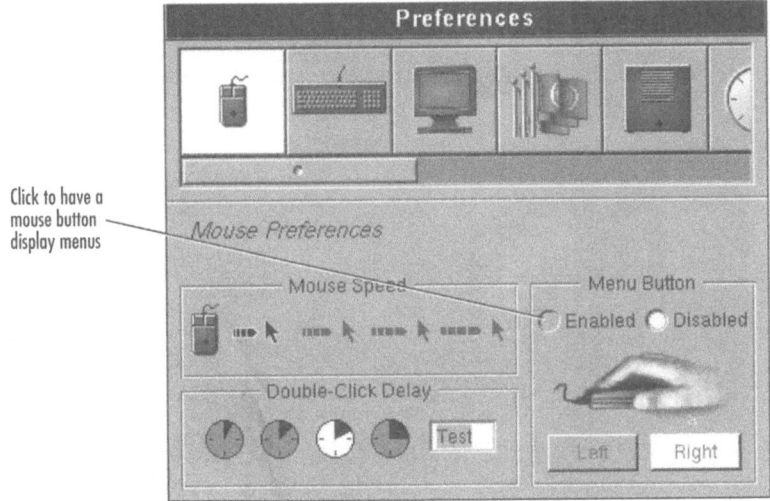

**Figure 11-8
Mouse Preferences**

Using Mouse Preferences, you can control the sensitivity of the mouse buttons and the cursor speed, as well as set one of the mouse buttons to display a menu when pressed.

Click to have a mouse button display menus

The double-click delay determines how much time may elapse between the first and second click of a mouse button for the action to be interpreted as a double-click. In contrast to the mouse speed, the slower settings are to the right, and the faster settings are to the left. The faster the settings, the less time you have to double-click a mouse button. If when you double-click a mouse button, NEXTSTEP often doesn't respond, set the double-click delay to a slower speed (farther to the right). A sample text field is provided so you can test the setting. Double-click the word *Test* in the text field several times at different speeds so you can determine the setting you prefer. When you double-click the word *Test* correctly, it will become selected. If the blinking insertion bar appears, you double-clicked too slowly. To fix it, select a slower setting or double-click the word faster.

NEXTSTEP allows you to use either mouse button to manipulate items on the screen. As a shortcut, you can display the main menu under the arrow cursor when a mouse button is pressed. Using this shortcut you can display and select a menu item without having to move the cursor. To enable this shortcut, select the Enabled button, then click Left or Right to indicate which mouse button you would like to use as the shortcut. The Left or Right button will be highlighted on the screen when selected.

11.1.1 Keyboard Preferences

The keyboard controls allow you to set the speed of the initial key repeat and key repeat rates (see Figure 11-9). The initial key repeat refers to the amount of time that will pass before a key that is held down begins to repeat on the screen. For example, if you hold down the period key on the keyboard, NEXTSTEP will wait for the amount of time indicated by the initial key repeat rate, before a second, third, and following period characters appear on the screen. Once the key begins to repeat, NEXTSTEP will continue to repeat the character according to the selection for key repeat rate. The faster the rate, the faster each successive character will appear. The slower settings are to the left, and the faster settings are to the right. A text field is also provided so that you can test your settings.

You may not consider key repeat rate to be important, but there is one key you probably use often in repeat mode, the Delete key. When you hold down the Delete key to delete several characters, the speed at which it begins to delete, and how fast it repeats are determined by these settings. Use the text field to enter several characters, and then delete them by holding down the Delete key to determine the settings that suit you best.

**Figure 11-9
Keyboard
Preferences**

Keyboard Preferences allow you to set key responsiveness.

Customizing the User Environment

11.1.2 Display Preferences

Selecting the display icon reveals several new options (see Figure 11-10). The first option is automatic dimming. NEXTSTEP automatically dims the screen after periods of inactivity. This prevents the monitor from becoming marked with a particular image that will never disappear. Dragging the slider sets the amount of idle time that must pass before the display is dimmed. The text field changes as you drag the slider to indicate the time you select in minutes. As a shortcut, you can type the time directly into the text field and press Return. The clock at the left of the slider will also change to reflect that selected time in minutes.

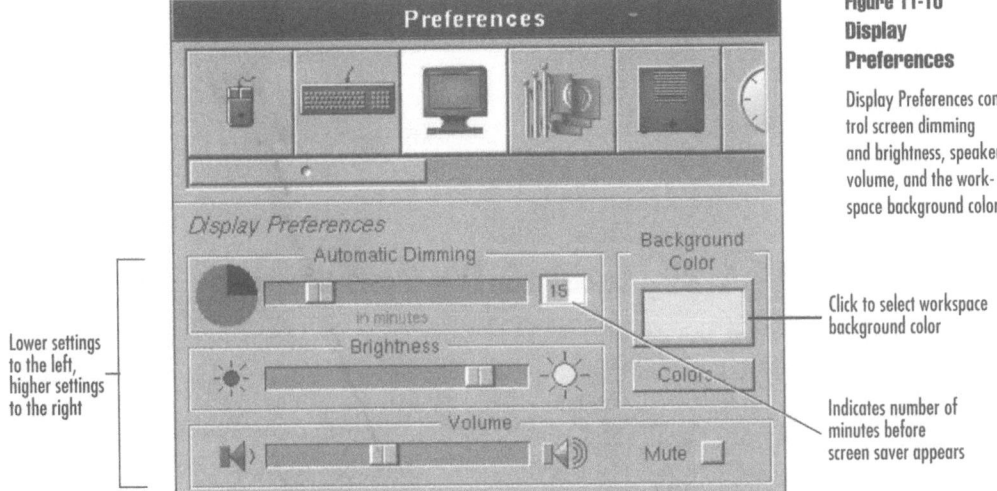

**Figure 11-10
Display
Preferences**

Display Preferences control screen dimming and brightness, speaker volume, and the workspace background color.

Lower settings to the left, higher settings to the right

Click to select workspace background color

Indicates number of minutes before screen saver appears

The brightness of the screen and the volume of the speaker are also controlled by sliders in this panel. Dragging the sliders to the right increases the brightness or volume while dragging to the left decreases them. (If you have a NeXT computer, you can also use the *volume* and *brightness* keys on the keyboard. Both perform the same function as the sliders, so use the control you prefer.) The mute switch in the display panel, when activated, turns off the computer's speaker.

A color well in the Display Preferences named Background Color, allows you to select a background color for the workspace. To select a new color, click the frame surrounding the color well and choose a color in the Colors panel (see Figure 11-11). The background changes instantly as you select colors in the Colors panel so you can see how your selection looks. NEXT-

You can preview colors without changing the background color by clicking the Colors button when the color well frame isn't highlighted.

Customization

STEP will continue to use this background color each time you log in until you change it. When you have made your color selection, click the Colors panel's close button to make the panel disappear.

Figure 11-11
The Workspace Background Color

To select a background color, click the color well frame and use the Colors panel to select a color.

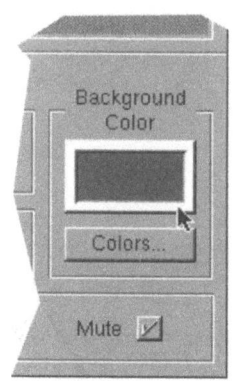
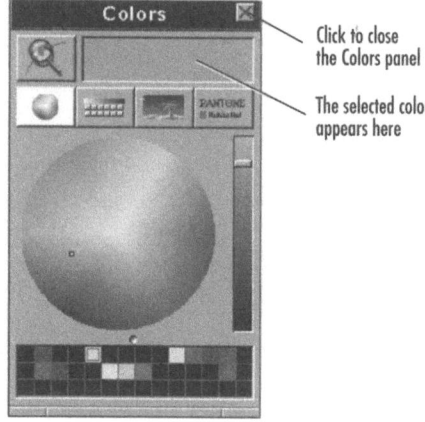

11.1.3 Localization Preferences

When you install NEXTSTEP, you are offered the opportunity to install several different language modules as well. If more than one language has been installed, you can select the one you would like NEXTSTEP to use in menus, panels, and applications. In the Preferences panel, click the flag icon to display the Localization Preferences options (see Figure 11-12). To select a language, drag the name of the language you prefer to the top of the languages list. Use the scroller to see languages that are out of view.

You'll also want to select a keyboard language to match the language you selected so that you can type the characters specific to the language. For example, when you select the Spanish keyboard language, you'll be able to use special characters such as ñ and ç in that language. To select a keyboard language, click the name of the language in the Keyboards list. You can view the characters available in the selected language by clicking Keyboard Panel. A panel containing a keyboard will appear in which you can type keys on the keyboard or click keys in the Keyboard panel to display sample text in the Keyboard panel's text field (see Figure 11-13). This way you can practice the keystrokes necessary to create special characters. You can even copy and paste them from the text field into a document. Don't forget that by holding down the modifier keys, such as Alternate, Control,

Customizing the User Environment

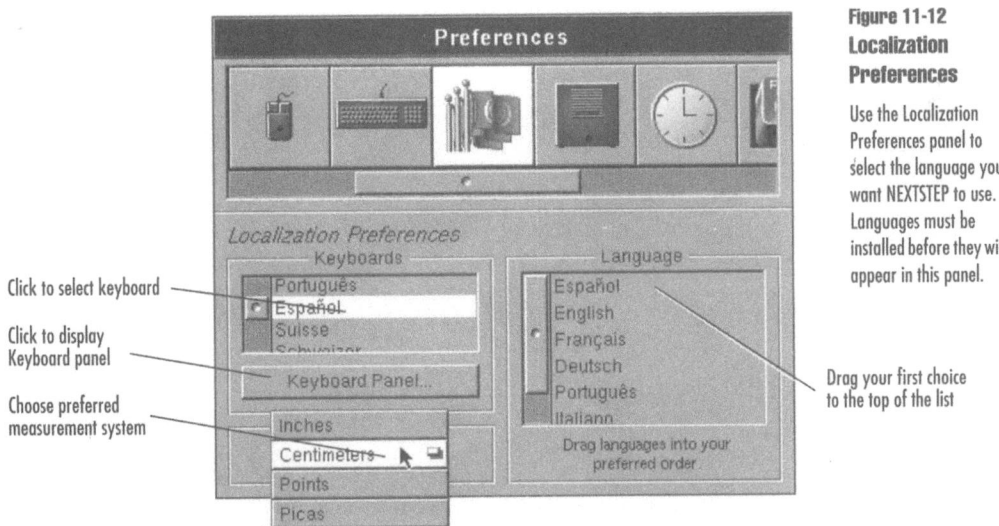

**Figure 11-12
Localization
Preferences**

Use the Localization Preferences panel to select the language you want NEXTSTEP to use. Languages must be installed before they will appear in this panel.

and Shift, you can see each of the font sets for a particular language. For example, typing 7 displays the numeral 7, typing Shift-7 displays an ampersand (&), and typing Alternate-7 displays a bullet (•). Not only can you preview each character set, you can also see how it will look in a particular font by clicking Set Font and choosing a font from the Font panel.

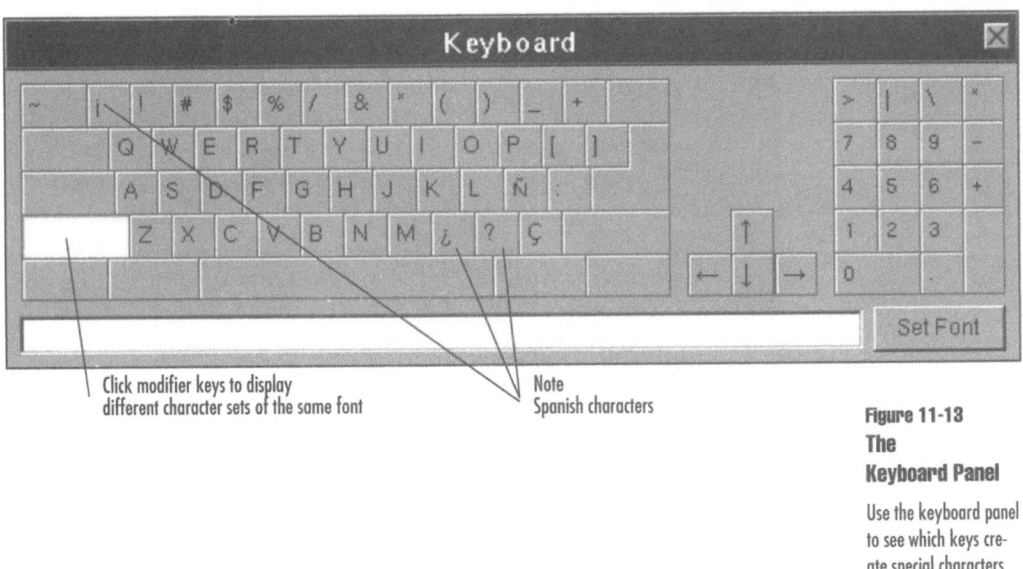

**Figure 11-13
The
Keyboard Panel**

Use the keyboard panel to see which keys create special characters.

287

Customization

Finally, if you want to use a measurement system other than feet and inches, you can select centimeters, points, or picas.

You can remap your keyboard to respond like the standard NeXT keyboard by choosing NeXTUSA. This mapping provides easier access to modifier keys (on both sides of the keyboard), and makes it easy to switch between using NeXT and PC keyboards.

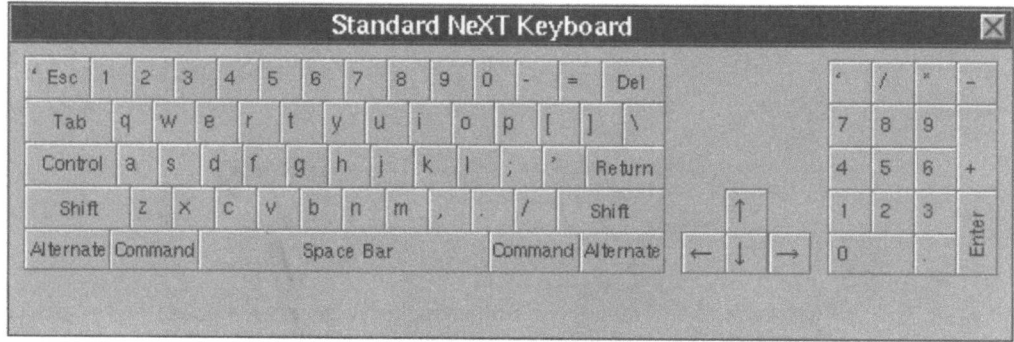

11.1.4 General Preferences

To see the General Preferences controls, click the NeXTcube icon. The general options allow you to view and set the default System, bold system, application, and fixed-pitch fonts required by NEXTSTEP, as well as the system beep sound (see Figure 11-14). To apply a font, select the way the font will be used in the pop-up list, and then click Font Panel to display the NEXTSTEP Font panel. Select the font you wish to use and click Set in the Font Panel to apply it. A small display area in the Preferences panel named Example: illustrates one of the ways the default font you select will appear and be used in NEXTSTEP. For example, the application font controls the typeface you see in the File Viewer, the system font controls how menus appear, and the bold system font is used in window title bars. To change a font size, select an item from the pop-up list, and then choose a font size in the Font Panel. You may need to log out and back in again to see some of your changes.

Customizing the User Environment

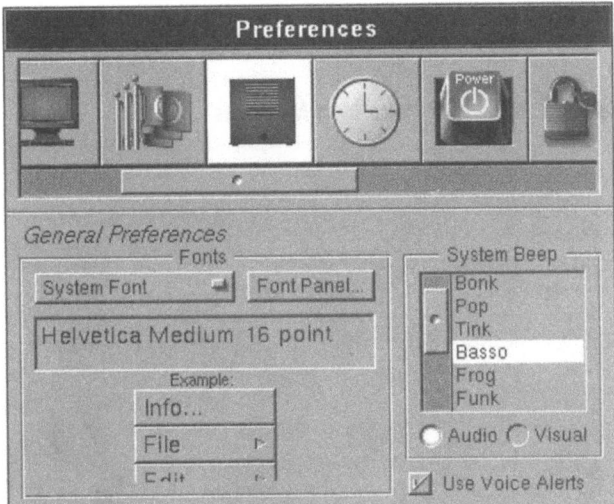

Figure 11-14
General Preferences

In the General Preferences panel, you can modify the system beep sound, turn voice alerts on and off, and select the default font for the system and for applications.

If you are using a NeXT computer, or a PC with a sound adapter installed, you can have NEXTSTEP play sounds to alert you to a mistake or problem. To hear sounds, highlight the audio button. You can also turn on a feature called Voice Alerts. When Voice Alerts are turned on, NEXTSTEP will play prerecorded voice messages to alert you to a printing problem. Voice alerts are played when a printing problem requires your attention, such as when the printer is out of paper or when the printer is ready for paper to be fed manually. Activating the Voice Alert switch turns voice messages on; deactivating voice alerts off. You can record you own voice-alert messages but you'll need to log in as **root** to install them or have the system administrator install them for you. Start the Sound application in **/NextDeveloper/Demos**, and record a new voice message as described in the paragraph above for creating a system beep sound.

To install the new message, copy the sound file into **/usr/lib/NeXT-Printer/English.lproj**. There are several messages that you can customize in this folder (see Table 11-1). Be sure to name your new message exactly the same as the one it replaces. If you would like to hear the voice messages, you don't have to wait for a printing problem to occur. Turn on the UNIX Expert switch as described in the Expert Preferences options, then locate the voice alert files in **/usr/lib/NeXTPrinter/English.lproj**. (If the

Customization

UNIX Expert switch is not on, you won't be able to see the **/usr** folder in the File Viewer.) Select a file, open the Contents Inspector, and click Play.

Table 11-1 NEXTSTEP Voice Alert Messages

File Name	Description
manualfeed.snd	Your printer is waiting for paper
nopaper.snd	Your printer is out of paper
paperjam.snd	Paper is jammed in your printer
printeropen.snd	Your printer cover is open

The beep sound can also be changed in the General Preferences panel. Several beep sounds are included as part of NEXTSTEP and appear in the scrolling list. You can add new sounds easily, using any sound application that can save sounds in snd format. NEXTSTEP includes a sound recording and editing application called Sound in **/NextDeveloper/Demos**. After recording a sound, install it by dragging the SND icon from the Untitled panel onto the **/LocalLibrary/Sounds** or **~/Library/Sounds** folders in a File Viewer. Each sound you place in these folders will appear in the General Preferences panel of the Preferences application. If you move or delete a sound file from one of these folders, it will also disappear from the list in the General Preferences panel. (NEXTSTEP also looks for sounds in the **/NextLibrary/Sounds** folder. Sounds located in this folder are provided as part of NEXTSTEP and are accessible only by the **root** user. They are rarely changed or deleted)

If you're using a PC and don't have a sound adapter, you can tell NEXTSTEP to alert you visually instead of using a sound. Click the Visual button instead of Audio. When in visual mode, NEXTSTEP will blink the NEXTSTEP logo in the application dock instead of playing a sound. This option may also be preferable in environments where sounds would be disruptive, or if you have impaired hearing and you might not hear the sound.

11.1.5 Date and Time Preferences

Clicking the clock icon in the Preferences panel displays the date and time options (see Figure 11-15). It is important for NEXTSTEP to know the current time and date because each time you save a file, NEXTSTEP stamps it with the date and time. Without an accurate date and time stamp, you may not be able to determine which files contain the most recent information. An accurate date and time stamp is also critical when making backups or restoring files from a backup. If the date and time stamp are incorrect, restoring files from a backup may overwrite newer information on your disk. NEXTSTEP requires the system administrator to set the date and time while logged in as **root**. If you are not the **root** user, you cannot set the date or time. Once the proper date and time are set, the computer will remember it even when the power is turned off.

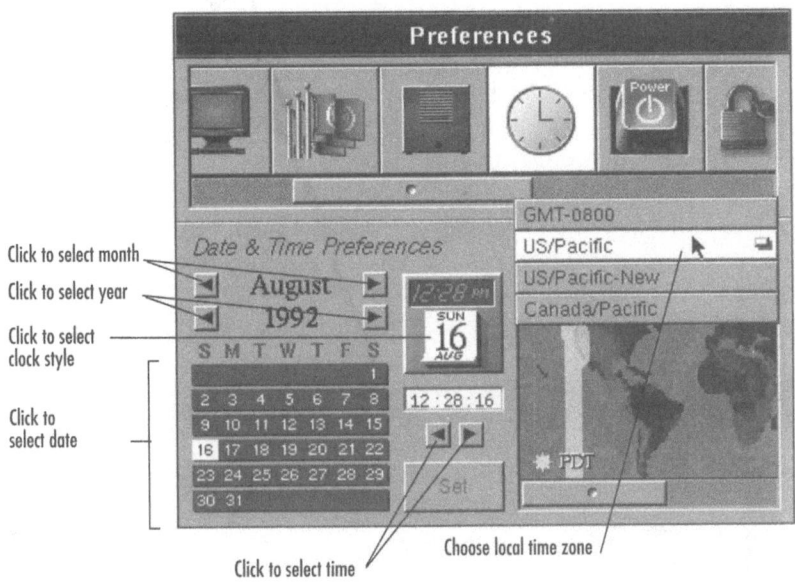

**Figure 11-15
Date and Time Preferences**

To set the date and time for your computer, use the Date & Time Preferences panel. When you have set the proper date and time, click Set.

If your computer system is connected to a network, the date and time setting may be controlled by a date and time server. In this case, Set is replaced by Synchronize in the Preferences panel. Clicking Synchronize will set the date and time to match that of the server.

If your computer is not connected to a server that maintains the date and time, you will have to set these attributes yourself. To set the date, click the arrows on either side of the month and year display. Clicking a day on

Customization

the calendar sets the day. To set the time, you can type the time in the time field or click the arrows on either side of the time display. Once the date and time have been correctly entered, click Set to apply them.

NEXTSTEP also provides a world map in which to set the time zone. Scroll the map to display your present location, and then click that location on the map to select your time zone. Should you live in an area that takes advantage of daylight savings time, use the pop-up list above the map to select your region within the time zone. NEXTSTEP uses this setting to adjust the time for daylight savings automatically. To indicate that a daylight savings region is selected, a small sun icon appears in the lower left corner of the world map.

11.1.6 Startup Preferences

If you have a late-model NeXT computer, you may be able to use the startup options to set a time and date for your computer to power on by itself. This may be handy if you're leaving the office for a trip but want your computer to power on Monday morning to receive electronic mail and incoming faxes, or simply make itself accessible to you and other users through a network. If this feature is available on your computer, you'll see the Startup Preferences panel (see Figure 11-16) when you click the Power icon. If it doesn't appear, you'll see an alert panel containing the message "that section could not be loaded."

**Figure 11-16
Startup
Preferences**

Use Startup Preferences. to set a date and time for you computer to power on by itself. You can also use it to set your computer to restart after a power failure.

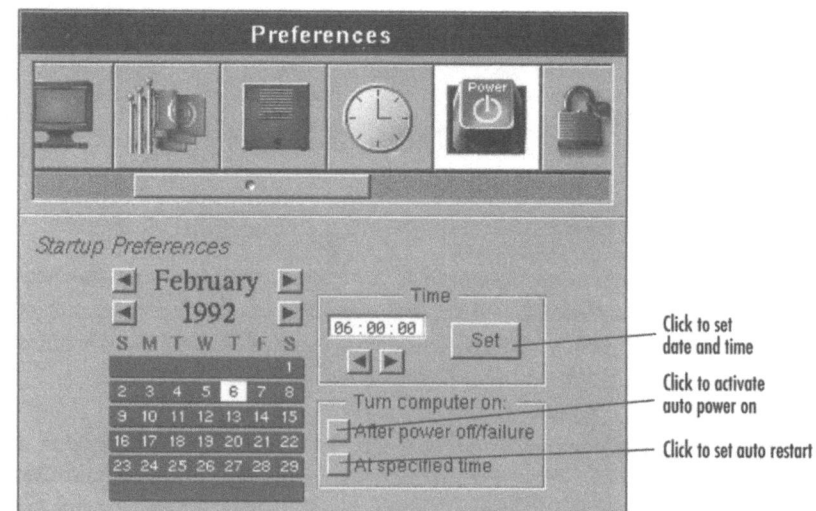

Customizing the User Environment

To set your computer to power on automatically, set a date and time just as described for the Date & Time preferences, and then click Set to set the date and time. To have the computer start up automatically at that time, turn the "At Specified Time" switch on.

You can also have your computer recover from a power outage automatically by turning on the "After power off/failure" switch. If the power should go out, or the computer be turned off accidentally, it will restart itself without any intervention when the power is restored. This is an especially useful feature for file, mail, and print servers, which can be critical to the operation of computer networks.

11.1.7 Password Preferences

To change your NEXTSTEP password, display the password preferences panel by clicking the padlock icon. You should change your password at least once each month, or as often as you require to ensure that your password has not been discovered.

To change your password, type your current password and then click OK (see Figure 11-17). If you did not enter a password to begin your NEXTSTEP session, don't enter anything, just click OK. The panel will change, requesting you to enter a new password. Your new password must be at least five characters long or the password panel will not accept it. Type a new password and click OK. You will asked to enter the new password a second time to verify that you entered it correctly and that you remember it. If you enter it differently the second time, your original password will not be changed. If the two passwords match, the password will be changed and you will need to use it the next time you log in.

The security of your files and of NEXTSTEP itself is directly related to your selection and use of passwords. Take the time to choose them well. Good passwords utilize upper- and lowercase letters, numbers, symbols, and spaces; cannot be found in dictionaries; and do not relate to the user. A good password might be **YoHum!**, **AnrIght**, or **W1#6a**. Of course, if you write down your password on a note and tape it to your computer, you might as well not use it at all! Don't write it down and store it near your computer or give it away to someone. Change your password often so that if it is discovered, the hacker will not be able to continue to use it.

Customization

**Figure 11-17
Password Preferences**

To create or change a NEXTSTEP password, use the password Preferences display.

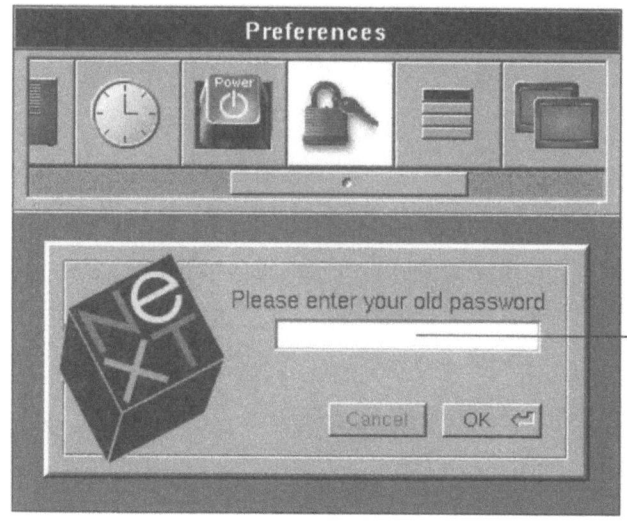

Type your current password, then type your new password twice.

Bad passwords would be **6/1/75** (a birthday), **Ken** (a spouse's name), and **Fido** (your pet's name). These passwords are easily guessed by a would-be hacker and shouldn't be used. Also, don't make minor changes to existing passwords. Some users diligently change their password each month but do so in a way that is easy to figure out. They use the same password each month and just add a number at the end relating to the current month. This is easy to remember, but it's also for a hacker to figure out too. Make every new password very different from the one that preceded it.

Passwords that are difficult to defeat are often difficult to remember. But a little effort spent in creating and changing passwords monthly can pay off by protecting against lost or stolen data. An excellent discussion of the use and abuse of computer passwords is provided in a book by Clifford Stoll named *The Cuckoo's Egg*.

11.1.8 Menu Preferences

The Menu Preferences panel allows you to change the default location of the main menu for the Workspace Manager and create and edit keyboard shortcuts. To change the default location of the main menu, drag the small image of the menu on the left side of the Menu Preferences panel (see Figure 11-18). As you drag it, the real main menu will move around the screen. This can be quite shocking if you're not expecting it. As you select

Customizing the User Environment

a new location for the main menu, remember that the application dock usually fills the entire right side of the display, so placing the menu along the right edge of the display may cover some of the dock icons. You may also have trouble seeing submenus if the main menu is placed too far to the right of the screen.

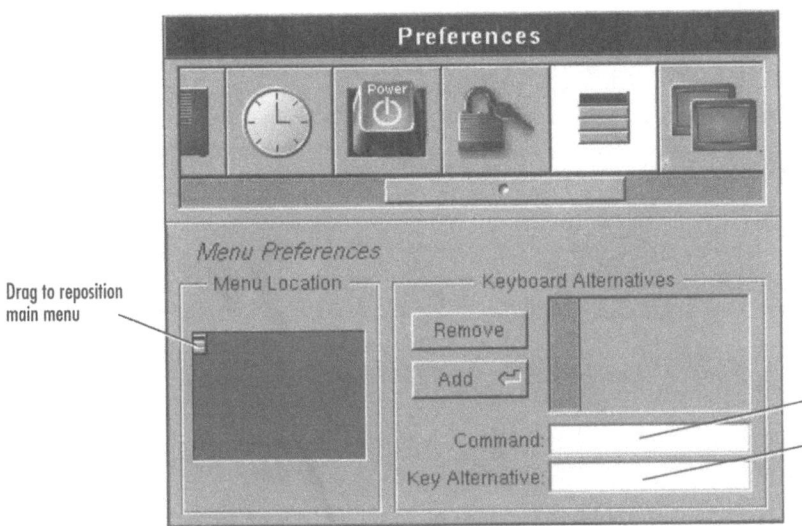

**Figure 11-18
Menu
Preferences**

You can change the location of the main menu of every application and create your own menu shortcuts using the Menu Preferences panel.

You can also use the Menu Preferences panel to create and edit keyboard shortcuts. To create or change a keyboard shortcut, type the name of the menu command and type the letter of the key you would like to be the shortcut. When creating your shortcut, remember that NEXTSTEP treats upper- and lowercase letters differently, so pay attention to the way a command name is displayed. The command name you type must match the real command name exactly for the shortcut to work. For example, entering S as a shortcut means you will have to type Command-Shift-S to use it. If you use s as a shortcut, you need only type Command-s to use it. After typing the menu command and shortcut key, click Add to enter it. If you enter a shortcut that's already in use, it will replace the one that already exists. To remove a shortcut, select it the shortcut list and click Remove. Remember that NEXTSTEP has many shortcuts already defined, so, to prevent confusion, be careful when assigning new ones.

Customization

11.1.9 Screens Preferences

It is possible, even desirable, to have more than one video display connected and in use on your computer. If your computer has more than one display, you can configure their arrangement using the Screens Preferences panel (see Figure 11-19). This panel will tell NEXTSTEP where items should appear when you drag them from one screen to another and which screen to use as the primary screen on which to display the login panel and the application dock. To set the display arrangement, drag the small screen icons in the Screens Preference panel. To determine which screen icon represents each real display unit, select a display from the scrolling list and click Locate. A spinning X will appear in the middle of the selected screen. Position the icons for each monitor just as the real monitors are positioned in relation to each other. NEXTSTEP treats multiple monitors as if they were part of a large single virtual monitor, so when you drag an item off one screen, it appears on the other.

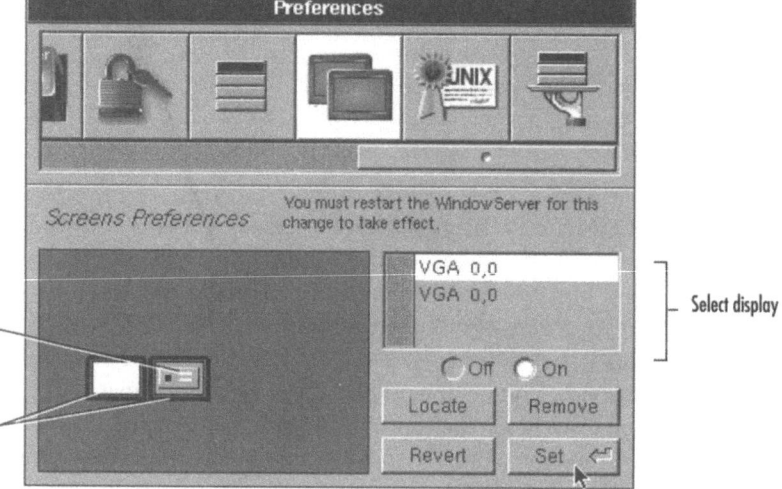

**Figure 11-19
Screens
Preferences**

Use the Screens Preferences panel to configure multiple displays. When you drag an item from one screen to another, it appears from the proper side of the display.

Drag to set primary monitor

Drag to arrange icons in the same manner as you have positioned the real displays

When you have the icons arranged in the desired fashion, click Set. If you have changed the screen icons but wish to return to the last saved setting, click Revert. Clicking Remove removes the selected screen icon from the Screens Preferences panel and disables the display it represents. At any time, you can disable every screen but the primary screen (which displays the login panel icon) by clicking the Off button below the scrolling list of attached displays

You can also drag the login panel icon, which appears in the middle of one of the screen icons, to another screen icon to make the login panel and application menus appear on that screen when you restart the computer.

11.1.10 Expert Preferences

The UNIX certificate icon in the Preferences panel is used to select the Expert Preferences. Expert Preferences should only be activated if you are familiar with the UNIX operating system. If you are not familiar with UNIX system commands, you may not only become confused by the results, but allow networked users control over your computer. Don't take a chance enabling an Expert option unless you are certain you know what you are doing. When you make a change to any of these options, the change will take effect the next time you log into your NEXTSTEP account.

The File Creation Mask (see Figure 11-20), which is very similar to the permissions matrix in the Attributes and Access Control Inspectors, is used to set the default permissions rather than the permissions for a selected file or folder. The permissions set here are applied automatically to every new file and folder you create. This can save you a significant amount of time verifying the permission of every new item you create. Some applications will override these default settings, so if you are in doubt, use the Attributes or Access Control Inspector to verify that the permissions are set correctly.

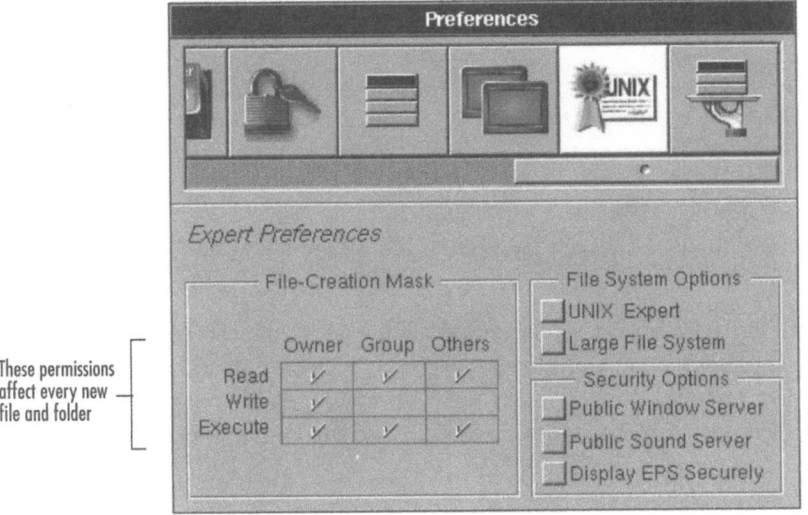

**Figure 11-20
Expert Preferences**

Expert Preferences are used to fine tune system performance and enable unique NEXTSTEP options but require a knowledge of UNIX commands.

Customization

The Expert Preferences panel also displays five switches that enable special features of NEXTSTEP. When UNIX Expert is activated, the entire UNIX file system is made visible in the File Viewer. This option is most useful for the **root** user who needs to see and modify UNIX files to configure a NeXT system. Unless you are a programmer or system administrator, there is rarely a need to activate this switch.

Activating the Large File System switch removes the triangle symbol that distinguishes folders from files in the File Viewer's browser. When this option is active, NEXTSTEP does not take time to display a folder's contents until you select it. This speeds the performance of the NEXTSTEP File Viewer when displaying disks that contain several hundred files or more but can slow scrolling through them. This option is best when you are navigating CD-ROMs or drives over 660 MB in capacity.

The following options allow other computer users connected to your computer over a network to control your computer. These options pose a security risk and should not be activated unless you assume the risk of other users controlling your computer.

The Public Window Server option allows users on remote computers network to access yours to run applications and open windows on your computer. It can be used to control a computer from across a network. One application of this option is to run applications on a remote computer that may have more disk storage, processing power, or time available for computing, and display the results on your own computer screen.

When Public Window Server is on, you can run a NEXTSTEP application on another computer, but have it displayed on your own. Log in to the remote computer using the **telnet** or **rlogin** command in a Terminal shell and on the remote computer, type the name pathname of the application followed by **–NXHost** and the name of your computer. For example: **/NextApps/Webster.app/Webster –NXHost myhost**

The Public Sound Server option allows users from across a network to use your NeXT computer's Digital Signal Processor chip and control the playing and recording of sounds on your computer. It's possible for a remote computer with this privilege to activate the built-in microphone on your

Customizing the User Environment

computer and listen in on your conversations. This feature is designed for intercom-type applications that allow voice communication over a computer network.

The Display EPS Securely option prevents hidden commands in Post-Script code from performing subversive tasks that might damage your system or lock you out.

11.1.11 Services Preferences

The Services Preferences options are a recent and welcome addition to NEXTSTEP. The services options allow you to customize the list of services that appear in the Services menu of applications. Recall that services are automatically loaded and placed in the Services menu by NEXTSTEP. Using the Services preferences, you can select the that services will appear in the menu (see Figure 11-21). This is handy if you don't wish to use some of the services that are automatically loaded by NEXTSTEP. For example, services such as HeaderViewer, Project, and Terminal are designed for programmers. You can disable these services so they do not clutter the Services menu and make it difficult to find the services you find most useful. You cannot customize each application's Services menu. The changes you make apply globally to every application's Services menu.

The services options appear in a two-column browser. To disable a service, click to highlight its name in the left column of the browser, and then click Disable. Repeat this procedure for each service you would like to remove from the Services menu. To enable a service, select its name and click Enable. In the Browser, disabled services appear in gray, enabled services appear in black.

If the service offers several commands, selecting the service's name will cause its commands to appear in the right browser column. To disable a particular command, select it in the right browser column and click Disable. You can enable a disabled service at any time by selecting a dimmed service command in the Services browser and clicking Enable. Changes made to services take effect immediately in every running application.

Customization

**Figure 11-21
Services
Preferences**

Using the Services Preferences panel, you can turn individual services on and off.

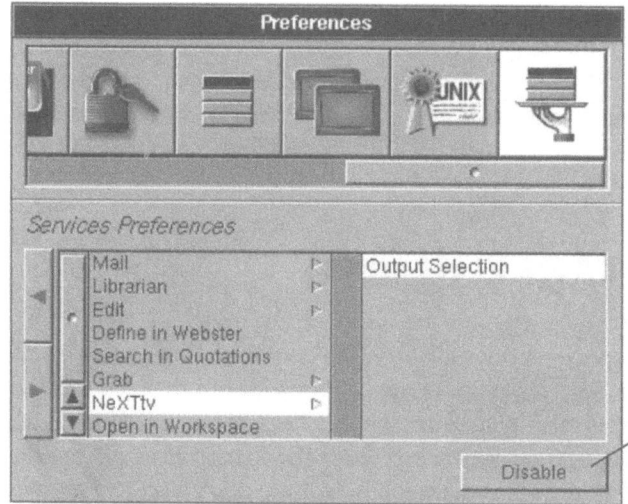

11.2 Installing New Fonts

One of the features many uses most want to customize on their computer is its collection of installed fonts. This, too, can be done in NEXTSTEP. NEXTSTEP uses only PostScript fonts, which are available from numerous dealers, mail-order companies, and computer stores, as well as directly from Adobe, the makers of PostScript. In NEXTSTEP, PostScript fonts can be installed three folders: **/NextLibrary/Fonts**, **/LocalLibrary/Fonts**, and **~/Library/Fonts**. Fonts installed in the folder **/NextLibrary/Fonts** are supplied by NeXT as part of NEXTSTEP and only fonts supplied by NeXT should be stored there. Fonts that are not included with NEXTSTEP that need to be made available to every user on the computer are placed in **/LocalLibrary/Fonts** but can only be installed by the **root** user. Fonts that should be available to only one user, should be installed in that user's **~/Library/Fonts** folder.

PostScript Type 1 fonts are available from many sources but not all are compatible with NEXTSTEP. The majority of PostScript fonts are used by Macintosh users and have been specifically designed for Macintosh systems. However, Adobe does make several font packages specifically for NEXTSTEP that contain a set of popular fonts for creating ads, flyers, memos, books, and other documents. Adobe fonts for NEXTSTEP not contained in Adobe's special font packages are distributed only by RightBrain Software, and are available by calling 800-4-RBRAIN. You can also purchase fonts directly from Adobe by calling 800-USA-FONTS. When you purchase fonts from Adobe or RightBrain, you will receive the font's outline, afm and bitmap files, and custom font installer application on one or more NEXTSTEP-formatted 3.5-inch HD floppy disks. This application makes installing PostScript fonts extraordinarily simple and also provides several extra features, such as the ability to download fonts to the printer, print a list of fonts installed in the printer, restart the printer, display the printer queue, and many more. Because Adobe licenses its fonts for use on a particular printer, not a computer, you may be able to copy your existing fonts to several machines without having to purchase extra licenses. The catch is that the fonts must all be used with the same printer. Refer to the license agreement that accompanies the fonts.

If you have already purchased PostScript fonts designed for other computer systems such as the Macintosh, or want to purchase PostScript Type 1 fonts from a company other than Adobe or RightBrain, there are several utilities available to convert them into NEXTSTEP format. Altsys sells an application called Metamorphosis for the Macintosh, which among other things, allows you to convert TrueType and PostScript Type 1 and Type 3 fonts for Macintosh into NEXTSTEP compatible format. This application requires a Macintosh. MetroSoft sells a utility named MetroTools for installing PostScript Type 1 fonts onto NEXTSTEP systems even though they were designed for the Macintosh. This application has the benefit of

Figure 11-22
Font Installers

The Adobe Font installer (top) is included when you purchase NEXTSTEP fonts from Adobe or RightBrain. If you want to install PostScript Type 1 fonts designed for the Macintosh, you can use MetroTools (bottom), a commercial utility.

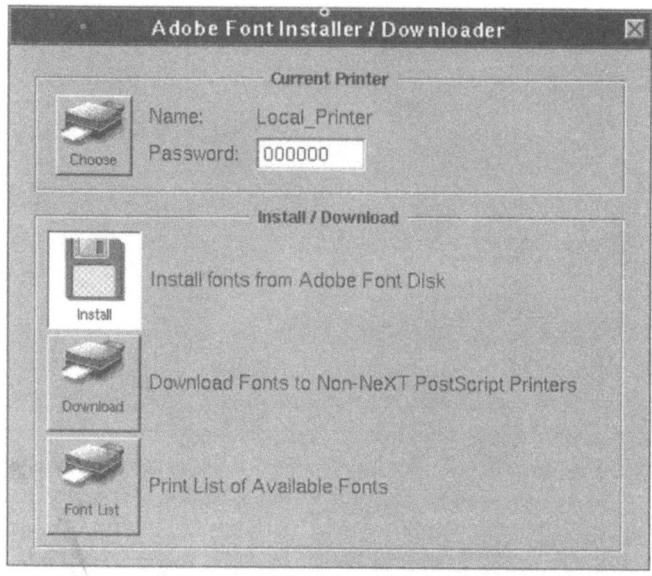

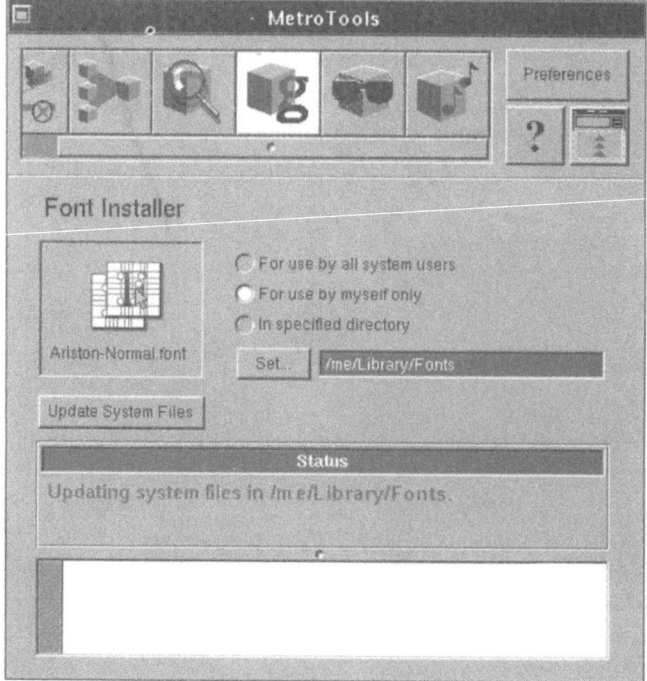

running under NEXTSTEP, but does not allow you to convert TrueType or PostScript Type 3 fonts. If you are planning to make use of many additional fonts, you would do well to purchase one of these two utilities.

11.2.0 Installing Fonts Manually

You can also install fonts manually by dragging them into an appropriate font folder. If you drag them into your **~/Library/Fonts** folder, the next time you start an application that uses fonts, the fonts will be indexed and incorporated automatically. If you are the **root** user, and install fonts manually into the **/NextLibrary/Fonts** or **/LocalLibrary/Fonts** folders so every user can access them, you will need to index the fonts manually. Type **buildafmdir** followed by the font directory pathname in a Terminal window. For example, to index new fonts in **/NextLibrary/Fonts**, you would type **buildafmdir /NextLibrary/Fonts**. In some cases, the new fonts will appear in the Font Panel but be marked as unusable. This can be fixed by typing **cacheAFMData** followed by the name or pathname of the AFM folder to be fixed.

In earlier versions of NEXTSTEP, the three components of a font—its AFM, outline, and bitmap files—were stored in separate folders within a font directory. Older NEXTSTEP applications running on NeXT computers may not work correctly if the fonts don't appear in these folders. If you have such an application, you can easily correct the problem by typing **font_update_2.0** in a Terminal window. This command will create symbolic links from each of the standard **.font** folders to an AFM, outline, and bitmap folder so older application can find the fonts you have installed.

11.2.1 Downloading Fonts

Unlike previous versions, NEXTSTEP 3.1 now automatically downloads fonts so they appear correctly in a printed document. If NEXTSTEP fails to do this correctly, you can download fonts manually using the **fontloader** command in a Terminal window.

The **fontloader** command creates a PostScript program that will download a font to the printer. Each time you download a font, it resides in the printer's RAM, so there is a finite amount of space in which to load fonts. If you run out of printer RAM, you have two choices: install more RAM in the

Customization

printer or use fewer fonts in the document you want to print. The printer's built-in fonts don't use the printer's RAM like downloadable fonts so use them as much as possible and use downloadable fonts only when necessary.

When you download a font, you must download each typeface one at a time. You cannot download an entire font family at once. A typeface consists of a family name followed by a specific typeface such as bold or italic. For example, Goudy Extra Bold, Goudy Italic, or Goudy Bold Italic. The names of each typeface can be found in the font directories **/NextLibrary/Fonts** (see Figure 11-23), **/LocalLibrary/Fonts**, and **~/Library/Fonts** or by reviewing the names listed in an application's Font Panel.

Figure 11-23
Font folders

Standard NEXTSTEP fonts are located in the /NextLibrary folder (top). You can examine individual font files by opening a font icon (bottom).

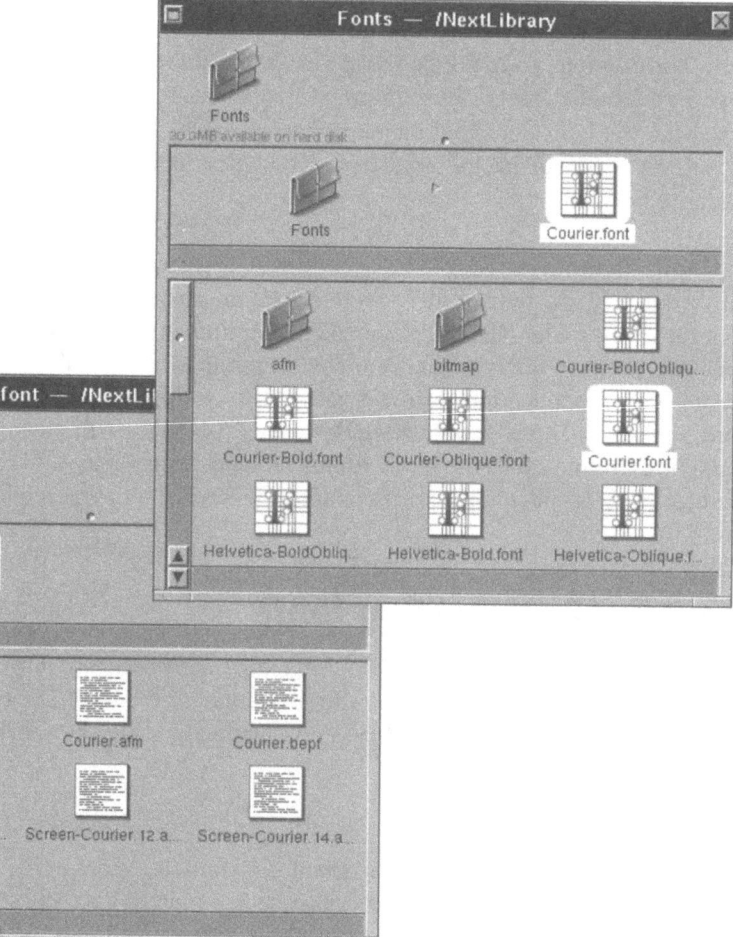

Installing New Fonts

To download a font to a non-NeXT printer, enter fontloader followed by the typeface name in a Terminal window. For example, to download the font named Futura Condensed Light Oblique, you would enter:

fontloader Futura-CondensedLightOblique

Notice how the typeface is separated from the font family name with a hyphen. This creates a PostScript program to download the font, but doesn't actually download the font. To download the font, you must send the PostScript program to the printer. This procedure can be simplified by combining the **Fontloader** and **lpr** (UNIX print) commands on the same command line using the UNIX pipe | symbol, which cause the output of one program to be used as input for another. Here is how the command to both would look:

fontloader Futura-CondensedLightOblique | lpr -P*name*

Be sure to replace *name* with the name of the printer to which the font should be downloaded. Also note that there is no space between the name of the printer and the **–P** option.

The fontloader command does not take effect instantly. NEXTSTEP will treat the print request it generates like every other print request and place it in the printer's queue. When the printer is ready, the print request is processed. Only after the print request has been completed can you print a document that utilizes the downloaded fonts. If there is a problem downloading the file, you'll never know because no messages are displayed on the screen. To verify that the font was downloaded successfully, check the file **/usr/adm/lpd–errs**. This file lists all printer errors. Since the last job sent to the printer was the font download request, you can skip to the end of the file and view the last 20 lines by typing **tail /usr/adm/lpd–errs**.

For each typeface you need downloaded, repeat the fontloader command, and replacing the name of the typeface each time. Downloaded fonts will remain in the printer until the printer is powered off or reset. In fact, this is the only way to remove a downloaded font. There is no way to selectively remove a particular downloaded font. If you make a mistake and download the wrong font, download too many fonts, or download the same font twice (**fontloader** doesn't check for fonts that have already been downloaded), the only way to clear the downloaded fonts is to turn off or reset the printer. Before you download fonts, take time to plan which are required and be careful not to duplicate download requests.

12

Networking

One of the primary design goals of NEXTSTEP was to allow transparent access to networked resources such as file servers, fax-modems, and printers. If you're familiar with DOS or Windows systems that use LAN Manager or Novell NetWare to share files and printers, you know how difficult they can be to set up and use. However, using NEXTSTEP to access similar networked resources is like using part of your own computer system. For example, using a remote printer or fax modem is absolutely transparent. You follow the same procedures for printing and faxing to a remote device as you to one attached directly to your own computer. Similarly, access to remote file systems utilizing the popular Network File System (NFS) from Sun Microsystems, can be accomplished using the standard NEXTSTEP File Viewer. For those without networks, transferring files to and from other computers using NEXTSTEP, DOS, or Macintosh file formats can be as easy as exchanging floppy disks.

In this chapter, we will examine how NEXTSTEP presents remote file systems and discuss several useful utilities for packaging and transmitting files between similar and dissimilar computer systems and how to open foreign files for use in NEXTSTEP. When describing networking, it's easy to get sidetracked describing the intricacies of network protocols, how background daemons maintain communication with other computers, and the details of print spooling. However, the emphasis on this chapter is to learn how to take advantage of these features, not how and why they work. For the sake of simplicity, let's assume that your computer is already properly connected to an Ethernet network that interconnects other computers running NFS and NetWare. If your computer is not connected to a network or you have never used a computer network, you will want to read on anyway. This chapter will give you an overview of the depth of resources available on a network and how easy it is to use them.

12.0 Network File System (NFS)

When a remote file system is mounted on your computer, it will appear "fat" (top) as compared with a folder stored on your own computer (bottom).

Included with every copy of NEXTSTEP is software to support Sun's Network File System (NFS), used to make file systems on remote computers appear as part of your own locally based file system. NFS is a de facto standard for networking UNIX-based systems, but software exists to allow Macintosh and DOS systems to use NFS as well. Using NFS, access to remote files is so simple you may not even know when you're using it. Like Novell NetWare, NFS is often configured to work in a client/server relationship where one machine (the server) acts as a central repository from which other machines (clients) access shared information. NFS can also be configured in a peer-to-peer fashion in which several machines act as both a server and a client to each other. Both the server and client NFS software is included with NEXTSTEP.

NFS file systems appear automatically when you log in and disappear when you log out. As a user, you don't have to do anything to make a remote file system available. Likewise, you can't do anything to make them available. Configuration of NFS file systems is performed by the system administrator of each user's machine that will share files. This is usually done prior to the computer being used for the first time.

The Net folder icon.

In general, remote file systems appear in the **/Net** folder on your computer. To traverse a remote NFS file system, locate and double-click the **/Net** folder icon in a File Viewer. Inside this folder, you will see the contents of one or more remote file systems that have been configured to share with your computer. Each remote computer's file system will be available through a folder in **/Net** that shares the same name as the remote computer it represents. This folder displays a special "fat" icon (see margin). Remote directories will appear as folders, and remote files will appear as normal NEXTSTEP document icons. You can treat these remote docu-

File Transfer Protocol (FTP)

ments and folders just as if they were part of your own computer—moving, copying, opening, editing, and printing them as usual. Even though remote files appear to be of your file system, they are still part of a remote machine and all rules of security still apply, so you may need to use the Attributes Inspector from time to time to determine which files you can modify and which you can't. Except for a slightly longer delay in opening and saving the files you find in **/Net**, you probably won't even notice when you are working with a remote file and when you are using one stored on your own hard disk.

12.1 File Transfer Protocol (FTP)

NFS is extraordinarily easy to use once the server and client machines are configured. However, NFS doesn't provide a solution for those occasions when you want to exchange a file with a remote computer that is not specifically configured to use NFS with your system. Recall that only the system administrator is able to configure NFS. Fortunately, a simple solution, known as File Transfer Protocol (FTP), allows you to transfer files to or from another computer that supports FTP and to which you have permission to exchange files. Many versions of FTP exist, allowing various computers system, including SUN, SGI, Macintosh and DOS, to exchange information.

One of the most popular uses of FTP is on a worldwide network of computers known as the Internet. There are literally millions of computers attached to the Internet. Using FTP, Internet users can collaborate on projects by exchanging data, reports, studies, and other information. Many of these computers attached to the Internet serve as bulletin boards containing documents, utilities, applications, images, sounds, and other electronic files that you can access without the need for a user name and password. These computers are known as FTP archives. Some FTP archives contain files specifically related to NEXTSTEP. From these machines, you can use FTP to collect items that interest you. The Internet is strictly for nonprofit use. There is no charge for using the Internet, but there may be charges for connecting to it, depending on who the connection provider.

Traditionally, FTP commands have been based on the command-line interface common to DOS and UNIX systems. To make FTP accessible to those unfamiliar with the command-line version, Charles G. Fleming and

Michael J. Mezzino wrote a very nice NEXTSTEP version of FTP named GatorFTP. Since it's significantly easier to use and makes use of the NEXTSTEP interface, we'll look at GatorFTP first.

12.1.0 GatorFTP

To install GatorFTP from the enclosed floppy disk, copy it to ~/**Apps** and decompress it. Be sure to check its permissions so that owner, group, and other have execute permission turned on. Then, double-click GatorFTP to start it. To save time later, you'll want to enter a default user name and password before you establish your first connection. Don't worry, even though you are setting a default name and password, you can change it easily when necessary. Entering a default name and password is simply a convenience. To set the default user name and password, choose Preferences from GatorFTP's Info menu. If you are going to connect to anonymous FTP sites for which you have no password, enter **anonymous** as the default user name, and your Internet mail address as the password. Internet mail addresses are of the form *user@host*. For example, if your NEXTSTEP account name is **sue** and you computer's name is **constellation.nyu.edu**, your Internet mail address would be **sue@constellation.nyu.edu**. If you are unsure of your Internet mail address, contact your system administrator to obtain it. Some FTP archives allow you to use **guest** as the password with the user name **anonymous**. When you have entered a name and password, click OK to save them. Each time you establish a connection to a remote computer this name and password will be entered for you.

Establishing a Session with a Remote Computer

GatorFTP has only one window, no panels, and few menu commands, making it very easy to use (see Figure 12-1). To establish a session with a remote computer, click to select a remote host name from the scrolling list in the upper left corner of the GatorFTP window. Several well-known NEXTSTEP-related archive sites are placed in the list to make it easy to access NEXTSTEP-related Internet archives. You can add your own list of host names as well, so that you can point and click to establish a session and avoid typing. When you have selected a host name, it will appear in the text field below the host name scrolling list (see Figure 12-2). If you want to remove the selected host name from the list, click Remove ftp site. If you want to add a new name, type it in the text field and then click Add

File Transfer Protocol (FTP)

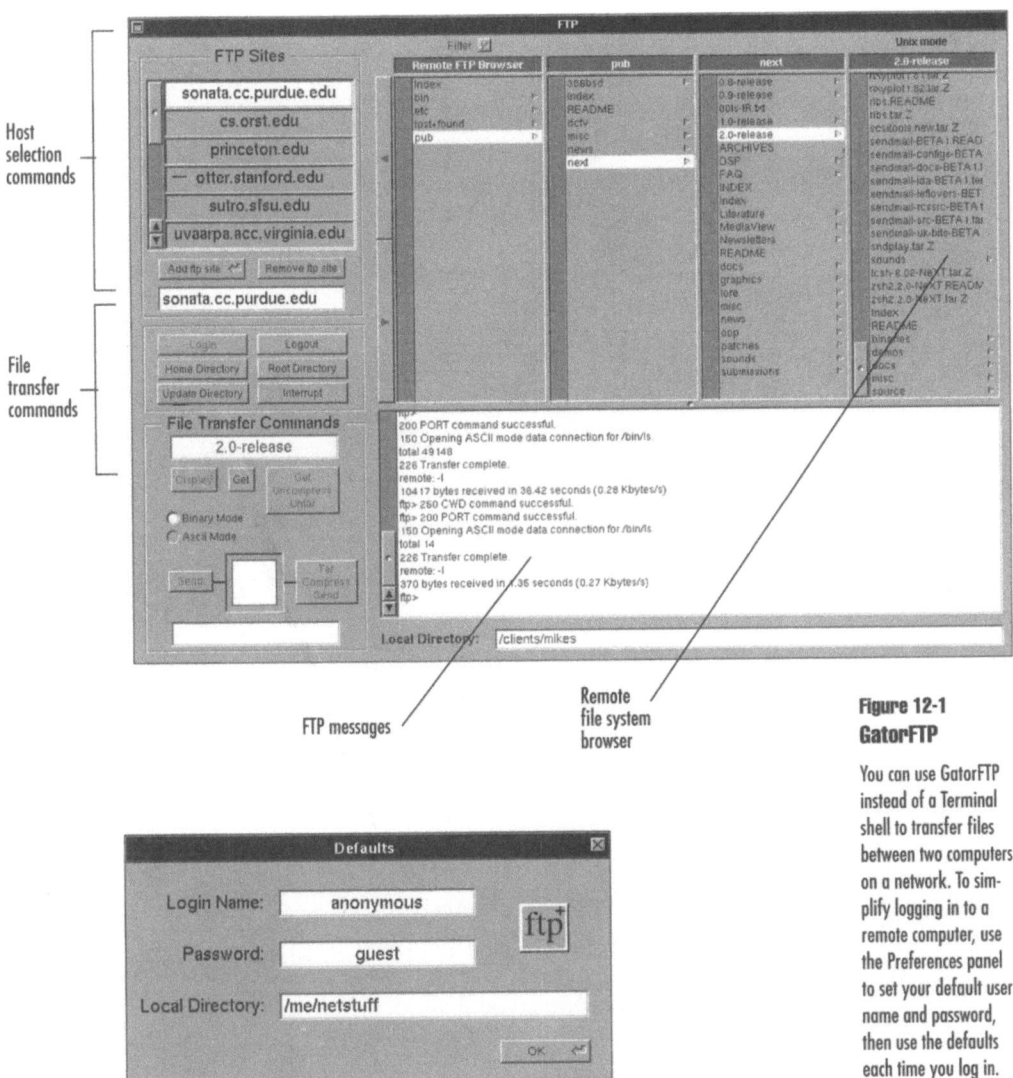

**Figure 12-1
GatorFTP**

You can use GatorFTP instead of a Terminal shell to transfer files between two computers on a network. To simplify logging in to a remote computer, use the Preferences panel to set your default user name and password, then use the defaults each time you log in.

ftp site. A list of Internet archives and their addresses can be found on-line at many archive sites. Many of the popular NEXTSTEP-related archives are listed in "Appendix B: Internet Archive Sites".

**Figure 12-2
An FTP Session
with GatorFTP**

Click a host name in the scrolling list or type one in the field to select a host, then click Login to begin an FTP session with it.

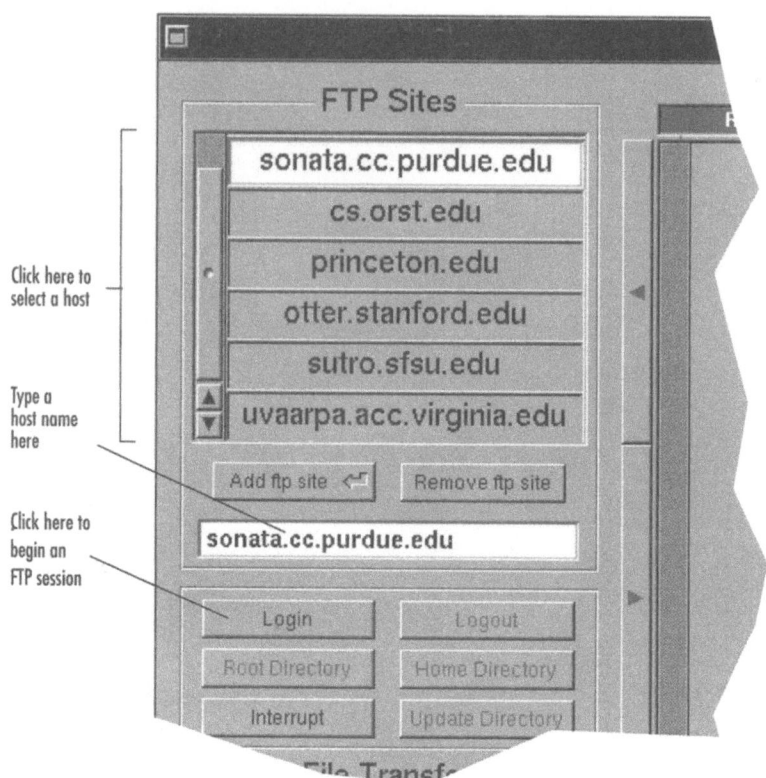

To gain entry into the computer you selected, click Login. GatorFTP's login panel will appear requesting a user name registered for the remote machine. If you have a user account on the remote computer, enter it and click OK. If you do not, you'll have to log in anonymously. Not every remote computer supports anonymous logins, so if your login attempt fails, contact the administrator of the remote computer for information about anonymous logins or attempt a connection to another host. To begin an anonymous login, enter **anonymous** as the user name and click OK. If you set the default user name to **anonymous**, you need only click OK. The GatorFTP password panel will appear requesting you to enter a password for the user account name you just entered. If you have a user account on the remote computer, enter the password for it and click OK. Otherwise, enter **guest** as the password and click OK. If the user name and password are accepted by the remote computer, you will see its file system displayed in the GatorFTP browser. If it is not, you can attempt to log in again or try to connect to another host.

Transferring Files

After you successfully enter a name and password for the remote computer system, its file system will appear in the GatorFTP browser. Use the browser to search the remote file system for files you want to copy or for a folder where you want to transfer files. Internet archives often store NeXT related files in **/pub/Next** although this is not true in every case. To get a file, locate the appropriate file in the browser, select the file transfer (usually binary) and click Get or Get Uncompress Untar to copy it to your home folder (see Figure 12-3). Unless you are sending ASCII text files, you should select binary mode transfers. Clicking Get causes the remote file to be transferred to your computer and placed in your home folder. Clicking Get Uncompress Untar transfers the file just as Get does but also uncompresses it and separates files bundled together into a single file. Archive sites typically compress and **tar** files together to make them easier to transfer. The term *tar* comes from tape archive, a UNIX command used to combines several files into a single file for easy backup onto magnetic tape. You can also use **tar** apart from tape storage. It is often used to keep collections of related files together and to prevent individual files that make up a program or project from getting lost or forgotten during an FTP session. To learn more about tar, type **man tar** in a Terminal window.

To transfer files, drag them from a File Viewer, drop them in the file well, select a transfer mode (usually Binary) and click Send or Tar Compress Send. The latter option combines the files into a single file and compresses that file before sending it. The message area below the GatorFTP browser will describe each file transfer as it occurs. Do not attempt another transfer until the **FTP>** prompt appears in the message area, as GatorFTP is still busy with your previous selection. To transfer the files into a particular folder on your computer, enter the pathname to the folder in the text field named Local Directory at the bottom of the GatorFTP window and press Return. If you do this correctly, a message indicating that you have changed your local directory will appear in the message area.

Figure 12-3
File Transfer with GatorFTP

To transfer a file to a remote host using GatorFTP, place its icon in the icon well and click the Send button (top). To transfer a file from a remote host to your computer, select the remote file in the File Viewer and click get (bottom).

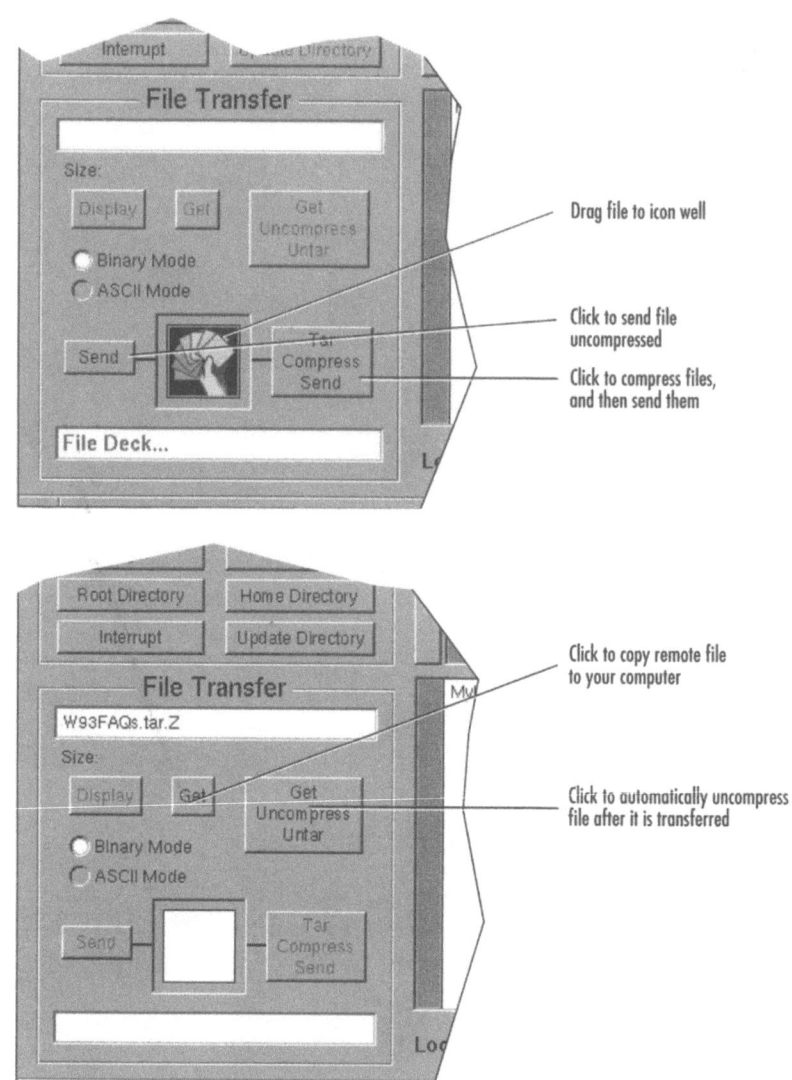

Files placed in Internet archives often have an associated ASCII, plain text file called **README** containing information about the application or utility in the archive. Before you transfer files to your computer, take a look at **README** files to determine if the other file contains something you want. This saves you the time and trouble of transferring large files only to discover that you didn't want them anyway. When you are receiving an

File Transfer Protocol (FTP)

ASCII document, such as a README file, you can transfer it to your computer and have it opened immediately in Edit by clicking Display instead of Get. GatorFTP will start Edit, if it is not already running, and transfer and open the file for you.

You can transfer as many files from an archive to your computer as your disk storage space allows. To transfer another file, select it in the browser and click the appropriate button to transfer it. When you have finished transferring files, click Logout to end your FTP session. Only a small number of users can access an archive at one time, so if you are finished transferring files, log out so others can gain access. When you have logged out, you can select another host from the scrolling list to establish another FTP session or choose Quit from GatorFTP's main menu to quit GatorFTP.

Readme files contain important information about the use of software, copyright notices and technical information that may be required to use the software they describe.

12.1.1 Command-line FTP

FTP consists of a group of UNIX commands used in a Terminal window. Start the Terminal application found in **/NextApps** and open a new window. To start using FTP, enter **ftp** followed by the Internet address of the computer to which you would like to begin a session. For example:

> ftp sonata.cc.purdue.edu

You will see the remote computer system's login message asking you to enter a user name and password similar to GatorFTP. Enter your user name and password or **anonymous** and **guest** to gain access to the remote file system. The prompt in the Terminal window will change to **FTP>** to indicate that only FTP commands may be entered. There are several FTP commands that you may use, but only a few that you should commit to memory. These are described in Table 12-1.

Table 12-1 Important FTP Commands

FTP Command	Description
binary	Changes the transfer type to binary.
cd path	Changes the current working directory on the remote file system.

Table 12-1 Important FTP Commands (Continued)

FTP Command	Description
dir	Displays a list of files and directories in the current working directory of the remote file system.
get file	Transfers the indicated file from the remote file system to the local file system into the default current working directory.
help command	Displays a one-sentence description of the indicated FTP command.
lcd path	Changes the local (default) directory.
?	Lists all FTP commands.
send file	Transfers the indicated file from the local file system to the current working directory of the remote file system.

The procedure for transferring a file is very similar to that described for GatorFTP except that you must enter each command using the keyboard instead of pointing and clicking with the mouse. So you can see what it might look like, a typical FTP session is shown in Figure 12-4. After logging in, set the transfer method to binary by entering the command **binary**. The normal response will read **Transfer Type set to I**. Next, use the **cd** and **dir** commands to navigate the remote file system and locate the file you want to get, or the directory in which you want to send a file. To transfer a file from your local file system to a remote file system, use the command **send** followed by the name of the file you wish to send. If the file is not in the current directory, enter its full pathname instead of just its name. To transfer a file from a remote file system to your local file system, enter the **get** command followed by the name of the file. Normally, the file will be placed in your current working directory but can change your current local directory using the **lcd** command so that you don't have to quit your FTP session to direct a file to another location.

When you are finished and want to end your session, enter **close**. If you want to begin another session immediately, you can enter **open** followed by the name of another computer. If you wish to stop using FTP, enter **quit**.

File Transfer Protocol (FTP)

Figure 12-4
A Typical FTP Session

FTP commands can be typed in a Terminal shell. In this example, the NewsGrazer applications is transferred from a remote FTP archive to the local directory named "download".

```
localhost> ftp sonata.cc.purdue.edu
Connected to sonata.cc.purdue.edu.
220 sonata.cc.purdue.edu FTP server (Version 5.1 (NeXT 1.0) Tue Jul 21, 1992) ready.
Name (sonata.cc.purdue.edu:me): anonymous
331 Guest login ok, send ident as password.
Password:
230 Guest login ok, access restrictions apply.
ftp> binary
200 Type set to I.
ftp> cd /pub/next/2.0/bin
250 CWD command successful.
ftp> lcd /me/download
Local directory now /me/download
ftp> get NewsGrazer72.3.tar.Z
200 PORT command successful.
150 Opening BINARY mode data connection for NewsGrazer72.3.tar.Z (187389 bytes).
226 Transfer complete.
local: NewsGrazer72.3.tar.Z remote: NewsGrazer72.3.tar.Z
187389 bytes received in 8.72 seconds (20.98 Kbytes/s)
ftp> close
221 Goodbye.
ftp> quit
localhost> cd /me/download
localhost> uncompress NewsGrazer72.3.tar.Z
localhost> tar -xf NewsGrazer72.3.tar
localhost>
```

12.1.2 File Compression

Many of the files you get from Internet archives are saved in a compressed format. If you routinely transfer a large number of files, you can compress the files you send, which shortens the time it takes to transfer files and reduces the disk space required to store them. Two UNIX commands allow you to combine and compress files: **tar** and **compress**. Files that have been combined using the **tar** command and compressed using the **compress** command can be identified by their **.tar.Z** suffix attached to the end of their names. Obviously, you should not use this suffix for files that have not been tarred and compressed. The **tar** suffix indicates that the file is actually a collection of files combined into one. The **Z** suffix means the file was compressed. Files can be compressed without being tarred, and vice versa, but the two are almost always used in combination.

You can compress a file before you transmit it to another computer, save it on a removable disk, or simply to regain hard disk space. To compress a file, select it in a File Viewer and choose Compress from the workspace File menu as described in "Compressing Files and Folders" on page 63. To decompress a compressed file, select it in a File Viewer and choose Decompress from the File menu. NEXTSTEP will decompress the file in the back-

Compressed files display this icon in the File Viewer.

ground as you continue to work. The result will be an decompressed file of the same name, but without the **Z** suffix. If the file has a **tar** suffix, it will need to be untarred before you can open it.

Decompress

You will need to decompress files having **.Z** suffixes before you can use them. If the file has a **.tar** suffix after being uncompresses, you'll also need to untar it to extract the individual files it contains. GatorFTP can all of this for you, or you can also do this yourself using the NEXTSTEP workspace. To decompress a **.Z** file, highlight it and display the Contents Inspector. A Decompress button will appear at the bottom of the inspector. Click this button to decompress the file. When you examine a **.tar** file using the Contents Inspector, a button named Unarchive will appear in the Inspector. Clicking this button will untar the file.

Tar

enTar (top) and Tarre (bottom) are two very popular tar and compress utilities.

A tar file is actually several files that have been placed into a single file. Tar is a UNIX command that was originally intended for creating tape archives and although using it is far from intuitive, its utility is not. Several shareware and public domain utilities—such as enTAR, Opener, and Tarre—are available to make tarring and compressing files easy to do. If you don't have access to one of these utilities, you can also use the UNIX **tar** command in a Terminal shell window. Start the Terminal application and use the UNIX **cd** command to make the directory containing the tar file, the present working directory. For example, if the tar file is in a folder in your home folder named **documents**, you would enter **cd ~/documents** in the Terminal window. To extract the files from the tar file, type **tar –xvf** followed by the name of the file in the Terminal window. For example, to untar a file named **demoapp.tar** you would type:

tar –xvf demoapp.tar

The options **–xvf** are three of many that can be used with tar. Specifically, **x** means extract the files, **v** means verbose and lists the results of the command on the display, and **f** means files and tells tar that the next name, **demoapp**, is the tar file to extract from. To learn more about tar, use the UNIX manual pages. For example, in the Terminal window, enter **man tar**. When you have untarred the files, you can quit Terminal and use a File Viewer to open and manipulate them.

12.2 Internet Etiquette

If you will be participating on the Internet, it is important to observe a few rules of conduct. Access to an Internet archive is a privilege, not a right, so be courteous in your use of an archive. The following general guidelines for using Internet archives, when followed, result in the least disturbance to other archive users and promote further expansion and support for the archive.

- ❖ Do not log in during peak hours. This means you should not try to access Internet archives between 8:00 A.M. and 5:00 P.M. at the remote computer's site. If you are connecting to a computer in Europe, for instance, be sure to calculate the time difference.

- ❖ Always log out after you've finished transferring files. Archives allow only a limited number of logins so if you fail to log out, you prevent others from gaining access to the archive.

- ❖ Do not use anonymous logins as an opportunity to hack, or break into folders that are locked. This is the fastest way to get in trouble with the authorities and force the computer's administrator to stop everyone using anonymous logins from accessing the archive.

- ❖ Do not transfer commercial applications or copyrighted information to an archive. All laws of ownership still apply on the Internet, and it is illegal to copy, distribute, or use applications, fonts, documents, and program code for which you do not have permission or a license.

12.3 Public Domain and Shareware

There are two popular methods for distributing applications and fonts on the Internet: as public domain software and shareware. Public domain software is absolutely free. You can use, copy, and distribute it at no charge, but you cannot claim it as your own. Many programmers place their work in the public domain as a benevolent service, for their own publicity.

Shareware is very much like public domain software in that it can be freely used, copied, and distributed, but it requires that you pay a small registration fee if you continue to use the software longer than a specified period of time. Typically a message will appear when you start a shareware application indicating the author's name, the length of time you may use the software at no charge, and the cost of the software. You are obligated to send the author the registration fee if you continue to use the software. It is also important to send the author the registration fee to encourage their development of the application. Many wonderful commercial applications began as shareware applications, and their further development was made possible only because the author received enough funds to continue the project. Although there is rarely any guarantee that shareware software will perform as advertised, shareware applications are often every bit as good as commercially available applications and although they are much smaller in scale, are even smaller in price, making them a great value.

12.4 Novell NetWare

NEXTSTEP does not limit you to only NFS and UNIX-based networking systems, but extends your reach by providing software to enable you to take advantage of network resources primarily intended for PCs. NEXTSTEP contains client software which enables you to access Novell NetWare file servers running version NetWare 286, version 2.15 or later, or NetWare 386, version 3.12. This allows you to take advantage of the many resources formerly available only to PCs on local area networks (LANs). When you log into a NetWare server, you can create, copy, delete, open and print files on a NetWare server just as if you were using a NetWare configured IBM PC. To manage NetWare access, NEXTSTEP includes a new application named NetWareManager in **/NextAdmin**.

Before you can log in to a NetWare server, you must enable NetWare for NEXTSTEP. To do so, start NetWareManager. If NetWare is not enabled, an attention panel will automatically appear asking if you want to enable it. Click OK to enable NetWare. As a reminder, another panel will then appear to inform you that NetWare will not become active until you restart the computer. Restart the computer when convenient so you can begin using a NetWare server.

Novell NetWare

12.4.0 Logging In

When the computer restarts, log into your NeXT account as usual, and then open the **/Net** folder in a File Viewer. You will see folders representing each of the NetWare file servers attached and running on the same network as your NeXT computer. To access a particular file server, double-click it in a File Viewer. If you are not already logged into the server, a NetWare Authentication panel will appear, requesting you to enter your NetWare user name and password provided to you by the administrator of the NetWare file server (see Figure 12-5). Do not enter your NEXTSTEP user name and password unless it happens to be the same as the one provided to you by the NetWare administrator.

NetWare folders look just like other NEXTSTEP folders in the File Viewer.

Enter your NetWare user name and password to gain access to your files on the server.

**Figure 12-5
NetWare Server Authentication**

When you select a NetWare server in a File Viewer to which you are not already logged in, the NetWare Authentication panel appears.

NEXTSTEP will allow you enter only 16 characters for a NetWare password even if the actual password is longer. If your NetWare password is longer than 16 characters, log in using a PC and change it, or have your NetWare administrator change it for you. Capitalization is not important when entering your NetWare user name and password, but if you make a mistake in the characters you type, the NetWare panel will blink and reappear with empty text fields so you can try again. You can be logged in concurrently to any number of NetWare file servers, but you should observe the courtesy of logging out from each one when you are finished using it to allow other users to access it. NetWare file servers allow a limited number of active users, so if you stay logged in but don't use it, you'll prevent someone else from logging in.

You can also log into a NetWare file server using NetWareManager. This method allows you to log in as usual, or change your log in without having to log out first. This may be necessary if you need to log in using the supervisor account and you are logged in as a normal NetWare user. To log in using NetWareManager, start NetWareManager, select a file server name in NetWareManager's Servers panel and choose Authenticate from the Server menu. The Authentication panel will appear (see Figure 12-6) in which you can enter your user name and password to gain access to the server. If you've entered a valid user name and password, you will see the contents of the file server when you open its folder in **/Net**.

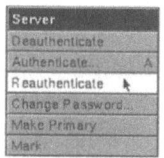

Reauthenticate saves you time by allowing you to log in as a different NetWare user without first logging out.

A more obscure but useful feature of NetWareManager allows you to log in as another NEXTSTEP user and then log into a NetWare server as a different NetWare user without having to log out of NEXTSTEP or NetWare (see Figure 12-8). This can happen when you log in as a different user in a Terminal shell using the UNIX **su** command to start a process as another user. For example, if you want to run a process or application as **root** and that process or application needs to use NetWare files, you'll need to log the **root** user into the NetWare server as well. To do this, choose New User in NetWareManager's Server menu. A NEXTSTEP authentication panel will appear first. Log in using a user name and password other than the one you are currently using. A new NetWare Servers panel will appear listing each of the available NetWare servers. Select a server then choose Authenticate from the Server menu to display the NetWare authentication panel and log in to the NetWare server.

12.4.1 Changing Your Password

You know that it is important to change your password from time to time, and this is true of NetWare passwords as well. To change your NetWare password using NEXTSTEP, start NetWareManager, select a server in the NetWare Servers panel, and choose Change Password from the Server menu. You must be logged into the NetWare file server to change your password to it. After choosing Change Password, enter your old password in the Password panel that appears, press Tab and enter the new password you would like to use. NetWare is not case sensitive so passwords such as **MyPass1** and **mypass1** are identical. NetWare passwords can contain any character except a slash (**/**) and can be no longer than sixteen characters. (NetWare passwords can be longer, but NEXTSTEP only supports passwords up to 16 characters long.) Click OK to enter your new password. If the old password you entered was correct, a new panel will appear asking

Novell NetWare

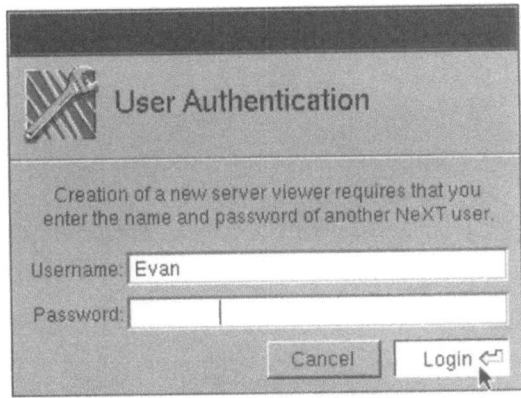

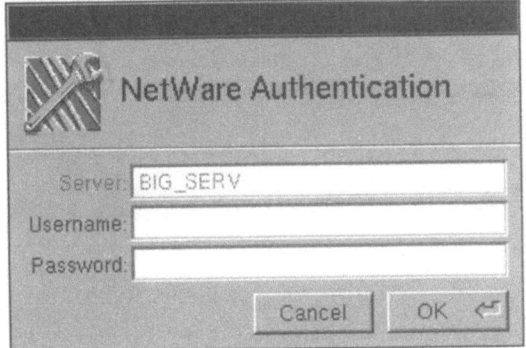

**Figure 12-6
Concurrent
NetWare Logins**

Using NetWareManager, you can log in to a NetWare server a second time as if you were a different NEXTSTEP user. First, choose New User from the Viewer menu, then log in using a different NEXTSTEP user name and password (top). When you have logged in successfully, a new NetWare Servers panel will appear (middle). Select a NetWare server and choose Authenticate to display the NetWare Authentication panel (bottom) where you can log in to NetWare as the other NEXTSTEP user.

you to enter your new password again for verification. This prevents you from making a mistake when typing in a new password and later being unable to gain access to the file server. After entering your new password a second time, an attention panel will appear to let you know that the password was changed successfully. You will need to use the new password the next time you log into this NetWare file server. If you entered the new password differently from the first time, an attention panel will appear to inform you the password change failed. Try changing the password again by choosing Change Password from the Server menu.

Don't let your NetWare password expire because you will not be able to change (update) your NetWare password from NEXTSTEP. If this happens, have the NetWare supervisor change your password for you, or use a NetWare-configured PC to change your password.

12.4.2 Logging Out

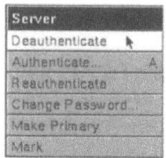

To disconnect from a NetWare server, choose Deauthenticate from the NetWareManager's Server menu.

Unless you log out, you will remain logged into a NetWare file server until you end your NEXTSTEP session. However, if you are logged in but not using a NetWare server, you may be preventing another user from gaining access to it, so as a courtesy to others, log out when you are finished using a NetWare file server. To log out from a NetWare file server, open NetWareManager, select the name of the file server you want to log out from in the NetWare Servers panel, and choose Deauthenticate from the Server menu. This is the equivalent of typing **logout** from a PC running NetWare client software. You can log out of several NetWare file servers by repeating this procedure. If you attempt to reopen the file server in the File Viewer, the NetWare login panel will appear again, requesting your NetWare user name and password. You can log in and out as many times as necessary. However, if you plan to use the NetWare file server often, it may be more convenient to remain logged.

12.4.3 Transferring Files

You can easily copy and move files between the two file systems by dragging their icons to another folder. Remember that because the format of the files may not be compatible with NEXTSTEP applications, conversion may be required before you can open a document stored on a NetWare server. You can save NEXTSTEP documents on a NetWare server, and these can be opened by double-clicking the document in a File Viewer. Like Macintosh files, you cannot double-click a DOS, Windows, or OS/2 file saved on a NetWare server to open it in an application. Those systems don't use the same file name extensions as NEXTSTEP to identify the applications that created them so NEXTSTEP will not know which application to start up, and will start Edit instead. If you have installed a NEXTSTEP application that can open the foreign file format, start it running first, then open the document from within the application.

12.4.4 Choosing File Names

NetWare servers can be configured to allow longer UNIX-style names, or restricted to allow only shorter DOS names. DOS file names can only be 8 characters long and have an additional extension of only 3 characters. This is commonly referred to as the 8.3 format. When you save a NEXTSTEP file on a NetWare server that is configured to use the DOS naming convention, you must use the 8.3 format. If you are not sure which naming convention is being used, contact your NetWare administrator or simply attempt to save a file using a name longer than 8 characters. If the DOS naming is being used, an attention panel will appear informing you that you cannot save the file with such a long name.

12.4.5 Understanding Permissions

NetWare file servers utilize numerous file and directory security permissions, which are both more extensive and different from those used in NEXTSTEP. When you log into a NetWare file server configured to allow DOS file names only, the entire NetWare server is assumed to be owned by you, the NEXTSTEP user. NEXTSTEP ignores folder permissions for group and other and uses only the owner permission. Use the Attributes Inspector if necessary to determine the ownership of folders. The following tables describe how NEXTSTEP permissions and NetWare permissions compare when the NetWare server is using DOS naming conventions.

Table 12-2 NetWare (DOS) and NEXTSTEP File Permissions

NEXTSTEP Permission	NetWare Permission
Read	Read and File Scan
Read	Read and File Scan
Write	Write
Execute	Doesn't apply

Table 12-2 NetWare (DOS) and NEXTSTEP File Permissions (Continued)

NEXTSTEP Permission	NetWare Permission
Assigned to file owner	Access Control
Don't apply	All other permissions

Table 12-3 NetWare (DOS) and NEXTSTEP Folder Permissions

NEXTSTEP Permission	NetWare Permission
Read and Execute	Read and File Scan
Write	Create, Erase, and Modify
Assigned to directory owner	Access Control
Supervisory and Write	Don't apply

When the NetWare server is configured to use UNIX names, you can create and save NEXTSTEP files on the NetWare server without having to modify their names at all. When you want to make a change to a file or folder on a NetWare server, you must have UNIX and NetWare permissions to do so. If either system's permissions prevent you from making a change, you will not be able to modify the file or folder. Table 12-4 and Table 12-5 describe how NEXTSTEP permissions compare with those of NetWare for files and folders when UNIX naming is being used.

Table 12-4 NetWare (UNIX Naming) and NEXTSTEP File Permissions

NEXTSTEP Permission	NetWare Permission
Read	Read
Write	Write

Table 12-5 *NetWare (UNIX Naming) and NEXTSTEP Folder Permissions*

NEXTSTEP Permission	NetWare Permission
Read and Execute	File Scan
Write	Create and Erase

12.5 Removable Disks

At times, a network is not available, or the network to which your computer is attached has failed and is not working. In these instances, your only resort may be to physically exchange compatible removable disks that both your computer, and the computer with which you want to exchange data can read. NEXTSTEP supports several different disk formats and removable media types.

Floppy Disks

If your computer isn't connected to a network, you may still be able to transfer data between yours and other computers. The simplest method is to copy the data onto floppy disks that both computer systems can read and physically transfer the disks from computer to the other so that they can exchange data. This is easy to do with DOS, Macintosh, and NeXT formatted floppy disks. UNIX file systems are not standardized so exchanging a floppy disk with another UNIX system not running NEXTSTEP is likely to fail. In this case, you'll have to resort to a network, as described in "File Transfer Protocol (FTP)" on page 309.

NEXTSTEP can read and write floppy disks in DOS, Macintosh, and NeXT formats.

NEXTSTEP not only works with DOS and Macintosh floppy disks, but with other storage devices as well. Many of these peripherals are based on the SCSI (Small Computer System Interface) standard. Your NeXT computer can also take advantage of Macintosh external storage devices, such as SCSI hard disk drives and CD-ROM drives by connecting them directly to a SCSI adapter in your computer. NEXTSTEP will mount these disks just like a NeXT formatted removable disk and allow you to copy files from them to the NeXT file system.

Bernoulli and SyQuest Disk Cartridges

A device that is extremely useful for transferring data between DOS, Windows, Macintosh, and systems running NEXTSTEP, is a removable hard disk drive. Two popular formats are Bernoulli and SyQuest. These manufacturer's drives work with PCs, Macintoshes and NeXT hardware, and feature capacities of up to 150 MB (Bernoulli) and 88 MB (SyQuest) per disk. When you attach one of these drives to your computer, you can insert a disk cartridges formatted for DOS, Windows, OS/2, Macintosh, or NEXTSTEP. You don't have to configure any software or add drivers to make them work. NEXTSTEP takes care of it for you.

NEXTSTEP can read CD-ROMs in High Sierra, Rock Ridge, ISO 9660, HFS, and NeXT formats

CD-ROMs

Data on CD-ROMs formatted in High-Sierra, ISO 9660, Rock Ridge, HFS, and NeXT formats can also be used with NEXTSTEP-compatible CD-ROM drives. There are a number of CD-ROMs in these formats that can be read by NEXTSTEP, but CD-ROMs are limited to read only. They do not allow you to transfer data you create only that which is imprinted on them by their manufacturer. These disks are mounted and unmounted just like any other removable disk (see "Mounting a Disk" on page 78 and "Unmounting a Disk" on page 79).

12.6 File Conversion

You may have thought that transferring data from one computer to another was the toughest part, but getting data onto a NEXTSTEP-readable disk is only half of the battle. After you have copied or mounted a foreign file, you must consider the file's format. Can it be opened by a NEXTSTEP application? Most applications store data in a unique way which is often incompatible with other applications. This is particularly true of applications designed for use with different system software. In an attempt to solve this problem, many NEXTSTEP applications—such as WriteNow, WordPerfect, Improv, and Illustrator—have built-in translators that enable them to open and edit files created by foreign applications, yet there are many foreign files that NEXTSTEP applications cannot read. Microsoft applications, very popular and widely available on PC and Macintosh systems, are not available for NEXTSTEP, so when transferring document made in these applications you'll need to convert them into a format NEXTSTEP applications can understand.

Emulators

One very popular application for converting files is MacLinkPlus/PC by Data Viz. MacLinkPlus provides over 400 translators to convert graphics and word processing files between Macintosh, Apple II, DOS, Windows, OS/2, Sun, and NeXT file formats. No translation software is able to translate documents with 100% accuracy, but MacLinkPlus comes very close, doing a remarkable job of retaining formatting features as well as text. After converting a file using any utility, be prepared to spend time adjusting fonts, correcting spelling mistakes, and formatting text.

If you don't have the MacLinkPlus program, you may be able to save documents in formats that NEXTSTEP applications can understand to avoid having to convert them. Microsoft, although it has no applications for NeXT computers, authored a file format standard called RTF that is widely used by NEXTSTEP application. You can save documents in many Microsoft applications in RTF format and transfer them to a NeXT computer on a floppy disk, removable hard disk, or across a network where they can be read by NEXTSTEP applications such as Edit, WriteNow, and WordPerfect. Fonts may not transfer because they are machine dependent, but the text will be intact as will most of the formatting. Another popular file format that is NeXT-compatible is PostScript and its close cousin, Encapsulated PostScript (EPS). Many PC applications are beginning to provide support for the PostScript file format, making it another good choice for when transferring data between systems. PostScript is especially popular with drawing applications such as Adobe Illustrator and Aldus Freehand on the Macintosh, CorelDraw and Illustrator for Windows on the PC, and just about every drawing application for the NEXTSTEP.

Apple uses a slightly different implementation of PostScript, so not every PostScript file generated on a Macintosh will be readable by a NEXTSTEP application. If you need to perform this conversion often, you may want to invest in EditBench, a $50 utility from Garfinkel and Associates, or Pixel Magician from Bachaus. Pixel Magician can perform numerous other conversions but at a cost of $300.

12.7 Emulators

While it is possible to convert documents so that they can be viewed or edited using NEXTSTEP applications, you cannot convert the applications to themselves. However, there are two emulators available for NEXTSTEP: SoftPC from Insignia Solutions and Executor from Abacus Research and

Development (ARDI). These applications allow you to run DOS, Windows, and Macintosh applications in a NEXTSTEP window. SoftPC simulates the DOS environment and Executor simulates a Macintosh environment. Emulators like these are not intended for heavy-duty everyday use, but offer an opportunity to migrate to NEXTSTEP without losing your investment in DOS, Windows, and Macintosh applications.

12.7.0 SoftPC

SoftPC is a NEXTSTEP application designed by Insignia Solutions, to emulate an Intel 80386-based computer. This same company is providing Microsoft with its DOS compatibility environment for Microsoft's upcoming Windows NT system. Currently, SoftPC is available as a separate commercial package, but a demonstration version will soon be included with every copy of the NEXTSTEP user environment. This version will be a fully working copy of SoftPC, but will only run for 20 minutes at a time. If you want to run SoftPC longer, you can purchase a license from Insignia to remove this limitation.

SoftPC provides a DOS protected-mode and Windows 3.1 standard-mode (Win-16) and runs on both NeXT and Intel hardware. When running a 486-based system, SoftPC delivers about 90% of the speed of the processor, losing little to overhead. In addition, SoftPC includes Windows-specific Graphics Device Interface (GDI) driver, which maps Microsoft Windows calls directly to the NEXTSTEP window server for top performance. You can create any number of virtual hard disk drives of any size based on the disk space you have available. NEXTSTEP treats each hard drive as a single file, so they can be easily managed. Both serial and parallel ports can be configured to work with those available on your native hardware, as well as floppy disk drives. You can even designate a NEXTSTEP folder as a virtual DOS drive so you can easily exchange documents between NEXTSTEP and DOS. SoftPC also includes support for the Microsoft Mouse, extended memory, VGA color, and the ability to increase the size of the screen 150% for easier viewing.

When you start SoftPC, you will see a window resembling a PC screen (see Figure 12-7). If you have DOS loaded, it will boot using its **config.sys** and **autoexec.bat** files as would a real PC. You can then run DOS application or start Microsoft Windows, or use the standard DOS utilities. To use a floppy

Emulators

disk, you'll insert the disk into a drive and allow NEXTSTEP to mount it. After the file is mounted in the workspace, you choose a menu command to make it available to SoftPC. Reverse the procedure to eject the disk.

Since NEXTSTEP is a multitasking, virtual memory operating environment, several DOS or Windows sessions can be run at once by launching several instances of SoftPC (see See "Learning Tricks" on page 116). If you need to transfer information from one document to another you can cut and paste text and graphics between DOS and Windows and NEXTSTEP.

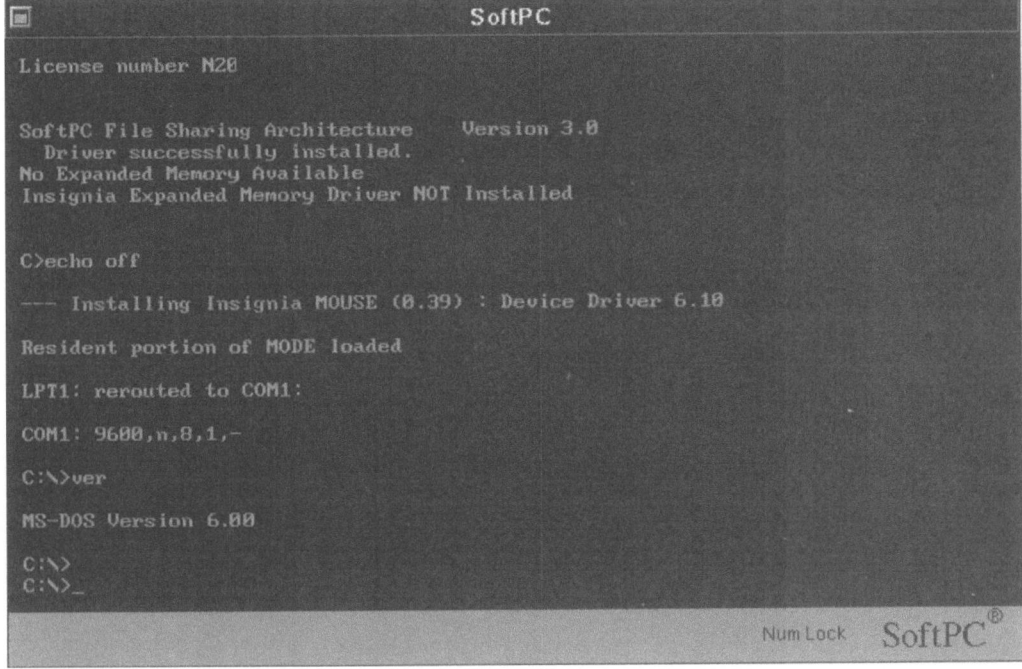

Figure 12-7
DOS Emulation

SoftPC emulates a full-featured Intel 386 environment in which you can run DOS or Windows applications.

12.7.1 Executor

Executor is a NEXTSTEP application that allows you to run a single Macintosh application at a time. It doesn't provide the Macintosh Finder (akin to the NEXTSTEP workspace) for locating and starting applications, support for color, or sound. ARDI designed it to work with Microsoft Word and Microsoft Excel, but Executor will work with many other Macintosh applications as well.

To open an application in Executor, you'll use a panel similar to the NEXTSTEP Open panel and the application starts immediately (see Figure 12-8). When you quit the application, Executor quits as well. To start up another Macintosh application, you run Executor again. This may seem like a step backward to those who are familiar with Multifinder, which allows you to quickly switch between running Macintosh applications, but it really isn't. You can easily run multiple Macintosh applications at the same time by starting several instances of Executor and running them simultaneously (see "Tricks" on page 124).

**Figure 12-8
Executor**

To start an application in Executor, you open it using a panel similar to the NEXTSTEP Open panel. When the application starts running, it appears in the Executor window.

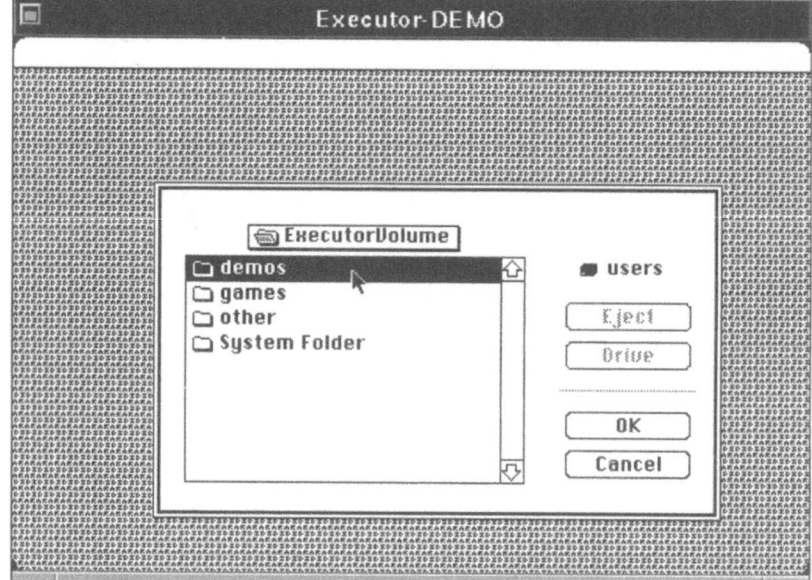

Emulators

In place of the Macintosh Finder, Executor provides an application named HFS_Xfer (pronounced "H F S transfer"). Using this application, you can transfer files between HFS (Hierarchical File System) Macintosh disks and NEXTSTEP. For the technically inclined, HFS_Xfer stores Macintosh files in Apple Double format, saving the resource fork. This means you can freely copy Macintosh files and applications to and from NEXTSTEP and Macintosh disks and they'll still work. HFS_Xfer is provided so that you can copy Macintosh applications, which you must purchase separately, into NEXTSTEP so Executor can use them. There are a couple of caveats with HFS_Xfer. It works only with Macintosh floppy disks, not with Macintosh hard drives, and it is limited to only those floppy disks that your computer can read. So for example, you can not read double-density, 800 KB Macintosh disks unless you have a special floppy disk drive. Most PCs have high-density 3.5-inch floppy drives which can only read high-density, 1.4 MB Macintosh floppy disks.

If you want to experiment with Executor before you buy it, you can obtain a trial version from most NeXT-related Internet archives, or call ARDI directly at (505) 766-9115. ARDI maintains a list of Macintosh applications known to work well with Executor, those that work only partially, and those that do not work at all. When you buy Executor, you pay a license fee for each application you want to run that appears on their "fully supported" list. A full-featured version with unlimited ability to run any Macintosh application is also available.

13

UNIX Commands You Should Know

Thus far we have concentrated on the NEXTSTEP graphical user interface to accomplish tasks, monitor the system, and control the computer. However, NEXTSTEP has a dual nature. You can control the computer using the graphical user interface, or by typing UNIX commands in a Terminal window. (If necessary, you can review the section on Terminal beginning on page 205) Most users feel the NEXTSTEP Workspace Manager is easier to use than UNIX commands, but this is not always the case. There will be times when only the command line interface will allow you to accomplish a task. For example, only with UNIX commands can you reassign the ownership of a file or folder to another user or log into a remote computer while continuing a NEXTSTEP session. Unless you purchase a NEXTSTEP application to create a backup of the file system to removable disks or tape cartridges, you will need to use UNIX commands to do so. Thus, it is important to know at least a few of the basic UNIX commands and those which allow you to accomplish tasks that cannot be done with the Workspace Manager.

To execute UNIX commands, you must start the Terminal application and open a Terminal window.

UNIX Commands You Should Know

UNIX is infamous for containing several hundred difficult commands and command permutations. The number of commands UNIX offers makes it a powerful system because there is a command to do just about anything, but choosing the appropriate command can also be overwhelming. You don't have to learn every UNIX command and option to be able to use UNIX. Instead, you can begin by learning several of the most often used UNIX commands, how to extend them with command options, and how to learn and use new UNIX commands. Depending on your experience with other UNIX systems or with DOS, you may find using the command line interface to be very straightforward. If you have been using a Macintosh or other GUI system, you may not be accustomed to typing commands. In this case, there are a few things you should know:

❖ When typing a command, nothing will happen until you press the Return key. This allows you to enter a command, review it, and make changes before you execute it. It is assumed that every command you type will be executed so although you will press Return after typing a command, the Return key symbol or character is not written as part of the command.

❖ You must be very careful to type each command exactly as it is presented. Upper- and lowercase letters are not equivalent and should not be transposed. Spaces are also very important. They must be entered exactly as shown. If you make a mistake while typing, press Delete to remove the character to the left of the cursor and retype the command correctly. If you want to cancel a partially typed command and start again, press and hold down the Control key and type **c**.

❖ When you enter a UNIX command, it is interpreted by a program known as a shell. There are several shells which can be used, and for each shell you use different commands. Commands entered into different shells may be interpreted differently so it's important to know which shell is being used. When a NeXT account is created, the system administrator will designate the shell you see each time you open a Terminal window. Typically, the administrator designates the C shell. For this reason, the commands described in this book pertain to the C shell. If you are not sure which UNIX shell you are using, you can force the computer to use the C shell by entering the command **csh** in a Terminal window.

13.0 UNIX Command Structure

UNIX commands are arranged in the following order: command, options, and arguments. Let's examine a typical UNIX command to see how it follows this form.

ls –l /Shared/documents

In this example, the command name is **ls**, which is used to display the contents of a folder. The **ls** command has many options, only one of which is used here. The **–l** option displays a *long* listing of the specified folder, **/Shared/documents**. Notice that the **l** option, like the name of the command, must be typed lowercase or it will not work. In this case, only one argument to the **ls** command is used, and it is represented by the pathname **/Shared/documents**, the folder whose contents we would like to see (see Figure 13-1). UNIX commands may differ as to how many options and arguments they contain but all follow this general form.

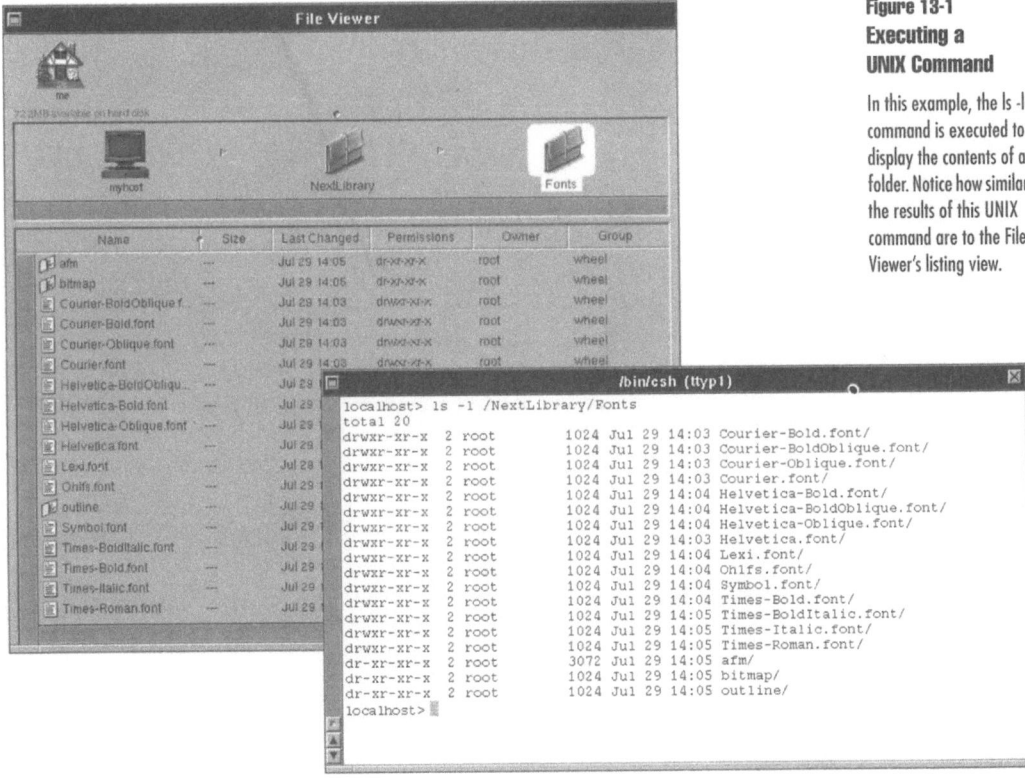

**Figure 13-1
Executing a
UNIX Command**

In this example, the ls -l command is executed to display the contents of a folder. Notice how similar the results of this UNIX command are to the File Viewer's listing view.

UNIX Commands You Should Know

13.1 Often-Used UNIX Commands

While there are hundreds of UNIX commands at your disposal, several are used so often that it they are worth committing to memory. These commands are listed in alphabetical order in Table 13-1 for easy reference.

Table 13-1 Basic UNIX Commands

Command	Description
cat file	Displays the contents of a file on the standard output. (By default, the "standard output" is the screen).
cat file1 file2 ...	Catenates several files and displays them on the standard output.
cd	Makes the home directory the current working directory.
cd pathname	Changes the current working directory to that specified by pathname.
chgrp -R group file	Recursively changes the group ownership of specified file (or folder) to the specified group. The group argument can be either the group name or group ID number. You must be the owner or superuser to change a file's group.
chown -R user file	Recursively changes the ownership of specified file (or folder) to the specified user. You must be the owner or superuser to change a file's owner.
cp file1 file2	Creates a copy of file1 named file2.
cp file pathname	Creates a copy of the file in the specified directory.
df	Displays the amount of free, used, and total disk space on mounted file systems, both local and remote.

Often-Used UNIX Commands

Table 13-1 Basic UNIX Commands (continued)

Command	Description
hostinfo	Displays information about the current host on the standard output, including CPU type, CPU speed, and available RAM. This command is useful in determining the computer's configuration.
kill *n*	Kills the process with ID *n*. Use the ps command to determine a process' ID.
kill -9 *n*	Kills the process with ID *n* no matter what (called a "sure" kill).
ln -s *source target*	Creates a symbolic (soft) link between the source file or directory and the target file or directory. Links cannot be created between files or folders on different file systems (drives, partitions).
lpq	Lists the status of the default printer's queue on the standard output.
lpq -P*printername*	Lists the status of the specified printer's queue on the standard output.
lpr *file*	Prints the specified file on the default printer.
lpr -P*printer file*	Prints the specified file on the specified printer.
ls	Lists the contents of the current working directory.
ls *pathname*	Lists the contents of the directory specified by pathname.
ls -C	Lists the contents of the current working directory in columns across the screen. Note that C is capitalized.

UNIX Commands You Should Know

Table 13-1 Basic UNIX Commands (continued)

Command	Description
ls -l	Displays a "long" listing of the contents of the current working directory.
ls -r	Lists the contents of the current working directory in reverse order. The r option can be combined with other options for more effective use of the ls command.
ls -s	Lists the contents of the current working directory including their size in kilobytes.
ls -t	Lists the contents of the current working directory sorted by time modifed (latest first).
man command	Displays the UNIX manual page describing the specified command, its options, and related UNIX commands.
mkdir name	Creates a new directory named name in the current working directory.
mkdir pathname	Creates a new directory specified by pathname. You must have write privileges in the folder specified by pathname.
mv file1 file2	Replaces file2 with file1. This command is often used to rename a file.
mv file pathname	Moves a file to a new location in the file system specified by the pathname.
nppower off	Turns off the power to the NeXT Laser Printer
nppower on	Turns on the NeXT Laser Printer
passwd	Allows you to change your current password.
ps -g	Lists all of the current processes on the standard output.

Table 13-1 Basic UNIX Commands (continued)

Command	Description
ps -u	Lists your current processes with headings on the standard output.
ps n	Lists the process with ID n on the standard output.
pwd	Lists the current working directory.
rlogin host	Attempts to log you into a remote computer named host using your current user name and password. The remote host must be configured to allow you to log in.
rm file	Removes (deletes) file from the NEXTSTEP file system.
su user	Allows you to temporarily login as user. This command is often used to login as root, without having to first log out.
telnet host	Attempts to log you into a remote computer named host. The remote computer need not have any special configuration, but you must have a valid user name and password to gain access to the remote host.
who	Displays a list of users currently logged into the computer on the standard output.
whoami	Lists who you are logged in as. This command is useful if you have used su to log in as another user and have forgotten which user you have logged in as.

13.2 Pathname Shortcuts

When using UNIX commands to control the computer, you will inevitably need to enter long pathnames. To make typing long pathnames easier, NeXT has provided several convenient shortcuts.

13.2.0 Auto-Completing a Pathname

NEXTSTEP monitors the text you type in the Save and Open panels and Terminal windows and can assist you in completing long pathnames. After you have partially entered a pathname, press the Escape key to have NEXTSTEP complete it. For example, if you were to type **/LocalL** and press Escape, NEXTSTEP would complete the pathname by typing **ibrary** for you. The only requirement for this to work is that the portion you type must uniquely identify the file or folder you are referring to. For example, if you type **/Local** and press the Escape key, NEXTSTEP will only play a beep sound to let you know it cannot figure out which file or folder you are trying to type. Because **/LocalApps** and **/LocalLibrary** both begin with **/Local**, NEXTSTEP cannot determine which pathname you are referring to, so it beeps at you instead. You can avoid this by entering another letter to uniquely identify the pathname you want to enter.

In the previous example, you could uniquely identify the **/LocalApps** folder by typing **/LocalA** and press Escape. If NEXTSTEP can only partially fill in the pathname, it will do so and wait for you to finish it. For example, assume there exists two files, **~/documents/memos/1memo** and **~/documents/memos/2memo**. If you type **~/d** and press Escape, NEXTSTEP will only enter **ocuments** and wait for you to type more. This happens because after you enter **~/documents**, there are two possible files you may be referring to. In this case, enter the number **1** or **2** and press Escape again to compete the pathname in the panel or Terminal window. Notice that you only have to enter 5 characters to type a 17 character pathname.

13.2.1 Cutting and Pasting Shortcut

Another shortcut for entering a long UNIX pathname or UNIX command after it has been typed in once, is to select it in the Terminal window, choose Copy from the Edit menu, click to place the insertion point at the prompt, and then choose Paste. This method is even faster when you use the keyboard equivalent for Copy, Command-c, and Paste, Command-v.

The copy and paste method is best used when a command has already been entered and is visible in the window, or when a pathname or file name has recently been displayed.

13.2.2 Dragging Shortcut

NEXTSTEP provides an even easier shortcut for entering long pathnames in a shell window. For example, locate the file, folder, or application in a File Viewer, drag its icon from a File Viewer onto a Terminal window (see Figure 13-2). NEXTSTEP will automatically type in its absolute pathname. You can also experiment with other applications to see how they respond when you drag an icon onto their documents.

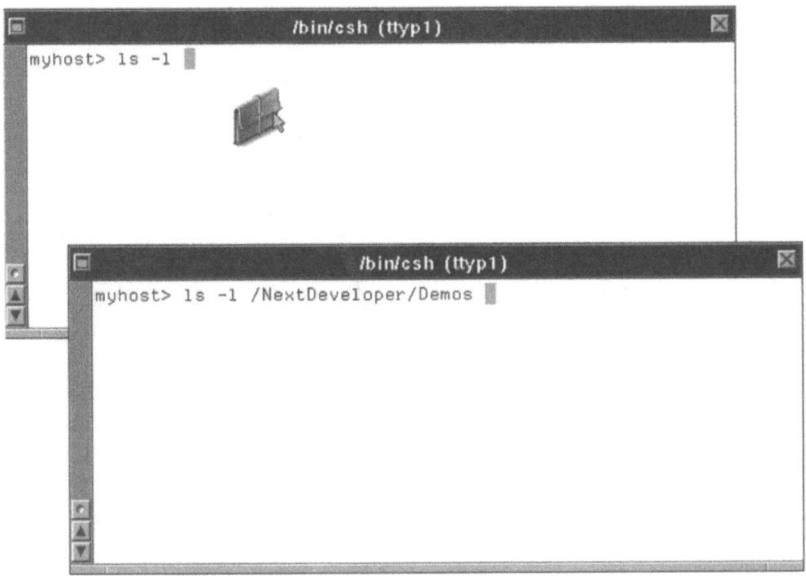

**Figure 13-2
Drag
Shortcut**

To enter a long pathname in a Terminal window, type the UNIX command you wish to use and drag the icon of the item on which you want to execute the command into the terminal window (top). Type the remaining portion of the command if necessary, then press Return to execute it (bottom)

13.3 Jargon

When you call on a system or network administrator, consultant, or even NeXT, for technical support, you will not want to waste time finding terms that each of you can understand. To make communication easier, take time to learn some of the popular jargon described below. It will allow you to get help faster and save you hours of possible frustration. (Reprinted with permission from the NeXT Support Bulletin.)

Table 13-2 *Popular Jargon*

Term	Description
Boot the machine single user	Type bsd -s in the ROM monitor window (on NeXT hardware only).
Run rc in the background	In single-user mode, type /bin/sh /etc/rc & at the # prompt.
R-login into the machine name	In a Terminal window, type rlogin name.
Type Command-tilde	Hold down the right Command key and then press the key in the upper-left corner of the numeric keypad.
Type Command-Command-tilde	Hold down both Command keys and then press the key in the upper-left corner of the numeric keypad.
Type Command-Alt-star	Hold down the left Command and Alternate keys and press the key in the upper right corner of the numeric keypad.
Halt the machine	While logged in as the root user, type the halt command in a Terminal window.
List the file systems that are mounted	Type the df or mount command in a Terminal window.

Jargon

13.3.0 General Tips

❖ When saying a pathname, don't pronounce the slashes between the pathname components. For example, **/usr/template/client/etc** is pronounced "user template client etcetera."

❖ When spelling a file name, assume each character to be lowercase. Indicate only when a character in a file name is uppercase.

❖ When entering a long file name in a Terminal window, it isn't usually necessary to type every character in the name. Use the shortcuts described in "Pathname Shortcuts" on page 342.

❖ You don't have to specify spaces in a UNIX command. For example, pronounce **ls –lg** as "l s dash l g".

Table 13-3 **UNIX File Name Pronunciations**

File Name	File Name Pronunciation
/etc	et-see or E-T-C or etcetera
/etc/passwd	password
/etc/exports	exports
/etc/fstab	F-S-tab
/etc/hosts	hosts
/etc/hostconfig	host config
/usr	user
/usr/adm	user A-D-M
/usr/adm/lpd-errs	user A-D-M L-P-D errors

Table 13-4 Command Pronunciations

Command	Pronunciation
exportfs	export F-S
fsck	fisk or F-S-C-K
ifconfig	I-F config or ifconfig
ls	list or L-S
ls –lag	L-S dash L-A-G
niutil	N-I U-til
nidump	N-I dump
ping	ping
su	sue or S-U
sync	sink

13.4 Special UNIX Commands

Among the many UNIX commands are several that are uniquely important as you learn about your NEXTSTEP system. These commands fall into two categories: NetInfo commands and backup commands. The first set allows you to manage the files that contain your system's configuration information, while the second allows you to make copies of this information, and even the entire file system, to ensure its safety should your computer or its components fail.

13.4.0 NetInfo Commands

Unlike other UNIX systems, NEXTSTEP relies on a proprietary database system known as NetInfo for maintaining system and network configuration information, such as host name, IP address, network routers, mail relays, shared printers, and remote systems with whom file systems may be

Special UNIX Commands

shared. Normally, this information is entered by the system or network administrator into text files contained in the /etc folder and read when necessary at boot time or when an application requires it.

It is common for those familiar with UNIX but unfamiliar with NEXTSTEP to enter the information in these files but forget to put it in the NetInfo database using the NetInfoManager application. This results in a system that appears to be configured correctly but does not work. If this happens, you can use the **niload** command to load the information from the text files into the NetInfo database. For example, printer configuration information is typically held in a the file **/etc/printcap** on most UNIX systems. If you entered information in this file on a NEXTSTEP system, you can then load the file into the NetInfo database by typing:

niload printcap *domain* **< /etc/hosts**

where *domain* is the name of the NetInfo domain to which your computer is a member. If your computer is not relying on a separate NetInfo server computer to provide its system configuration information, then the domain is called "local" and is represented by a period. For example, the previous command would be entered:

niload printcap . < /etc/hosts

The **niload** command can be used to load many different configuration files, including aliases, exports, fstab, group, hosts, networks, passwd, services, and others. You can use the **man** command to learn more about niload. Remember, you must be logged in as the root user for the **niload** command to work. If this were not so, any user could change critical system information and cause the computer to fail when it is rebooted.

NEXTSTEP also includes a command to save NetInfo information into text files so you can transfer the information to other systems or so you can easily record it in an easy-to-read format. To dump information from the NetInfo database to a file, use the **nidump** command. For example, to save information about other hosts on a shared network from the local domain's NetInfo database to a text file, you would enter:

nidump hosts . > /etc/hosts

If you leave off the last part of the command, **> /etc/hosts**, which redirects the output into a text file, the information will be displayed in the Terminal window instead of being placed in a file.

NEXTSTEP also includes a command named **niutil** so that you can edit the NetInfo database directly, without having to use NetInfoManager. This command can be further explored using the UNIX manual pages, but is generally only needed by system administrators.

13.4.1 UNIX Backup Commands

It is very important to make copies of critical files at regular intervals to ensure that these files will not be lost should the hard disk fail, the computer be lost or damaged, or the data be deleted accidentally. Because of file permissions, backing up files from a multi-user system such as NEXTSTEP is a bit more intricate than with single-user systems such DOS or Macintosh computers. A user can only access his or her own files. For the entire system to be accessible, the root user must perform the backup. While the system is being backed up, other users cannot be allowed access to the system or a file might be changed while it is being backed up and either be corrupted or miss the latest modifications. Also, the massive size of the file system, at least 80 MB for the user environment, and 250 MB or more for the developer environment, requires a high-capacity backup device. This device must also be reasonably fast to make backups timely.

Types of Backups

Backups are of two types: full and incremental. Both full and incremental backups contain a copy of every file in the file system on one or more disks, called volumes. The difference between the two is apparent only when a subsequent backup is made. If changes are made to the file system and another backup is made, using the full backup technique would require the entire file system to be copied to the backup volumes again, even if most of the files have not changed. In contrast, a subsequent incremental backup copies only those items which have changed since the last backup and leaves unchanged items on the backup volumes untouched. Generally, fewer files are copied using an incremental backup so the time spent backing up is less than with a full backup. Both full and incremental backups can also be performed on a subset of the entire file system such as a user's home folder or a specified collection of folders.

Special UNIX Commands

No matter which method you use, at least one backup should be made that contains every item in the file system. If you haven't made many modifications to your system, you can use the NEXTSTEP CD-ROM in place of your full backup. Remember that this disc doesn't have the documents you have created on it. They must be stored separately. To restore information, from the CD-ROM, a CD-ROM drive is required. If you have significantly modified your NEXTSTEP file system, such as configuring an Internet address and NFS file sharing or making changes to the NetInfo database, you should make a backup of at least those files which have been modified. Most of these files are contained in **/etc** so making a backup of these files is relatively simple. If necessary, you can dump your system's configuration from the NetInfo database into text files in **/etc** as described in "NetInfo Commands" on page 346.

What to Use for Backup Volumes

To hold the backed up files, you can use just about any storage device including a hard disk drive, 8mm tape drive, DAT tape drive, or other removable storage media such as floppy disks, optical disks, and removable magnetic hard disks. Each type of media has its good and bad points. An external hard drive is expensive, but very fast. DAT tapes can hold over 1 gigabyte of data, are very reliable, and several can be used to hold a single backup. The drive however is currently very expensive, about $1,500-$2,500, and somewhat slow. Magneto-optical disks can also hold a large amount of data, 128 MB for 3.5 inch disks, and 650 MB for five disks. They are much slower than a hard disk drive, but faster than tape. Floppy disks are the most inexpensive alternative, but they often fail, resulting in lost data, and they hold so little data that they are typically only used for backing up a few files at a time. DAT offers an excellent combination of speed, capacity, and reliability. For smaller capacity systems, a magnetic removable disk drive such as an Iomega Bernoulli transportable is a good choice. Not only is it very reliable, but disks of varying capacities can be used in this drive to provide virtually unlimited storage. Another feature of the Bernoulli drive is that it can be used with various systems including, Sun, Macintosh, PC, and even NeXT computers.

Which Files to Back Up

The most critical changes to the NEXTSTEP file system are made in **/private/etc**, **/LocalApps**, **/NextApps**, **/usr/local** and **/private/etc/NetInfo**. If these have not been altered significantly, the NEXTSTEP CD-ROM will suffice as a backup. If the computer is rendered unbootable, it can also be started using the CD-ROM. The BuildDisk or NEXTSTEP 3.1 Installer applications can then be used to replace the files on the hard drive from the CD and the few modifications that were lost can be restored manually. If the time it would take to rebuild and modify the system files is more than would be required to make and restore a backup copy, make a backup copy of the entire file system or at least the folders that contain changes.

Simple Backup Procedure

The most rudimentary backup method is to drag an icon to a floppy disk, preferably the larger-capacity 2.8 MB or 1.4 MB disks. For backing up a few files or a small folder, this works very well. Applications do not require backup. They can always be reinstalled from the original factory disk. If you make changes to the contents of folders not in your home folder, back them up as well. To back up system files to floppy disk, log in as the **root** user, or have the root user drag the **/private/etc** folder onto a floppy disk. If you cannot see the **/private/etc** folder in the File Viewer, turn on the UNIX Expert switch using the Preferences application. The **/private/etc** folder is important because it contains the NEXTSTEP network and system configuration information that would be critical to restoring your system should it need to be reinstalled from scratch. To restore your computer to service it after rebuilding its file system from scratch, copy the **/private/etc** files back onto the boot disk in the **/private/etc** folder and restart the computer. This will restore the system's local and network configuration, but will not restore each user's home folders or customized folders, such as **/LocalApps** or **/LocalLibrary**.

Only a complete file system backup will allow you to recover user home folders and other customized folders. To create a complete file system backup, you must log in as the **root** user. Use a third-party NEXTSTEP utility, such as SafetyNet or BackupMaster or the **tar** or **dump** commands. For a complete discussion of creating and restoring backups using **tar** and **dump**, refer to the *NEXTSTEP Network and System Administration* manual.

13.4.2 How to Learn New Commands

Because there are so many UNIX commands and options, on-line help is provided to assist you in selecting and building an appropriate UNIX command. You can use the **man** and **apropos** (pronounced ap ra poe') commands to learn more about a UNIX command or discover which command is appropriate for the task at hand.

Special UNIX Commands

13.4.3 The man Command

Due to the number of options and the obscure naming of UNIX commands, even veteran UNIX users forget how to use or spell a command, or which letters to use as options. However, the voluminous nature of UNIX necessarily requires a set of manuals that would weigh well over 30 pounds, contain information about more than 1,000 commands and topics, and take up numerous volumes. To save trees, shipping costs, and shelf space, the original authors of UNIX provided on-line help called UNIX manual pages, or man pages for short. Manual pages are ASCII files, generally in nroff or troff format (popular document formatting systems), that are displayed using the UNIX **man** command in the Terminal application. This allows you to access them quickly and easily when you need them. Manual pages describe mostly UNIX commands and only a few NEXTSTEP topics.

To view the manual page for a particular command, double-click the Terminal application icon to display a Terminal window, and then enter **man** followed by a space, followed by the name of the command. For example, to learn more about the **chown** command described in section 13.0, enter **man chown**. The message "please wait, reformatting man page..." will appear as the page is readied for display in the Terminal window. After a moment, you will see the manual page as shown in Figure 13-3.

You can also access manual pages using the Digital Librarian. This is described in section "UNIX Manual Pages" on page 368.

Most manual pages contain more text than will fit in a window, so the text is broken up into pages. To go forward and view the next page, press the space bar or type **f**. One line of text from the previous page will appear at the top of the window for the sake of continuity, followed by the text on the next manual page. To go backward and review a previous page, type **b**. You can also drag a scroller knob to review information that has scrolled out of the window. If you have found what you are looking for, you don't need to forward through the entire manual entry to continue. Type **q** to quit viewing a manual page and continue entering other UNIX commands.

Figure 13-3
UNIX Manual Pages

You can review UNIX manual pages on-line using the man command in a Terminal window. In this example, the Terminal window displays the first page of the ls command.

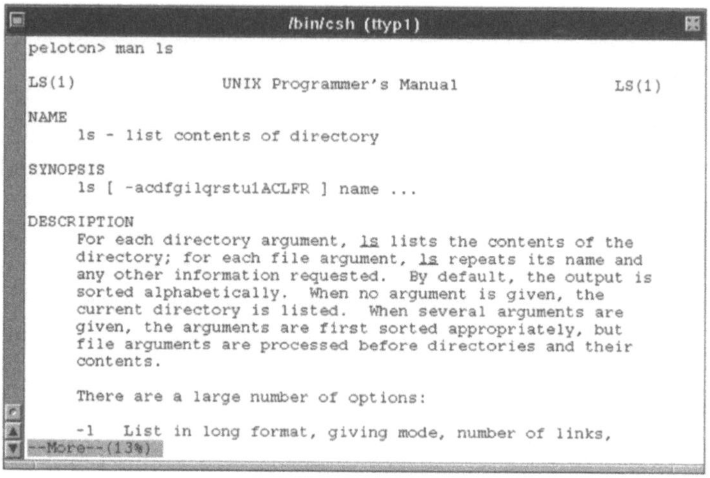

```
/bin/csh (ttyp1)
peloton> man ls
LS(1)              UNIX Programmer's Manual              LS(1)
NAME
     ls - list contents of directory
SYNOPSIS
     ls [ -acdfgilqrstu1ACLFR ] name ...
DESCRIPTION
     For each directory argument, ls lists the contents of the
     directory; for each file argument, ls repeats its name and
     any other information requested.  By default, the output is
     sorted alphabetically.  When no argument is given, the
     current directory is listed.  When several arguments are
     given, the arguments are first sorted appropriately, but
     file arguments are processed before directories and their
     contents.

     There are a large number of options:

     -1   List in long format, giving mode, number of links,
--More--(13%)
```

13.4.4   The apropos Command

The ability to view a manual page for a UNIX command is wonderful, but only if you know the name of the UNIX command you want to read about. If you don't know the name of the command you are looking for, you have a serious problem! Fortunately, UNIX provides an **apropos** command, which lists commands that relate to a particular topic. For example, if you don't know which UNIX commands are used to set the ownership of a folder, you could type **apropos owner** in a Terminal window to display a description of UNIX file ownership, and list several UNIX commands related to viewing and changing ownerships. You can then use **man** to view detailed information about one of the commands found using **apropos**. If you request information about a topic that does not exist or relate to a UNIX command, you will see the message "topic not found" after entering the apropos command. Try **apropos** again using another topic. There is no workspace equivalent for the **apropos** command.

14

NEXTSTEP First Aid

This chapter will teach you how to recover from problems as simple as an application freezing or as daunting as a total system failure. It is included in this book because the unexpected crash, failure, or problem always seems to occur when no one is around to help, the technical support telephone line is busy, and the project you're working on is due in an hour. The techniques we'll discuss are well known to veteran NEXTSTEP users and not unusually difficult to perform. However, it's best to take a moment to calm down, write down what you were doing when the failure occurred, and patiently call a knowledgeable NEXTSTEP guru for assistance or call NeXT at 1-800-848-NeXT. If you can't wait and aren't afraid to attempt repairs on your own, then this chapter is for you.

If you've used any computer for any length of time, you know that sooner or later something goes wrong. Invariably, you'll find yourself in a situation from which you cannot proceed or retreat. Such situations are colloquially referred to as a crash, freeze, or hang. The symptoms of a crash include but are not limited to the inability to select a menu command, the cursor freezing, a window not being drawn correctly, and the application disappearing. Application crashes can have varying degrees of severity, ranging from the almost trivial loss of a print request to the total inability to continue using any application or the workspace. With single-tasking systems such as DOS, a system freeze often necessitates restarting the computer, and in the process, losing all of your work in progress that had not been previously saved to disk. In contrast, NEXTSTEP rarely suffers from a total system crash from which you cannot escape—really. More often than not, it is only a particular application that hangs or freezes, leaving the other running applications free from harm and allowing you to recover using the NEXTSTEP workspace. Let's examine how you might recover from some typical problems, and then proceed to techniques for recovering from more severe problems.

14.0 Frozen Applications

One of the great advantages of NEXTSTEP is that when an application crashes, it doesn't necessarily stop the entire computer from functioning. How can you tell when an application crashes? A common symptom of a crash is that you cannot choose a menu command, such as Quit or Save, or the spinning disk cursor never changes back to the arrow cursor. If this happens, you should wait a couple of minutes just to be sure the computer isn't working on a background task. If you're convinced the application has crashed, you can often work around it simply by ignoring it and switching to another application. If you need to continue using that application, you'll have to clear it from the computer's memory so you can start it again. This is called killing an application.

Spinning Disk Cursor

To kill a crashed or frozen application, you'll use the Processes panel. From the crashed application, double-click the NeXT logo in the dock or click a window belonging to the workspace. If this doesn't make the Workspace Manager the current application, the application has crashed the entire system and you'll need to resort to methods described in "System Crash Recovery" on page 355. Thankfully, this is a rare event, and the workspace will usually become active. Display the Processes panel using the Tools menu or by pressing Command-P and select the name of the application in the panel. To clear the application from memory, click Kill. An attention panel will appear to verify that you are sure you want to kill the process. Click Kill again in the attention panel. Killing an application process does not quit it gracefully: temporary and other working files are left open, and you will not be able to save the documents you were working on. However, if the application has crashed, you can't save your work anyway, so you have nothing to lose by killing it. For these reasons, never kill an application instead of using the Quit command.

14.1 System Crash Recovery

> If you need to use one of the recovery procedures described below, attempt them in the order they are described. As you progress further down the list of techniques, you increase the potential for data loss and file system corruption. If you are unsure about the implications of any of these procedures, do not attempt to perform them. Call for help from an experienced system administrator or call NeXT at 800-848-NeXT.

When NEXTSTEP encounters a fatal error from which it cannot recover, you will either see a special attention panel named Panic, or you will not be able to choose menu commands or buttons in any running application. In either case, you won't be able to use even the workspace, so recovery is more difficult. You'll need to take drastic measures to regain control of your computer. If you see a Panic panel, write down the information it contains for later reference. It may help you determine the problem that caused the crash. Your first step after a fatal crash should always be to attempt a normal shutdown. Although it may not work, it's always the best method for powering off as it ensures that data in RAM is saved on the disk. If that doesn't work, you can force NEXTSTEP to shutdown ungracefully by pressing the key to the right of the space bar and the key in the upper left corner of the numeric keypad (see Figure 14-1) simultaneously.

**Figure 14-1
Displaying the Restart Panel**

After a crash, you can press the keys shown here in white to display the Restart panel and restart or power off the computer.

A panel should appear in the middle of the screen asking you "Restart or Halt? Type r to restart, or type h to halt. Type n to cancel" (see Figure 14-2). Try to restart first. If that doesn't work, try halting the computer. Wait a few moments to see what happens. If the system restarts or powers off you've fixed the problem. Skip to "Starting Up After a Crash" on page 359 to get NEXTSTEP started again. If nothing happens after a few minutes, try this procedure again. If still nothing happens, you'll need to take further measures as described in the next section.

**Figure 14-2
Using the
Restart Panel**

Using the Restart panel, you can restart or power off a crashed system. If you displayed the Restart panel by mistake, you can cancel by typing n.

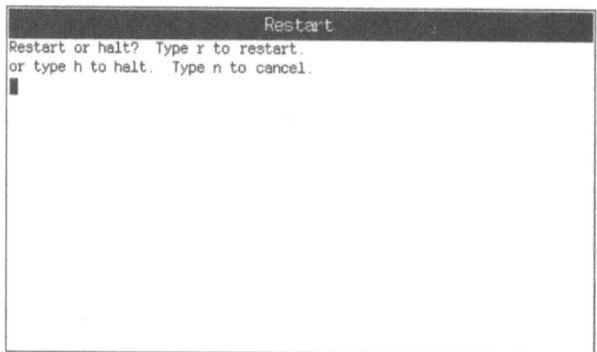

14.1.0 Forcing NeXT Computers to Power Off

If you are using a NeXT computer, press the key in the upper left corner of the numeric key pad and both keys on either side of the space bar to display the NMI Mini-Monitor (see Figure 14-3 and Figure 14-4). The Mini-Monitor is typically used by programmers to debug applications, but can also be used to restart your computer. In the NMI Mini-Monitor panel, type **halt** to power off the computer or **reboot** to power it off and then restart it. Both of these commands will power off the computer gracefully. You can also type **?** to see a list of other NMI Mini-Monitor commands.

**Figure 14-3
Restarting
the Computer**

If your computer crashes, you can press the keys shown here in white to display a panel with which you can restart or power off the computer.

System Crash Recovery

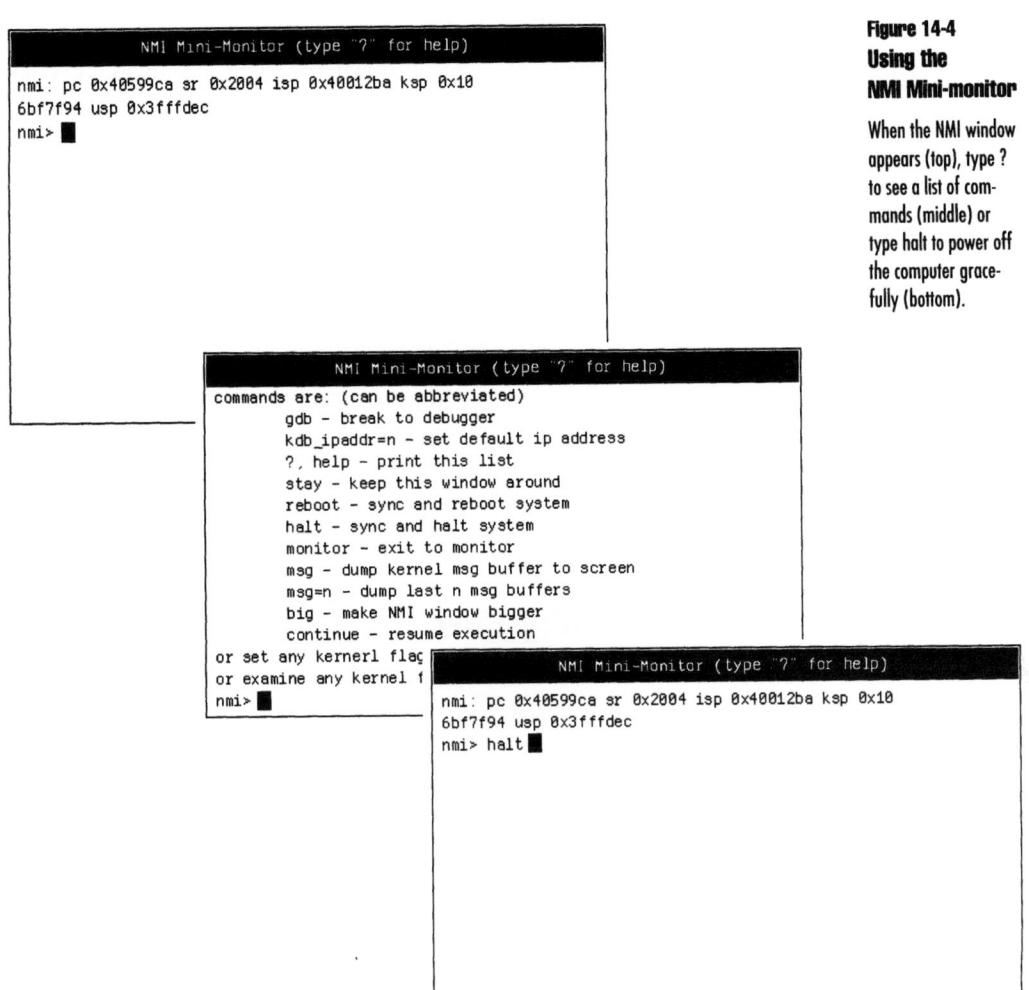

**Figure 14-4
Using the
NMI Mini-monitor**

When the NMI window appears (top), type ? to see a list of commands (middle) or type halt to power off the computer gracefully (bottom).

If the **halt** command has no effect, type **mon** to display the ROM Monitor. When you press these keys on a NeXT computer, you'll see the ROM Monitor. Using the ROM Monitor window, you can force NEXTSTEP to boot from a particular disk. For example, to boot from a SCSI disk, enter **bsd**. To boot from a CD-ROM drive, type **bcd**. You should see the system respond by restarting as if you had just powered on.

When the computer is running smoothly, you can also use the ROM monitor to modify or inspect the boot process. You can see the ROM monitor when the system boots by holding down the right Command key and pressing the key in the upper left corner of the numeric keypad after the "Testing System" message is replaced by the "Loading from Disk message". To change the start up process, type **P** at the **NeXT>** prompt and press Return to inspect or change system parameters such as which disk drive to boot from (SCSI disk = **sd**, twisted-pair Ethernet = **tp**), whether to run diagnostics, list all of the startup activity rather than displaying the spinning disk icon, and other parameters. If you are the curious type, you may want to turn on the verbose mode. This causes the computer to display a window listing all of the startup tasks as the NeXT computer boots the operating system instead of the spinning disk icon. You'll see quite a few things happen by watching this list. No wonder it takes so long to power on! After getting to know more about the NEXTSTEP boot process, turn the verbose mode off using the ROM Monitor's **p** command again.

14.1.1 Manually Powering Off

Failing all of these solutions, you can always power off manually on any system using the power switch. This is the worst possible way to restart the computer, as it is very likely that the file system will be corrupted in some way. However, if the system has crashed and the previous procedures have not worked, you have little choice other than waiting for someone more expert to assist you.

On a NeXT computer, press the press the left Command key, left Alternate key, and the key in the upper left corner of the numeric keypad at the same time (see Figure 14-5) to manually power off the computer.

**Figure 14-5
Forcing
Power Off**

On NeXT computers, you can force a power off by pressing each of the keys shown here in white at the same time.

14.1.2 Starting Up After a Crash

After forcing a PC system to power off, turn off the power switch, wait a minute or so and turn the power switch back on to restart the system. It will take a little longer to start up after a crash as it must verify the state of the file system and make repairs. When it's ready, you'll have the opportunity to boot from one of several partitions (if partitions exist on your hard disk) or alter the normal NEXTSTEP boot procedure. For example, after choosing to boot to the partition containing NEXTSTEP, the prompt **boot:** appears. At this prompt you can enter **mach_kernel –s** which will boot the computer into single-user mode. This mode logs you in as **root** and displays only a command-line prompt. It is often used by system administrators to effect repairs to a system. These commands are discussed in more detail in the on-line documentation contained in the developer environment.

> If the hardware configuration files have been changed corrupted preventing NEXTSTEP from booting properly, you can force NEXTSTEP to use a default configuration. Type **–s config=Default** at the **boot:** prompt. This will usually allow NEXTSTEP to boot so that you can run the Configure application and correct the problem.

After powering off a NeXT computer, press the power key on the keyboard to turn it back on. When you start or restart a NeXT computer, it will also take a little longer to display the login panel as it must verify the state of the file system and make repairs. When that is accomplished, log in again as usual and continue your NEXTSTEP session.

Booting a NeXT Computer from a Different Hard Disk

Recovering a nonstarting PC or Macintosh is as easy as inserting a bootable floppy disk and restarting the computer. However, the only way to start a NeXT computer without using its internal hard disk is to attach a bootable external disk drive or CD-ROM drive containing the NEXTSTEP disc. Even a 2.88 MB floppy disk is not large enough to hold the information required to boot and repair a corrupted NEXTSTEP file system. To force the computer to reboot using a different disk drive when you can't use the Workspace Manager, or to reboot in single-user mode to perform specialized administrative tasks, such as restoring a lost root user password, use the ROM monitor.

You should have more than a passing acquaintance with UNIX commands and the UNIX file system to attempt the following repair. However, if you do not have an administrator handy, and the computer is not working, you have little to lose by trying. If nothing else, by trying, gain valuable knowledge and be better prepared when you call NeXT or another source for help, and the technician suggests you to enact a procedure while on the phone. A complete discussion of system recovery using the ROM monitor is provided in the *NEXTSTEP Network and System Administration* manual. If in doubt, call for help from a system administrator or a NeXT Authorized Service Center.

To restart the NeXT computer from an external hard disk, attach a bootable NEXTSTEP drive to its SCSI port and set its SCSI ID to zero. NeXT computers will always attempt to boot from the device using the lowest SCSI ID unless you have set it to act differently. Attempt to restart the computer as usual, but remember, you'll have to use a user name and password for the bootable disk. If you don't have a password for the bootable disk, display the ROM monitor and enter **bsd −s** (note the space before the hyphen). This command will cause the computer to reboot in single-user mode, bypassing the graphical user interface and the need for a password. When the **#** prompt appears, you will be the root user and you can perform repairs. Do not attempt to fix the system unless you are familiar with the UNIX file system and UNIX commands.

15

The World of NEXTSTEP

If you want to learn more about NEXTSTEP and related products, there are several good sources for information. However, you may not know quite where to find them. This chapter describes some of the materials that are available, how to get them, and a brief description of the information they contain. If you need specific information about a NeXT product, you can call NeXT directly at 1-800-848-NeXT (in the USA). This telephone number will connect you with NeXT's information hotline, designed specifically to help you get the information you need about NeXT and NeXT products, and help you find an authorized NeXT dealer near you.

15.0 Contacts at NeXT

NeXT, Inc. is pleased to provide information at your request. Some of their publications include, but are not limited to, independent studies describing the advantages of NEXTSTEP over competitive systems, white papers that describe in detail issues such as developing NEXTSTEP database applications, open system standards, NEXTSTEP connectivity, and more. NeXT also offers video and audio cassettes that discuss object-oriented computing, success stories, and NeXT products.

There are a number of ways for you to for contact NeXT, including telephone, electronic mail, and fax but NeXT makes it easy by providing a central, all-purpose telephone hotline. If you need information regarding a purchase, product information, technical assistance, or any other information, contact NeXT at:

in North America:

NeXT, Inc.
900 Chesapeake Drive
Redwood City, CA 94063
USA
1-800-848-NeXT

in Europe:

NeXT Computer Germany GmbH
Oskar-Messter-Strasse 24
8045 Ismaning
Germany
+49/89.996.5310
FAX: +49/89.961.2392

To report NeXT software problems and suspected bugs, send Internet mail to **bug.next@next.com**. If you're willing to pay a small fee, you can ask a question of NeXT's developer technical support staff by sending Internet mail to **ask.next@next.com**.

To ask questions, provide input or ideas for NeXT's quarterly bulletin, or to ask programmatic questions regarding NeXT Authorized Service or Support Centers, call 415-438-4331, send a fax to 1-800-228-NeXT, or write:

Service Operations
NeXT, Inc.
980 Mission Court
Fremont, CA 94539

15.1 Information in Print

If you're interested in reading more about NEXTSTEP, there are several good sources of material. This section describes several manuals, book, and journals in print, that relate to NEXTSTEP and NeXT computers.

15.1.0 NEXTSTEP Manuals and References

With each copy of NEXTSTEP, you'll receive printed reference manuals and electronic documentation designed for both new and experienced NEXTSTEP users. In the NEXTSTEP user environment package you'll find, along with registration and license materials, a small quick-start manual named *Here's How*, a *User's Guide* describing the general use of NEXTSTEP, an installation guide, *Installing and Configuring NEXTSTEP Release 3.1 for Intel Processors* (or NeXT computers), and Release Notes.

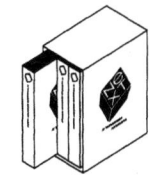

The *NEXTSTEP Network and System Administration* manual, which was included with previous versions of NEXTSTEP is still included with Release 3.1, but only in electronic format. It can be found in **/NextLibrary/Documentation/NextAdmin** and reviewed using the Digital Librarian or Edit applications. If you are not the **root** user of your computer, you probably won't need to concern yourself with the *NEXTSTEP Network and System Administration* manual, although it's a great source for learning more about the details of NEXTSTEP administration.

15.1.1 The NeXT Developer Series

Addison-Wesley, a well-known publisher of technical computing books, recently began publishing a series of books on programming in NEXTSTEP. These books were written by NeXT, and originally available only to registered developers who attended NeXT's Developer Camp in Redwood City, California. They are now available to the public through bookstores and computer retail outlets. You can also order them directly from Addison-Wesley at 800-447-2226. These are highly technical books intended for the serious programmer who wants to write applications for NEXTSTEP. A subset of these manuals is also included when you purchase the NEXTSTEP Developer Environment.

Table 15-1 NeXT Developer Books

Title	Product Number	Retail Price
NEXTSTEP Network and System Administration	473893	$28.95
NEXTSTEP Programming Interface Summary*	63253	$30.95
NEXTSTEP Operating System Software	473872	$24.95
NEXTSTEP Object Oriented Programming and the Objective C Language	63251	$24.95
NEXTSTEP User Interface Guidelines*	63250	$24.95
NEXTSTEP General Reference Volume 1*	62220	$44.95
NEXTSTEP General Reference Volume 2*	62221	$44.95
NeXT Development Tools and Techniques*	63249	$30.95
Sound, Music and Signal Processing on NeXT: Reference	433033	$39.95
Sound, Music and Signal Processing on NeXT: Concepts	433028	$19.95

* Included with the NeXTSTEP Developer Environment.

15.1.2 Books in Print

The Design and Implementation of the 4.3 BSD UNIX Operating System
Samuel J. Leffler, Marshall K. McKusick, Michael J. Karels, and John S. Quarterman, Addison-Wesley, 1988.

The Design of the UNIX Operating System
Maurice J. Bach, Prentice-Hall, 1986.

Information in Print

NEXTSTEP Programming: Concepts and Applications
Alex Duong Nghiem, Prentice-Hall, 1993.

NEXTSTEP Programming Volume One: Object-Oriented Applications
Simson L. Garfinkel and Michael Mahoney, Springer-Verlag, 1993.

Practical UNIX Security
Simson L. Garfinkel and Gene Spafford, O'Reilly & Associates, 1991.

Taking the Next Step: The Buyer's Guide to NEXTSTEP Computing
Seth Ross & Daniel Miles Kehoe, Albion Books, 1993.

UNIX System Administration Handbook
Evi Nemeth, Garth Snyder, and Scott Seebass, Prentice-Hall, 1989.

Writing NeXT Programs
Ann Weintz, Boardwalk Publishing, 1991.

15.1.3 Magazines in Print

NeXTWORLD

NeXTWORLD Magazine is one of the best sources for information about the NeXT and NEXTSTEP-compatible products. Each issue includes several in-depth features on new hardware and software, lively editorials, both positive and negative, about the state of NEXTSTEP, product reviews, and how-to's. Each issue also includes mail-order advertisements, and classified ads that describe products, job opportunities, and services.

NeXTWORLD is printed in full color, on oversized glossy paper. Each issue costs $4.95 (U.S.) and subscriptions are available for $39.90 (U.S.). Issues are delivered each month. For subscription information, contact *NeXTWORLD* magazine at:

NeXTWORLD Magazine / Subscriber Services
P.O. Box 56429
Boulder, CO 80322-6429
Internet mail: **subsrip@nextworld.com**
1-800-755-6398
FAX: 415-442-1891

NeXTReview

NeXTReview is a monthly newspaper style publication designed for the NEXTSTEP professional. It includes features, reviews, descriptions of new products, editorials, product advertising, and technical discussions. NeXTReview is not sponsored or endorsed by NeXT. NeXTReview also provides a bulletin board service (BBS) to its subscribers and advertisers. The cost of each issue is $4, and subscriptions are $45 (U.S.) and $75 (Canada). You can contact NeXTReview at:

NeXTReview
12416 Hymeadow Drive
Austin, TX 78750-1896
512-250-9023
FAX: 512-331-3900

15.1.4 User Group Newsletters

Many NeXT user groups distribute newsletters to their users. Popular, well designed and informative newsletters are produced by VNUS, the Vancouver NeXT Users Group and BaNG, the Bay Area NeXT Users Group. Newsletter articles contained in user group newsletters are insightful, concise, and not afraid to tell it like it is. User group newsletters often contain ads for new and used equipment and software, tips and tricks, and minutes from the last user group meeting, as well as an obligatory request for membership and dues. Many NEXTSTEP users find they cannot attend regular meetings, but still wish to be active members of the group and stay informed of its activities. User groups acknowledge this and distribute a newsletter just for this reason. Many user groups also post their newsletters on-line at Internet archive sites. At the Purdue archive site, you can often find newsletters from VNUG, rmNUG, and SCAN, and others.

BaNG

Bay Area NeXT Users Group, one item on-line on Purdue. Edited by Robert Nielson (**nielsen@everest.portal.com**).

NeXUS

Published bi-monthly for $36/year. Contact Alfonso Guerra at **{emory | gatech}!nanovx!nexus**.

rmNUG NeWS
Rocky Mountain NeXT Users Group newsletter, latest issue May 1991 (monthly). Edited by David Bowdish (**73340.2146@compuserve.com**).

SCaNeWS
Southern California NeXT Users Group newsletter. First issue came out January 1991. Edited by Mike Mahoney (**manhoney@beach.csulb.edu**)

What's NeXT?
The Boston Computer Society NeXT User group produces a NeXT newsletter called *What's NeXT?* BCS can be reached at 1 Center Plaza, Boston, MA 02108.

15.2 Information in Electronic Format

One of the difficulties with printed material is that it must be searched sequentially. Most manuals and references include a table of contents and index, but few are comprehensive and you must often refer back to them several times until you find reference you are looking for. A better solution for finding information is to use an electronic search that can employ various search techniques very quickly, and which allows you to manipulate the information after it is found. For this reason, NeXT distributes its manuals pre-indexed in Digital Librarian format and on-line help using hypertext links between key words and related information. With hypertext links, clicking a key word within the text automatically displays information related to that word. You do not have to search an index, scan a table of contents, or read through a chapter of text to find it. Distributing information electronically not only serves as written instruction, but also allows graphics, motion video, and sound. There are several products—such as MediaView, MediaStation, and CraftMan—that take this multimedia approach to providing information.

15.2.0 On-Line Help

One of the best sources for information while using NEXTSTEP is on-line help. On-line help is easy to access, displays information directly related to the object you select on the screen, and provides examples and related topics. Because applications use the same kind of Help panel, learning how to

manipulate the Help panel controls in one application will apply to the Help panels in every other application that uses the standard Help panel. To learn how to use the Help panel, see "The Help Panel" on page 119.

15.2.1 UNIX Manual Pages

You can access UNIX manual pages, more commonly referred to as man pages, using the Digital Librarian (see Figure 15-1), as well as with the UNIX **man** command in a Terminal window (see "The man Command" on page 351). The bookshelf containing the man pages is located in **/NextLibrary/Bookshelves** and is named **SysAdmin.bshlf**. Opening this system administration bookshelf in the Digital Librarian allows you to browse the man pages. This is the easiest way to find and view a man page. You can use Librarian to search another topic, list the man pages topics, and read man page listings. You may even want to keep Librarian running all the time for quick access, and hide it when it's not in use.

**Figure 15-1
Accessing UNIX
Man Pages**

You can find the man pages in Digital Librarian format in /NextLibrary/Documentation/ManPages. Drag the man pages icon onto the Digital Librarian bookshelf and use a key word search to find the information you need.

15.2.2 Internet Archives

Currently, very few books exist that describe how to use the NEXTSTEP user environment. Most of the information you might like to know that is not in this book or in the *NEXTSTEP User's Guide*, is located on-line in Internet archives. Several NeXT-related archives exist on the Internet and

Information in Electronic Format

do not require you to enter a user name or password. NeXT archives contain technical notes, public domain and shareware applications, utilities, fonts, demonstration applications, artwork, editorials, typical user questions and answers, and much more. If you are able to connect to this network, or know someone who can, you have access to the largest available collection of information about NEXTSTEP and related issues. A list of NeXT-related Internet archive sites is provided in "Appendix B: Internet Archive Sites". To access information on an Internet archive, use Gator-FTP+ as described in "GatorFTP" on page 310 (see Figure 15-2).

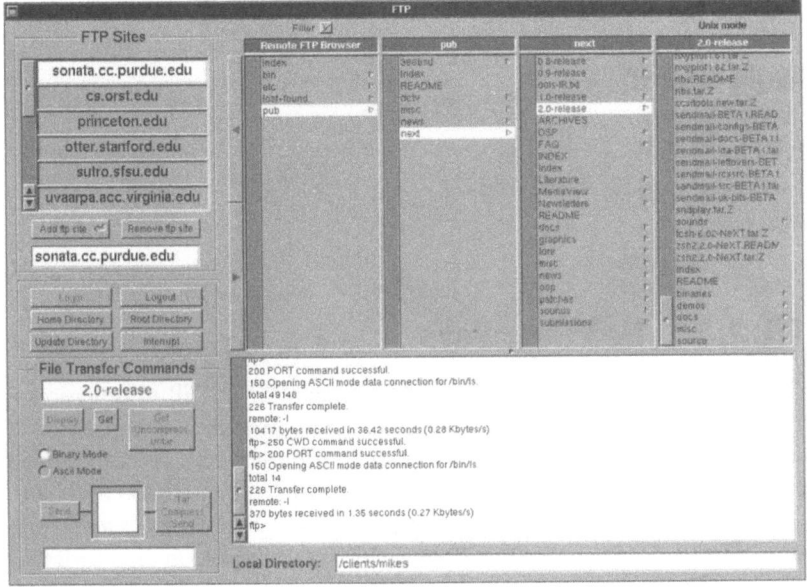

**Figure 15-2
Accessing
Internet Archives**

Using the GatorFTP+ application provided on the enclosed disk, you can access thousands of documents, articles, reviews, images, sounds, applications, demos, and news.

If you don't have access to the Internet, you can purchase a CD-ROM containing most of the NeXT-related information from Internet archives. Several discs are available, such as Jewel of the Matrix by Object Horizons, The Internet Unplugged by ISOMEDIA, and The Big Green CD by Skylee Press. Each of these discs costs about $100 and contains public domain, shareware, and demonstration applications, fonts, images, sounds, utilities, documents, programming samples, and the files normally found on the Internet at NeXT-related archives. Each disc contains a maximum of 600 MB of information.

Jewel of the Matrix
Object Horizons Ltd.
167 Milk St., Ste. #212
Boston, MA 02109-4315.
617-499-9523.

The Internet Unplugged
ISOMEDIA Inc.
14808 NE. 31st Circle
Redmond, WA 98052
206-869-5411 or 800-468-3939.

The Big Green CD
Skylee Press
PO Box 471645
San Francisco, CA 92147-1465
415-474-7803.

15.2.3   NeXTanswers

One of the best sources for up-to-the-minute NEXTSTEP information is NeXTanswers, a free document retrieval system provided by NeXT. NeXTanswers is available 24 hours a day by fax or Internet mail. You can request information about NEXTSTEP for Intel Processors configuration and hardware compatibility, installation instructions, lists of known bugs and workarounds, articles from *NEXTSTEP In Focus*, and information on a variety of other NEXTSTEP topics.

By Fax

Using a touch-tone phone, call 415-780-3990. You'll be asked for your fax number, a number to identify your fax, such as your phone extension or office number, and the ID numbers of the documents you want. Ask for document 1001 for a complete list of available documents. When you finish entering the numbers of the documents you want, hang up the phone and the documents will be faxed to you. You can call any time to request more documents.

Information in Electronic Format

By Internet Mail

If you prefer, you can request a NeXTanswers document using Internet mail. Send a mail message to **NeXTanswers@next.com** and include the document's ID number in the subject line or body of the message. To receive a complete list of available documents, include the keyword **index** in the Subject line or body. You can ask for multiple documents in the same request message. The documents are sent as NeXTmail attachments. If you can't receive NeXTmail, include the word **ASCII** in the subject line or body of the message. The documents will be sent as ASCII text instead.

If you want more detailed instructions for using NeXTanswers, send a mail message that includes **help**. If you continue to have problems using NeXTanswers, send a request for help to **NeXTanswers-request@next.com**.

15.2.4 Questions and Answers

NeXTanswers used to be a collection of typical questions and answers about NeXTSTEP and NeXT computers located at several Internet archives and available in the NeXT *SupportBulletin*. These files are now called Questions and Answers. You can copy them from an Internet archive to your computer using the GatorFTP+ application as described in section "GatorFTP" on page 310. If you don't have access to Internet, you can also receive them as part of NeXT's *NEXTSTEP in Focus* newsletter.

When you receive the Questions and Answers files, start the Digital Librarian and drag the folder containing them onto the Librarian shelf then double-click it to display Digital Librarian's Inspector panel. Choose Index from the Inspector's pop-up list, and then click Set Up to create an index. Indexing will only take a moment, then you can begin searching search using a keyword of your choice to learn about a particular subject. If you prefer to browse, click List Titles in Digital Librarian to see a list of document titles, then double-click a title to view the document.

15.2.5 NEXTSTEP in Focus

NeXT's quarterly bulletin, *NEXTSTEP In Focus—Support Bulletin for Users and System Administrators*, provides timely, in-depth technical information to NeXT users and system administrators. Topics range from new product updates to tips on system administration to explanations of system internals. Each NEXTSTEP *In Focus* issue includes a floppy disk that contains an electronic version of the bulletin. To subscribe to the bulletin, send Internet mail to **support_bulletin@next.com** or call 1-800-848-NeXT. From outside North America, call +1-415-424-850.

15.2.6 TechSupportNotes and MiniExamples

NeXT also distributes TechSupportNotes and MiniExamples. These collections include technical information intended for advanced users, system and network administrators, and programmers. Both of these items are stored in compressed form and can be found on Internet archives. Table 15-2, "Location of TechSupportNotes and MiniExamples" describes where to find them. Each TechSupportNote uses about 100 KB after being uncompressed, and each MiniExample generally uses less than 50 KB of disk space after being uncompressed.

Table 15-2 Location of TechSupportNotes and MiniExamples

Host Name	Location
cs.orst.edu	/pub/next/documents/NeXTanswers/MiniExamples
cs.orst.edu	/pub/next/documents/NeXTanswers/TechSupportNotes
sonata.cc.purdue.edu	/pub/next/docs/MiniExamples
sonata.cc.purdue.edu	/pub/next/docs/TechSupportNotes

15.2.7 Using E-mail to Obtain Internet Files

Many institutions have access to the Internet, yet not every NEXTSTEP user belongs to one of these institutions. If you are in this group, you can still obtain files from the Internet using electronic mail. Purdue maintains an e-mail-based archive server for those without FTP access. To obtain information about how to get a file using e-mail, send an e-mail message with the text **help** to **archive–server@cc.purdue.edu**. If your electronic mail is routed through one or more other mail systems before it gets to Purdue, it may no longer contain your e-mail address in Internet format. The

Internet format for electronic mail addresses is **user@host.type** where **user** is your user name, **host** is the IP name of the host where you have your user account, and **type** is the type of host, such as **edu**, **com**, **mil**, and so on. If this happens, the server at Purdue will not be able to return your mail. To correct the problem, include your Internet address as a part of your mail message. For example, use *path name@site.edu* or *path wellknownsite!yoursite!yourname@uunet.uu.ne*. but do not use *name@site.bitnet* or *name@site.UUCP*.

15.2.8 CompuServe

For those without access to the Internet, there is a commercial source for on-line electronic information called CompuServe that requires only a modem and a telephone line. CompuServe provides access to information, technical assistance, friendly user conversation, and other aspects of the NeXT culture by connecting your computer to archive-like resources called bulletin boards maintained by CompuServe (see Figure 15-3).

```
                         IComm
Press <CR> for more :

Be Sure To Attend The NeXT Conference! Thursday's At 10:00pm EST!

Press <CR> !
NeXT Users Forum Menu

 1 INSTRUCTIONS

 2 MESSAGES
 3 LIBRARIES (Files)
 4 CONFERENCING (0 participating)

 5 ANNOUNCEMENTS from sysop
 6 MEMBER directory
 7 OPTIONS for this forum

 8 JOIN this forum

Enter choice !
```

**Figure 15-3
NeXT Forum
on CompuServe**

CompuServe is very easy to access using any computer and modem. To review NeXT-related information, type GO NEXT.

CompuServe charges a fee for the use of its service, not including the cost of the phone call, but it's accessible to anyone with a computer, modem, and telephone line. To help you get started, CompuServe offers NeXT users and developers a special free membership and $15 credit so you can learn how to use the system. Contact CompuServe at 1-800-848-8119 and ask for representative #235 for this offer. If you're living or working outside the U.S., call +49-89-66-550-111. Here is a brief description of the CompuServe NeXT forum that was published on the Internet:

The forum contains: Message Section, Library Section, & Conference.

Message Section: This section allows you to leave messages, announcements, questions, answers, and general NeXT trivia.

Library Section: This section offers a place to upload and download programs and other files in any on of several categories.

Conference Section: This section allows for "live" computer conferences with other NeXTer's from around the country (world). Conferences will be scheduled on a regular basis.

CompuServe Advantages:
Until now, the only way that NeXTer's could get together via modem nationally, has been through Internet. However, Internet's access is limited and most of the new purchasers of NeXT do not have access to Internet, Usenet, or ftp'ing. On CompuServe over 90% of the NeXT users will have local number access where they can ask questions, get programs and information, and exchange idea's with other NeXT users. Much like an national user's group, only better.

David Bowdish - Sysop of the NeXT Forum
76711.143@compuserve.com
rmNUG NeWS Editor
Rocky Mountain NeXT Users Group Executive Board member

15.2.9 E-Mail Special Interest Groups

If you are able to send mail on the Internet or BITnet networks, you can share information with other NEXTSTEP users by subscribing to a Special Interest Group (SIG). A SIG is a collection of computer users who trade information, news, rumors, and tips using electronic mail. Many other electronic subscription services, such as AppleLink and CompuServe, can also send mail to Internet and BITnet networks. If you are not sure if you can send messages to these systems or don't know how, contact your ser-

Information in Electronic Format

vice provider. To subscribe to a SIG, send an e-mail message to one of the addresses shown in Table 15-3. For the most recent list of SIGs, call NeXT or send mail on the Internet to **user_groups@next.com**.

Table 15-3 NeXT-Related Special Interest Groups

SIG	Electronic Mail Address
Adobe Illustrator NeXT SIG	jchin@wcraft.wimsey.bc.ca
AFS NeXT SIG	info-afs-next-request@transarc.com
Classroom: NeXT Courseware SIG	e-mail the text: "SUBSCRIBE next-classroom <your name>" to MAILSERV@gac.edu
Communications/TeleCommunications SIG	nextcomm-request@marble.com
Create Interest Group (CIG)	Create-request@mcs.anl.gov
Data GROUP NeXT SIG	data_group@dazzl.com
DataPhile Interest Group (DIG)	DataPhile-request@mcs.anl.gov
Executor SIG	executor-request@ictv.com
Finnish: FUNeXT (Finnish Users of NeXT)	mailserver@lists.funet.fi and write in body text: HELP LIST SUB FUNeXT
FUN (Frame Users Network)	Frameframers-request@drd.com
Frame User Network - New England (FUNNE)	funne@srbci.mv.com
GIS (Geographical Information Services) SIG	next-gis-request@deltos.com
Icon	NeXT-icon-Request@bmt.gun.com

Table 15-3 NeXT-Related Special Interest Groups (continued)

SIG	Electronic Mail Address
Improv User Group	improv-request@calvin.tamu.edu
Japanese: Kanji and Japanese on the NeXT	next-nihongo-request@pinoko.berkeley.edu
Mathematica Special Interest Group	mathgroup-request@yoda.physics.unc.edu
Medical: NeXTMed SIG	NeXTMed-request@ulnar.biostr.washington.edu
Music: NeXT Music SIG	nextmusic-request@wri.com
Network and Security Management for Installed Labs and Large Installations	next-lab-request@cs.ubc.ca
NexLAW - Legal NeXT User Group	NexLAW-request@techlaw.com
NeXTManagers (quick & technical answers)	next-managers-request@stolaf.edu
NeXT Q&A's	email the text: "SUBSCRIBE NEXT-L <your> <name>" to LISTSERV@BROWNVM.BROWN.EDU
NeXT Nugget News	nugget-request@next.com
Programmers/Developers: NeXT Programmers SIG	next-prog-request@cpac.washington.edu
Publishing Interest Group	publish-request@chron.com
SCIENCE NeXT User Group (SNUG)	snug-requests@whitewater.chem.wisc.edu
United Kingdom SIG	uk-next-users-request@ohm.york.ac.uk and next-uk-usergroups-request@asmec.co.uk

15.2.10 UseNet News

A running dialog of news, information, tips, suggestions, and commentary takes place each day on the Internet. This "news feed" is called UseNet news, and can be read using the NEXTSTEP application named News-Grazer (see Figure 15-4). Currently, NewsGrazer runs only on NeXT computers. UseNet news, in practical terms, is a bulletin board system maintained by volunteers, that is available through the Internet and through private bulletin board systems. You can post comments, suggestions, complaints, questions, or editorials on public electronic bulletin boards and carry on conversations or electronic meetings with computer users from around the world. You can also gain a great deal of insight on problems and solutions not generally known to the general public, all for free. NewsGrazer is a NEXTSTEP UseNet reader that requires your computer be connected to the Internet and that your site have a news server. Contact your local network administrator for more information about UseNet news service.

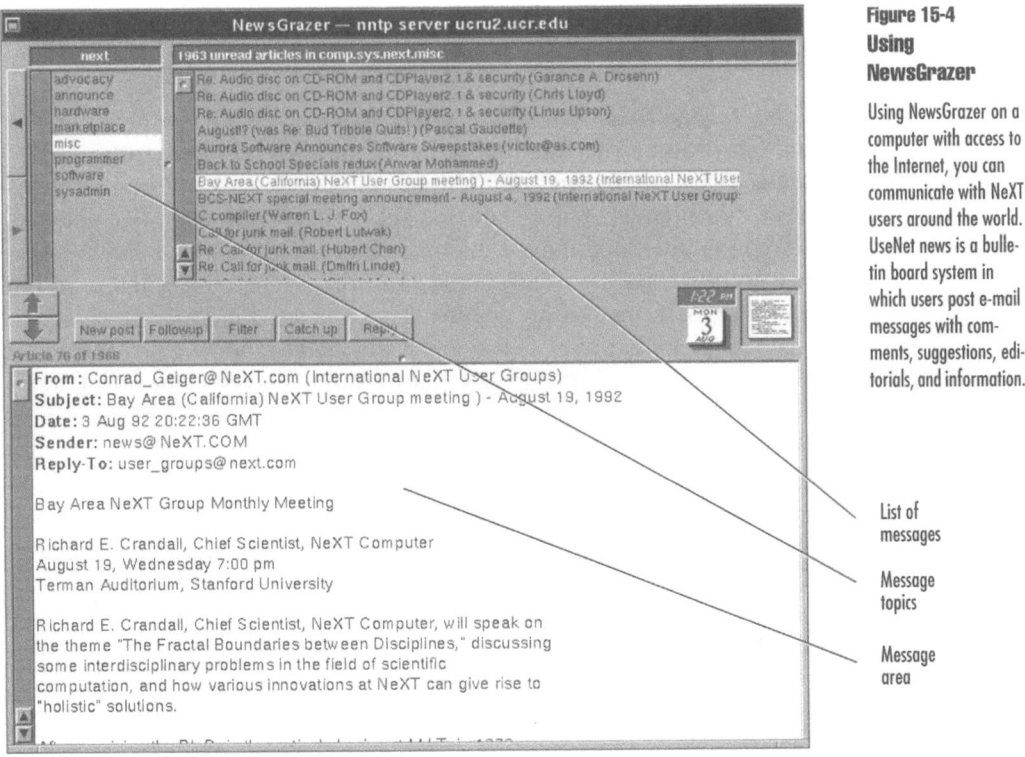

**Figure 15-4
Using
NewsGrazer**

Using NewsGrazer on a computer with access to the Internet, you can communicate with NeXT users around the world. UseNet news is a bulletin board system in which users post e-mail messages with comments, suggestions, editorials, and information.

List of messages

Message topics

Message area

15.2.11 Frequently Asked Questions (FAQs)

A collection of questions and answers provided by NeXTSTEP users is posted on many FTP archive sites named FAQs. FAQs are also available on UseNet News. FAQs are a collection of ASCII documents that can be read using Edit, WriteNow, WordPerfect, or any other word or text processor, and are divided by subject. FAQs exist for programming languages, compatibility, peripherals, memory, printing, upgrades, utilities, and more. Using Digital Librarian, you can index the FAQ folder and search for particular topics of interest. FAQs are maintained by volunteers who make every effort to provide accurate information. However, there is no guarantee that this information is correct or current. If in doubt, verify the information with a second source. FAQs are provided as a service to the NEXTSTEP user community for the NEXTSTEP user community. If you have comments or suggestion for information that you would like to see included in future FAQs, contact the FAQ moderators whose names and e-mail addresses appear at the end of each FAQ document.

15.2.12 On-Line Technical Documents

Other technical documents can also be found at Internet archives. Part of the fun of using the Internet is the joy of finding hidden treasures like these. Don't be discouraged if it seems difficult to find and transfer items from the Internet, it is a skill that takes time to develop. For practice, search the Internet using the information provided in "Appendix B: Internet Archive Sites" for a copy of the most recent FAQs. If you find anything else that looks interesting, transfer it to your machine too. Be careful—some items are not free. These are clearly marked, however, so read all of the **README** files you see. Because this Internet is not commercial, items you find are provided as is with no warranty, guarantee, or implied support. Browsing the Internet is very much like shopping antique stores. There is much available, most of which you might consider junk. However, if you are looking for something in particular and find it, you would probably say the work was worth the reward. Consider yourself fortunate if for every ten files you transfer from the Internet, you find one or two worth keeping.

15.2.13 Shareware and Public Domain

Internet archives contain more than just technical documents; they also contain many shareware and public domain applications, demonstration applications, utilities, fonts, images, sample code, and more. You use the same procedure to transfer applications using FTP as you do to transfer documents. You should be aware of the legal issues regarding the use of these resources before you download them to your computer. An item placed in the public domain is provided at no charge. You can use and distribute it without cost but you cannot claim it for your own. Shareware items can be used freely for a specified period of time, but if you continue using the software after the time period expires, you are obligated to send the author a (usually) small fee. How do you know if an item is in the public domain or shareware? It's the responsibility of the author to clearly identify items as shareware, and it's illegal for anyone to remove this notification. Most authors indicate that their work is shareware in attached **README** files, Info panels, or Help panels. If you don't see a copyright notice, trademark, or shareware notice, you can generally assume the item is in the public domain and free to use. In the even that the item has not been placed in the public domain, but is available on the Internet, you are still liable. Once in a while commercial software finds its way onto the Internet, but just because it's easy to copy does not mean it is free. Read the notices included with the software carefully.

Shareware is an affordable method of distribution used by many private programmers who cannot afford to market their work commercially or perhaps through good will want to make their applications widely available. The shareware system allows you to try software before you buy it. This is great if you can't afford to purchase nonrefundable software, which may end up not suiting your needs. Many shareware products become so popular that they are developed into commercial products with advanced features, regular updates, and complete documentation. Supporting the shareware concept by sending in your fee benefits everyone by providing incentive to programmers, inexpensive software, and the ability to try before you buy. Pay for shareware you continue to use.

15.3 User Groups

Over 430 NeXT User Groups, or NUGs, as they are known, exist across the globe in over 25 countries including Australia, Brazil, Canada, Germany, Japan, Rumania, Russia, Sweden, and the U.S, and constitute over 20,000

NEXTSTEP users. An umbrella organization named NoIR, the NeXT Organizations InteRnational is responsible for encouraging the growth and creation of user groups worldwide. NoIR also represents user groups and serves to bring user group issues and concerns to NeXT for action. To contact NoIR, send Internet mail to Dan Lavin at **dlavin@nextworld.com**.

If you want to get connected with the NeXT user culture, user group membership is definitely the best method. User groups can greatly assist you no matter what your skill level. If there is one near you, by all means join it. The small annual dues required by most user groups are more than worth the information, camaraderie, and encouragement you will receive.

User groups generally meet once each month at locations such as libraries, churches, and schools. Vendors often demonstrate their hardware and software, and NEXTSTEP tips and tricks are passed among members. You can also get copies of public domain software and obtain discounts on applications and peripherals.

Because new user groups are continually forming, contact NeXT at 1-800-848-NeXT, or send electronic mail to **user_groups@next.com** to obtain the most up to date information about the user groups in your area. If you are interested in forming a user group, ask to speak with Conrad Geiger, the NeXT User Group liaison.

15.4 Conferences and User Training

15.4.0 NeXTWORLD Exposition

In January of 1992, NeXT, *NeXTWORLD* magazine, and WorldExpo, Inc., presented the first annual NeXTWORLD Expo. The three-day conference consisted of two days of vendor exhibits, two days of user conferences, a one-day user group meeting, and a three-day developer conference in Moscone Center in San Francisco, California. This continuing event is the premiere gathering of NeXT users, developers, product distributors, and NeXT employees from all around the world.

Admission to the exhibits only is $25, $40 on-site registration. The user conference costs $195, $245 on-site, and the cost of the developer conference is $695, $745 on-site. NeXTWORLD Expo is presented once each calendar year. Contact NeXT at 1-800-848-NeXT for information about future NeXTWORLD expositions.

15.4.1 Training Courses

NeXT relies heavily on its partners to provide training to users and administrators, but also offers courses of its own. These seminars are taught by NeXT in Redwood City, California and Chicago, Illinois, and discuss how to use and configure NEXTSTEP systems. If you can afford the cost of admission, travel, and a stay in a local hotel, this is an excellent opportunity to learn about NEXTSTEP computing from the experts.

To register or obtain more information about these and other classes, contact NeXT at 1-800-848-NeXT and select option 2 for training. When calling from outside the U.S., dial +1-415-780-3707.

Table 15-4 NeXT Training Courses

Title	Description	Days	Cost
Introducing NEXTSTEP	A workshop for technical evaluators and programmers introducing the user and developer environment.	5	$1,500
Programming NEXTSTEP	An introduction to the tools and techniques for developing applications from scratch. Intended for application developers of all kinds.	5	$1,800
Programming Database Kit	An introduction to the architecture and features of the Database Kit and enable students to write applications to retrieve and display information from databases.	2	$1,100

Table 15-4 NeXT Training Courses (continued)

Title	Description	Days	Cost
Advanced NEXTSTEP	A workshop describing advanced programming techniques. Prerequisite: Programming NEXTSTEP.	5	$1,800
Configuring NEXTSTEP Systems	An introduction to hardware assembly and configuration techniques and the installation of NEXTSTEP.	2	$500
NEXTSTEP Administration	A workshop to provide information for planning, configuring, and maintaining systems in a NEXTSTEP network.	4.5	$1,500
Fast-track System Administration	A workshop that provides system administration information and experience specifically related to NEXTSTEP-specific system software.	3	$900

15.4.2 Where to Find NEXTSTEP Products

AppWrapper

The AppWrapper is a catalog of NeXTSTEP products, printed quarterly by Paget Press. It contains advertisements and product descriptions of over 500 items, and includes a CD-ROM containing demonstrations of many of the applications described in the catalog. You can purchase products by mail and can license software contained on the CD-ROM by phone. Subscriptions to the AppWrapper cost $36 per year within the U.S., and $50 per year outside the U.S.

Paget Press, Inc.
2125 Western Avenue, Suite 300
Seattle, WA 98121-2136
206-448-0845
Internet mail: **eaw@paget.com**

Font Hotline

To purchase fonts prepared especially for NEXTSTEP, call the Font Hotline run by RightBrain Software at 800-525-FONT. If you live outside the United States, you can write to order from RightBrain Software

RightBrain Software
132 Hamilton Avenue
Palo Alto, CA 94301
USA
1-800-525-FONT

NeXT Authorized Dealers

NEXTSTEP can be purchased through university bookstores (if you are affiliated with a university), through independent dealers, and from NeXT itself. Dealers offer you the best opportunity to learn about NeXT and NeXT-related products, as their responsibility is to provide information, training, and post-sale support. Many users groups are associated with dealers that provide them a place to meet and equipment to use in exchange for assistance for their customers. Look in the phone book for your NeXT authorized dealer, or call NeXT at 1-800-848-NeXT.

NeXTConnection

If you are unable to find a NeXT software retailer in your vicinity, you can call NeXTConnection, a mail-order catalog warehouse of NeXT-related products. You can call NeXTConnection to order, or to request a free catalog of products.

NeXTConnection
9 Mill Street
Marlow, NH 03456
800-800-NeXT or 603-446-7771
Fax 603-446-7791
Internet: **nextconnection@nextconn.com**

Reference

Appendix A:
Supported Printers

NEXTSTEP supports a wide variety of printers and is constantly adding support for new and existing printer models. The list provided on the following pages reflects the printers supported at the time of this writing. If you don't see a particular printer in this table call NeXT at 1-800-848-NeXT or the printer manufacturer to see if one is available. Remember that if you choose to use a non-PostScript printer, you'll need to license it's use of NEXTSTEP's built-in PostScript. This license can be purchased directly from NeXT for about $75.

Appendix A

Table A-1 Printers Supported in NEXTSTEP 3.1

Manufacturer	Printer Model
Agfa	Compugraphic 9400P Matrix ChromaScript TabScript C500 PostScript Printer
Apple	LaserWriter LaserWriter II NT LaserWriter II NTX LaserWriter II NTX v51.8 LaserWriter II NTX-J v50.5 LaserWriter IIf LaserWriter IIg LaserWriter Personal NT LaserWriter Plus LaserWriter Plus v42.2 Personal LaserWriter NTR
APS	PS PIP with APS-6-108 PS PIP with APS-6-80 PS PIP with LZR 1200 PS PIP with LZR 2600
AST	TurboLaser-PS
Canon	LBP-4 PS-2 LBP-8IIIR PS-1 LBP-8IIIT PS-1 LBP-8III PS-1 PS-IPU Color Laser Copier PS-IPU Kanji Color Laser Copier
Colormate	PS
Compaq	Pagemarq 15 Pagemarq 20

Table A-1 Printers Supported in NEXTSTEP 3.1 (continued)

Manufacturer	Printer Model
Dataproducts	LZR-2665 LZR 1260 LZR 1560 LZR 960
Digital	DEClaser 1150 DEClaser 2150 DEClaser 2250 PrintServer 20 PrintServer 40 Plus
Epson	EPL-7500 LP-3000PS F2 LP-3000PS F5 PostScript CARD 510/NeXT
Fujitsu	RX7100PS
GCC	BLP Elite BLP II BLP IIS Business LaserPrinter
Gestetner	GLP800-Scout
Hewlett-Packard (HP)	LaserJet IID PostScript Cartridge LaserJet III PostScript Cartridge LaserJet III PostScript Plus LaserJet IIID PostScript Cartridge LaserJet IIID PostScript Plus LaserJet IIIP PostScript Cartridge LaserJet IIP PostScript Plus LaserJet IIISi PostScript LaserJet IIP PostScript Cartridge LaserJet 4 PostScript Cartridge PaintJet XL300

Appendix A

Table A-1 Printers Supported in NEXTSTEP 3.1 (continued)

Manufacturer	Printer Model
IBM	4019, 17 fonts 4019, 39 fonts 4029, 18 Fonts 4029, 39 Fonts 4216-020 4216-030 ProPrinter 24P/NeXT
Linotronic	100 200 200 v49.3 300 300 v49.3 330-RIP 30 330 500 530-RIP 30 530 630
Monotype	ImageMaster 1200 Imagesetter
NEC	Colormate PS/40 Colormate PS/80 SilentWriter 95 Silentwriter2 990
NeXT	400 dpi Level II Printer NeXT Color Printer
Océ	Color G5242 PostScript Printer
OKI	MICROLINE 801PS+F OL830-PS OL840-PS
Panasonic	KX-P4455

Table A-1 **Printers Supported in NEXTSTEP 3.1 (continued)**

Manufacturer	Printer Model
QMS	ColorScript 100 ColorScript 100 Model 10 ColorScript 100 Model 20 ColorScript 100 Model 30 PS Jet PS Jet Plus PS 1700 PS 2000 PS 2200 PS 2210 PS 2220 PS 410 PS 800 PS 800 Plus PS 810 PS 810 Turbo PS 815 PS 815 MR PS 820 PS 820 Turbo PS 825 PS 825 MR
Qume	ScripTEN
Ricoh	PC Laser 6000-PS
Scantext	2030-51
Schlumberger	5232 Color PostScript Printer
Shinko	Color CHC-746PSJ PostScript Printer
Silentwriter	2, Model 290 2, Model 90 LC 890 LC 890XL

Table A-1 **Printers Supported in NEXTSTEP 3.1 (continued)**

Manufacturer	Printer Model
Texas Instruments	2115 13 fonts 2115 35 fonts OmniLaser 2108 microLaser16 Turbo microLaser6 Turbo microLaser9 Turbo microLaser PS17 microLaser PS35 microLaser XL PS17 microLaser XL PS35
Tektronix	Phaser III PXi Phaser III PXiJ Phaser II PXe with 17 fonts Phaser II PXe with 39 fonts Phaser II PXi Phaser II PXiJ Phaser IISD Phaser 200e Phaser 200i
Unisys	AP9210 17 Fonts AP9210 39 Fonts AP9415
Varityper	4200B-P 4300P Series 4000-5300 Series 4000-5330 Series 4000-5500 VT-600P VT-600W VT4510-A VT4990 4000-L300 4000-L330 4000-L500 4000-L530

Table A-1 **Printers Supported in NEXTSTEP 3.1 (continued)**

Manufacturer	Printer Model
VT4	53EA
	53EB
	530A
	530B
	530C
	533B
	533C
	550A
	550B
	550C
	551A
	563A
	563B
Xerox	DocuTech 135
	DocuTech 85
	DocuTech 90

Appendix B:
Internet Archive Sites

The following Internet archive sites provide public access to NeXT-related files accessible using FTP on a computer connected to the Internet. If you have a computer connected to the Internet, you may be able to access and download files stored at these sites. This list is only a starting point—there are thousands of archive sites. Unfortunately, because sites are added and removed often., this list includes only sites which are well-known and stable. For other sites, search the Purdue archive in **/pub/next/ARCHIVES**.

Appendix B

Primary NEXTSTEP Archives — Directory

cs.orst.edu	pub/next
etlport.etl.go.jp	
otter.stanford.edu	(mathematica)
pellns.alleg.edu	pub (academic apps)
sonata.cc.purdue.edu	pub/next
src.doc.ic.ac.uk	

European NEXTSTEP Archives — Directory

atlas.physchem.chemie.uni-tuebingen.de	
fiasko.rz-berlin.mpg.de	
ftp.informatik.uni-muenchen.de	/pub/next
rusvm1.rus.uni-stuttgart.de	/pub/next

Other NEXTSTEP Archives — Directory

aeneas.mit.edu	
akbar.cac.washington.edu	
archive.umich.edu	
astro.princeton.edu	pub/rtf2TeX.tar.Z
athena-dist.mit.edu	(XNeXT, athena)
boombox.micro.umn.edu	pub/gopher/NeXT
budapest.math.macalstr.edu	
calvin.stanford.edu	NeXT and pub/Khoros
cameron.egr.duke.edu	pub/NeXT
ccrma-ftp.stanford.edu	
ftp.cica.indiana.edu	
coyote.cs.wmich.edu	pub/NeXT
cs.orst.edu	pub/next
cs.ubc.ca	tmp/NeXT
csus.edu	pub/NeXT/sounds
dagon.acc.stolaf.edu	
dehn.mth.pdx.edu	
ee.uta.edu	
eesun1.arl.utexas.edu	public/NeXT
emx.utexas.edu	pub/next
etlport.etl.go.jp	

Other NEXTSTEP Archives (continued) — Directory

Site	Directory
f.ms.uky.edu	pub/next
fiasko.rz-berlin.mpg.de	
forwiss.uni-passau.de	pub/next
ftp.byu.edu	
ftphost.cac.washington.edu	
ftp.informatik.uni-muenchen.de	pub/next
ftp.ncsa.uiuc.edu	
ftp.uni-kl.de	pub/next
greyrock.mso.colostate.edu	
heplib.slac.stanford.edu	
iesd.auc.dk	pub/next
isca.uiowa.edu	
iuvax.cs.indiana.edu	pub/graphs/NeXT
java.cc.mcgill.ca	pub/NeXT
j.cc.purdue.edu	
kalikka.jyu.fi	pub/next
math.utexas.edu	pub/next
media-lab.media.mit.edu	pub/next
midway.uchicago.edu	pub/NeXT
mrcnext.cso.uiuc.edu	
ncar.ucar.edu	ncarg/unix3.01/NeXT
nic.funet.fi	pub/next
nic.stolaf.edu	pub/ps
nisca.acs.ohio-state.edu	pub/next
nova.cc.purdue.edu	pub/next
nugget.rmnug.org	pub/NeXT
otter.stanford.edu	
peanuts.pst.informatik.uni-muenchen.de	pub/next
plethora.media.mit.edu	pub/next
prep.ai.mit.edu	pub/gnuprinceton.edu
ronin.css.itd.umich.edu	pub/next
roxette.mty.itesm.mx	pub/next
sachiko.acc.stolaf.edu	
saqqara.cis.ohio-state.edu	next
slc2.ins.cwru.edu	pub/next
snekkar.ens.fr	pub/next
solaria.cc.gatech.edu	pub/next

Other NEXTSTEP Archives (continued) — Directory

Host	Directory
sonata.cc.purdue.edu	pub/next
spinner.gac.edu	pub/next
src.doc.ic.ac.uk	next
sumex.stanford.edu	pub
sutro.sfsu.edu	pub
ucbvax.berkeley.edu	pub/tiff
uhunix2.uhcc.hawaii.edu	pub/next
umaxc.weeg.uiowa.edu	pub/next
umd5.umd.edu	NeXT
unmvax.cs.unm.edu	
uvaarpa.acc.virginia.edu	
venera.isi.edu	
yak.macc.wisc.edu	pub/kermit
zaphod.ncsa.uiuc.edu	misc/file.formats/graphics.formats

Appendix C:
Buried Treasures

NEXTSTEP includes many interesting items that are often overlooked because they are either buried deep within the file system or in the **/Next-Developer** folder where you may not think to look. There are also many useful applications available on the Internet at various FTP archive sites. This section describes a few of the more interesting and useful treasures you can find hidden in the NEXTSTEP user environment and on the Internet. For your convenience, you'll find some of the applications discussed in this chapter on the floppy disk included with this book.

Archie

The Internet connects several hundred thousand computers across the world so finding a particular file on the Internet is like finding the proverbial needle in a haystack. But, there are so many useful things to be found on the Internet, several special network servers, called Archie (short for Archive) servers have been created to assist users in finding the files they are looking for. To make use an Archie server, you'll want to get a copy of Archie from one of the NeXT-related archive sites. Archie is a public

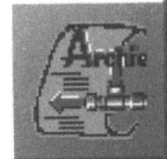

Appendix C

domain NEXTSTEP application available on the Internet, which works only on NeXT computers. If you have a NeXT computer attached to the Internet, you can use Archie to find a list of archive sites that contain a file you are looking for and then transfer the file from those sites using Archie, FTP or GatorFTP.

After starting Archie, choose Preferences from the Info menu. In the Preferences panel that appears, select an appropriate Archie server, or if you have an archive server specific to your institution, enter its Internet address in the Custom Host Field (see figure below). Click Save to save the settings and close the Preferences panel.

The Archie Preferences

Use the Preferences panel to indicate which archive server you want Archie to use when locating items on the Internet. Click Save to save the new settings.

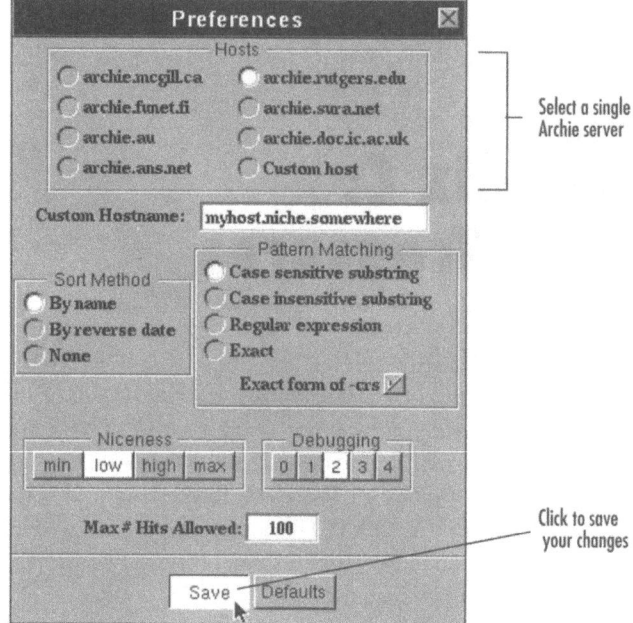

To begin a search, called a query, enter the name of the file you are looking for in the Query String field, and click Query in the Archie window. The Archie Query panel will appear indicating the status of the search. Because of the large number of Internet hosts and files they contain, the search may take several minutes. Feel free to continue working on another project as Archie searches the for the file. It will continue its search even when hidden or in the background of the workspace. When Archie has finished its search, it lists the names of every host known to have a file matching the name you entered in the Archie panel, up to the "maximum number of hits allowed" setting in the Preferences panel. To examine the location of the file or retrieve it from a host, select the file in the Archie panel browser. When you select the file, detailed information about that file will appear in the lower half of the Archie panel.

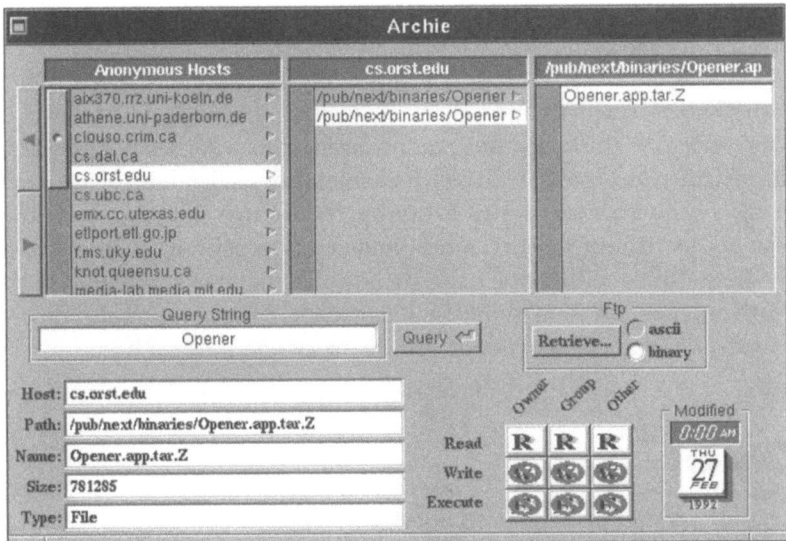

Using Archie

To find a file on the Internet, enter part or all of its name and click Query. If the search is successful, a list of hosts will appear in the Archie panel (top). To retrieve a file, select it in the Archie browser and click Retrieve. The Archie FTP Progress panel (bottom) will appear so you can monitor the progress of the transfer.

Archie is not only able to help you find a file, but also to transfer it to your computer. To transfer a file, select it in the Archie panel browser and click Retrieve. The Archie FTP Progress panel will appear and display the status of the file transfer. Some anonymous FTP sites require you to enter your complete Internet address as a password. If this is the case, Archie may not be able to log into the FTP archive and begin the file transfer. You can solve the problem by entering your complete Internet address using the Set Login command in Archie's Info menu. For example, you would enter

Appendix C

robert@dogpound.tsm.com instead of **robert@dogpound**. You only have to enter this once. Archie will remember it even if you log out or turn off the computer. By default, Archie will transfer the file from the remote host to your home folder. If you want Archie to transfer the file to a particular folder, choose Set Local Dir in the Archie menu and select the appropriate folder. You'll have to reset this each time you use Archie, or transferred files will appear in your home folder.

Sometimes Archie will find a directory instead of a file that matches your query string. In this case, the contents of the directory may not appear in the Archie panel browser. To see the contents of such a directory, select it in the Archie browser and click Listing. Notice that the Retrieve button changes its name to Listing when a directory is selected in the Archie browser. Archie will contact the host to determine the contents of the directory, then list them in the Archie browser. You can repeat this process as many times as necessary to browse directories on Internet hosts.

Clip Art

Euphonium

Clip art isn't an application, but a buried treasure. The Digital Webster application includes with some of its definitions, pictures that you can use in your own documents. For example, define the following words using Digital Webster: *afghan hound, manual alphabet, turban, torii, wormfence,* and *zebu.* Each of these definitions includes a picture. Digital Webster stores these pictures in the **/NextLibrary/References/Webster-Dictionary/Pictures** folder. If you want to use them in a document, just drag or import the appropriate TIFF or EPS file containing the image you want into your document. Even if you don't find these images useful, they are certainly fun to look at.

Digit

On the floppy disk included with this book, you'll find a wonderful scientific calculator named Digit. This calculator application was written by Mark G. Tacchi and is provided for free. You can use Digit just as you would a typical hand-held pocket calculator. Digit features many scientific functions, works in degrees and radians, octal, decimal, hexadecimal, and binary too. If you find Digit useful and use it often, you may want to place it in your dock and have it start automatically each time you log in.

Buried Treasures

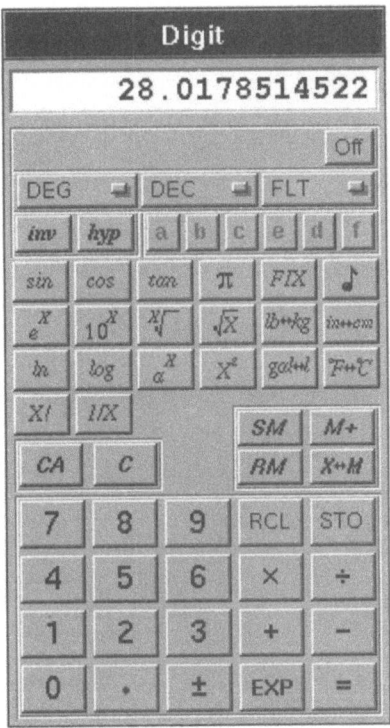

Digit

Digit simulates a typical hand-held scientific calculator. You can even copy and paste the contents of its display into other applications

BackSpace Screen Saver

The NEXTSTEP developer environment includes a very entertaining screen saver named BackSpace. BackSpace is used to display animated images after a period of inactivity to prevent a single image from burning itself into the screen. It's not only a screen-saver, it can also play while you work, replacing the workspace background color with its animation. Back-Space is very popular among NEXTSTEP users because it's easily customized to display new and entertaining images.

BackSpace can be found in the **/NextDeveloper/Examples/AppKit** folder of the developer environment, but the original code can be freely distributed and compiled into an application, so have a friend compile it for you or keep an eye out for it on the Internet. It can also be found on the CD-ROMs described on page 370. The illustration below shows what some of the BackSpace modules look like.

Appendix C

The BackSpace Screen Saver

When Backspace is running and there has been a period of inactivity, it will display an animated image to prevent the screen from being burned-in with a particular image. To continue working, press any key or drag the mouse. Three of the customizable BackSpace modules are shown in this figure: Bezier (top left), World Space (top right), and Boink (bottom right). To select a particular module, click its name in the BackSpace Settings panel (bottom left).

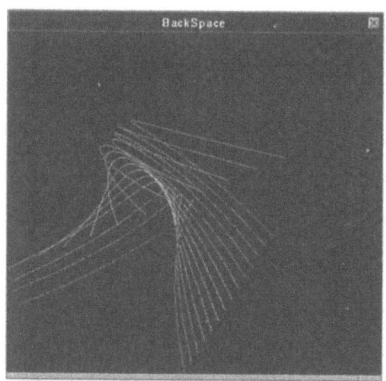

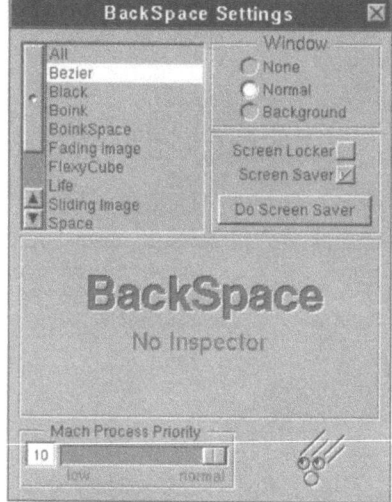
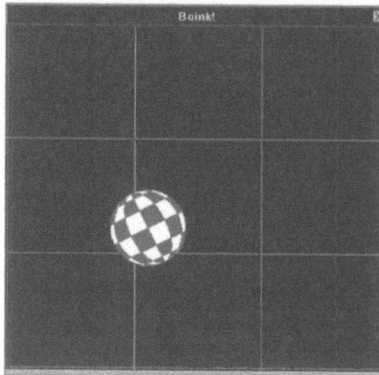

ImageViewer

ImageViewer isn't included as part of NEXTSTEP, but it's so useful that it deserves special mention. When the NEXTSTEP Inspector cannot display a thumbnail of an image, you can use this public domain application to view it. ImageViewer is available from many NeXT-related FTP archives and CD-ROMs. With ImageViewer you can open and display image files in numerous image formats, including those used on other computer systems. To open an image file, double-click the ImageViewer application icon to start it, then choose Open from the Image menu. You can also convert the image to another format using the Save As command in the File menu.

Buried Treasures

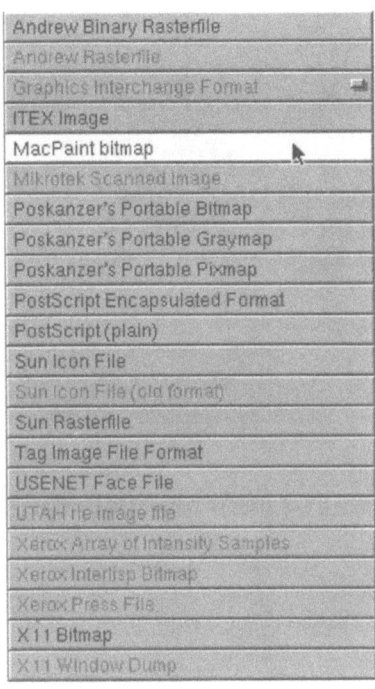

Image Viewer File Formats

ImageViewer is capable of reading many image file formats used on NeXT systems and many others. Some of the more popular file formats include Mac-Paint (Macintosh), SUN Rasterfile, TIFF, and GIF.

Opener

Opener is able to compress and decompress files using various compression formats. What makes Opener wonderful is that it supports compression formats on DOS, Macintosh, and other systems as well as those used in NEXTSTEP. Opener is a public domain application available on the Internet, but unfortunately, only runs on NeXT computers.

To compress a file using Opener, start Opener, and drag the file or files onto the Opener icon. A panel will appear in which you can choose the type of compression you would like to use. Select the compression scheme from the pop-up list and click okay (see figure below). Opener will create a new compressed file containing the items you dropped onto its icon. When it's finished, an attention panel will appear to inform you of the pathname of the compressed file. Opener usually stores its files in **/tmp**. To save the compressed file, drag it to a floppy disk icon or into your home folder.

Appendix C

Opener Compression

To compress files using Opener, drag a file, folder, or multiple file icon onto a running Opener icon. Opener will display this panel so you can select a compression method.

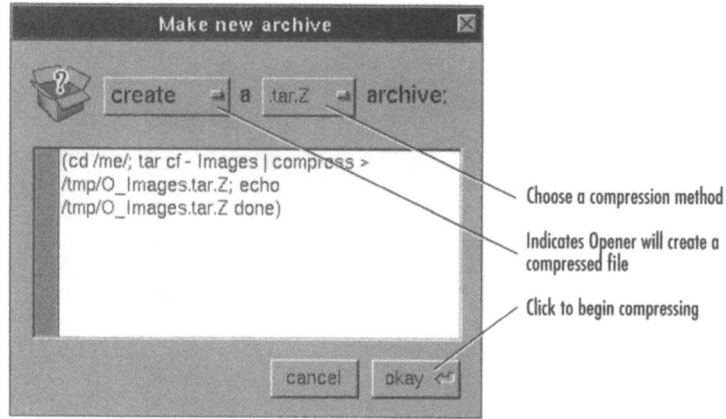

Choose a compression method

Indicates Opener will create a compressed file

Click to begin compressing

Table C-1 Formats Supported by Opener

Platform	File Formats Supported
All	PS
DOS	arc, zip, zoo
Macintosh	bin, hqx, sit
UNIX	lzh, shar, tar, uu, Z

To decompress a file using Opener, choose Open from the File menu and select the file you want to decompress. Opener will begin decompressing in the background so you can continue working. If Opener is able, when the file has been decompressed, it will automatically open an application and display the file. If not, Opener will display the file in a new File Viewer instead. If you want to save the decompressed file, choose the Save command from the application in which it was opened, or drag the file from the File Viewer into your home folder. You can also decompress files when you double-click them using the Tools Inspector as described in "Tools Inspector" on page 95.

TeX

Unless you are looking for it, you probably won't notice that TeX is included with NeXTSTEP. TeX, pronounced "tek", was designed by Donald E. Knuth of Stanford University to prepare documents for typesetting. In particular, TeX was designed so that it could easily typeset complex mathematical equations. Since its inception, TeX has become very popular with scientists, mathematicians, engineers, and researchers. If you are required to submit documents in TeX format, or read TeX documents from others, you will find NeXT's implementation of TeX very familiar yet easier to use.

In general, you will create text documents in ASCII format that contain TeX commands. You can then use TeX to read the file, interpret the commands, and produces an output file containing only formatted text. While TeX is not capable of many of the complicated formatting of today's Desktop Publishing (DTP) systems, it does surpass them in certain areas. TeX is significantly better at formatting mathematical equations, handling ligatures and kerning, and is excellent at determining automatic page and line breaks. One of TeX's greatest advantages is that it supports numerous fonts, and that its output files are device independent. For this reason, TeX's output files are called DVI files. (DVI stands for device independent.) Because the file is device independent, the document will appear the same whether printed on a dot-matrix printer, laser printer or typesetting machine.

TeX is contained in a package on the NEXTSTEP user environment CD-ROM. You can find it in the **/NeXTCD/Packages** folder. To install it, you'll need to log in as the root user, then double-click it to start the Installer program. TeX is about 5.5 MB when compressed, and uses about 10.4 MB when it is installed. After installing TeX, you'll notice a new application in **/NextDeveloper/Demos** named TeXview. Using this application you can read, write, and edit DVI files, and can easily convert them to PostScript format.

A document is available on-line to help you learn how to use TeXview, but not TeX itself, nor METAFONT, an integral part of TeX. To read the on-line documentation for TeXview, conveniently formatted using TeX, choose View Manual from TeXview's Info menu. You can print it (about 120 pages) using the usual Print command in the main menu. To learn more about TeX or METAFONT, refer to the TeX Book and the METAFONT Book, by Donald E. Knuth, published by Addison-Wesley.

Appendix D:
Hardware Compatibility

NEXTSTEP was originally designed to run on very specific hardware configurations manufactured by NeXT. However, with the release of NEXTSTEP for Intel Processors, many different models can now be used to run NEXTSTEP. However, not every combination will work. This appendix presents a preliminary list of hardware compatible with NEXTSTEP for Intel Processors and is based on a prerelease document provided by NeXT. First, you will find a general description of the types of hardware and peripherals compatible with NEXTSTEP for Intel Processors, followed by charts describing specific configurations.

NeXT and third-party manufactures are constantly adding new and existing hardware support to NEXTSTEP so you can choose from the widest possible range of products. In fact, the NEXTSTEP Hardware Compatibility Guide is updated every two weeks! If you don't see an item you are looking for in the list, contact NeXT or the manufacturer of the hardware to find out about NEXTSTEP compatibility. NeXT is also happy to provide you with their most current version of the *NEXTSTEP for Intel Processors Hardware Compatibility Guide*. Calling them toll-free at 1-800-848-NeXT. If you prefer, you can have the information sent to you immediately by fax or electronic mail using the NeXTanswers information service as described in "NeXTanswers" on page 370.

Central Processors

Personal computers are differentiated primarily by their central processing unit (CPU). NEXTSTEP for Intel Processors, as its name implies, requires a PC that uses an Intel 80486 CPU. This includes 486SX, 486DX, and 486DX/2 CPU models. Intel 486DX and 486DX/2 CPUs are recommended for better performance. NEXTSTEP 486 uses several 486 specific features that enhance the performance of NEXTSTEP. NEXTSTEP 486 will *not* run on 386 machines, nor will it run on the Cyrix 486SLC based system because it is not a true 80486. However, as new CPUs are developed by Intel, NEXTSTEP 486 will not only support them, but will also take advantage of their performance enhancements.

Hard Disk Storage

The NEXTSTEP user environment requires a minimum of 120 MB of hard disk storage. For the developer environment, you'll need a 330 MB or larger hard disk. The two editions are additive. To use the developer environment, you'll first need to install the user environment. Larger disks are recommended for standalone systems, because they cannot share files from a central file server.

Graphics

NEXTSTEP for Intel Processors also uses the Display Postscript system and can be used with both monochrome and color monitors. For 2-bit (four-shade) grayscale support, such as that provided on NeXTcube and NeXTstation Monochrome systems, the PC can use most VESA (Video Electronics Standards Association)-compatible VGA or Super VGA graphics adapter cards, including super VGA cards from manufactures such as Orchid, ATI, Paradise, Video Seven, and Compaq. These graphics adapters are supported at resolutions of 640x480, 800x600, and 1024x768. Resolutions at or above 800x600 are recommended for optimal display. Grayscale systems must also include at least 8 MB of RAM, with 12 MB or more highly recommended.

For 16-bit (65,536 colors) color support, a PC will require a high performance workstation-style graphics adapter. Many new graphics systems are being introduced that meet these requirements, including Intel JAWS (such as DeLL Processor-Direct Graphics), Chips and Technologies Wing-ine, and certain Local Bus Graphics adapters. Depending upon the size of available VRAM (video RAM), resolutions of 800x600, 1024x768, 1120x832, and 1280x1024 will be supported. To maintain performance, at least 16 MB of RAM must be installed in a color system, but 24 MB or more is highly recommended.

Disk Interface

NeXT computers have always utilized a SCSI bus to connect peripherals such as scanners, CD-ROM drives, and hard disks. However, because few PCs have a SCSI bus built into them, they require a SCSI adapter. PCs running NEXTSTEP for Intel Processors can use either IDE and SCSI hard disk interfaces or both. SCSI adapters from Adaptec and DPT (for both ISA and EISA) are supported. Support for others will be added in the future.

Pointing Devices

Another integral feature of a computer running NEXTSTEP is a pointing device. This has traditionally been a mouse, but can include other devices too. Microsoft and Logitec bus-compatible mice are supported as are PS/2 port and serial mice. Graphics tablets are also supported.

Printer Support

NEXTSTEP boasts support for numerous printer models, listed in Appendix A. Support of only a few non-PostScript printers is included in the initial release of NEXTSTEP for Intel Processors, but more may supported in a future release.

Networking Support

ISA and EISA-based network adapter cards are compatible with NEXTSTEP for Intel Processors, including Ethernet and Token Ring Cards from vendors such as SMC (Western Digital), Intel, and 3Com. A network adapter card is required only if the PC will be networked to other computers. A network adapter is not required on standalone systems.

Sound Support

Most popular PC sound cards will be supported for both playback and recording. These include PC sound adapters, such as the Sound Blaster, MediaVision Pro Audio Spectrum, and Integrated Business Audio from Compaq. A sound card is not required.

Certified Hardware

NeXT has certified particular PC system configurations to works with NEXTSTEP for Intel Processors, and will continue to do so for numerous others with each new release of NEXTSTEP. Several agreements have been signed by NeXT and hardware manufacturers, such as Compaq, DeLL, Data General, Epson, Hewlett-Packard, NEC, and Siemens, to manufacture NEXTSTEP-compatible hardware and in some cases, provide NEXTSTEP preloaded and ready to run on these machines right out of the box. NeXT will soon be porting NEXTSTEP to Hewlett-Packard's RISC-based Progression Architecture (PA) workstations. Many of these systems have yet to be announced at the time of this writing, but a smaller list of computer systems has been published by NeXT. The tables at the end of this appendix describe some of the system configurations that are known to work upon the initial release of NEXTSTEP for Intel Processors. Remember that the list of compatible hardware is updated every two weeks. There may also be other combinations of equipment that will work with NEXTSTEP for Intel Processors, but aren't yet certified.

Hardware Compatibility

Desktop Systems

System Vendor	Model	Expansion Bus	CPU Speed	Graphics Architecture	Notes	16bit Color Graphics Resolution 800x600	16bit Color Graphics Resolution 1024x768	16bit Color Graphics Resolution 1120x832	2bit Grayscale Graphics Resolution 640x480	2bit Grayscale Graphics Resolution 800x600	2bit Grayscale Graphics Resolution 1024x768
					Color Desktop Systems require 16MB RAM and 120MB Hard Disk Min						
Compaq	Deskpro 33M	EISA	33	Add-on QVision	Requires Compaq QVision 1024/E	■					
Compaq	Deskpro 50M	EISA	50	inc. QVision	Requires Compaq QVision 1024/E	■					
Compaq	Deskpro 50L	EISA	50	Add-on QVision	Requires Compaq QVision 1024/E	■					
Compaq	Deskpro 66M	EISA	66	inc. QVision	Requires Compaq QVision 1024/E	■	■				
DELL	DE/2 DGX	EISA	50	JAWS			■				
DELL	ME Series	EISA	50,66	Add-on EISA Card	Requires Compaq QVision 1024/E or ATI Graphics Ultra Pro EISA Version with 2MB VRAM	■	■				
Epson	Progression	ISA	25,33,66	Wingine	1MB VRAM Version supports 800x600, 2MB VRAM Version Supports 1024x768	■					
Gateway	486/50,66V	ISA	50,66	VL-Bus ATI Mach 32	Requires 2MB VRAM	■	■				
Intel	GX/Professional Workstation	EISA	33,50,66	LocalBus ATI Mach32	Requires Hi-Res RAMDAC and 2MB VRAM	■	■	■			
Lucky Goldstar	LG 486NX	ISA	50, 66	Wingine		■					
NEC	PowerMate Express DX2/50,66e	EISA	50,66	Add-on EISA Card	Requires Compaq QVision 1024/E or ATI Graphics Ultra Pro EISA Version with 2MB VRAM	■	■				

Appendix D

							16bit Color Graphics Resolution		2bit Grayscale Graphics Resolution		
	System Vendor	Model	Max Disk / RAM	CPU	Display	Notes	800x 600	1024x 768	1120x 832	640 x480	800x 600	1024x 768
AC Powered Portables		Model	Max Disk / RAM	CPU	Display	All Portables require 8MB RAM and 120MB Hard Disk Min. A SCSI adapter and SCSI CD-ROM are required to install NeXTSTEP						
	Compaq	486M/33	200 / 32	33 DX	1MB VGA							
		486C/33	200 / 32	33 DX	1MB Color VGA							
		486M/66	525 / 32	66 DX2	1MB Color VGA							
		486C/66	525 / 32	66 DX2	1MB Color VGA							
	Toshiba	T6400DX	200 / 36	33 DX	1MB Color VGA							
		T6400DXC	200 / 36	33 DX	1MB Color VGA							
	NEC	Prospeed 486C	200 / 20	25 SX	1MB Color VGA	Floating Point Processor recommended						
Battery Powered Portables	System Vendor	Model	Max Disk / RAM	CPU	Display	Battery Powered Portables require a Docking Station with SCSI adapter and SCSI CD-ROM to install NeXTSTEP						
	Altima	433D	160 / 20	33 DX	1MB VGA							
	Compaq	LTE Lite 4/25C	210 / 20	25 SL	1MB VGA							
	Toshiba	T4400SX	120 / 20	25 SX	1MB VGA	Floating Point Processor recommended						
		T4400SXC	120 / 20	25 SX	1MB VGA	Floating Point Processor recommended						
		T4400C	200 / 20	25 DX	1MB VGA							

Hardware Compatibility

Category	Interface	Bus	Vendor	Model	Cache	Notes	16bit Color Graphics Resolution 800x 600	16bit Color Graphics Resolution 1024x 768	16bit Color Graphics Resolution 1120x 832	2bit Grayscale Graphics Resolution 640 x480	2bit Grayscale Graphics Resolution 800x 600	2bit Grayscale Graphics Resolution 1024x 768
Hard Disk Controllers	IDE					Systems with IDE Hard Drives will require a SCSI Interface and SCSI CDROM drive for the initial installation of NeXTSTEP.						
	SCSI	ISA	Adaptec	1542B	No							
		EISA	DPT	2011B	512K-16M							
			DPT	2012B	512K-16M							
Local Area Network Adapters	Protocol	Bus	Vendor	Model								
	EtherNet	ISA	Intel	EtherExpress 16		Available with Twisted Pair or Thin Lan						
			SMC	Ethercard Plus Elite 16		Available with Twisted Pair, Thin Lan or both						
PC Sound Cards	Type	Bus	Vendor	Model								
	8 bit	ISA	MediaVision	ProAudio Spectrum Plus		Support will be available with an update disk shortly after Beta Release						
Pointing Devices	Type	Interface	Vendor	Model								
	Mice	PS/2	Microsoft	MS Mouse		Also Supports Microsoft Compatible PS/2 mice						
			Logitec	Mouse Man								
		Bus	Logitec	Mouse Man								
Misc Devices	Type	Interface	Vendor	Model	Notes							
	Interfaces	Serial				Support will be available with an update disk shortly after Beta Release						
Supported Printers	Type	Interface	Vendor	Model	Notes							
		SCSI	NeXT Color Printer									
	Interfaces	Serial	Adobe Postscript Level II Printers									
		Parallel	Adobe Postscript Level II Printers			Support will be available with an update disk shortly after Beta Release						

D-7

Appendix D

	Type	Interface	Architecture	Vendor	Model	Notes	16bit Color Graphics Resolution			2bit Grayscale Graphics Resolution		
							800x 600	1024x 768	1120x 832	640 x480	800x 600	1024x 768
Color Graphics Adapters	16 Bit Color Linear Frame Buffer	CPU Board	JAWS	Dell	DGX				■			
			C&T Wingine	Epson	Progression 1MB VRAM		■					
				Epson	Progression 2MB VRAM			■				
			LocalBus ATI Mach32	Lucky Goldstar	Wingine			■				
				Intel	GX / Professional		■					
		EISA	QVision	Compaq	QVision 1024/E 1 MB VRAM			■				
			ATI Mach32	ATI	Graphics Ultra Pro	Requires 2MB VRAM for 1024x768		■				
		VL-Bus	ATI Mach32	ATI	Graphics Ultra Pro	Requires 2MB VRAM for 1024x768		■				
	Type	Interface	Architecture	Vendor	Model							
Grayscale Graphics Adapters	2 Bit Grayscale	CPU Board	Super VGA	Dell	ET-4000							■
		ISA	VGA							■		

Glossary

active application The application that you're currently working in. It's the only application with any menus showing, and it's the one that contains the key window.

application A program with a graphical user interface that you can run from the workspace, such as Edit, FaxReader, or Preferences.

application dock (dock) The column of up to 13 icons along the right edge of the screen. It contains application icons that you can use to start up applications. It also contains the recycler.

arrow keys Four keys, labeled with arrows, that cause movement (usually of the insertion point) in the indicated direction.

ASCII characters A subset of the characters that can be typed from your keyboard.

attention panel A panel that requires you to perform an action in it before you can continue to work in an application. It can't be covered by any other window or icon.

©1993 NeXT, Inc. All rights reserved. Entries from the NeXT Glossary reprinted with permission.

Glossary

bookshelf A collection of targets in a digital library, in which Digital Librarian searches the targets you select.

brightness keys The two keys that control the brightness of the screen. The upper key increases the brightness, the lower key decreases it.

browser A multiple-column area of a window in which you can browse through hierarchically organized information by clicking names in the columns.

busy cursor A spinning disk that means the application you're working in is busy and you have to either wait or switch to another application.

button A graphic object that you click to make something happen, or press to cause a continuous action. Buttons are labeled with text, graphics, or both.

byte A unit of information in the computer. In a plain ASCII file, for example, each character occupies one byte.

click To position the cursor on something and, without moving the mouse, press and release a mouse button.

close To make a window disappear from the workspace when you're done using it. Closing a window that contains a file puts the file away, usually giving you a chance to save changes first.

close button A button in a window's title bar that, when clicked, closes the window. When the close button is partially drawn, it means that the window contains unsaved changes or that its contents aren't up-to-date.

CMYK color model A method of mixing colors that involves mixing cyan, magenta, yellow, and black inks.

command A word or phrase in a menu that describes an action an application can take, or names a submenu or panel it can open.

current folder The folder that you're currently working in. If you're working in a file, the current folder is the one containing that file. In the File Viewer, the current folder is usually the rightmost folder in the icon path.

cursor The image on the screen that moves as you move the mouse. It's usually an arrow.

Glossary

Delete key A key used to remove individual characters, words, graphics, or other items.

detach To drag a submenu away from its associated menu.

digital library An on-line collection of information—such as, reference works, documentation, and literature—that you can access with a NEXTSTEP application designed for that purpose.

dimmed Gray, faded, or otherwise made to recede into the background. You can't choose a command or operate a button when it's dimmed.

disk A magnetic medium on which the computer stores information. See also *floppy disk* and *hard disk drive*.

dock See *application dock*.

dot file A file or folder whose name begins with a period and which typically contains information that you don't need to access. Dot files are normally hidden from view in Workspace Manager folder windows.

double-click To click twice in quick succession on the same object. A double-click often extends the action caused by a click.

drag To press and hold down a mouse button, move the cursor by sliding the mouse, and then release the mouse button.

EPS Encapsulated PostScript, a format for storing graphics.

extension The last period in a file name and all characters that follow. A file's extension indicates the type of information in it and the applications that can open it.

file A collection of related information stored on a disk, such as a document, report, letter, or application.

file package A special folder containing files that aren't normally shown in folder windows. Instead, a file package looks and behaves like a file (when you open it by double-clicking, for example).

file system The collection of all the files you can access through your computer. See also *hierarchical file system*.

File Viewer A Workspace Manager window that gives you access to all the files in the file system.

Glossary

flppy disk A plastic disk, encased in a protective cartridge, that holds information a floppy disk drive can read or write.

flppy disk drive A mechanism that can store and retrieve information from a floppy disk.

folder A place in the file system that contains files and other folders. Opening a folder displays the names of the files and folders it contains.

font A set of properties that describe the appearance of text: font family (such as Times), typeface (for example, **bold** or *italic*), and size (in points).

font family A collection of characters with a consistent design. Examples are Helvetica and Times.

group A class of users for which permissions are assigned to a file or folder. A group is set up by a system administrator.

group address A shorthand address used in the Mail application to identify a single user or a group of users.

hard disk drive A device that can store and retrieve information from metal disks permanently encased within it. A hard disk drive is usually installed inside your computer.

hide To temporarily remove the windows of a running application from view in the workspace.

hierarchical file system A file system in which folders can contain other folders, down to any number of levels.

highlight To make something such as a command, text, icon, or title bar stand out visually. Highlighting usually indicates that something has been chosen to perform an action, or selected to receive an action.

home folder Your home base in the file system. Your home folder holds your personal files. Its name is the same as your user name.

host name The name by which a computer on a network is known to the other computers on the network. The host name is assigned by the system administrator and appears at the top of the login window.

HSB color model A method of mixing colors that involves adjusting hue, saturation, and brightness. See also *hue*, and *saturation*.

Glossary

hue The name of a color, such as red, green, or yellow.

icon A small pictorial representation of an application, file, folder, disk, or other item.

icon path An area in the File Viewer that displays the selected file or folder and the folders along its branch of the file system hierarchy.

initialize To prepare a disk so it can hold information. When you initialize a disk, any information already on it is destroyed.

insertion point The place where text and graphics may be entered; usually represented by a blinking vertical bar.

key window The standard window or panel that currently receives keystrokes. Its title bar is highlighted in black. You make a window the key window by clicking in it.

keyboard alternative A combination of keys, including the Command key, that you can use instead of the mouse for choosing a command.

kilobyte 1024 bytes.

link A special file that looks and acts like an ordinary file or folder. But when you open it, you access the contents of a file or folder that's somewhere else in the file system.

log in To gain access to a computer by providing a user name and a password.

log out To quit all running applications and (if you had to log in to use the computer) return to the login window.

mailbox A file package (in the Mailboxes folder in your home folder) in which the Mail application stores messages. Everyone has an Active mailbox where all incoming messages are delivered.

main menu The menu that appears in your workspace when an application is active. Its title bar displays the application's name (or an abbreviation).

main window The standard window that you're currently working in. If it's not also the key window, it has a dark gray title bar and receives any action performed by a panel.

menu A window that contains a vertical list of commands.

miniaturize button A button in a window's title bar that, when clicked, shrinks the window into a miniwindow.

miniwindow An icon that represents a miniaturized window.

mouse buttons The two buttons on the mouse.

open To put up a window in your workspace. Opening a file or folder puts up a window that displays the contents of the file or folder.

owner The person (represented by user name) who created a file or folder. The owner may also be a class of users for which permissions are assigned to a file or folder.

panel A window that typically appears in response to a command and provides information about the application or lets you control what the application does.

password A sequence of characters that you must enter along with your user name when logging in. It can consist of letters, numbers, symbols, and spaces, and should be known only to you.

pasteboard The place where the computer stores what you last cut or copied with the Cut or Copy command.

pathname A name, or a sequence of names separated by a slash (/), that specifies a file or folder in the file system.

permissions Characteristics of a file or folder that determine what certain users can do with the file or folder—for example, whether they can view a file's contents or remove a file from a folder.

pixel The smallest unit of measurement on a computer's screen. The NeXT MegaPixel Display measures 1120 by 832 pixels and has approximately 92 pixels per inch.

plain text A data format consisting solely of characters from the ASCII character set. These include text characters (with no font properties) and control characters.

point A unit of measurement equal to 1/72 of an inch.

pop-up list A list of options that you can choose from to set a state. You open the list by pressing a button with a ▇ on it.

Glossary

press To position the cursor on something and, without moving the mouse, hold down a mouse button and keep it down until the desired effect is achieved.

program A set of coded instructions that a computer follows to perform a specific task.

public sound server A NEXTSTEP computer whose sound recording and playback features can be accessed by other computers over a network.

public window server A NEXTSTEP computer that can display the windows of an application that's running on another computer on a network.

pull-down list A list of commands that you can choose from to cause an action. You open the list by pressing a button with a ▼ on it.

read-only A file that has read permission, but not write or execute permission, for one or more classes of users is a read-only file for those users. Those users can see the file's contents, but they can't save changes to it.

read permission A characteristic of a file or folder that allows certain users to view its contents. See also *permissions*.

recycler An icon, in the dock that you use to delete files and folders from the file system.

resize bar The narrow strip at the bottom of a window that you can drag to change the size of the window.

resolution The number of dots per inch of images on a display screen or in printed output. The higher the resolution, the clearer the image.

Return key A key used to start a new line or paragraph. You can also press Return to operate a button with a ↵ on it.

RGB color model A method of mixing colors by blending red, green, and blue lights.

root folder The folder at the top of the file system hierarchy. This folder is represented by a slash (/). It's physically located on the startup disk.

RTF Rich Text Format, a text format that includes font and formatting properties.

Glossary

saturation The intensity of a color—how much of a particular hue is in the color. See also *hue*.

save To store information on a computer's disk.

scroll To move through information in a window or section of a window when there's more than can be displayed at one time, so that a different part of the information is visible.

scroll button A button, usually in a scroller, that you click or press to scroll by small increments, or that you Alternate-click to scroll by a windowful.

scroll knob A variable-sized box in a scroller that moves as you scroll and that you can drag to scroll. Its length indicates how much of the scrollable contents are currently displayed, and its position indicates what part of the contents are displayed.

scroller A dark gray vertical or horizontal bar containing a scroll knob and scroll buttons. Scrollers appear along the left side or bottom of an area that you can scroll through.

server A computer on a network that contains files and folders that other people on the network can access.

shelf An area along the top of the File Viewer where you can keep files and folders that you access frequently.

Shift key The key used to produce the capital letters on letter keys and the upper character on keys labeled with two characters.

slider A control that lets you set a value in a range by dragging a knob within a bar.

startup disk The disk that contains the system files that your computer needs in order to operate. It's usually a hard disk inside your computer.

submenu A menu that's opened by a command in another menu (usually the main menu).

system administrator The person in charge of a computer network or of a computer that's been set up to be used by more than one person.

system files Files that the computer needs in order to operate and that must be loaded into the computer after it's turned on.

Tab key A key used to move to the next stopping point in a sequence, such as a tab stop in a document or a text field in a panel.

text field A white box where you can enter text. A text field is usually labeled with text that identifies what information should go in it.

TIFF Tagged Image File Format, a format for storing graphics.

title bar The strip at the top of a window that contains its title and possibly buttons for manipulating the window. It's highlighted in black if it's the key window, or dark gray if it's the main window but not the key window.

typeface A variation of a font family, such as **Bold**, *Italic*, or ***Bold Italic***.

user name The name by which the computer identifies you. This is the name you log in with, the name used to identify you as the owner of files and folders, and the name of your home folder.

volume keys The two keys that control the volume of NeXT computer's speaker. The upper key increases the volume, the lower key decreases it.

window A rectangular area in which information is presented on the screen. See also *standard window* and *panel*.

word Any sequence of characters between spaces or punctuation marks, selected with a double-click.

workspace The screen environment in which you do your work on a NEXTSTEP computer.

write permission A characteristic of a file or folder that allows certain users to change its contents. See also *permissions*.

Index

A

Access Control Inspector, see Inspector:Access Control
account, see also user accounts 2
active application 45
active partition 4
Adaptec SCSI adapter card D-3
ADB keyboard 119
adding a mail address 189
adding sound to a mail message 191
address book 98
    adding members 102
    creating groups 100
    dumping to text file 104
    inspecting 99, 104
    locations in file system 98
    modifying an entry 100
    modifying RTF file template 104
    removing a member 102
    silent destroy 102
    sorting member list 104
    standard RTF template 105
Address Inspector 98
Addresses folder 50

Adobe 301
afm file 301
aliases 347
Alternate key 24, 67, 128
anonymous login 312
app wrapper 267
Apple II
    converting files to NEXTSTEP 329
Apple LaserWriter II 163
AppleLink 374
application
    auto-starting 115, 276
    crash 354
    creating another instance of 116
    dock, see dock
    dots 108
    hiding 114
    killing 354
    monitoring 112
    search path 110
    setting default 109, 111
    starting 108, 111
    starting as root user 244
    starting remotely 240
    tile 108

Index

unhiding 108, 114
applying a color 141
applying a font selection 135, 136
Apps folder 52, 108, 270
Appsoft Draw 17
Appsoft Image 246
apropos command 350, 352
Archie
    application C-1
    query C-2
    server C-2
Archive.mbox 195
Arrange in Front command 47
arrow cursor 13, 14, 66, 126, 221, 222
arrow key 43, 126
ASCII 94, 314, C-9
assigning permissions 96
attention panel 118
Attributes Inspector 87, 88
audio cassettes 361
Audio Spectrum D-4
auto-completing a pathname 342
auto-starting an application 115
available disk space 42

B

BackSpace C-5
BackupMaster 84, 350
backups
    floppy disk 64
    full 348
    incremental 348
    organizing files 52
    using Tar command 350
    using UNIX commands 348
beep sound 288, 290
Bernoulli removable disk cartridge 77
    as backup volume 349
Big Green CD 369
Billiards 222
bitmap files 303
BITnet 374
BoinkOut 224
Bookshelves folder 209
booting
    NEXTSTEP 4
    single-user 359
    to DOS 4, 8
    using default configuration 359

brightness keys 285
browser 33
    Adjusting column width 278
    scroller 32
    triangle symbol 32
bsd -s command 360
bug reporting 224
BugNeXT 224
buildafmdir command 303
BuildDisk application 350
bullet character 287
bullet symbol
    NeXTmail 192
bulletin board system (BBS) 309, 377

C

C programming language xxiii, xxv
C shell 336
cacheAFMData command 303
canceling a font selection 138
cd command 318
CDPlayer application 226
CD-ROM 77, 280
    Big Green CD 369
    finding files on 55
    formats 328
    High-Sierra format 328
    Internet Unplugged 369
    ISO 9660 format 328
    Jewel of the Matrix 369
    Macintosh HFS format 328
    navigating 31
    NEXTSTEP 349, 359
    PhotoCD 245
    playing audio CDs 226
    public domain 369
    Rock Ridge format 328
changing a NEXTSTEP password 293
Chess 227, 228
chown command 90
chunks, see multi-volume copy
Clean Up Icons command 34
clearing the pasteboard 131
close button 22, 43, 47
    icon 22
    on submenu 26
Close command 47
CMYK 145
color model 140

Index

CMYK 145
color wheel 143
grayscale 144
HSB 145
PANTONE List 148
RGB 144
selection buttons 141
Color panel xxiii
color swatches 142
color well 141
color wheel 143
Colors panel xxiv, 139
    applying a color 141
    CMYK 145
    color swatches 142
    color well 141
    color wheel 143
    controls 140
    grayscale 144
    HSB 145
    magnifying glass 140
    PANTONE List 148
    resizing 142
    RGB 144
Command key 27
Compaq D-2, D-4
complete works of Shakespeare 210
compress (UNIX) command 317
Compress command 63, 317
compressed file icon 64
compressing files and folders 63, 82
CompuServe 373
CompuServe NeXT forum 374
Compute Size button 88
configuring a NetWare printer 176, 177
configuring a printer (general) 172, 178
Contents Inspector, see Inspector/
    Contents
context sensitive help 119
Control key 71, 204
converting file formats 328
Copy command 131, 153, 342
copy cursor, see cursor: copy
copying
    files and folders 66
    files to removable disks 81
    link 72
    multiple files 62
CopyOf file name prefix 68
CorelDraw 329

CPU
    Cyrix 486SLC D-2
    Intel 486DX D-2
    Intel 486DX/2 D-2
    Intel 486SX D-2
    Intel 80386 D-2
    Intel 80486 D-2
creating a fax cover sheet, see also Draw application 168
creating a group address 190
creating a link 71
creating a NeXTlink, see NeXTlinks
creating a PostScript file 163
creating a printer definition 174
creating fax cover sheet templates 232
cursor 12
    arrow 13, 14, 66, 126, 221, 222
    busy/spinning disk 354
    copy 66, 82
    I-beam 126
    link 71
    move 65
    pointer 221
customizing a keyboard map 234
customizing folder icons 306
Cut command 130, 131

D

daemons 5, 7
DAT tape drives 349
Date and Time preferences 291
date and time server 291
Decompress command 64, 317
default application 43, 109
default permissions 97
defining a word in Digital Webster 217
Delete key 129
deleting
    files 30
    files and folders 73
    text 129
Desktop Publishing (DTP) C-9
Destroy command 72, 74, 75, 102
    shortcut 74
diagnostics 358
diamond (link) button 157
Dictionaries folder 138
Digital Librarian 25, 55, 209, 371
    auto-updating an index 214

Index

creating a Bookshelf file 210
creating a target 210
index symbol 213
indexing a target 213
language Inspector 216
opening a Bookshelf file 210
searching a target 211
Searching Inspector 213
Digital Quotations application 150
Digital Signal Processor (DSP) 298
Digital Webster application 150, 217, C-4
dir.tiff file 48
directory, see folder
disk
    duplicating 84
    ejecting 79
    how it appears in File Viewer 280
    initializing 80, 81
    mounting 78
    unmounting 79
Disk menu 79
Disk Options 78, 280
Display PostScript, see PostScript
    Display
Dock 29, 108, 276
    arranging icons 30
    icons 29
    positioning 108
    removing icons 30
Dock Options 115
document, see file
DOS 4
    converting files to NEXTSTEP 329
    file naming 325
    FTP software 309
dot file 186
DOTS printer drivers 175
downloading fonts 303
drag and drop
    in the Open panel 125
    in the Save panel 125
    on an application tile 243
    pathname shortcut 343
Draw application 169, 170, 230
    creating a fax cover sheet 232
    text editing 231
    tools 231
Duplicate command 67
duplicating
    files and folders 67

floppy disks 84
DVI files C-9

E

Edit
    application 104, 117, 186
    Developer Mode 186
Edit menu 130, 131, 153
editing a SND file 253
Eject command 79
ejecting a disk 79
ElectroFile 55
electronic mail, see NeXTmail
e-mail, see NeXTmail
Empty Recycler command 30, 74
Encapsulated PostScript
    cross-platform compatibility 329
enTAR 84, 318
EPS file format 91
Epson 510 printer 174
erasing files 30
Escape key 342
etc folder 347, 349
Ethernet 308
    3com adapter D-3
    booting from 358
execute permission 89
executing a UNIX command 336
Expert preferences 297
extending a selection 61, 128

F

fax
    address book 98
    addressing 102
    archiving 180
    inspecting queue 207
    removing a request from the queue 209
    selecting a fax modem 165
    sending 165, 170
    sending delayed 170
fax modem 165
    adding users 182
    Modem Options 179
    Printing Options 183
    Recordkeeping Options 180

Index

sharing 178
speaker control 179
user permissions 181, 182
Fax Modems panel 178
Fax panel 98, 165, 197
   adding a user 166
   cover sheet 168
   entering a fax number 166
   Fine button 168
   Modem button 165
   Options 167
   previewing a fax 167
   receipt 168
   removing a user 167
FaxReader
   application 197
   fax log 202
   reading an incoming fax 197
field 5
FIFO - First In First Out 171, 209
file
   compressing 63, 82
   conversion 328
   copying 66
   copying to removable disk 81
   CopyOf name prefix 68
   creation mask 297
   creation mask, see also permission :default 297
   deleting 30, 73
   DOS names 325
   duplicating 67
   extensions 16, 109
   grouping 58
   moving 65
   opening 124
   saving 122
   special characters 48
   table of common extensions 17
   viewing contents 91
file and folder linking 72
File menu 100
file name extension 109
file organization strategies 53—55
file package 268, 270
file system 15, 18, 32, 90
   different views of 33
   hierarchy 18
   navigating 31, 43
File Transfer Protocol (FTP) 309

File Viewer 15, 58, 280
   Browser 33
   changing root folder 44
   close button 43
   icon spacing 33
   icon view 43
   invisible grid 33
   navigating 31
   opening a new 43
   selecting files 42
   shelf 39
   sorting 35, 36
   spacing icons 34
filter service 93
filter-service 245
Find panel 132, 133
Finder command 56
Finder options 279
Finder panel 57, 132, 209, 279
   adding a target 56
   Find button 57
   keyboard shortcut 56
   removing target 57
   Stop button 57
   target 56
finding a file or folder 55
finding text within a document 132
   Ignore Case option 133
   Regular Expression option 133
   searching backward 133
fixed disks 281
floppy disk
   as backup 349
   as it appears in File Viewer 280
   HD (High-Density) 301
   table of supported formats 78
   UNIX format 327
floppy disk drive
   CubeFloppy external 78
   TurboFloppy external 78
folder
   compressing 63
   copying 66
   copying to removable disk 81
   creating 48
   customizing icon 306
   deleting 73
   duplicating 67
   grouping 58
   hiding 50

inspecting 33, 88
merging 67
moving 65
naming 48, 49
reserved 50
sorting contents of 93
special characters 48
font hotline 301, 383
Font panel 134
   applying selection 135
   cancelling a selection 138
   dimple 137
   previewing a selection 134
   resizing 137
   shortcut 134
font_update_2.0 command 303
fontloader command 303
fonts
   afm file 301
   bitmap file 301
   converting 301
   downloading 303
   installer applications 300
   PostScript 301
   TrueType 301
   Type 1 301
   Type 3 301
   typefaces 134
Fonts folder 51, 270, 303
Fortran programming language xxv
fractals 236
FrameMaker 252
Freehand 329
Frequently Asked Questions (FAQs) 209, 378
fstab file 347
FTP 310, 313, 315
   archives 309
   commands 315, 316

G

games 224
GatorFTP 310, 369
Generate RTF File command 104
generic application icon 18
GNU chess 227
Grab application 150, 220
grayscale 144
group file 347

group permission 88, 89, 90
grouping adjacent icons 59
grouping nonadjacent icons 61
GUI - Grapical User Interface xxiii

H

halt command 344
hand icon 62
Header Viewer 299
Help command 120
Help key 119
Help panel
   Backtrack button 121
   diamond icon 120
   link button 120
   navigating 120
   navigation controls 119
   shortcut 119
   text area 119
   tips for using 121
hidden folders 50
Hide command 114
Hide Links command 155
hiding and unhiding applications 114
home folder 2, 33, 40, 48, 56
   abbreviation 19
hosts file 347
HP LaserJet III 163
HSB 145
hypertext documents 157
hypertext links 121

I

I-beam cursor 126
IBM ProPrinter 174
icon 16
   open icon 65
   sparkle 65
   tile 108
Icon Path 15, 39, 40, 102
   scroller 39
Icon View 43
   file name abbreviations 34
   setting title width 279
IconBuilder 246
IconBuilder application 48
Illustrator 164, 328, 329

Index

Image Agent 93
ImagePac 245
ImagePac file 245
ImageViewer C-6
Improv 252, 328
Info view 271
initial key repeat 284
Initialize disk panel 81
initializing a disk 80
inserting text 126
insertion point 126
inspecting the boot process 358
Inspector
    Access Control 95, 297
    Address 98
    Attributes 87, 88, 90, 91, 96, 297
    Contents 36, 87, 91, 93, 94
    Link 155
    Tools 87, 109
Inspector command 92
Installer
    application 244, 268
    Info view 271
    Log panel 273
    Progress display 273
    removing applications 273
installing fonts 300
Internet 379, C-1
    etiquette 319
    FTP archives 310, 368
    mail address 310
Internet network 309
Internet Unplugged CD-ROM 369
IP address 346, 349

J

Jewel of the Matrix CD-ROM 369
Jobs, Steve xxii
JPEG compression 246

K

key window 45, 47
keyboard
    creating shortcuts 295
    equivalents 27
    initial key repeat 284
    navigation 42

NeXT ADB 119
    Preferences 284
    repeat rate 284
    shortcuts 27
Keyboard application 234
Keyboard panel 235, 286, 287
keyboard shortcuts
    creating 294
killing an application 354
Knuth, Donald E. C-9

L

language preference 286
Large File System option 298
Library folder 50
link button 158
link cursor, see cursor :link
Link Inspector 155
    command 155
    shortcut 156
Link menu 153
linking an image, see NeXTlinks
linking files and folders in the file system 70
links 71, 72, 88
Lip Service 191
Listing command 37
Listing View
    dragging icons 38
Loading from Disk message 358
LocalApps folder 52, 108, 269, 349
Localization Preferences 235, 286
LocalLibrary folder 52
Log Out command 6
logging into a NetWare file server 321
logging into NEXTSTEP 1, 5
logging out from a NetWare file server 324
login panel 2, 5
Logitec mouse D-3
lpr command 305
ls -l command 37

M

Mach operating system xxii
Macintosh
    color picker 143
    converting files to NEXTSTEP 329
    FTP software 309

Index

icons 33
MacLinkPlus 329
magnetic tapes 77
magneto-optical disk 77
magnifying glass 140
Mailboxes folder 50
man Command 351
man pages 351, 368
Mandelbrot 236
merge folders 67, 68
METAFONT (see also TeX) C-9
Metamorphosis 301
MetroSoft 301
MetroTools 301
microphone
    built-in 252, 298
Microsoft Windows
    converting files to NEXTSTEP 329
miniaturize button 21
Miniaturize command 47
MiniExamples 372
miniwindow 22
modifier keys 235
Molecule 238
monitoring applications 112
monitoring background tasks 113
mounting a disk 78
mouse D-3
    buttons 13, 283
    clicking buttons 13
    defining button action 14
    double-click buttons 13
    dragging the mouse 13
    modifier keys 15
    Preferences 282
    tips for using 14
moving files and folders 65
multiple undo 130
multitasking xxii
multi-volume copy 82
multi-volume set 82

N

naming a folder 48, 49
naming files
    extensions 18
    special characters 18
Net folder 308, 321
NetInfo
    database 346, 347, 349
    domain 178, 248, 347
    server 347
NetInfoManager application 90, 347
NetWare 4, 320
    286 version 320
    changing password 322
    logging in using File Viewer 321
    logging in using NetWareManager 322
    logging out 324
    multiple logins 322
    passwords 321
    transferring files 44
    user names 321
NetWareManager 240, 244
NetWareManager application 320
network administrator 248, 377
Network File System (NFS) 308, 349
New Folder command 48
New Group command 100
New Link command 72
New Viewer command 43
NewsGrazer 377
NeXT authorized dealers 382
NeXT cube icon 288
NeXT logo icon 108, 221
NeXT technical support hotline 355
NeXT user groups (NUG) 379
NeXT, Incorporated 361, 362
NeXTanswers 209, 370
NeXTConnection 383
NeXTcube 239, 250
NeXTdimension 239, 250
NeXTlinks 152
    Break All Links command 155
    Break Link command 155
    breaking a link 156
    creating a link 156
    diamond icon 157
    Hide Links command 155
    hiding visible links 155
    identifying links 155
    inspector 155
    link button 158
    Link Inspector command 155
    Link menu 153
    linking an image 153
    Open Source command 155
    Paste and Link command 153, 158

Index

Paste Link Button command 158
Publish a Selection command 154
publishing a link 154
repairing broken link 158
Update from Source command 155
update methods 156
updating 156
NeXTmail 2, 150, 187, 224, 252, 372
   adding an address 189
   blind carbon copy 189
   bullet symbol 192
   carbon copy 188
   compacting a mailbox 194
   creating a group address 190
   creating a new mailbox 193
   deleting messages 194
   forwarding a message 192
   Lip Service 191
   preferences 192
   removing an address 189
   replying 189
   sending non-NeXT mail 195
   sorting 193
   triangle symbol 192
NeXTstation icon 18, 39
NEXTSTEP
   bundled applications 185
   developer environment 209
   DOS support 77
   logging in 1
   version 2.1 xxiv
NEXTSTEP CD-ROM, see CD-ROM NEXTSTEP
NEXTSTEP for Intel Processors
   EISA bus support D-3
   IDE hard disk support D-3
   ISA bus support D-3
   JAWS video support D-2
   network support D-3
   non-PostScript printer support D-3
   SCSI support D-3
   sound cards supported D-4
   Super VGA support D-2
   VGA support D-2
NEXTSTEP logo icon
   blinking 290
NEXTSTEP Manuals 363
NEXTSTEP menus 24
   positioning 26
   preferences 294

   setting default position 294
NEXTSTEP release 3 Installer application 350
NEXTSTEP windows 20
   close button 22, 47
   features 21
   key window 45
   miniaturize button 21
   resize bar 24
   selecting background window 45
   title bar 21, 26, 43
NeXTtv 239, 240
NeXTWORLD Expo 380
NeXTWORLD magazine 365
NFS 10, 242, 307, 308, 309
NFSManager 240, 244
nidump command 347
niload command 347
niutil command 348
No Contents Inspector message 93
NoIR (NeXT Organizations InteRnational) 380

O

Objective C programming language xxiii
object-oriented design xxiii
OCR Servant 151, 168
On-Line help 367
Open as Folder command 44, 66
Open panel
   browser 124
   Home button 125
Open Sesame 240
Open Source command 155
open.dir.tiff file 49
Opener application 318
opening a file 124
optical disks 280
OS/2, converting files to NEXTSTEP 329
other (world) permission 90
owner permission 88, 89
Oxford Dictionary of Quotations 219

P

padlock icon 293
panel
      Colors 139

Fax 165, 197
Find 132, 133
Finder 209
Font 134
Keyboard 235
Print 162, 197
Save 122
Panic window 355
PANTONE
   list 148
   numbers 148
   selecting a color by number 148
PANTONE Color Matching System xxiii
Pascal programming language xxv
passwd file 347
password 1, 2
   changing 293
Password Preferences 293
Paste and Link command 153, 158
Paste command 131, 342
Paste Link Button command 158
pasteboard 131, 153, 220, 221
   clearing 131
pathname 19
   auto-completion 342
   pronunciation 345
   root or 39
   shortcuts 19, 342
pausing a background task 113
permission 89, 96
   assigning 90, 96
   default 97
   execute 89
   fax 181
   group 89, 90
   inspecting 88, 95
   matrix 90, 96
   owner 89
   read 89
   world 90
   write 89
PhotoAlbum 245
PhotoCD 245
   multi-session 247
   preferences 247
   standard sizes 247
   thumbnail 245
PhotoGrade 163
pipe (example) 305
playing a sound (SND) file 251

PMS, see PANTONE
pointer cursor 221
pop-up list 86
   icon 86
   in Finder panel 57
PostScript
   cross-platform compatibility 329
   Display xxv, D-2
   Level II xxv
PostScript Printer Definition (see PPD file) 173
Power key 7, 359
power off procedure 7
Power panel 8
PPD file 173, 174
Preferences
   Disk options 280
   Finder options 279
   Localization 235
Preferences application 14
   Date and Time 291
   Display preferences 285
   Expert preferences 297
   General preferences 288
   Keyboard preferences 284
   Localization preferences 286
   Menu preferences 294
   Mouse preferences 282
   Password preferences 293
   Screens preferences 296
   Services preferences 299
   Startup preferences 292
Preview application 164, 195
previewing a font selection 134, 137
previewing printer output 164
primary screen 296
Print command 163
Print panel 162, 197
   Fax button 165
   Options button 162
   Preview button 164
   Save button 163
printing 160
   configuring a printer 172, 178
   deleting a request in the queue 209
   inspecting queue 207
   Print command 163
   to disk, see also Print panel: Save button 163
PrintManager 171, 176, 207

Index

creating a printer definition 174
    removing a printer definition 174
private/etc folder 349
processes 112
Processes panel 67, 69
    copy progress (pie) indicator 69
    Pause button 69
    repeat switch 73
    Resume button 69
    shortcut 112
    Stop button 69
Project (service) 299
public domain 319, 379
Public Sound Server option 298
Public Window Server option 241, 298
Publish Selection command 154
publishing a link 154
pull-down list 87

R

RAM - Random Access Memory 4
read permission 89
reading a fax message 197
README file 314
Receipts folder 274
recording a sound 252
recovering from a non-booting disk 359
recycler 30, 73, 102
    destroying a link 71
    emptying 30, 74
    icon 73
    retrieving items from 30, 74
    vs. Destroy command 75
    window 30
redirecting output to a file, see Print panel:-
    Save button
regular expression 133, 211
removable disk 280
    cartridges 77
    definition 77
    icons 77
removing a mail address 189
removing a printer definition 174
rendering server 248
RenderMan 253
RenderManager 248, 249
repairing a broken NeXTlink 158
repeat switch 73
Replace All, see Find panel

replacing text 129, 133
reserved folders 50
resize bar 24
resizing the Shelf 41, 66
Restart panel 8
restricted user 181
retrieving items from the recycler 74
Return key 5, 43, 336
RGB 144
rhosts file 240, 241
RIB file 253
Rich Text File (RTF) format 94
RightBrain 301
rlogin 205, 344
ROM monitor 359, 360
root folder 18, 39, 53
root user 2, 3, 18, 53, 240, 241, 244, 291,
    298, 301, 322, 350
RTF file format 91, 104, 329
RTFD file format 91

S

SafetyNet 84, 350
Save command 122
Save panel 122
    browser 122
    Home button 123
    tips for using 123
saving a file 122
saving colors, see color swatches
screen
    brightness 285
    dimming 285
screen saver
    BackSpace C-5
    built-in 5
Screens preference 296
ScreenScape 250
    Controls 251
scroller 22, 23
    buttons 23
    knob 22
SCSI 327
    configuring SCSI ID 360
searching with Digital Librarian 211
Select All command 61
selecting
    adjacent Items 58
    entire document 129

Index

fax cover sheet 168
fax modem 165
file 58
keyboard map 235
PANTONE color 148
paragraph 129
text 127
self-diagnostics 4
sending a fax 170
Services 150
    customizing menu 299
    disabling 299
    menu 150
    Preferences 299
    using 150
Services menu 242
setting the default application 109, 111
SGI (Silicon Graphics Incorporated) 309
shareware 319, 379
Shelf 39, 40, 102
    adding an icon 39
    dimple 41, 277
    File Viewer 15
    hidden icons 41
    messages 42
    removing an icon 40
    resizing 41, 66
    setting title width 277
    starting an application from 40
Shelf options 277
shell 205, 336
    C shell 336
Shift key 128
shortcuts
    application 116
    Command key 28
    Font Panel 136
    Help panel 121
    pathname 342–343
    Tools Inspector 111
Show Links command 155
silent destroy 102
single user 344, 359, 360
slash (/) character 19
SMTP - Simple Mail Transfer Protocol 187
SND file
    format 290
    playing 91, 93
software license 52, 270
software objects xxiii, xxiv

Sort command 36, 93
Sort Icons command 91
sort key 36
sorting files 93
sorting icons 35
    choosing a sort method 36
sorting mail messages 193
Sound application 251, 290
    editing a sound file 253
    playing a sound 253
    recording a sound 252
Sound Blaster D-4
Sounds folder 51, 270
speaker
    third-party external 226
    volume controls 93
special characters
    assigning to keys 234
    foreign language 286
Special Interest Groups (SIGs) 374
spell checking 138
spinning disk cursor 354
starting an application 108
Starting NEXTSTEP 4
stopping a background task 113
storage devices 77
su command 322
submenu
    close button 26
    detaching 26
    hiding 26
Sun 308, 349
    converting files to NEXTSTEP 329
super user, see system administrator and root user
Syquest removable disk cartridge 77
system administration 3, 240
system administrator 2, 52, 90, 91, 269, 291, 308, 310, 336, 348
system beep
    recording a new sound 252
    selecting beep sound 288

T

Tab key 5, 162
tar command 317
tar file name suffix 318
tar.Z file name suffix 317
target 56

Index

copying files 62
    Digital Librarian 210
    when moving files 65
Tarre 318
Tech Support Notes 372
Terminal application 96, 205
    customzing shell window 207
    Service 299
Terminal window 90
Terminal window, see also shell
Testing System message 358
text editing 126
    deleting text 129
    extending selected text 128
    inserting text 126
    replacing text 129
    selecting a entire document 129
    selecting a paragraph 129
    selecting text 127
text fields 126
TeXview C-9
The Installer, see Installer:application 270
TIFF file format 91
TIFFany application 246
tilde (~) character 20
title bar 21, 26, 43
Token Ring D-3
Tools Inspector 87, 109
    shortcut 111
    starting an application 111
Tools menu 69, 85
triangle symbol
    NeXTmail 192
trusted user 181
turning off the computer, see also Power key 10
typefaces 134
Typesetting mathematical equations C-9

U

Undo command 130
unhiding an application 108, 114
UNIX
    certificate icon 297
    permissions 89
UNIX commands 335
    common 338—341
    executing 336
    format of 337

UNIX Expert option 350
unknown application icon 18
unmounting a removable disk 79
unrestricted user 181
unselecting files and folders 59
Update from Source command 155
updating a NeXTlink 156
user accounts 1, 2
user group newsletters 366
User.addresses file 56
UserManager application 90
using Services 150
usr/adm/lpd-errs file 305

V

Video Cassette Recorder (VCR) 239, 250
View command 33
voice alerts 289
VRAM (Video RAM) D-3

W

Webster's Collegiate Thesaurus 217
Webster's Ninth New Collegiate Dictionary 217
wheel group 241
White Papers 361
Who's Calling 55
Window menu 46, 93
WordPerfect 328
workspace 5, 29, 108
    setting a background color 285
Workspace Manager 11, 24, 46, 98
    Preferences panel 275
workspace preferences 275—281
world (other) permission 90
world map 292
write permission 89
WriteNow 328
WYSIWYG xxvi

Z

Z filename suffix 317
Zilla 256, 257, 258

MIX
Papier aus verantwortungsvollen Quellen
Paper from responsible sources
FSC® C105338

If you have any concerns about our products,
you can contact us on
ProductSafety@springernature.com

In case Publisher is established outside the EU,
the EU authorized representative is:
**Springer Nature Customer Service Center GmbH
Europaplatz 3, 69115 Heidelberg, Germany**

Printed by Libri Plureos GmbH
in Hamburg, Germany